The Asian Way to Peace

THE ASIAN WAY TO PEACE

A Story of Regional Cooperation

Michael Haas

PRAEGER

New York
Westport, Connecticut
London

Library of Congress Cataloging-in-Publication Data

Haas, Michael, 1938–
The Asian way to peace : a story of regional cooperation / Michael Haas.
p. cm.
Bibliography: p.
Includes index.
ISBN: 978-0-275-93216-9
1. Asia – Foreign relations. 2. Regionalism (International organization) I. Title.
JX1569.H29 1989
341.24 – dc20 89-32262

Library of Congress Catalog Card Number: 89-32262

First published in 1989

Praeger Publishers, One Madison Avenue, New York, NY 10010
A division of Greenwood Press, Inc.

Printed in the United States of America

The paper used in this book complies with the Permanent Paper Standard issued by the National Information Standards Organization (Z39.48 – 1984).

10 9 8 7 6 5 4 3 2 1

For Werner Levi

CONTENTS

Figures *ix*

Tables *xiii*

Preface *xvii*

Abbreviations *xxi*

1 The Asian Way to Peace 1

2 Foreign-Aid Publicity (but Not Planning) from Colombo 23

3 A Paper Tiger and a Radar Tiger 31

4 Casting a Wide Net (with Many Holes) toward Africa 52

5 Tokyo and Seoul Bid for Leadership 65

6 When Japan Listens, Who Talks in Southeast Asia? 91

7 ASEAN: A Spirit of Cooperation to Be Emulated 118

8 Clones of ASEAN in Southeast Asia 149

9 Multilateral Money Management in Asia 182

10 Getting the Word Out in Asia 206

11 The "OPECization" of Asia 219

12 Conferocracies 250

13 Continuing Vitality in Asian Regional Cooperation 265

14 The "ASEANization" of Asian Regional Cooperation 282

Bibliography *289*

Index *291*

FIGURES

2.1	Organization of the Colombo Plan	25
3.1	Organization of the South-East Asia Treaty Organization	35
3.2	Organization of the Anglo-Malayan and Anglo-Malaysian Defence Agreements	41
3.3	Organization of the Five Power Defence Arrangements	45
4.1	Organization of the Asian-African Legal Consultative Committee	54
4.2	Organization of the Afro-Asian Rural Reconstruction Organization	61
5.1	Organization of the Asian Productivity Organization	67
5.2	Organization of the Asian-Pacific Parliamentarians' Union	70
5.3	Organization of the Asian and Pacific Council	76
5.4	Organization of the Cultural and Social Center for the Asian and Pacific Region	78
5.5	Organization of the Food and Fertilizer Technology Center for the Asian and Pacific Region	81
5.6	Organization of the Economic Cooperation Center for the Asian and Pacific Region	84
5.7	Organization of the Registry of Scientific and Technical Services for the Asian and Pacific Region	85

6.1	Organization of the Ministerial Conference for the Economic Development of Southeast Asia	93
6.2	Organization of the Southeast Asian Fisheries Development Center	95
6.3	Organization of SEAFDEC: Secretariat	95
6.4	Organization of SEAFDEC: Training Department	97
6.5	Organization of SEAFDEC: Marine Fisheries Research Department	99
6.6	Organization of SEAFDEC: Aquaculture Department	101
6.7	Organization of the Southeast Asian Agency for Regional Transport and Communications Development	104
6.8	Organization of the Regional Organization for Inter-Governmental Cooperation and Coordination in Family and Population Planning in Southeast Asia	108
6.9	Organization of the Study Group on Asian Tax Administration and Research	111
6.10	Organization of the Southeast Asian Promotion Centre for Trade, Investment and Tourism	113
7.1	Organization of the Association of Southeast Asia	121
7.2	Organization of Maphilindo	125
7.3	Organization of the Association of South East Asian Nations	127
7.4	Organization of ASEAN: Foreign Ministers' Side	128
7.5	Organization of ASEAN: Economic Ministers' Side	130
7.6	Organization of ASEAN: Secretariat	130
7.7	Organization of the ASEAN Inter-Parliamentary Organization	142
7.8	Organization of the Meeting of the Chiefs of National Police of the ASEAN Countries	144
8.1	Organization of the Southeast Asian Ministers of Education Organization	151
8.2	Organization of the Southeast Asian Ministers of Education Secretariat	152
8.3	Organization of the SEAMEO Regional Center for Tropical Biology	157
8.4	Organization of the SEAMEO Regional Center for Educational Innovation and Technology	158
8.5	Organization of the SEAMEO Regional Centre for Education in Science and Mathematics	160
8.6	Organization of the SEAMEO Regional Language Centre	162
8.7	Organization of the SEAMEO Southeast Asian	

	Regional Center for Graduate Study and Research in Agriculture	163
8.8	Organization of the SEAMEO Regional Centre for Archaeology and Fine Arts	166
8.9	Organization of the SEAMEO Regional Tropical Medicine and Public Health Project	167
8.10	Organization of the Regional Institute of Higher Education and Development	170
8.11	Organization of the Tripartite Council	174
8.12	Organization of the Conference of the Foreign Ministers of Kampuchea, Laos, and Vietnam	177
9.1	Organization of the Central Banks of Southeast Asia, Australia and New Zealand	184
9.2	Organization of the Asian Development Bank	187
9.3	Organization of the South-east Asian Central Banks Group	194
9.4	Organization of the Asian Clearing Union	197
9.5	Organization of the Asian Reinsurance Corporation	201
10.1	Organization of the Asian-Pacific Postal Union	207
10.2	Organization of the Asia-Pacific Institute for Broadcasting Development	212
10.3	Organization of the Asia-Pacific Telecommunity	215
11.1	Organization of the Asian and Pacific Coconut Community	221
11.2	Organization of the Association of Natural Rubber Producing Countries	224
11.3	Organization of the Asian Vegetable Research and Development Center	227
11.4	Organization of the International Pepper Community	231
11.5	Organization of the Asian Rice Trade Fund	233
11.6	Organization of the Southeast Asia Tin Research and Development Centre	236
11.7	Organization of the Association of Tin Producing Countries	240
12.1	Organization of the Informal Meeting of Directors General of Civil Aviation, Asia and the Pacific	251
12.2	Organization of the Asian Judicial Conference	254
12.3	Organization of the Conference of Asian and Pacific Labor Ministers	256
12.4	Organization of the Association for Science Cooperation in Asia	258
12.5	Organization of the Taxation and Customs Cooperation Conference	261
13.1	Organization of the Bangkok Agreement	267

13.2 Organization of the Centre on Integrated Rural Development for Asia and the Pacific 270
13.3 Organization of the Asian and Pacific Development Centre 274
13.4 Organization of the South Asian Association for Regional Cooperation 278

TABLES

1.1	Asian Regional Organizations: Formation and Termination	11
2.1	Colombo Plan: Membership, Bureau Assessments, and Colombo Plan Staff College Assessments, ca. 1985	26
3.1	Military Organizations: Years of Membership	36
3.2	South-East Asia Treaty Organization: Assessments	38
3.3	Five Power Defence Arrangements: External Contributions	46
4.1	Asian-African Legal Consultative Committee: Membership and Assessments	55
4.2	Afro-Asian Rural Reconstruction Organization: Membership and Assessments	62
5.1	Asian Productivity Organization: Membership and Assessments	68
5.2	Asian-Pacific Parliamentarians' Union: Membership in the Union and Its Subsidiary Bodies	72
5.3	Asian-Pacific Parliamentarians' Union: Assessments	73
5.4	Asian and Pacific Council: Formation and Termination of Centers	77
5.5	Cultural and Social Center for the Asian and Pacific Region: Membership and Assessments	80
5.6	Food and Fertilizer Technology Center for the Asian and Pacific Region: Membership and Assessments	81

5.7	Registry of Scientific and Technical Services for the Asian and Pacific Region: Membership and Assessments	86
6.1	Ministerial Conference for the Economic Development of Southeast Asia: Formation and Termination of Subsidiary Bodies	92
6.2	Ministerial Conference for the Economic Development of Southeast Asia: Membership	93
6.3	Southeast Asian Fisheries Development Center: Membership and Secretariat Assessments	96
6.4	Southeast Asian Fisheries Development Center: Department Budgets	96
6.5	Southeast Asian Agency for Regional Transport and Communications Development: Membership and Assessments	106
6.6	Regional Organization for Inter-Governmental Cooperation and Coordination in Family and Population Planning in Southeast Asia: Membership and Assessments	109
6.7	Study Group on Asian Tax Administration and Research: Membership	111
6.8	Southeast Asian Promotion Centre for Trade, Investment and Tourism: Membership and Assessments	114
7.1	Association of South East Asian Nations and Related Organizations: Membership	122
7.2	Association of South East Asian Nations: Secretariat Assessments	133
8.1	Southeast Asian Ministers of Education Organization: Formation and Transformation of Subsidiary Bodies	152
8.2	Southeast Asian Ministers of Education Organization: Membership and SEAMES Assessments	153
8.3	Southeast Asian Ministers of Education Organization: Budgets of Subsidiary Bodies	155
8.4	Regional Institute of Higher Education and Development: Membership and Assessments	170
8.5	Tripartite Council: Membership	175
8.6	Conference of the Foreign Ministers of Kampuchea, Laos, and Vietnam: Membership	178
9.1	Central Banks of Southeast Asia, Australia and New Zealand: Membership	185

9.2	Asian Development Bank: Membership and Subscriptions	189
9.3	South-east Asian Central Banks Group: Membership and Assessments for SEACEN Centre	195
9.4	Asian Clearing Union and Asian Reinsurance Corporation: Membership	198
10.1	Asian-Pacific Postal Union: Membership, Assessments for the Central Office, and Cost Sharing for the Asian-Pacific Postal Training Centre	208
10.2	Asia-Pacific Institute for Broadcasting Development: Membership and Contributions	213
10.3	Asia-Pacific Telecommunity: Membership and Assessments	216
11.1	Asian and Pacific Coconut Community: Membership and Assessments	222
11.2	Association of Natural Rubber Producing Countries: Membership and Assessments	224
11.3	Asian Vegetable Research and Development Center: Membership and Assessments	228
11.4	International Pepper Community: Membership and Assessments	231
11.5	Asian Rice Trade Fund: Membership	234
11.6	Southeast Asia Tin Research and Development Centre: Membership and Assessments	237
11.7	Association of Tin Producing Countries: Membership and Assessments	241
11.8	Membership in Three Informal Commodity Communities: Government Consultation Among Jute Producing Countries; Intergovernmental Consultative Forum of Developing Tropical Timber Producing/Exporting Countries; and Regional Consultative Group on Silk	243
12.1	Informal Meeting of Directors General of Civil Aviation, Asia and the Pacific: Membership	252
12.2	Asian Judicial Conference: Membership	254
12.3	Conference of Asian and Pacific Labor Ministers: Membership	257
12.4	Association for Science Cooperation in Asia and Taxation and Customs Cooperation Conference: Membership	260
13.1	First Agreement on Trade Negotiations Among Developing Member Countries of the Economic and	

Social Commission for Asia and the Pacific: Membership 267
13.2 Centre on Integrated Rural Development for Asia and the Pacific: Membership and Assessments 272
13.3 Asian and Pacific Development Centre: Membership and Amounts Pledged 274
13.4 South Asian Association for Regional Cooperation: Membership and Assessments 279

PREFACE

Regional cooperation developed in every continent of the world before coming into its own in Asia. Asian countries could thus take advantage of experience gained elsewhere, and they have now compiled an impressive record of achievement that can be emulated.

My purpose in examining regional organizations is to see in microcosm how nations conduct their foreign relations in Asia. For many observers, Asian regional cooperation is synonymous with the Association of South East Asian Nations (ASEAN) and possibly the South Asian Association for Regional Cooperation (SAARC), since the other organizations are so technical that little is generally known about them. Large numbers of international interactions involve trade and technical matters, however, so Asian regional cooperation in my opinion is best typified by the activity of the less conspicuous yet highly successful functional bodies.

In 1971, with funding from the Carnegie Endowment for International Peace and the United Nations Institute for Training and Research (UNITAR), I visited ten countries to begin to learn more about international organizations headquartered in Asia. It was my belief that one can only generalize about such notions as functional integration, international cooperation, and regionalism by going directly to the major hubs of such activity – offices of specific organizations. Since 1971, I have interviewed nearly 500 persons in 15 Asian countries about 53 regional intergovernmental organizations headquartered in Asia. My research culminated at the Institute for Southeast Asian Studies on a Fulbright Research Grant during midsummer 1987, when I wrote up the results of nearly two decades of research on Asian regional cooperation, then condensed the manuscript in the fall of 1988.

This volume is an effort not only to provide details on organizations whose existence is largely unknown but also to put into perspective a number of issues on regional cooperation. I have sought to sketch out a theory of regional cooperation known as the "Asian Way," a political culture that was cultivated carefully and now flourishes in the region.

A few remarks by way of definition are in order at this point. By "Asia" I refer to the region from the Afghanistan-India-Pakistan land mass to China on the east, along with associated islands and archipelagos, including Japan, the Philippines, Indonesia, Sri Lanka, and the Maldives. I include one organization headquartered in Iran, since it has the word "Asia" in its title, but other Tehran-based organizations are not included because their membership consists of one or more countries in the region often called the "Middle East." This volume describes intergovernmental organizations whose decision making is largely independent of the United Nations system or any other organization headquartered outside Asia. To be a regional organization, I required that intergovernmental bodies had at least three members in Asia. Some Asian organizations lack basic charters or headquarters; between 1967 and 1976 ASEAN had neither, yet could hardly be excluded from consideration. I included formal organizations as well as organizations that often consisted merely of annual meetings, as long as there was a regular title to these less formalized but regular conferences and representation of officials at the rank of minister or department head. This may cast a wider net than most scholars are prepared to tolerate, but the spirit of regional cooperation in Asia includes both formalized and more informal organizations, so it would be procrustean to define the scope of my endeavors otherwise.

I begin with a chapter on the "Asian Way," the theme of the volume and the spirit behind efforts at regional cooperation. I then devote chapters to various categories of organizations, concluding with the thesis that Asian regional cooperation has become "ASEANized."

The source of information consists largely of interviews and primary documents. References for each organization are cited together near the beginning of each section, as I have pledged confidentiality to the interviewees, and the primary materials are found elsewhere in my multivolume *Basic Documents of Asian Regional Organizations* or in unpublished manuscripts housed at the Asia Collection, Hamilton Library, University of Hawaii, the most complete repository for these materials in the world. Other scholars working in the field have, in my experience, seldom relied on these basic and essential sources, so one contribution of this volume is to bring to light information that I have been collecting for many years.

Earlier versions of Chapters 1 and 14 appeared in *Pacific Community* and *Asia Pacific Community*, respectively, both defunct publications of the Asia Club, Tokyo; I am grateful for the permission of the Club to reprint large portions of the original essays. Although this volume updates Volume 8 of my *Basic Documents of Asian Regional Organizations*, published by Oceana Publications, the analysis is more analytically focused herein.

I would like to dedicate the book to Werner Levi, who recruited me to the University of Hawaii in 1964. On one occasion in the late 1960s, he noted that no one was studying the important topic of Asian regional organizations, a point that I recalled subsequently when I was deliberating topics to pursue during my first sabbatical. Werner has been a delightful colleague and stimulating scholar throughout the years.

ABBREVIATIONS

AAC	Agricultural Advisory Council (of SEARCA)
AALCC	Asian African Legal Consultative Committee
AARRO	Afro-Asian Rural Reconstruction Organization
AATC	Afro-Arab Training Centre (of AARRO)
ABA	ASEAN Bankers Acceptance scheme
ABU	Asian Broadcasting Union
ACC	Asian Coconut Community
ACC	Asian Cultural Center (of APU)
ACCC	Association of Canadian Community Colleges
ACDA	Asian Centre for Development Administration
ACTAR	Asian Center for Tax Administration and Research (proposed)
ACU	Asian Clearing Union
ADB	Asian Development Bank
ADC	Asian Development Center (of APU)
ADEF	Asian Development Equity Fund (of ADB)
ADF	Asian Development Fund (of ADB)
ADI	Asian Development Institute

ADIPA	Association of Development Research and Training Institutes of Asia and the Pacific
AEM	ASEAN Economic Ministers Meeting
AFC	ASEAN Finance Corporation
AfDB	African Development Bank
AFIC	Asian Finance and Investment Corporation (proposed)
AIBD	Asia-Pacific Institute for Broadcasting Development
AIC	ASEAN Industrial Complementation Project
AIDS	acquired immune deficiency disease
AIEDP	Asian Institute for Economic Development and Planning
AIJV	ASEAN Industrial Joint Venture
AIP	ASEAN Industrial Project
AIPO	ASEAN Inter-Parliamentary Organization
AIT	Asian Institute of Technology
AJC	Asian Judicial Conference
AMDA	Anglo-Malayan Defence Agreement (before 1963); Anglo-Malaysian Defence Agreement (from 1963 to 1971)
AMM	ASEAN Annual Ministerial Meeting
AMU	Asian Monetary Unit
ANRPC	Association of Natural Rubber Producing Countries
ANZAC	Australia and New Zealand Asian Command
ANZAM	Australian, New Zealand, and Malayan area
ANZUK Force	Australian, New Zealand, and United Kingdom Force
ANZUS	Security Treaty Between Australia, New Zealand, and the United States
AOPTS	Asian-Oceanic Postal Training School
AOPU	Asian-Oceanic Postal Union
APATO	Asian and Pacific treaty organization (proposed)
APCC	Asian and Pacific Coconut Community

APCC	Asian-Pacific Cultural Center
APC-HRD	ASEAN-Pacific Cooperation in Human Resources Development Project
APCWD	Asian and Pacific Center for Women and Development
APDAC	Asian and Pacific Development Administration Centre
APDC	Asian-Pacific Development Center (of APPU)
APDC	Asian and Pacific Development Centre (Kuala Lumpur)
APDI	Asian and Pacific Development Institute
APDO	ARCAFA Project Development Office
APEID	Asian Program of Educational Innovation for Development
APIRLAS	ASEAN Program on Industrial Relations and Labor Studies
APMCS	Asian and Pacific Maritime Cooperation Scheme
APO	Asian Productivity Organization
APPTC	The Asian-Pacific Postal Training Centre
APPU	Asian-Pacific Parliamentarians' Union
APPU	Asian-Pacific Postal Union
APT	Asia-Pacific Telecommunity
APTIRC	Asian-Pacific Tax and Investment Research Center
APU	Asian Parliamentarians' Union
AQD	Aquaculture Department (of SEAFDEC)
ARCAFA	SEAMEO Regional Center for Archaeology and Fine Arts
ARPLA	Asian Regional Center for Strengthening Labor and Manpower Administration
ARSDEP	Asian Regional Skill Development Program
ARTEP	Asian Regional Team for Employment Promotion
ARTF	Asian Rice Trade Fund
ASA	Association of Southeast Asia
ASAIHL	Association of Southeast Asian Institutions of Higher Education
ASAS	Association of South-East Asian States (proposed)

ASCA	Association for Science Cooperation in Asia
ASEAN	Association of South East Asian Nations
ASEANAPOL	Meeting of the Chiefs of National Police of the ASEAN Countries
ASF	Agricultural Special Fund (of ADB)
ASI	Asian Statistical Institute
Asian Re	Asian Reinsurance Corporation
ASOD	ASEAN Senior Officials on Drug Matters
ASPAC	Asian and Pacific Council
ATC	Arab Training Centre (of AARRO)
ATN	Asian Telecommunications Network
ATPC	Association of Tin Producing Countries
AVRDC	Asian Vegetable Research and Development Center
Bangkok Agreement	First Agreement on Trade Negotiations Among Developing Member Countries of the Economic and Social Commission for Asia and the Pacific
BIOTROP	SEAMEO Regional Center for Tropical Biology
BIS	Bank for International Settlements
CALM	Conference of Asian Labor Ministers
CAPLM	Conference of Asian and Pacific Labor Ministers
CCB	Central Coordinating Board (of TROPMED)
CCM	Consultative Committee Meeting (of the Colombo Plan)
CDM	Center Directors Meeting (of SEAMEO)
CERTA	Closer Economic Relations Trade Agreement
CGDK	Coalition Government of Democratic Kampuchea
CIP	Centro Internacional de Papas (International Potato Center)
CIRDAP	Centre on Integrated Rural Development for Asia and the Pacific
CO	Central Office (of APPU)
COCI	Committee on Culture and Information (of ASEAN)
Cocopep	Permanent Coconut Production and Productivity Panel

Cocotech	Permanent Panels of Coconut Technology (of APCC)
COFAB	Committee on Finance and Banking (of ASEAN)
COFAF	Committee on Food, Agriculture and Forestry (of ASEAN)
COIME	Committee on Industry, Minerals and Energy (of ASEAN)
Comintern	Communist International
COORDCOM	Coordinating Committee of Southeast Asian Senior Officials on Transport and Communications
COSD	Committee on Social Development (of ASEAN)
COST	Committee on Science and Technology (of ASEAN)
COTAC	Committee on Transportation and Communications (of ASEAN)
COTT	Committee on Trade and Tourism (of ASEAN)
C-Plan	The Colombo Plan for Co-operative Economic and Social Development in Asia and the Pacific (Colombo Plan for Co-operative Economic Development in South and South-East Asia before 1977)
CPSC	Colombo Plan Staff College for Technician Education
CRO	common rule of origin
CTC	Combined Tin Committee
CULSOCEN	Cultural and Social Center for the Asian and Pacific Region
DGCA	Informal Meeting, Directors General of Civil Aviation, Asia and the Pacific
EAIC	East Asian Insurance Congress
EC	European Community
ECAFE	Economic Commission for Asia and the Far East (of the UN)
ECDC	economic cooperation among developing countries
ECE	Economic Commission for Europe
ECOCEN	Economic Cooperation Center for the Asian and Pacific Region

EEC	European Economic Community
EEZ	exclusive economic zone
EPA	European Productivity Agency
ESCAP	Economic and Social Commission for Asia and the Pacific (of the UN)
FAO	Food and Agriculture Organization of the United Nations
FEFC	Far Eastern Freight Conference
FFTC	Food and Fertilizer Technology Center for the Asian and Pacific Region
FPDA	Five Power Defence Arrangements
GATT	General Agreement on Tariffs and Trade
GCJPC	Government Consultation Among Jute Producing Countries
GNI	gross national income
GNP	gross national product
GSP	generalized system of preferences
HOM	High Officials Meeting (of SEAMEO)
IACP	International Association of Chiefs of Police
IADS	Integrated Air Defence System
IAU	International Association of Universities
IBFD	International Bureau of Fiscal Documentation
IBRD	International Bank for Reconstruction and Development
ICA	International Cooperative Alliance
ICAO	International Civil Aviation Organization
ICCDA	Inter-Regional Coordinating Committee of Development Associations
ICFDTTP/EC	Intergovernmental Consultative Forum of Developing Tropical Timber Producing/Exporting Countries
ICJ	International Court of Justice
ICM	Informal Consultative Meeting (of SEATAC)

ICSID	International Center for Settlement of Investment Disputes
IDA	International Development Association
IDACA	Institute for the Development of Agricultural Cooperation in Asia
IFC	International Finance Corporation
IGCC	Regional Organization for Inter-Governmental Cooperation and Coordination in Family and Population Planning in Southeast Asia
IJO	International Jute Organization
ILC	International Law Commission
ILO	International Labor Organization
IMCO	International Maritime Consultative Organization
IMF	International Monetary Fund
IMO	International Maritime Organization
INNOTECH	SEAMEO Regional Center for Educational Innovation and Technology
INRA	International Natural Rubber Agreement
INTERPOL	International Criminal Police Organization
IPC	International Pepper Community
IPTAR	Institut Penyiaran Tun Abdul Razak
IPU	Inter-Parliamentary Union
IRD	integrated rural development
IRRDB	International Rubber Research and Development Board
IRRI	International Rice Research Institute
IRSG	International Rubber Study Group
ISA	International Silk Association
ITA	International Tin Agreement
ITC	International Tin Committee (before 1956)
ITC	International Tin Council (since 1956)
ITRC	International Tin Research Council

ITRDC	International Tin Research and Development Council
ITRI	International Tin Research Institute
ITSG	International Tin Study Group
ITTO	International Tropical Timber Organization
ITU	International Telecommunication Union
JACPP	Japan-ASEAN Cooperation Promotion Program
JCRR	Sino-American Joint Commission on Rural Reconstruction
JPC	Japan Productivity Center
JSF	Japan Special Fund (of ADB)
LAWASIA	Law Association for Asia and the Pacific
LDP	Liberal Democratic Party (of Japan)
Maphilindo	Mushawarah Maphilindo
MFA	multifiber arrangements
MFRD	Marine Fisheries Research Department (of SEAFDEC)
MOP	margin of preference
MPSF	Multi-Purpose Special Fund (of ADB)
MSA	Malacca Strait Authority (proposed)
MSC	Malacca Straits Council of Japan
NACA	Network of Aquaculture Centers in Asia (of FAO)
NATO	North Atlantic Treaty Organization
NIEO	new international economic order
NPO	national productivity organization
NTB	nontariff trade barriers
NZForsea	New Zealand Force Southeast Asia
OPEC	Organization of Petroleum Exporting Countries
PC	Pepper Community
PDM	Project Directors/High Officials Meeting (of SEAMEO)
Peppertech	Pepper Technical Panel
PICC	Philippine-Indonesian Coconut Commission

PIPA	Pacific Islands Producers Association
PMC	Postministerial Conference (of ASEAN)
PRK	People's Republic of Kampuchea
PTA	Preferential Trading Arrangements (of ASEAN)
RCD	Regional Cooperation for Development
RCGS	Regional Consultative Group on Silk
RECA	Research and Education Center for Asia (of AARRO)
RECSAM	SEAMEO Regional Centre for Education in Science and Mathematics
Registry	Registry of Scientific and Technical Services for the Asian and Pacific Region
RELC	SEAMEO English Regional Language Centre (before 1977); SEAMEO Regional Language Centre (since 1977)
RIHED	Regional Institute of Higher Education and Development
RRIM	Rubber Research Institute of Malaysia
SAARC	South Asian Association for Regional Cooperation
SAFG	South Asian Federation Games
SAFSR	South Asian Food Security Reserve
SARC	South Asian Regional Cooperation
SDR	special drawing right (of IMF)
SEAC	South-East Asia Command
SEACEN	The South-east Asian Central Banks Group
SEACEN Centre	The South-east Asian Central Banks Research and Training Centre
SEACOR	Southeast Asian Community Organization (proposed)
SEAFDEC	Southeast Asian Fisheries Development Center
SEAFET	Southeast Asian Friendship and Economic Treaty (proposed)
SEALPA	South East Asian Lumber Producers' Asociation
SEAMCED	Ministerial Conference for the Economic Development of Southeast Asia

SEAMEC	Southeast Asian Ministers of Education Council
SEAMEO	Southeast Asian Ministers of Education Organization
SEAMES	Southeast Asian Ministers of Education Secretariat
SEAMHO	Southeast Asian Medical and Health Organization (proposed)
SEAMIC	Southeast Asian Medical Information Center
SEANWFZ	Southeast Asian Nuclear Weapon Free Zone
SEANZA	Central Banks of Southeast Asia, Australia and New Zealand
SEAPCENTRE	Southeast Asian Promotion Centre for Trade, Investment and Tourism
SEARCA	SEAMEO Southeast Asian Regional Center for Graduate Study and Research in Agriculture
SEASAME	Southeast Asian Science and Mathematics Experiment (of RECSAM)
SEATAC	Southeast Asian Agency for Regional Transport and Communications Development
SEATO	South-East Asia Treaty Organization
SEATRAD Centre	Southeast Asia Tin Research and Development Centre
SEDF	SEAMEO Educational Development Fund
SGATAR	Study Group on Asian Tax Administration and Research
SGO	Senior Government Officials meeting (of IGCC)
SIAP	Statistical Institute for Asia and the Pacific
SNEP	SEAMEO Nonformal Education Project
SOM	Senior Officials Meeting (of ASEAN)
SOM	Senior Officials Meeting (of TC)
SPAFA	SEAMEO Regional Project in Archaeology and Fine Arts (before 1986); SEAMEO Regional Centre for Archaeology and Fine Arts (since 1986)
SPARTECA	South Pacific Regional Trade and Economic Cooperation Agreement
SPF	South Pacific Forum

SWDCAP	Social Welfare and Development Center for Asia and the Pacific
TAC	Technical Advisory Committee (of FFTC)
TASF	Technical Assistance Special Fund (of ADB)
TC	Tripartite Council
TCCC	Taxation and Customs Cooperation Conference
TCDC	technical cooperation among developing countries
TD	Training Department (of SEAFDEC)
TNG	Trade Negotiations Group
TOP	Thailand Outreach Program (of AVRDC)
TPA	Tin Producers' Association
TPNG	Trade Preferences Negotiating Group (of ASEAN)
TRI	Tin Research Institute
TROPMED	SEAMEO Regional Tropical Medicine and Public Health Project
TSS	Traffic Separation Scheme (of TC)
TVIS	tropical vegetable information service (of AVRDC)
U.K.	United Kingdom of Great Britain and Northern Ireland
UN	United Nations
UNCITRAL	UN Commission on International Trade Law
UNCTAD	UN Conference on Trade and Development
UNDP	UN Development Program
UNESCO	UN Educational, Scientific, and Cultural Organization
UNGOM	UN Good Offices Mission
UNIDO	UN Industrial Development Organization
UNIPOM	UN India-Pakistan Observation Mission
UNITAR	UN Institute for Training and Research
UNMOGIP	UN Military Observer Group in India and Pakistan
UPU	Universal Postal Union
U.S.	United States of America

USAID	United States Agency for International Development
World Bank	International Bank for Reconstruction and Development
ZOPFAN	Zone of Peace, Freedom and Neutrality (of ASEAN)

1 THE ASIAN WAY TO PEACE

ASIAN INTERNATIONAL HISTORY

Attempts to unify Asia date back some 2,500 years to a period of hierarchically organized state relations. More specifically, as early as ca. 1500–1100 B.C., the Shang dynasty of China established a pattern of imperial control over adjacent mainland Asian territories, with tribute paid even by Japan; a peaceful hegemony in East Asia continued until the early nineteenth century. By the fourth century B.C., centralized rule was established in India, but Muslim armies were able to destroy the Indic empire in a period of struggle from the eighth to the sixteenth centuries. During these eras, archipelagic Southeast Asia was able to flourish on its own, and the Srivijaya Kingdom deterred potential invading armies from China as well as India.

War, by no means absent in Asia over the centuries, was engaged in less often by Asians than by Europeans until the advent of European imperialism.[1] Gunpowder, a Chinese discovery used for ceremonial purposes, was put to military use by the Europeans. By the nineteenth century the relentless search for markets on the part of European companies caused their governments to seek stability for commercial activities by dispatching armed contingents throughout nearly all countries of Asia. Europe sought to dominate Asia at this stage of world history and therefore had to be expelled, by force wherever necessary, for Asia to return to its former position of eminence in the world.

A new era in the history of Asia began after the end of World War II, as the imperial powers of the West withdrew from Asia, granting or yielding independence to their former colonies. Just as the advent of

Western influence was associated with warfare in Asia, so also was there a temptation among the new states of Asia to embark upon war in order to settle festering international disputes, which in many instances were legacies of colonial boundaries. Indeed, since 1946 Asia has been a battleground for about one-third of the wars fought around the world.[2]

What developments have occurred within Asia to cope with such a high level of interstate conflicts? How has Asia responded to the need for machinery and procedures for conflict resolution? In the years immediately after 1946, many Asian countries were content to look upon such events as the partition of India and Pakistan as a natural consequence of decolonization and the growth of nationalism. Although the United Nations Military Observer Group in India and Pakistan (UNMOGIP) was set up in 1948 primarily to deal with the disputed territory of Kashmir, Asia's reliance on the United Nations (UN) declined thereafter. The only UN peacekeeping organ sent to Asia between 1948 and 1988 was the UN India-Pakistan Observation Mission (UNIPOM), which operated in 1965–66. The UN Good Offices Mission (UNGOM) sent to Afghanistan in 1988 was formed mainly to permit the superpowers to extricate themselves from an Asian conflict.

One of the main correlates of the low profile of the UN in Asian conflict resolution is the gradual development of a unique approach to international relations known as the "Asian Way." The Asian Way of settling international conflicts has served to supplement the UN in matters of international politics while stimulating the growth of Asian regional cooperation and intergovernmental organizations. The Asian Way did not spring into action overnight, and it is therefore useful to describe how the Asian Way originated, how it has been promoted, and how it has been utilized. This chapter traces the development of the Asian Way, relating it to conditions in the past and present, as a new approach for bringing about world peace through the establishment of bonds of cultural affinity. In this manner it is possible to claim that the Asian Way not only constitutes an important contribution as a tool of international statecraft but also operates to bring about peaceful relations among Asian countries. Through the Asian Way, Asia is now beginning once again to influence world history in a dramatic manner. The remaining chapters note specific organizational manifestations of the Asian Way.

THE "ASIAN WAY"

Despite geographic and historical diversity, the peoples of Asia share a common culture in regard to international relations. One aspect of culture is the set of shared beliefs and sentiments that serve to orient leaders of states to their roles as international actors. The similar roles of leaders of Asian states reflect shared cultural orientations regarding precolonial, colonial, and postcolonial development. The reason for this convergence is that historical conditions shaped a common interest in peaceful modes of state behavior. Interlopers from outside the region further underscored the virtues of peaceful statecraft, and the destiny of the countries of Asia has come to depend more and more upon efforts to forge a common identity and a compatible operational code in foreign policy.

The Asian Way developed in the years after World War II, as Asian leaders began to deal directly with one another; it is not an indigenous pre-historical cultural concept. The Asian Way arose because it was gradually realized that many so-called principles of international relations observed in Western political experience could not be applied satisfactorily in an Asian context. In order to trace the development of the Asian Way, therefore, it is necessary to explain how Anglo-European practices have been unlearned and how traditional Asian methods for conflict resolution have been invented or rediscovered and readapted to the contemporary world.

The traditional cultures of Buddhism, Confucianism, Hinduism, and Islam provided Asia with a complex set of norms of international relations in which peace was considered more normal than war. When the West began its imperialist encroachment, the lack of a strong military tradition in Asia meant that colonial control could be obtained easily through force of arms. Whatever contact existed between Asian countries was interrupted, as trade and communication was established between metropolitan and colonial nodes in a network of imperialist domination.

Political independence did not bring economic independence in Asia. Colonial governors were withdrawn, but corporations with head offices in metropolitan countries remained. Insofar as the interests of corporations were entrenched before political independence, the economies of what were to be called "developing countries" were vertically integrated into a world capitalist system in which Asia exported raw materials at unfavorable terms of trade. History provided two models for economic development: capitalist prosperity through a long period of economic ups and downs and the Soviet Union's remarkable success in modernizing quickly through state direction of the economy in just 30 years. The victory of the forces of Mao in China by 1949 frightened capitalist countries in Asia—both the imperial powers that still maintained anachronistic control over various enclaves and territories and the newly independent states that had indigenous pro-Communist insurgents. The result was increased bilateral aid, the development of programs of multilateral economic assistance through various UN agencies, and an extension of the cold war to Asia. Institutionally, the UN Economic Commission for Asia and the Far East (ECAFE) in Bangkok, known as "the economic parliament of Asia,"[3] began in 1947 to formulate ambitious plans for economic development.

The nature of the rhetoric in ECAFE, Western-oriented and -dominated as it then was, contrasted with the more relaxed diplomacy conducted bilaterally within and between Asian countries, often inspired by Buddhist, Confucian, Hindu, Muslim, and other indigenous influences. The tradition of sharp disputation in the West clashed with the Asian need to save face, for example. A process of unlearning Western practices was associated with a rediscovery (selective, of course) of more traditional Asian methods for conflict resolution; this learning process proceeded quietly and without fanfare throughout the 1950s. In time, the new style of diplomacy was described as the Asian Way, though old styles have persisted as well.

No single individual is responsible for codifying or defining the Asian Way. The process of developing the Asian Way was spontaneous and almost simultaneous throughout the capitals of Asia. Inasmuch as China, Japan, and Thailand never entirely lost their independence, one might presume that they would be in the forefront of the development of the Asian Way. But China was isolated diplomatically. Japan's attempts to assume the role of Asian superpower, both past and present, were alien to the more equalitarian elements at the core of the concept. Thanat Khoman, Thai Foreign Minister during the 1950s, encouraged the development of a uniquely Asian method of diplomacy, but so did many other leaders.

U Nyun, who became the Executive Secretary of ECAFE in 1959, coined the term Asian Way. His aim was explicitly political: to steer discussion away from the concerns and priorities of the countries outside Asia and toward the aspirations and needs of developing countries inside Asia. U Nyun was careful not to define the Asian Way in specific terms; he was not declaring that there was a kind of anthropologically derived set of principles of Asian diplomacy to be contrasted with Western diplomacy, though this was an unmistakable implication of his repeated references to the Asian Way during ECAFE meetings. His objective to encourage outside countries to be more attentive to and respectful of statements of Asian delegates was largely successful at ECAFE. The Asian Way was practiced outside UN organs in the quiet diplomacy of regional cooperation during the 1960s as well. In 1967, principles identified with the Asian Way motivated the foreign ministers of five Southeast Asian countries to form the Association of South East Asian Nations (ASEAN), an institution that embodies the spirit of the Asian Way more fully than U Nyun's ECAFE, which is currently known as the Economic and Social Commission for Asia and the Pacific (ESCAP). The Asian Way has thus served to define a new political culture within which Asian diplomacy has been pursued in more recent years.

To determine the components of the Asian Way, we cannot rely on any single primary source. The actions, speeches, and writings of U Nyun, Thanat Khoman, and others have provided clues.[4] But the Asian Way appears to be a syncretic synthesis of many traditional approaches that has been reconstructed for a purpose that is politically motivated. Insofar as international relations are concerned, it would be inaccurate to say that the Asian Way is the sole cultural standard today, but it has made such dramatic inroads into the consciousness of diplomats in the region in the last three decades that it is now the most prominent norm of diplomacy in regard to methods for conflict resolution in Asia.

There are two levels and six principles to consider in any effort to understand the Asian Way. The first level consists of general beliefs and orientations toward human and international relations. The second level consists of practices and specific procedures followed in concrete situations. In both senses, the Asian Way constitutes an operational code that explains how Asian statesmen ideally prefer to conduct their affairs today at the international level.

Asian Solutions to Asian Problems

In regard to general principles, the Asian Way is largely a recognition that there must be "Asian solutions to Asian problems," a slogan popularized by Japan in the 1920s but also a tenet of Thai foreign policy, which has endeavored to avoid reliance on outside powers. This principle means that Asians prefer to solve their own problems in their own way, rather than inviting Western countries to proffer advice about policies concerning national development and international conflict. The phrase "Asia for the Asians," used by Claro Recto of the Philippines, conveys a similar view that the outsider is viewed as having too marginal an interest or understanding of Asian problems to be in a position to make a genuine contribution to Asia, except under very limited and temporary circumstances.

The principle may be traced in concrete terms to the Lahore Convention, adopted at the annual meeting of ECAFE in 1951. Before 1951, Western countries and their colonies had more votes in ECAFE than Asian countries, and they insisted on controlling the outcome of meetings by overparticipating in debates, calling for votes, and by pressuring Asian countries into adopting particular positions. As a result, ECAFE was unable to act positively for the best interests of the peoples of Asia. The Lahore Convention sought to end Western interference of this sort by declaring:

> the time has come when clearer recognition should be given to the principle that member countries belonging to the region should make their own decisions in the Commission on their own economic problems. . . . In pursuance of this principle the member countries of the Commission not in the region would be willing, as a general rule, to refrain from using their votes in opposition to economic proposals predominantly concerning the region which had the support of a majority of the countries of the region.[5]

The stress on self-reliance is based on what Emmanuel Pelaez has called "a deeply-ingrained Asian ethnic that you hear about family matters from family members, not outsiders."

Equality of Cultures

As Thanat Khoman stated, the Asian Way comprises a "spirit of tolerance and partnership" that contrasts sharply with the "concept of domination and subjection" that typified the imperialist powers in their dealings with Asian peoples.[6] Given ethnic divisions and national rivalries, international relations should not be likened to fights, to games, or to debates but instead to informal discussions in which each party is accorded equal status. There is no acceptance in Confucian doctrine, for example, of the Western concept of *raison d'etat*, the view that states are not bound by norms applied to individuals. Instead of Westerners' *Gesellschaftish* penchant for rational and impersonal calculations preparatory to agreements, it is necessary for Asians to develop personal relationships with one another in order to develop a *Gemeinschaftish* mutual trust, from which agreements become possible. According to the Indonesian notion of *mushawarah* (an Arabic-derived word), consensus-building discussion takes place not as between opposites but as between friends and brothers. Asians feel uncomfortable in situations in which the prerogatives of status inhibit the free expression of ideas.

The equality principle is manifest in at least three ways. First, Asians are reluctant to join or form international organizations that are likely to be dominated by a big country, including Japan. Second, although diplomats accept the Confucian principle that big countries should exercise restraint in dealing with weaker states while small states should look up to larger states as big brothers, equalitarian relationships are preferred. Japan, the richest country in Asia, has often tried to play an equal role by declining to exercise leadership in discussions at multicountry conferences, but it has not been easy for Tokyo to do so. Third, the principle of equality recognizes that very often it is difficult for an envoy to change positions during an international conference. Hence countries that hold contrary views avoid stating differences in a harsh or inflexible manner; all sides at a conference learn to respect one another's views, referring to the experience as an "exchange of views."

Consensus Decision Making

The equality principle is related to a third facet of the Asian Way. Power plays, trade-offs, and deals that produce temporary compromises and modi vivendi in Anglo-European bargaining are eschewed by the Asian Way, which operates on the basis of a principle of unanimity. A decision is the outcome of a consensus, a flexible accommodation of opposites that is built gradually on the basis of what all parties can endorse. The Pilipino term *pakikisama*, the emphasis on observing correct interpersonal relations, well illustrates the basis for the need for unanimous consensus. This differs from the Western tendency toward rigid confrontation of divergent positions followed by a compromise calculated by an implicit mathematical-type algorithm. In the Asian Way no decision is made unless each party can support the decision in principle. *Mufakat*, to use another Arabic-derived Malay term, refers to the process of building unanimity through discussion rather than majority voting. This consensus-building principle, rooted as it is in principles of etiquet, is also consistent with the Lahore Convention, which developed in reaction to the stormy sessions in the early years of ECAFE. In those sessions, when Western countries called for votes that compelled Asian countries to take sides on particular issues, some countries voted with the Western powers in order to avoid unpleasant castigations from their principal sources of capital aid and technical assistance. Tension between pro-West and neutralist countries, in turn, served to divide Asians.

Today, decisions in Asian international organizations are made unanimously without a count of votes. Deliberations are informal in tone, conducted usually in private, and with no formal records kept of the proceedings until a public session is held. Malaysia's former Prime Minister Tun Abdul Razak once contrasted Asian "sports-shirt diplomacy" with the formality of Western "business-suit diplomacy."[7] As a result of the principle of unanimous consensus, conflict that might result in loss of face can be softened, and a joint responsibility for progress emerges from discussions. Decisions are based more on "give" (rather than the Western "give-and-take") and coercive tactics are avoided in diplomacy. If friction is anticipated at a forthcoming meeting, the meeting is postponed. If a country cannot accept or go along with a popular view in a diplomatic conference, no decision is made.

Thus, in contrast to the Western principle of majority rule and the Quaker principle of having the collective wisdom and judgment of a majority brought to bear in order to shame or ostracize a recalcitrant individual or state, the Asian Way is grounded in the belief that no majority has the right to rule or shame anyone. Everyone is entitled to the dignity of their own position and need not lose face. It should be pointed out that the two times when international organizations pointed a collective finger at an Asian country were at Japan in the early 1930s and at China in the early 1950s. In both cases, the result was that the countries turned inward and decided to go it alone; the outcome was more intense conflict in the region.

Informal Incrementalism

There is a recognition that shared objectives, such as the desire for an Asian common market, can be achieved most effectively through small steps rather than by drawing up grand blueprints or timetables. Governments and international organizations proceed with caution, in other words, mindful of the famous Chinese proverb that a journey of 10,000 *li* begins with the first step. Care is necessary in order to secure a solid political backing throughout each stage of a project. This Asian incrementalism differs from Western incrementalism, notably of the Fabian variety. The latter sets up an institution and endows it with a mission in a carefully worded constitution or charter. Asian incrementalism instead stresses the utility of noninstitutional frameworks for discussion, while operational activities are entrusted to organizations without elaborate constitutional specifications.

This nonlegalistic incrementalism results from the fact that Asian governments must often try to obtain popular consent without the benefit of strong political parties, pluralistic interest groups, and an informed citizenry. Such conditions require government leaders to engage in a complex process of consultation with organized interests, while attempting to anticipate the reactions of those who lack group memberships to represent their views, those who are unaccustomed to working through formal structures, and those who only make their views known after specific actions have been taken. Rather than exerting political pressure over proposals in parliaments, Asians prefer to respond to concrete results of decisions. Hence, if there are local political centers of authority, national leaders must approach them for support before launching a five-year plan. In ECAFE's twenty-fifth-year report, this principle is stated with considerable cogency:

> Priorities of developmental work are determined by the needs of the countries and their willingness to participate. A project will be successful only when there is general understanding of its nature and a conviction of its worth by the countries concerned. As the United Nations has no power of sovereignty,

this means working at it, but often also proceeding slowly until a better understanding is developed and national positions and policies are favorable.[8]

Asian incrementalism recognizes the inherent limitations of any government in a developing country as a catalyst for developmental objectives.

Primacy of Politics over Administration

Matters of implementation are separated from matters of principle in the Asian Way. Asian diplomats obtain a commitment to abstract goals first, such as ASEAN's concept of the neutralization of Southeast Asia, leaving questions regarding the feasibility of putting lofty ideals into practice as matters to be left out of political discussions. Implementation is assigned to administrative subordinates, who are not supposed to throttle the attainment of political objectives. Thus, Asian political leaders intend to keep the primacy of politics above the prerogatives of bureaucracies. Asian leaders will not allow a lack of development capital or other economic difficulties to weaken their political resolve. Secretariats of international organizations in Asia, thus, are usually modestly staffed and carefully monitored by member governments at annual meetings, but the management is more macro-level than micro-level. The Western preference for making decisions only about matters that can be quickly and optimally translated into action is not part of the Asian Way. Instead of focusing attention on problems related to lack of resources, as a Western feasibility study would do, Asian diplomats prefer to make decisions in principle in order to concentrate on objectives and solutions that transcend current limitations.

Pan-Asian Spirit

Finally, the Asian Way is a pan-Asian spirit that allows wide latitude for subregional efforts. The Asian Way is not aimed against any state or group of states but instead is based on the notion of *bayanihan*, the Pilipino term for collective self-help at the local level, or *gotongroyong*, the Indonesian equivalent. Within Asia, an entire community will provide assistance in projects that benefit individual members, such as moving a family's house by having several dozen persons carry the load on their shoulders over the distance to the new location. This collective interdependence and responsibility to others contrasts with the mind-your-own-business individualism and impersonal character of much of Western society.

Accordingly, there is a general recognition that international decisions may often have to precede national development planning, as there should be an end to wasteful economic competition in the respective countries' efforts to sell product at home or abroad. Regional and subregional economic cooperation will lack credibility as long as political rivalries remain between states. So the Asian Way encourages leaders to accept an international status quo concerning borders, while adapting national development plans to a future international division of labor among the countries of Asia, which must begin at the subregional level before growing. The freezing of the Malaysian-Philippine territorial dispute over Sabah after 1963 should be viewed in this context. Unlike the Anglo-European experience, political leaders in Asia operate without much interference from national economic interests and instead focus on responding to competition from foreign and multinational corporations on a regional and national basis. That many countries are now seeking cooperative strategies is important for our purposes, indicating that the common culture forged by the Asian Way will point to peace rather than in the direction of costly conflict in the years ahead. And peace is seen as the normal condition of international relations.

Each of the six principles above, in sum, reverses an axiom that might be used to describe how Westerners would handle public policy matters, although these principles, to be sure, are not alien to Western societies. The Asian Way arose as steps were taken to cope with the international problems of states that had achieved political but not economic independence after World War II. Having found that Anglo-European methods can abet even further conflict in many instances, the Asian Way emerged as an amalgam of the teachings of Buddha, Confucius, and Mohammed, adapted to modern times. The Asian Way is more likely to be a model of performance in Asian public and private life, which those in the West endeavor to keep as separate realms.

ASIAN REGIONAL ORGANIZATIONS

How has the Asian Way served to bring about the framework for a more lasting peace? The main achievement of the Asian Way is the growth of new intergovernmental organizations and agencies with headquarters in Asian countries, within which the Asian Way is practiced.

It is, therefore, appropriate to ask how international organizations can succeed in bringing about peace, while national governments, the members of the organizations, are the parties to conflict situations that have all too often erupted in wars. What are the specific mechanisms or devices employed by international bodies? With which problems do they cope most successfully? Why have they only recently been established? There are about 40 regional organizations today with predominantly Asian membership. Most have been formed since 1960, and about half of the total were formed after 1965 (see Table 1.1). Indeed, during the 1960s, Asia saw such organizations increase at a faster rate than any other region in the world.[9] What accounts for this momentum? One way to answer these questions is to review them with special attention to wellsprings of leadership in their formation.

Table 1.1
Asian Regional Organizations: Formation and Termination

Year	Organizations Formed	Organizations Terminated
1950	C-Plan	
1951		
1952		
1953		
1954		
1955	SEATO	
1956	ALCC[a]	
1957	AMDA,[b] SEANZA	
1958		
1959		
1960		
1961	AOPU,[a] APO, ASA,[b] DGCA	
1962	AARRO	
1963	AJC	
1964		
1965	ADB, APU,[a] SEAMEO	
1966	ASPAC, CALM,[a] SEACEN, SEAMCED	
1967	ASEAN, COORDCOM,[b] SEAFDEC	ASA
1968	ACC[a]	
1969		
1970	FFTC, RIHED	
1971	ANRPC, AVRDC, CULSOCEN, ECOCEN, FPDA, IGCC, Registry, SGATAR, TC	
1972	ASCA, PC,[a] SEAPCENTRE TCCC	ASPAC
1973	ARTF[c]	AJC
1974		Registry
1975	ACU, AIPO, Bangkok Agreement	ECOCEN, SEAMCED, TCCC
1976		SEATO
1977	AIBD, SEATRAD Centre	
1978	CIRDAP	SEAPCENTRE
1979	APT, GCAJPC	
1980	IFMC	
1981	ASEANAPOL, Asian Re,	
1982	ICFDTTP/EC, RCGS	IGCC
1983	APDC, ATPC, SARC[a]	
1984		
1985		RIHED
Totals	53 organizations	11 organizations

[a]Acronym or name changed later
[b]Superseded by another organization
[c]Currently dormant

There were some false starts in the development of regional cooperation in Asia. The Congress of the Nations of the Orient, convened by the Communist International (Comintern) at Baku in 1920, called upon the peoples of Asia to rise up against the imperialist powers. The Pan-Asiatic Conference of 1926 at Nagasaki enabled Japan to unveil the concept of a Greater East Asia Co-Prosperity Sphere, but this vision turned into a justification for Japanese aggression in the following decade. The Far Eastern Commission, which supervised Japan's military occupation after World War II, had a wide range of countries as members, but the very title (far from what?) showed that the initiative was outside Asia.

Efforts at leadership may be placed into at least nine categories. The earlier attempts were less consequential than the later ones, as the Asian Way had to be learned through a trial-and-error process.

External Initiatives

Cooperation between external and internal pressures for regional institutions started the ball rolling. ECAFE was set up in 1947 at the insistence of a UN delegate from China, who pressed the case in the General Assembly. Western countries at first opposed the ECAFE idea but changed their minds as an Economic Commission for Europe (ECE) gained acceptance. ECAFE became ESCAP in 1974.

The Colombo Plan for Co-operative Economic Development in South and Southeast Asia came into being in 1950, initially as a product of the British Commonwealth of Nations, with strong backing from Australia, India, and Ceylon (which became Sri Lanka in 1972). Eventually, the Colombo Plan was transformed from having a "very British" tone to one corresponding to the concept of the Asian Way, and in 1977 it became the Colombo Plan for Co-operative Economic and Social Development in Asia and the Pacific (C-Plan).

Military-oriented organizations in Asia also had joint support from countries inside and outside Asia. The Australian, New Zealand, and Malayan Defence Committee (ANZAM Defence Committee) was established in 1948 at Canberra to coordinate use of the Commonwealth Far East Strategic Reserve, under the command of the British Commander-in-Chief, Far East, at Singapore. The South-East Asia Treaty Organization (SEATO), formed in 1955 and the Anglo-Malayan Defence Agreement (AMDA) of 1957 were supported financially by Western powers. Both of these were viewed as stopgaps until Asia gained more self-reliance to provide for itself. AMDA became the Anglo-Malaysian Defence Agreement in 1963 and was superseded by the Five Power Defence Arrangements (FPDA) of 1971, which by 1987 had a greatly reduced external presence. SEATO shut down on the first day of 1977, having run counter to the Asian Way.

Indian Leadership

India was the first Asian country to exert leadership within the region. A nongovernmental Asian Relations Organization was formed at New Delhi in 1947 but was premature. The Indian government sought to build a nonaligned movement in Asia, and Sri Lanka responded by convening the first of three meetings in 1954 and 1955 to launch the movement. Known as the Colombo Powers Conferences, they were clearly so anti-Western that they mirrored the contentiousness eschewed by the Asian Way.

Two Afro-Asian organizations were established with headquarters in Asia. The Asian Legal Consultative Committee (ALCC), formed in 1956 at New Delhi, became the Asian African Legal Consultative Committee (AALCC) the following year. In 1962, Indian leadership sparked the formation of the Afro-Asian Rural Reconstruction Organization (AARRO), a second organization headquartered in New Delhi with a core of Asian countries. AARRO eventually oriented itself more toward Africa and the Middle East (the latter sometimes called "Western Asia"). The failure of India and other countries to mobilize a large bloc of Afro-Asian countries was due to the heterogeneous character of the Third World. There is no truly "Afro-Asian Way," as the champions of the movement discovered; instead, common political motivations were shared but not an underlying cultural resonance. New leadership, therefore, was required in order to create organizations based on the Asian Way.

Northeast Asian Initiatives

The next set of organizational initiatives came from northeast Asia. In 1957, two years after Allied occupation of Japan ended, Prime Minister Nobusuke Kishi proposed three banking organizations: an Asian commercial fund for short-term loans, an Asian development fund for long-term loans and technical assistance, and an export credit fund. As these ideas appeared to recall the concept of the Greater East Asia Co-Prosperity Sphere, they got nowhere. Instead, two organizations originally conceived as nongovernmental efforts were launched as intergovernmental entities. The Asian Productivity Organization (APO) was founded in 1961, and the Asian Parliamentarians' Union (APU) began in 1965. (By 1980 the latter had become the Asian-Pacific Parliamentarians' Union, or APPU.) Northeast Asia became the focal point for initiatives because Japan was able to ensure the financial success of any organization that might interest the rest of the countries of Asia. Both organizations receded into the background of Asian regional cooperation precisely because of the increasing disparity between Japan and other Asian countries, which is contrary to the Asian Way principle of equality.

The establishment of diplomatic relations between Japan and the Republic of Korea in 1965 was one in a series of steps by the latter to end its diplomatic isolation. Seoul, in close consultation with Tokyo, launched an ambitious effort toward regional cooperation in 1966 with the establishment of the Asian and Pacific Council (ASPAC). ASPAC was too cold war–oriented; it collapsed in 1972, when many of its members preferred to develop warmer relations with the People's Republic of China than could be tolerated by Seoul and its more faithful de facto regional ally, the Republic of China. Before folding, however, ASPAC gave birth to several autonomous organizations: the Cultural and Social Center (CULSOCEN) in 1968, the Food and Fertilizer Technology Center (FFTC) in 1969, the Economic Cooperation Center (ECOCEN) in 1970, and the Registry of Scientific and Technical Services and the Asian and Pacific Maritime Cooperation Scheme (APMCS) in 1971. When ASPAC collapsed, only two organizations survived: CULSOCEN and FFTC, headquartered respectively at Seoul and Taipei. Although elements of the Asian Way were practiced, ASPAC's underlying political motives were alien to it.

In 1966, with the war in Vietnam producing fears throughout Asia of a "row of dominoes" falling to Communist regimes, Japan decided that its new "Asian diplomacy" would be most effectively implemented through plans to finance aid to Southeast Asia. The first meeting of the Ministerial Conference for the Economic Development of Southeast Asia (SEAMCED) convened at Tokyo in 1966. Japan expressed an interest in financing projects proposed by Southeast Asian countries. The first new organization, the Southeast Asian Fisheries Development Center (SEAFDEC), came in 1967. A Coordinating Committee of Southeast Asian Senior Officials on Transport and Communications (COORDCOM) began in 1968, becoming the Southeast Asian Agency for Regional Transport and Communications Development (SEATAC) by 1972. In the field of population and family planning, the Inter-Governmental Coordinating Committee (IGCC) was formed in 1971, becoming the Regional Organization for Inter-Governmental Cooperation and Coordination in Family and Population Planning in Southeast Asia (still IGCC) in 1973. The Study Group on Asian Tax Administration and Research (SGATAR) convened in 1971. The Southeast Asian Promotion Centre for Trade, Investment and Tourism (SEAPCENTRE) started in 1972.

But the inequality in wealth between Japan and the countries of

Southeast Asia and the involvement of Indochinese countries in all these organizations presented three dilemmas. First, the Asian Way could not be practiced where there was a sharp distinction in roles between aid donor and aid recipient, so Japan had to keep a low profile. Second, what happened if Japan did not finance an organization or pulled out later? Third, what was to be done when the Indochinese countries were inactive after 1975? The first casualty of the change of regimes in Indochina was SEAMCED (by 1975). SEAFDEC retained Japanese support but attracted other funds. SEATAC sought aid from non-Japanese sources. IGCC also got financing from other donors, but shut down in 1982 when external funds dried up. SGATAR, lacking support from Japan, has continued without any central office. Ninety percent of SEAPCENTRE support was from Japan, but the organization was discontinued in 1978, when the programs it supported became fully funded by Japan as part of its aid to ASEAN. The conjunction of the Japanese Way and the Southeast Asian Way did not exactly add up to the Asian Way; the former had yet to learn from the latter.

Southeast Asian Leadership

Subregional organizations in Southeast Asia, at first modest in scope, increasingly proved to be the most dynamic. The Association of Southeast Asia (ASA) had an auspicious start in 1961, with the Asian Way in the forefront, but formation of Malaysia provoked conflict over territories in Borneo claimed by Indonesia and the Philippines. Maphilindo, launched in 1963 by Indonesia, Malaya, and the Philippines, was an effort to freeze the conflict; but as soon as Malaysia was finally formed, ASA was put on ice, and Maphilindo was stillborn. Then a new regime in Indonesia began to develop a "good-neighbor" policy toward the region, an embodiment of the Asian Way par excellence, ultimately resulting in the establishment in 1967 of ASEAN, an organization of such political importance that it now overshadows all other Asian regional bodies. ASEAN's success, due in large part to the application of Asian Way principles on a systematic basis, in turn inspired the formation of the ASEAN Inter-Parliamentary Organization (AIPO) in 1977 and the Meeting of the Chiefs of National Police of the ASEAN Countries (ASEANAPOL) in 1981. Neither AIPO nor ASEANAPOL has been recognized as part of the structure of ASEAN, though their formation proves that the application of the Asian Way has spilled over into new areas for cooperation.

Yet another example of spillover was in the field of education. The Southeast Asian Ministers of Education Organization (SEAMEO) was formed in 1968. Under SEAMEO, seven regional centers of excellence and regional projects have been formed within its member countries. In

1971, Indonesia, Malaysia, and Singapore formed the Tripartite Council (TC) to coordinate policies toward the straits of Malacca and Singapore. In 1980, after Vietnam's army had largely removed the threat of Pol Pot from neighboring Cambodia (then called Kampuchea), the first in a series of meetings known as the Conferences of the Foreign Ministers of Laos, Kampuchea and Vietnam was held, an Indochinese counterpart to and would-be interlocutor with ASEAN.

Banking Organizations

Bankers in Asia, particularly in Japan, wanted a regional bank. Since 1956, an Australian-sponsored series of biennial training programs had been operated by the Central Banks of Southeast Asia, Australia and New Zealand (SEANZA). Since SEANZA was not set up to undertake the task of developing the framework for a regional bank, ECAFE leadership brought bankers together to form the Asian Development Bank (ADB) in late 1966. While ECAFE consulted throughout the region concerning ADB, some of the central bank governors that had been participating in SEANZA held a meeting on their own at Bangkok in early 1966 to consider provisions for the proposed ADB. The banking officials then constituted a South-east Asian Central Banks Group (SEACEN), which formed the South-east Asian Central Banks Research and Training Centre (SEACEN Centre) 11 years later, in 1977. Meanwhile, ECAFE (now ESCAP) prepared the way for the Asian Clearing Union (ACU) in 1975 and the Asian Reinsurance Corporation (Asian Re) in 1978.

Communication Organizations

Several UN Specialized Agencies had a catalytic role in promoting Asian regional cooperation, leaving most of the leadership to countries in the region, who were pursuing the Asian Way with greater success. The Philippines took the initiative in starting the Asian-Oceanic Postal Union (AOPU) in 1962, a "restricted postal union" in accord with policies of the Universal Postal Union (UPU) at Berne. Although AOPU only had four members up to 1968, by 1975 its membership was sufficient to take over operation of the Asian-Oceanic Postal Training School (AOPTS) from the UN Development Program (UNDP), and in 1981 AOPU became the Asian-Pacific Postal Union (APPU). The UN Educational, Scientific, and Cultural Organization (UNESCO) asked UNDP to fund a Malaysian broadcasting training center as a prototype for a regional organization, and the Asia-Pacific Institute for Broadcasting Development (AIBD) emerged on its own in 1977. ESCAP then teamed up with the International Telecommunication

Union (ITU) to devolve the former's concept of an Asian "telecommunity" into a self-sustaining Asia-Pacific Telecommunity (APT) in 1979.

Commodity Communities

Commodity-producing countries were next in line. Problems in maintaining prices for primary products in the region had interested ECAFE's economists for many years, but now the prodding came more from the countries than just from the staff at Sala Santitham (Peace Hall, where ECAFE offices were originally located) in Bangkok. After the formation of ASEAN, the practice of having new organizations drawn up by ECAFE, then negotiated to exist on their own, had become a more familiar pattern. ECAFE first launched the Asian Coconut Community (ACC) in 1969 (becoming APCC, the Asian and Pacific Coconut Community, in 1975). Although ECAFE had studied problems of natural rubber in the region, the ASEAN countries, minus the Philippines, took their own initiative in forming the Association of Natural Rubber Producing Countries (ANRPC) in 1970, along with India and Sri Lanka. In 1972, Robert Chandler retired as Director of the nongovernmental International Rice Research Institute (IRRI) in order to head the new Asian Vegetable Research and Development Center (AVRDC). ECAFE next tried to get support for the Pepper Community (PC), which was approved in 1972 but languished until the mid-1970s. Begun on an interim basis, PC was retitled the International Pepper Community (IPC) in 1980, thereby attracting Brazil as a member the following year. The Asian Rice Trade Fund (ARTF), meanwhile, was formed at ESCAP in 1974 but never got off the ground. Then ESCAP and UNDP assisted Indonesia, Malaysia, and Thailand in forming the Southeast Asia Tin Research and Development Centre (SEATRAD Centre) in 1979. ESCAP continued to form commodity communities on an informal basis, and in 1979 the Government Consultation Among Jute Producing Countries (GCJPC) was formed. In 1982, ESCAP initiated two bodies – the Intergovernmental Consultative Forum of Developing Tropical Timber Producing/Exporting Countries (ICFDTTP/EC) and the Regional Consultative Group on Silk (RCGS). The Association of Tin Producing Countries (ATPC) emerged in 1983, primarily after efforts that began within ASEAN, though ATPC membership extends to Africa as well.

Conferences without Headquarters

Some Asian organizations never quite congealed; in these cases, leadership came from the Philippines, but funding sources were never found. Just as ASEAN had no secretariat in its first decade, some groupings of Asian countries have met together at regular intervals without a central office. There have been reasons to meet but no funds to support large projects, so these ministerial-level conferences continue to form a part of the corps of Asian regional organizations, sustained more by the Asian Way than by formalisms or donors.

The first of these bodies, the Informal Meeting, Directors General of Civil Aviation, Asia and the Pacific (DGCA), began in 1961; in time the Bangkok office of the International Civil Aviation Organization (ICAO) agreed to provide secretariat services for their meetings. Supreme Court chief justices met regularly from 1963 to 1973 under the aegis of the Asian Judicial Conference (AJC). The Conference of Asian Labor Ministers (CALM) came together in 1966, then retitled itself the Conference of Asian and Pacific Labor Ministers (CAPLM) in 1976, and has continued ever since with regular participation by the Bangkok office of the International Labor Organization (ILO). The Association for Science Cooperation in Asia (ASCA) brought together scientists working on government research projects and others with related interests in 1972; Seoul has provided a coordinating office since 1988. The Taxation and Customs Cooperation Conference (TCCC) existed from 1972 to 1975. These conferences were convened with invitations from the Philippines, but only TCCC had a secretariat at Manila.

Later Organizations

Some of the later organizations do not fall into the categories above. They attest, nonetheless, to the vitality of Asian regional cooperation. ESCAP furnishes the secretariat for the First Agreement on Trade Negotiations Among Developing Member Countries of the Economic and Social Commission for Asia and the Pacific, known as the Bangkok Agreement, of 1975. The Bangkok office of the Food and Agriculture Organization of the United Nations (FAO) convened meetings leading to the formation of the Centre on Integrated Rural Development for Asia and the Pacific (CIRDAP) in 1979. After a long history as an ECAFE/ESCAP project, the Asian and Pacific Development Centre (APDC) emerged on its own as an independent regional organization in 1983.

The newest regional organization is perhaps the most tenuous in the minds of many, yet potentially could prove the most successful. Bangladesh, feeling that South Asia should have the benefits of an ASEAN-type organization, developed the concept of a South Asian regional institution in the mid-1970s, then sold the idea to its neighbors. After meetings with foreign secretaries and foreign ministers from April 1981 to May 1985, the South Asian Association for Regional Cooperation (SAARC) was officially approved by a summit conference of the heads of government of seven countries in December 1985. Subject to many strains in its short existence, SAARC's initial stress on building a common culture holds a potential for proving once and for all that the Asian Way is the surest pathway to peace in Asia.

CONFLICT RESOLUTION THROUGH THE ASIAN WAY

The main principle underlying the growth of new international organizations in Asia is that peace may be achieved through the cultural affinity cultivated by the Asian Way. This is perhaps an indirect approach to peace, for it rests on the assumption that causes of war in Asia can be attacked by bringing about a common culture, which in turn can spill over into economic and political cooperation. The Asian Way has had an impact on conflict resolution in at least three ways: by favoring economic cooperation over political disputes, by providing informal networking at technical conferences, and by infusing political organizations with the principles of the Asian Way.

Primacy of Economics over Politics

In choosing to control their own destinies together, Asian countries have gradually come to the realization that they must work together economically on a truly multilateral basis if they are ever to make progress separately. Although economic competition keeps prices of primary products down in the First World, cooperation serves the best economic interests of the developing countries of Asia. Thus, a major reason for the dynamism of new Asian regional organizations is that most are concerned with economic issues and with the desire to have a multiplier effect through joint projects. Then, while mutual benefits are derived through cooperation, divisive conflicts and disputes are not on the agenda and thereby recede from attention. Border and other disputes are soft-pedalled whenever countries with outstanding political differences decide to join hands in new international institutions on behalf of a common mission. India and Pakistan, to name two countries often at odds in public, do not quarrel with each other within these bodies. Disputes along the borders of ASEAN countries have been handled through bilateral mechanisms in order to ensure continued progress at economic cooperation.

Technical Organizations as Arenas for Conflict Resolution

Technical organizations can serve as arenas for resolving disputes. It was at an early meeting of SEAMEO that representatives from Malaysia and the Philippines agreed to a détente regarding conflicting claims to Sabah, which continued until 1987, when the Philippine Constitution gave up all claims to the territory. But the greatest impact is in the development of cross-national ties at a personal level between younger technical experts. Eventually, these individuals can and do rise to important positions, where they must inevitably consider the policy of their country toward another in human terms as affecting persons whom they met as co-participants in past conferences. Border disputes between China and India, China and Laos, China and Vietnam, the two Koreas, Japan and the Soviet Union, and Laos and Thailand remain precisely because at least one of the parties in the conflict belongs to few regional organizations and thus lacks access to informal discussions that could ease the situation.

Role of Political Organizations

Political organizations that practice the Asian Way have been successful as conflict-management arenas. ASEAN, which served the immediate political objective of ensuring peace among Indonesia, Malaysia, and the Philippines in 1967, has built political solidarity over the past two decades on a variety of issues. SAARC devotes most of its public agenda to technical-assistance projects; in private, intra-SAARC tensions have been defused since the inception of the organization. Indian troops went to Sri Lanka in 1987 and the Maldives in 1988 with the tacit approval of fellow SAARC countries. ASPAC and SEATO, which failed to follow Asian Way principles, no longer exist.

THE ASIAN WAY AS A NEW THEORY OF INTERNATIONAL COOPERATION

The exemplary character of Asian regional cooperation is primarily due to a new form of international statecraft in the region. This innovation, known as the Asian Way, goes beyond previous theories of international integration.

The Asian Way represents a new stage in the development of theories of regional cooperation.[10] *Functionalist theories*, identified with David Mitrany,[11] envisage that a proliferation of technical organizations may achieve world peace by prompting nations to transfer small slivers of their sovereignty to technical experts in myriad functional areas. Such *neofunctionalist theorists* as Ernst Haas[12] point to the experience in forming the European Economic Community (EEC), noting that collective political resolve was an important precondition to the development of European functional organizations, which in turn was expected to spill over into more sensitive areas and snowball into a larger politically inclusive union. Functionalists, in short, see nonpolitical cooperation as a precondition to political cooperation; neofunctionalists argue that the two aspects should be reversed. *Communication theorists*, particularly Karl Deutsch and associates,[13] argue that the cultural affinity evidenced by dense social communications of ordinary people must precede progress in national and international integration, both in political and more technical matters. The Asian Way agrees with neofunctionalists that the leaders of nations must first recognize common interests, and it agrees with communication theorists that a common culture must be forged. However, it argues that a common method for diplomacy, based on the best elements of diverse cultural and religious value systems, is a precondition to political and technical cooperation from which social communications between peoples will grow.

The theory of the Asian Way, in short, is a *cultural theory of international cooperation*. Having laid a foundation of cultural affinity, a network of social communications among technical experts will lead to expanding neofunctionalist political cooperation and into functionalist economic and technical areas. The net result of collaborative efforts of the Asian Way has been a fuller respect for the integrity of other countries, a spirit of solidarity and sharing, a belief that intense conflict is unacceptably fratricidal and unprofitable, and thus the development of a peaceful community among Asian countries. Countries outside the web of interrelationships forged by the Asian Way continue to be plagued with economic, political, and technical difficulties in their efforts to achieve economic development.

These generalizations require us to look more carefully at each Asian regional institution. We find in the detailed workings of these bodies the full scope of cooperation and the extent to which regional cooperation penetrates almost every sphere of life in Asia.

NOTES

1. Quincy Wright, *A Study of War*, 2nd ed. (Chicago: University of Chicago Press, 1965), pp. 641–45.
2. Istvan Kende, "Wars of Ten Years (1967–1976)," *Journal of Peace Research*, 15(3) (1978): 227–42.
3. David Wightman, *Toward Economic Cooperation in Asia* (New Haven, CT: Yale University Press, 1953).
4. See Michael Haas, "The 'Asian Way' to Peace," *Pacific Community* (Tokyo), 4 (Fall 1974): 498–514.
5. Ibid., p. 503.
6. Ibid.
7. Ibid., p. 504.
8. Ibid.
9. "The Geography of International Organization," *International Associations*, 24 (March 1972): 175.

10. For a summary of theories of regional integration, see Charles Pentland, *International Theory and European Integration* (New York: Free Press, 1973). For a detailed presentation of the need for elites to forge unity among disparate peoples, see Estrella D. Solidum, *Towards a Southeast Asian Community* (Quezon City: University of the Philippines Press, 1974).

11. David Mitrany, *A Working Peace System* (Chicago: Quadrangle, 1966).

12. Ernst B. Haas, *Beyond the Nation-State* (Stanford: Stanford University Press, 1964).

13. Karl W. Deutsch, *Political Community at the International Level* (Garden City, NY: Doubleday, 1954).

2 FOREIGN-AID PUBLICITY (BUT NOT PLANNING) FROM COLOMBO

The first meeting of foreign ministers of the British Commonwealth of Nations after World War II was scheduled to convene at Colombo, Ceylon, in January 1950. A general discussion of international relations, with particular attention to Asia, was originally envisaged. The dramatic success of the Communist revolution in China, however, gave some urgency to the meeting.

As the meeting began, Ceylon's Prime Minister, D. S. Senanayake, spoke first, stressing that Asian problems were more economic than political. His Finance Minister, J. R. Jayawardene, proposed a Commonwealth "Marshall Plan" for Asia. Since Australia had already prepared a similar proposal, consensus was present, and the idea was accepted by the foreign ministers, who then set up a Commonwealth Consultative Committee to develop the framework of the organization.

THE COLOMBO PLAN FOR CO-OPERATIVE ECONOMIC AND SOCIAL DEVELOPMENT IN ASIA AND THE PACIFIC (C-PLAN)[1]

The inaugural Commonwealth Consultative Committee meeting at Sydney in May 1950 decided that developing member countries in attendance should develop six-year development plans and then present them to a second Consultative Committee meeting to be held at London from September 25 to October 5, 1950. The set of reports, together with a proposed Constitution of the Council for Technical Co-operation in South and South-East Asia, were then approved at the London conference. Since the plans of Ceylon, India, and Pakistan did not lend themselves to an integrated multilateral aid program but instead to a set of bilateral programs between each country and the donors (Australia, Canada, New Zealand, and the United Kingdom), a scheme including a central office (the Bureau) and a coordinating organ (the Council) in Colombo was thought most appropriate. The organization, originally called the Colombo Plan for Co-operative Economic Development in South and South-East Asia, went into effect July 1, 1951, for a five-year trial. At the end of each subsequent five years C-Plan was renewed for another five-year period until 1980, when it was extended for an indefinite time period. In 1977, the organization was retitled The Colombo Plan for Co-operative Economic and Social Development in Asia and the Pacific to reflect the new concerns with social issues and an extension in geographic scope to include island nations in the South Pacific.

According to the original Constitution, the Council was "to assist in the economic development of South and South-East Asia by the promotion of technical assistance" (Article 1). When the Constitution was revised in 1977 to apply to all organs of the Colombo Plan, three purposes were specified:

> (a) To promote interest in and support for the economic and social development of Asia and the Pacific, (b) to keep under review economic and social progress in the region and the flow of developmental assistance under the Colombo Plan from member Governments with a view to accelerating development through cooperative effort; and (c) to facilitate development assistance to and within the region.

The Commonwealth Consultative Committee was the initial organ of the C-Plan, but the word "Commonwealth" was dropped in 1951, when non-Commonwealth countries expressed an interest in membership. The Consultative Committee Meeting (CCM) occurs biennially (annually up to 1984) for about a week; it is attended by ministers and senior officials from the member countries (see Fig. 2.1). A preparatory Meeting of Senior Officials of Member Countries convenes for the first two or three days of the week, clearing the way for an efficient plenary session.

The Council has one delegate from each member country. Diplomatic representatives of member countries posted in Colombo, plus special representatives sent occasionally by countries lacking diplomatic missions in Sri Lanka, attend Council sessions. Originally, the Council served in a coordinating role, with frequent meetings; today, it meets for morning sessions on a quarterly basis, primarily to review reports from the Bureau, to adopt the budget, and to prepare for the CCM.

The Bureau for Technical Co-operation in South and South-East Asia (shortened to "Bureau" in 1977), was set up in 1951 to receive requests

Figure 2.1
Organization of the Colombo Plan

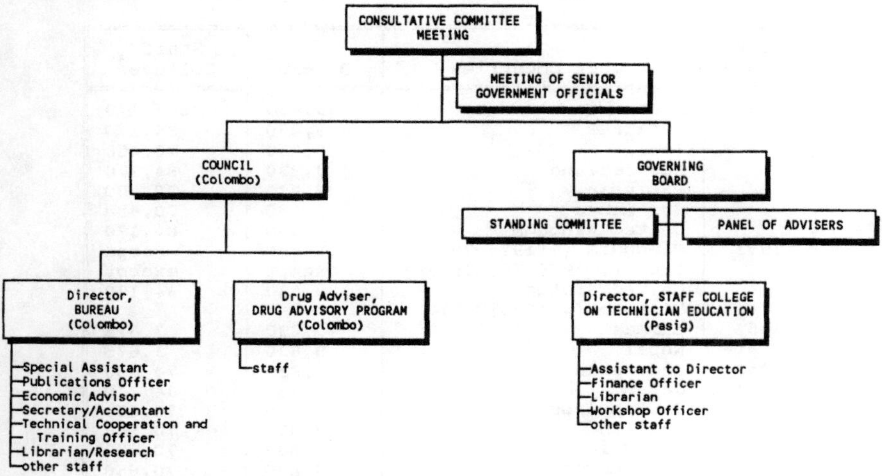

for capital aid and technical assistance, presenting them to the Council and notifying countries of the awards. In 1953, an Information Unit was also established at Colombo separate from the Bureau, but in 1957 the two organs merged, and the Bureau became the secretariat for the Council. Bilateral aid requests were then routed to the CCM, leaving the Bureau the task of publicizing C-Plan and handling other duties assigned to it by the CCM.

The Bureau's head is a Director. A Regional Population Adviser was posted at the Bureau from 1969 to 1975. A Drug Advisory Program has been attached to the Bureau since 1973.

The initial attendance at the Commonwealth Consultative Committee meeting in 1950 consisted of seven representatives from the Commonwealth (see Table 2.1). North Borneo and Sarawak were also at the original meeting but did not attend later meetings of the CCM. Since then, membership has increased to include more than two dozen countries, including Japan and the United States as donors.

Originally, aid to countries was monitored for South and Southeast Asia, called the Colombo Plan Region. Through this definition of scope, C-Plan could refuse to admit both regimes claiming to represent China. The pan-Asian principle of the Asian Way resulted in extending the region to include Korea in 1962, and the admission of Fiji in 1972 and Papua New Guinea in 1973 resulted in the renaming of the region to encompass Asia and the Pacific. China still has not become a member.

Table 2.1
Colombo Plan: Membership, Bureau Assessments, and Colombo Plan Staff College Assessments, ca. 1985

Year Joined	Member Countries	Bureau[c]	Staff College[d]
1950	Australia	$9,830	$84,170
	Canada	9,830	84,170
	India	9,830	70,650
	New Zealand	9,830	84,170
	Pakistan	9,830	70,650
	Sri Lanka	9,830	70,650
	United Kingdom	9,830	84,170
1951	Cambodia (i 1975-79)	exempt	exempt
	Laos (i 1975-79, 1981-)	exempt	exempt
	United States	9,830	84,170
	Vietnam (w 1978)[a]		
1952	Burma	9,830	3,675
	Nepal	9,830	3,675
1953	Indonesia	9,830	70,650
1954	Japan	9,830	84,170
	Philippines	9,830	70,650
	Thailand	9,830	70,650
1957	Malaysia	9,830	70,650
1959	Singapore[b]	9,830	70,650
1962	Bhutan	9,830	3,675
	South Korea	9,830	70,650
1963	Afghanistan	9,830	3,675
	Maldives	9,830	3,675
1966	Iran	9,830	70,650
1971	Bangladesh	9,830	3,675
1972	Fiji	9,830	3,675
1973	Papua New Guinea	9,830	35,295
Totals	27-1=26 Members	$235,920	$1,272,540

[a]Joined as Republic of Vietnam
[b]Absorbed by Malaysia in 1963; expelled from Malaysia 1965; rejoined 1966
[c]Totals exclude amounts for the Drug Advisory Program
[d]Basic Operating Costs only
Key: i = inactive
w = withdrew

In 1978, Vietnam, notifying the organization that it considered its membership to have ended when the Republic of Vietnam ceased to exist in 1975, attended the CCM as an Observer. Laos sent a delegation as well to the 1978 meeting. In 1980, when Laos returned as an Observer, the Cambodian seat was occupied by Democratic Kampuchea, the regime associated with Pol Pot that was no longer in control of most of the country. Laos has not attended since, though it is still a C-Plan aid recipient. Representatives of the coalition of forces allied with Pol Pot took over the Cambodian seat in 1982.

Each country has generally contributed an equal share to pay for the costs of the Bureau in accordance with the Asian Way principle of equality (Table 2.1). In 1971–72, countries with gross national products (GNPs) over $1 billion paid equal shares that accounted for two-thirds of the expenses, while those below that figure paid equal shares of the remaining one-third, although worldwide inflation soon made the distinction untenable. In 1973, the Council decided to allow relief to certain members as it deemed appropriate. Cambodia and Laos have been exempted from annual assessments since that time. The Drug Advisory Program, set up in 1973, is financed separately; donations totaled $245,000 for 1988–89. Australia, Japan, and the United States contribute most of the funding, which goes for fellowships for training courses and seminars, narcotics control equipment, and publications to disseminate information on measures employed for drug control in member countries.

C-Plan assessments primarily fund publications that promote the flow of aid to the region. Annual reports of the Council contain a tally of bilateral aid from the various donor countries to recipient countries. From 1950 to 1988, C-Plan reported that about $65 billion in capital aid and $6 billion in technical assistance had been received in the region. In 1988, for the first time, more than half of the aid came from Japan.

Technical assistance consists of experts, volunteers, and equipment as well as human resources development, that is, providing fellowships and training places for students in the educational institutions of donor countries. There are three types of training: training in institutions external to the region, intraregional training (where the donor is inside the region), and third-country training (where the institution is inside the region but funds are from countries outside the region). The Bureau also sponsors occasional expert conferences.

COLOMBO PLAN STAFF COLLEGE FOR TECHNICIAN EDUCATION (CPSC)

Since its inception, C-Plan has provided technical assistance involving trainers from developed countries and trainees from developing countries. In 1964, the position of Adviser on Intra-Regional Training was set up at the Bureau to promote the use of trainers from the Colombo Plan region. By 1973, some 7,300 persons had received training in this manner, with India being the principle donor, but there was no institution in the region to improve the quality of training itself. During the third Colloquium on Intra-Regional Technician Training in April 1969, an Asian solution to an Asian problem arose – the idea of a regional center to train technician education teachers. After discussion by the Consultative Committee and further study in 1970–71, the Council set up a Working Party of Experts in February 1972, which drew up a plan for a technician education training institution that was approved by the CCM in December 1972. A Memorandum of Understanding to create the Colombo Plan Staff College for Technician Education (CPSC) was approved during the December 1973 CCM, and CPSC began functioning in late 1974 after the Consultative Committee approved its Constitution. The position of Adviser on Intra-Regional Training at the Bureau was then abolished.

According to the Constitution, the purpose of CPSC is "to assist the member countries of the Colombo Plan in the improvement of the quality of technician education and training in the countries of the region." To this end, CPSC is to "(i) undertake programs in staff development and training, and development and research; (ii) serve as a regional forum for discussion; and (iii) provide an advisory and resource service" [Article III(1)].

CPSC was originally located in Singapore. In 1987, it was relocated to Pasig, Metro Manila. A Governing Board was established by the CCM to oversee operations; it includes one representative from each participating government, with the Bureau Director and CPSC Director as ex officio members. A Standing Committee of the Governing Board reviews various matters preparatory to Governing Board action. The Governing Board selects a Panel of Advisers, consisting of about two experts in technician education from developed and three from developing participating countries, to provide technical evaluation of the work of CPSC. The full-time professional staff of the college makes up the Academic Board, which meets about once each month to finalize courses, review research projects, and select applicants for admission. CPSC reports each year to the CCM.

All members of C-Plan are eligible to participate in CPSC. Most joined in 1974, but Vietnam withdrew in 1980, New Zealand followed suit in 1983, and the United States pulled out in 1986. Hongkong, a non–C-Plan member, first participated in 1976.

There are three parts to the budget: basic operating costs, core faculty costs, and fellowship costs (Table 2.1). Basic operating costs are based on a two-tier formula: countries with a GNP of $1 billion or more contribute a full share, those below provide a half share. The Governing Board allows a few smaller countries (Afghanistan, Bangladesh, Bhutan, Burma, Fiji, Maldives, and Nepal) to make "symbolic contributions."

Four types of activities have been handled by CPSC: college-based activities, in-country workshops, developmental projects, and consultancy services to upgrade the skills of trainers at technician education institutions. CPSC also provides courses for training administrators and managers.

SUMMARY AND CONCLUSIONS

C-Plan initially was a reaction to the fear that countries in Asia would become engulfed in revolutions that would bring Communist regimes to power, as happened in China. The theory was that empty bellies will support political forces that offer to provide basic necessities for all, and thus that Marxist ideology would win if capitalist Asia remained poor. The United States had assisted Europe for much the same reason through the Marshall Plan, but it was reluctant to support Asia in a similar manner, and Washington did not become a serious participant until the end of C-Plan's first decade of operation. Thus, C-Plan could not fulfill its founders' most ambitious aims.

Rather than becoming a multilateral program, C-Plan's unique contribution was that, during the lengthy CCMs, countries in need could contact donor countries in order to secure capital aid for particularly urgent projects. No other aid "supermarket" was available at the time, and no similar institution exists in Asia today. Technical assistance, concerned mostly with training of technicians in First-World institutions and at their expense, was also left entirely as a bilateral effort, with the Bureau relegated to the role of publicizing the flow of aid that it did not itself control. The "Colombo Plan" label became a convenient way to package bilateral aid, which was somewhat eclipsed when the UN began a more prestigious program of multilateral aid. U.S. aid to Burma, for example, was handled entirely under the Colombo Plan so that Burma would not feel compromised as a nonaligned nation begging for aid from the leader of the First World.

In time, Third-World countries, using the forums of C-Plan, began to make useful suggestions for changes in the methods by which aid programs were administered. India sought to be an aid donor, and the resulting program on intraregional aid enabled Third-World countries to help each other, an Asian solution to an Asian problem in accordance with the Asian Way. By the mid-1970s, the UN Conference on Trade and Development (UNCTAD) flattered C-Plan by dignifying this concept as "technical cooperation among developing countries" (TCDC), a major component of the New International Economic Order (NIEO) launched in the mid-1970s. C-Plan was thus a decade ahead of its time. In 1987–88, TCDC aid was $6.7 million, compared to developed-country technical assistance of $1 billion and capital aid of $5.8 billion.

C-Plan is thus not a plan and there is no central direction from Colombo, but it continues because of the success of the CCM supermarket and the way in which bilateral aid dresses up as multilateral aid. Starting as a British Commonwealth initiative, Japan provides the majority of aid today. C-Plan's TCDC, one of the most visible efforts to implement NIEO in the world today, meanwhile, has become globalized.

NOTE

1. For references to Colombo Plan documents, see Michael Haas, *Basic Documents of Asian Regional Organizations* (Dobbs Ferry, NY: Oceana Publications), vol. 5, pp. 20–44. For a bibliography of secondary sources, see pp. 6–19.

3 A PAPER TIGER AND A RADAR TIGER

Concerned over the implications of Japanese aggression in Manchuria in 1933, Australia proposed a security pact for Asia in 1936, inviting China, France, Japan, the Netherlands, the Soviet Union, and the United Kingdom to participate, but there was no response. Japan, meanwhile, proposed a Greater East Asia Co-Prosperity scheme, promising to help countries in the region to overthrow colonial rule in exchange for participation in a wider economic market.

When World War II broke out in the Pacific, France was to handle the defense of Indochina (but dropped out when Paris surrendered to Germany in 1940), the United Kingdom was responsible for the recapture of Burma and Malaya, and the United States focused on the Philippines and Pacific islands. After France fell under Vichy rule in 1940, Prime Minister Winston Churchill and President Franklin Roosevelt met in Quebec in August 1943. They agreed to establish a South-East Asia Command (SEAC) and a Southwest Pacific Command. Lord Louis Mountbatten was appointed Supreme Allied Commander in South East Asia. General Douglas MacArthur, named Supreme Allied Commander in the Southwest Pacific, ultimately extended his control over Japan itself.

SEAC had jurisdiction over civilian and military operations; it allocated food supplies and transported coal and freight for civilian and military purposes in an effort that integrated countries of the region for the first time. The unified Australia and New Zealand Asian Command (ANZAC) formed a part of Lord Mountbatten's troops during the war. In the ANZAC pact of January 21, 1944, Australia and New Zealand agreed on a wide range of issues, including a pledge to consult each other regarding any postwar settlement in Asia. After the war, SEAC was converted into the Far East Strategic Reserve.

In 1947, Australia revived the idea of a security pact, and such countries as the Philippines, the Republic of China, and South Korea also were in favor of some such arrangement. Instead of a broad military alliance, three sets of agreements arose. One started the South-East Asia Treaty Organization (SEATO). A second set dealt with Malaya and later Malaysia (AMDA and FPDA). The third pact was the Security Treaty Between Australia, New Zealand, and the United States (ANZUS). This chapter deals with the first two arrangements. ANZUS is beyond the scope of this volume.[1]

SOUTH-EAST ASIA TREATY ORGANIZATION (SEATO)[2]

As World War II ended, Communist armies were achieving victories in China, and guerrilla movements, inspired by nationalism and Marxism, gathered strength in Malaya, the Philippines, and Vietnam. When Australia renewed its call for a military pact in 1947, London was cautious about extending itself beyond Malaya, the largest British colony left in Asia. Washington, while maintaining bases in the Philippines, did not wish to alienate Asian nations, opposing what they called "neocolonialism." President Syngman Rhee of South Korea, President Chiang Kai-Shek of the Republic of China, and Philippine President Elpidio Quirino were also considering regional security schemes. After an initial meeting between Chiang and Rhee in early 1949, as Communist forces were achieving victory in China, the two proposed a regional mutual security pact. In July 1949, Chiang visited Quirino, who in turn invited Asian countries to a conference at Baguio, the Philippines, in 1950, when he hoped that a Pacific union would be organized for purposes of military security. Rhee supported the Quirino initiative, but Prime Minister Jawaharlal Nehru of India, preferring to leave breaches of the peace to the UN, suggested instead that an Asian union should concentrate on economic problems. Inasmuch as Burma, Ceylon, Indonesia, and Pakistan supported India, Quirino modified the agenda of the Baguio conference, which discussed only cultural, economic, and social matters.

War broke out in Korea in June 1950. Since the Soviet Union was boycotting the UN Security Council, the body authorized a UN Command, which was led by General MacArthur. Rather than restoring the status quo antebellum, UN forces crossed over the 38th parallel into North Korea later in 1950. India thereupon withdrew support from the UN action for taking sides in an East–West military confrontation, contrary to principles of nonaligned nations. The Republic of China and South Korea, however, were all the more intent upon a Pacific security pact. When the second Baguio conference opened later in 1950, Australia, Pakistan, the Philippines, and Thailand were strongly in favor of a military pact, but nonaligned Ceylon, India, and Indonesia were firmly opposed, though neither a military pact nor a nonmilitary Asian union were even discussed at sessions of the contentious meeting.

U.S. policy shifted significantly in 1950, and the United States quickly arranged for a peace treaty with Japan. As a condition of Australia's support for the peace treaty, the United States agreed in 1951 to the ANZUS pact. The United States then signed bilateral security treaties with Japan and the Philippines in 1951, South Korea in 1953, and the Republic of China in 1955.

Although Britain and France considered various forms of regional defense arrangements for Southeast Asia at the end of World War II, Australia was excluded from these discussions, and the United States did not want to participate in any effort that could be perceived as preserving colonialism. Indeed, the United States insisted that the United Kingdom could not attend ANZUS meetings, even in the role of an Observer. In May 1951, however, U.S. Observers went to a military conference arranged by the United Kingdom at Singapore, and a follow-up conference was convened at Washington in January 1952.

When Dwight Eisenhower became U.S. President in 1953, his Secretary of State John Foster Dulles pursued a policy of establishing a ring of military alliances around the Soviet Union and its allies. A Five-Power Staff Agency was formed in January 1953, with representation from Australia, France, New Zealand, the United Kingdom, and the United States; its terms of reference covered all countries of Southeast Asia. The agency met at Singapore and Honolulu until mid-1954. After the victory of Ho Chi Minh over France at Dien Bien Phu in June 1954, the agency convened in Washington, where the five countries agreed to seek a general guarantee for the peace of Southeast Asia.

Thai Foreign Minister Prince Wan Waithayakon then offered Bangkok as the headquarters for a new military security organization. Dulles responded by seeking a great-power guarantee for peace in a postcolonial Southeast Asia, and he obtained the support of British Prime Minister Anthony Eden and French Premier Georges Bidault in midsummer 1954. Dulles hoped that a Southeast Asian pact would eventually expand to encompass all countries of Asia.

The South-East Asia Collective Defense Treaty Conference next convened in Manila on September 8, 1954. Countries of the region were invited, including the colonial powers, but Indochinese countries were excluded so that the meeting would not appear to violate terms of the 1954 Geneva peace treaty on Indochina. Malaya demurred, as it was still a colony of the United Kingdom. Burma, Ceylon, India, and Indonesia were invited, but as expected did not attend. Pakistan, interested in a security guarantee vis-à-vis India, was also interested in a defense pact. The result was the signing of the South-East Asia Collective Defense Treaty. Dulles insisted that the new arrangement, limited in scope as it was, should not be equated with the North Atlantic Treaty Organization (NATO), and so he called the arrangement "ManPac." In 1955, when the Council established by the Manila treaty met for the first time, the delegates agreed to form a more permanent body, known as the South-East Asia Treaty Organization. The acronym SEATO thus emerged.

According to the treaty, its purpose was to strengthen the ability to resist aggression, both individually and collectively, with an added provision on economic and technical assistance. In case of armed attack, the parties pledged to refer the matter to the UN Security Council. Short of overt aggression, the countries agreed to consult together to take action, with the approval of the country affected. The United States attached a one-paragraph reservation to the treaty, known as the Understanding of the United States, stating that countermeasures for aggression only applied to Communist aggression. This provision assured India that the United States would not defend Pakistan in case of a war between the two countries. Other countries gave India similar assurances, though less formally.

The Protocol to the South-East Asia Collective Defense Treaty extended the treaty area to encompass Cambodia, Laos, and South Vietnam. Although the Geneva Accords of July 1954 appeared to preclude the participation of the three Indochinese countries in the Manila treaty, the countries at the conference hoped that they would eventually sign the treaty.

Philippine President Ramon Magsaysay, still pursuing the concept of a Pacific union along the lines of the Baguio conferences, drafted a set of principles known as the Pacific Charter, which the Manila conference endorsed. This third document sought to counterbalance the military character of the treaty, already accused of being neocolonialist, with support for the principle of national self-determination and the utility of international cooperation in the cultural, economic, and social fields.

The Council of Ministers, the only organ designated in the treaty, was attended by foreign ministers or their deputies; it was to "be so organized as to be able to meet at any time" (Article V). In practice, it met at least once each year for two to three days (see Fig. 3.1).

During the inaugural Council in 1955, France insisted that all Council decisions be by a unanimous vote, contrary to the Asian Way principle of consensus decision making without votes. In March 1961, France then proceeded to veto the use of SEATO troops in Laos. France's veto soured Bangkok on the utility of SEATO. Accordingly, in March 1962, U.S. Secretary of State Dean Rusk met with Thai Foreign

Figure 3.1
Organization of the South-East Asia Treaty Organization

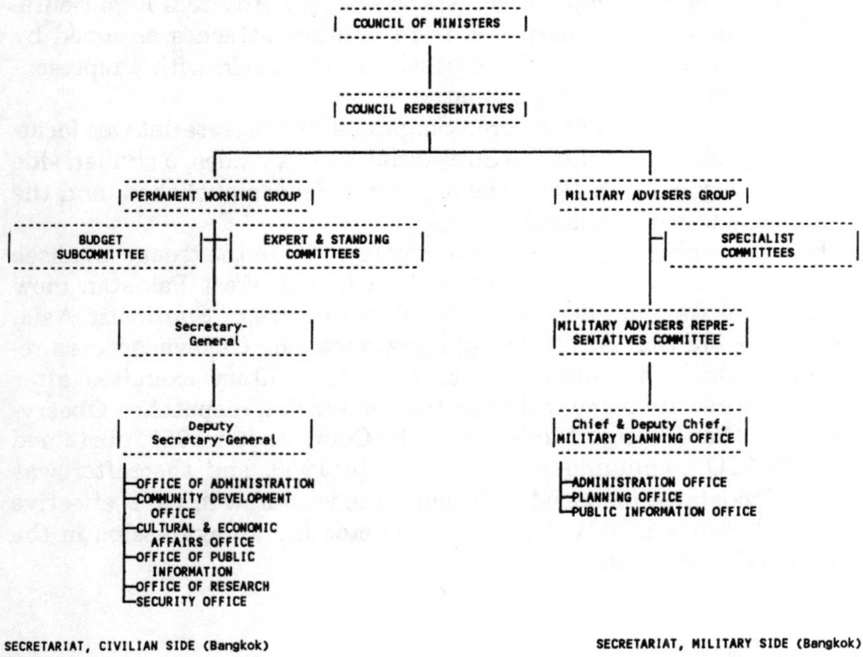

Minister Thanat Khoman; the resulting Rusk-Thanat communiqué effectively cancelled France's veto by providing that the United States was pledged to come to the support of any victim of aggression in Southeast Asia, whether the support was collective or bilateral. Australia then associated itself with the communiqué.

In accordance with the continuous-consultation provision of Article V, the Council established the Council Representatives. Composed of ambassadors (or their deputies) at diplomatic missions of member countries in Bangkok, with a special representative from the Thai government, this body met about once each month for a one-day session from 1955 to 1976. In 1960, during the crisis over Laos, the Council Representatives met 48 times. The Council Representatives was immediately subordinate to the Council of Ministers and was responsible for setting policy for the Secretariat.

The Council Representatives relied on two bodies to oversee details of Secretariat operations. The Permanent Working Group supervised civilian operations; the Military Advisers Group handled military matters. Each member country had a representative on both bodies. The Permanent Working Group met about once each week. The Military

Advisers Group met only twice each year; it consisted of a high-ranking officer (the Military Adviser) from each member country. Between Military Advisers Group meetings, the Military Advisers Representative Committee met, constituted from military attachés assigned by each member country to their embassies at Bangkok, with a representative from the Thai defense ministry.

Although Great Britain favored Singapore, the Secretariat was located in Bangkok. Originally, the Secretariat had two sides: a civilian side and a military side. In 1973, the military side was abolished, and the civilian side was reorganized.

SEATO membership was open to any country in the treaty area (see Table 3.1). Only three countries in Asia joined; West Pakistan (now Bangladesh) was, in effect, considered to be part of Southeast Asia. France, hoping that SEATO would guarantee the Geneva Accords regarding Indochina, ceased participation in military exercises after 1962, withdrew its personnel from the Secretariat, dispatched Observers rather than Foreign Ministers to the Council after 1963, abstained from SEATO communiqués from 1964 to 1966, and thereafter was absent. Pakistan announced its intention to withdraw in 1972, effective in 1973, because SEATO had failed to deter Indian aggression in the Bangladesh war of 1971.

Table 3.1
Military Organizations: Years of Membership

Organization	Year Joined	Member Countries	Year Withdrew
SEATO	1954	Australia	1977
		France	1977 (i 1966-)
		New Zealand	1977
		Pakistan	1973
		Philippines	1977
		Thailand	1977
		United Kingdom	1977
		United States	1977
AMDA	1957	Malaya	
		(Singapore)	1965 (u)
		United Kingdom	
	1959	Australia (a)	
		New Zealand (a)	
		Singapore	1965
FPDA	1971	Australia	
		Malaysia	
		New Zealand	
		Singapore	
		United Kingdom	

Key: a = associated power
i = inactive after 1966
u = status uncertain after independence

Regarding the Protocol states of Indochina, the neutralization of Laos, effected by the Geneva Conference of 1962, removed that country from the protection of the Protocol. Cambodia's Prince Norodom Sihanouk formally renounced the guarantees afforded by the Protocol in a letter sent in April 1964 to the SEATO Secretary-General, who replied in 1965 that no action involving the Protocol could be taken without the consent of the country involved. When Lon Nol ousted Sihanouk in 1970, the new government stated that it wished to remain outside the protection of the Protocol as well. Although U.S. President Lyndon Johnson stated in 1966 that U.S. troops in Vietnam carried out formal commitments under SEATO, no SEATO decision ever called for such an action. Under the terms of the Paris peace settlement of 1973, Vietnam was removed from the scope of the Protocol as well.

The treaty area was defined to include the Western Pacific (south of Hongkong and Taiwan) as well as Southeast Asia. Five of the eight members fell within this zone, including Pakistan. The area was drawn to include Brunei, Burma, Indonesia, Malaya, Nauru, Papua New Guinea, Portuguese Timor, Sabah, Sarawak, and Singapore as well, but in the Indonesian–Malaysian confrontation of 1963–67 the United States invoked ANZUS rather than SEATO guarantees. Malaya, although welcome to join, awaited independence in 1957, by which time AMDA had been negotiated. Since Australian, British, and New Zealand troops were already involved in combatting a Communist insurgency in Malaya, Kuala Lumpur felt that it needed no additional guarantees. Although neither Burma nor Indonesia accepted SEATO, they did not renounce its guarantees, and their military sent Observers to SEATO military exercises in Thailand on a few occasions. In 1958, delegates from an Indonesian insurgent group unsuccessfully sought recognition from the SEATO Council.

SEATO's Secretariat received generous contributions. In the first fiscal year (up to mid-1958) the budget was $787,145. A maximum of $1.5 million was set informally, based on the 1968–69 budget. In 1973, when the staff was reduced in a major reorganization, the budget was still $1.35 million. When civilian technical-assistance projects began, they were financed by the Secretariat budget; after a project became operationally viable, it was financed by participating member countries outside the framework of SEATO. Most SEATO projects were civilian in nature, and about eighty-five percent of the budget was for civilian purposes. Each government defrayed its own expenses in SEATO military exercises.

Contributions to the Secretariat were based on relative national incomes rather than on the Asian Way principle of equality (see Table 3.2). France and Pakistan ended yearly contributions in 1973; their portions were then divided among the remaining countries.

Table 3.2
South-East Asia Treaty Organization: Assessments

Member Countries	Assessment (1973)
Australia	13.5%
France	13.5
New Zealand	8.0
Pakistan	8.0
Philippines	8.0
Thailand	8.0
United Kingdom	16.0
United States	25.0
Total	$1.35 million

SEATO financed but did not staff several civilian institutions between 1959 and 1965. The Asian Institute of Technology (AIT) is probably the most famous of these efforts. In addition, SEATO supported trade schools, textile training centers, an apprentice training program, a textile training center, an agriculture research project, a scholarship program, a fellowship program, literary awards, publications series, and conferences on cultural and educational themes.

About four military exercises occurred each year, testing the ability to conduct joint military operations in the air, on land, and on the sea. There was no SEATO military force. A military technical training school was set up at Bangkok in 1960, including a motor vehicle training center in 1969.

SEATO never authorized military action. Under terms of the Rusk-Thanat communiqué, however, Thailand asked for troops to deter an impending attack by the Pathet Lao in May 1962. Within forty-eight hours, Australia, New Zealand, the Philippines, the United Kingdom, and the United States dispatched combat forces, and the threat was averted. But this grandstanding of a crisis was in contradistinction to the incrementalism of the Asian Way, which prefers careful, constant, and modest diplomacy.

When Australia threatened to pull out of SEATO in 1973, the United States responded by saying that it would reconsider continuing ANZUS, whereupon Australia demurred. In July 1975, when it became clear that SEATO was an obstacle to normal relations with the new Indochinese communist regimes, Philippine President Ferdinand Marcos and Thai Prime Minister Kukrit Pramoj agreed to a joint communiqué calling for an end to SEATO. The Council agreed to dissolve SEATO's Secretariat and projects when it met two months later, leaving an interim period to wind down operations. On January 1, 1977, the Secretariat closed its doors. SEATO was said to exist no more. The guarantees under the South-East Asia Collective Defense Treaty remain, however, and the Council could reconvene at any time. The so-called farewell address of the final SEATO Secretary-General contained a plea to have the Association of South East Asian Nations (ASEAN) fill the role of SEATO, a comment that, of course, contradicts the nonmilitary character of ASEAN.

ANGLO-MALAYAN DEFENCE AGREEMENT (AMDA)[3]

In March 1946, the South-East Asia Command established by Churchill and Roosevelt was abolished. British troops stayed on in Malaya within the Commonwealth Far East Strategic Reserve, which consisted of a U.K. infantry brigade and various air and naval units, with a battalion each from Australia and New Zealand, under the British Commander-in-Chief, Far East.

The Union of Malaya was established in April 1946. Great Britain urged various states in Malaya to form a federation to supersede the Union. The Union provided internal self-government for British territories on the Malay peninsula, while London conducted foreign affairs for the region through the Governor-General of Malayan and Borneo Territories, a post set up in May 1946, with headquarters at Singapore. The Federation of Malaya came together in February 1948, with Singapore excluded from its scope, although Malaya continued to have its foreign affairs handled by London.

An increase in activity by Communist party of Malaya guerrillas on the border with Thailand in March 1948 resulted in the declaration of the Malayan Emergency three months later. A Chiefs of Staff Defence Committee, to coordinate military operations among the countries already involved in the Commonwealth Far East Strategic Reserve, was established in May 1948; it was technically under the command of the British Commander-in-Chief, Far East. Inasmuch as the Committee directed joint military exercises of the Reserve in the Australian, New Zealand, and Malayan (ANZAM) area, it was known as the ANZAM Defence Committee. Military chiefs of staff from Australia, New Zealand, and the United Kingdom attended its meetings, which rotated among the participating countries but never met in public. By 1955, the ANZAM Defence Committee undertook the coordination of counterinsurgency efforts in Malaya, since the Commonwealth Far East Strategic Reserve had been fused with the ANZAM structure. Thereafter, ANZAM Defence Ministers met on a regular basis at least once each year.

In October 1957, the Federation of Malaya was granted full independence, so a new military arrangement was necessary. On independence day, the Federation of Malaya and the United Kingdom signed the Agreement Between the Government of the United Kingdom of Great Britain and Northern Ireland and the Government of the Federation of Malaya on External Defence and Mutual Assistance, known as the Anglo-Malayan Defence Agreement (AMDA), superseding the ad hoc ANZAM framework for the defense of Malaya. Since Australia and New Zealand were involved in ANZAM, they exchanged separate sets of letters with Malaya during March and April 1959, associating themselves with AMDA. Singapore became self-governing in June 1959, but it was neither fully independent nor covered by AMDA, though it remained the headquarters for the Commonwealth Far East Strategic Reserve and hence was included in the scope of ANZAM. In July 1960, when the Malayan Emergency was declared at an end, the Commonwealth Far East Strategic Reserve was set up as an arm of the ANZAM Chiefs of Staff.

Malaya became Malaysia in September 1963, adding Sabah, Sarawak, and Singapore as states to the new Federation of Malaysia. According to the Agreement Relating to Malaysia of July 1963, AMDA was revised and applied to all states of Malaysia (Article VI) when the new Federation went into effect in September 1963. Australia and New Zealand then exchanged letters with Malaysia to update their association with the revised AMDA.

In August 1965, however, the Prime Ministers of Malaysia and Singapore signed An Agreement Relating to the Separation of Singapore from Malaysia as an Independent and Sovereign State. Article VIII provided that the new state of Singapore would undertake to negotiate a new agreement on its own to replace AMDA and similar international agreements. Singapore promised to indemnify Malaysia for any associated damages, liabilities, or obligations. An amendment to the Malaysian constitution then provided that Malaysia would have the right to continue to maintain bases and other facilities in Singapore and that the United Kingdom had the right to use Commonwealth troops in Malaysia for the defense of Singapore.

According to AMDA's preamble, its purpose was twofold: "to preserve peace and to provide for . . . defence." The Commonwealth Far East Strategic Reserve, the principal organizational component of AMDA, was headquartered at Singapore (see Fig. 3.2). It consisted of troops from Australia, Malaya, New Zealand, and the United Kingdom, led by the British Commander-in-Chief, Far East. The ANZAM Chiefs of Staff Committee, consisting of the chiefs of staff of Australia, New Zealand, and the United Kingdom, met to coordinate AMDA activities, in particular joint military exercises that occurred from time to time.

British bases were maintained despite the independence of Malaya in

Figure 3.2
Organization of the Anglo-Malayan and Anglo-Malaysian Defence Agreements

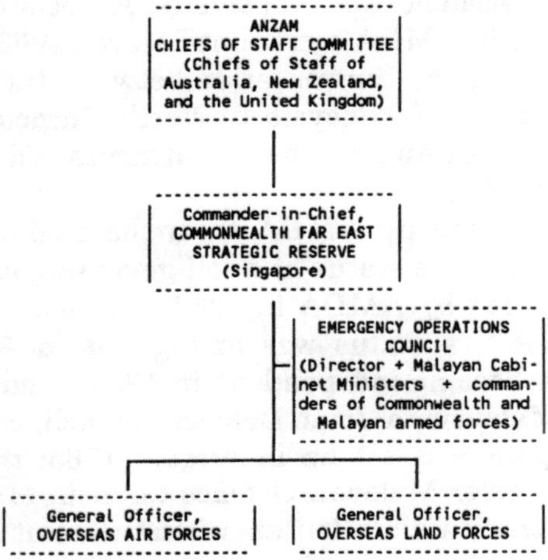

1957. Originally, Butterworth Air Force Base was British. The Australian air force deployed a squadron of jet fighters at Butterworth from July 1958. In 1970, Great Britain turned over the base to Malaysia, which in turn agreed to set up a joint operation of the base with Australia. In Singapore, the Tengah Air Force Base was originally British, and Australian aircraft were first deployed there in July 1950. When Singapore became independent in 1965, the base became Singaporean. A detachment of aircraft has been assigned to Tengah from the Butterworth base. Woodlands Naval Base, Singapore, was transferred to Malaysian control in 1963, then Singapore took it over in 1965 on the condition that Malaysia be allowed to train at the base thereafter. Army bases existed in several locations. The 28th Commonwealth Brigade, for example, was at Taiping in the 1950s; it moved to Terendak, Malacca, in 1961. Pulada, a jungle warfare training school, has operated at Ulu Tiram, Johore Bahru, Malaya.

AMDA shifted operations under the Emergency from British to Malayan control in keeping with the incrementalism of the Asian Way. An Emergency Operations Council was set up under the control of the Malayan government, with a Director of Emergency Operations in charge (see Fig. 3.2). Although the Director did not have operational command of Commonwealth overseas forces, the commanders of these forces were to coordinate activities with the Director. The chain of command of overseas forces extended directly to Canberra, London, and Wellington for the individual services. Britain's Commander-in-

Chief, Far East, served as adviser to Malaya's National Defence Council until August 1966, when Malaysia terminated the advisory role.

Malaya and the United Kingdom were the primary members of AMDA. Australia and New Zealand were considered Associated Powers. Australia kept its status in AMDA secret until March 1963, when information leaked out during the confrontation between Indonesia and Malaya over the extension of Malaysia to North Borneo; the news leak aimed to alert Jakarta of Australian commitments and thereby to deter Jakarta from aggression.

Singapore was covered by AMDA from the beginning, even after 1959, when it achieved the status of a self-governing colony. Although Singapore was covered by AMDA in 1963 as a new state in the Federation of Malaysia, its status was ambiguous in AMDA (but not ANZAM) when it became independent in 1965. Under terms of the separation from Malaysia, a Joint Defence Council, composed of Malaysia and Singapore, was set up in August 1965; the body was an expansion of the former Malayan Defence Council. Malaysia voted to veto Singaporean trade with Indonesia when the Joint Defence Council met in March 1966, whereupon Singapore withdrew from the Council. Although U.K. bases became Singaporean on independence day in 1965, they were in principle available for use under the terms of AMDA. Malaysian troops, accordingly, remained at the air force, army, and naval bases in Singapore, but Singapore declared the troops to be "temporary," and Malaysia finally withdrew them at the end of 1967, although Malaysia still trains at Woodlands Naval Base.

Each external country was responsible for paying military personnel of its own armed forces. The United Kingdom defrayed the cost of military training of the Malayan armed forces. No rent was charged for the use of bases by armed forces external to Malaya, Malaysia, or Singapore.

AMDA's primary aim was to provide for the defense of peninsular Malaya against external attack. Since the Commonwealth Far East Strategic Reserve existed not only for external Malayan defense but also for regional defense under ANZAM, Singapore was covered by the latter arrangement. Malaya was eager to extend AMDA in 1963 to support the creation of Malaysia, which was opposed by an advance of Indonesian troops.

The Commonwealth Far East Strategic Reserve engaged in military exercises on several occasions. Key provisions of AMDA provided that consultations would be held with Malaya (later Malaysia) in case of threats from outside forces in order to determine the nature of any joint response. In addition, troops of the four countries participated in counterinsurgency operations against the Malayan Communist party during the Emergency. Yet another element, military training of Malayan armed forces by U.K. instructors, played an important role throughout AMDA, but AMDA's "elder brother" elements did not conform to the equality principle of the Asian Way.

FIVE POWER DEFENCE ARRANGEMENTS (FPDA)[4]

One of the British Labour Party's campaign promises before being elected in 1966 was to reduce military spending. A 1967 Defence White Paper, *Britain East of Suez*, stated London's intention to phase out most military commitments in Asia by 1971, inasmuch as they constituted nearly half of the entire British defense budget. Australia, Malaysia, New Zealand, and Singapore (the last in doubt about the status of AMDA and ANZAM since it gained independence in 1965) were concerned that something should be established to replace AMDA and ANZAM. Malaysian Prime Minister Tunku Abdul Rahman proposed a five-power conference in July 1967. Singapore's Prime Minister Lee Kuan Yew also appealed to Australia and New Zealand for assistance. Perhaps the last straw occurred in March 1968, when a flotilla of Soviet warships first paraded through the Indian Ocean.

In early 1968, the British Commander-in-Chief, Far East, established three advisory working groups composed of military officers from Australia, Malaysia, New Zealand, Singapore, and the United Kingdom. The Air Defence Advisory Working Group recommended the establishment of an integrated air defense system. The Army Advisory Working Group agreed that there should be joint military exercises and a multinational jungle warfare training school. The Naval Advisory Working Group noted that Malaysia and Singapore desired to continue using Woodlands Naval Base and to develop similar facilities for coastal defense. The reports of the three bodies were submitted to the prime ministers of the five countries, who met at Kuala Lumpur during June 1968 with the objective of superseding AMDA and ANZAM. London offered to provide financial aid totalling $125 million to the region in order to mitigate the economic effects of the planned withdrawal of British forces from the area. The five powers authorized a joint military exercise for 1970, code-named Bersatu Padu, so an exercise planning staff met at Kuala Lumpur shortly after the meeting to organize the exercise.

When Australian Prime Minister John Gorton and his New Zealand counterpart Keith Holyoake announced in February 1969 that their troops would remain in the region even if British troops were evacuated completely, the stage was set for serious consideration of a multilateral arrangement. The five countries met again during June 1969 at Canberra, agreeing to set up a joint service advisory working group to consider various problems affecting more than one service; the working group then convened after the joint exercise in 1970. Great Britain's *Supplementary Statement on Defence Policy* in October 1970 promised that some U.K. troops would remain in Southeast Asia if terms of a new five-power arrangement were satisfactorily negotiated. After a meeting of senior officials in Singapore in January 1971, a final preparatory meeting was held in London in April 1971. The Five Power Ministerial Meeting on the External Defence of Malaysia and Singapore then met at Kuala Lumpur on June 10–11, 1971, to set up an Integrated Air Defence System (IADS), effective September 1, 1971, and to have the Five Power Defence Arrangements (FPDA) supersede AMDA on November 1, 1971, although they were not adopted until December 1, 1971. By the end of the year, Britain evacuated facilities in Singapore but retained military troops in the region as contributions to the Australia-New Zealand-United Kingdom (ANZUK) force, the successor to the Commonwealth Far East Strategic Reserve.

The third paragraph of the April 1971 communiqué regards "the defence of Malaysia and Singapore as indivisible." Paragraph six then states the aim of FPDA as "the external defence of Malaysia and Singapore." Accordingly, there are two objectives set forth in the founding documents of FPDA:

> to continue to cooperate closely in defence arrangements [and] . . . in the event of any form of armed attack externally organized or supported or the threat of such attack against Malaysia or Singapore their Governments would immediately consult together for the purpose of deciding what measures should be taken jointly or separately in relation to such attack or threat.

Due in part to continuing but muted rivalries between Malaysia and Singapore, the three external powers negotiated separate arrangements with the two Southeast Asian countries, making a total of six agreements in the FPDA. Although adopted on December 1, 1971 they were deemed to have entered into force on November 1, 1971.

Although the April 1971 communiqué establishing FPDA anticipated the need for future ministerial conferences, no such meetings have yet been held. A Joint Consultative Committee, established in 1971, provides a forum for consultation at the senior official level for all three branches of the military services; this body meets for at least one day each year and is the equivalent of the former ANZAM Defence Council, though it is now composed of permanent secretaries of defense (see Fig. 3.3).

The Air Defence Council, set up by the 1971 meeting, manages IADS and gives direction to its commander; this body meets four times each year for one day, alternating venues between Kuala Lumpur and Singapore. Its composition is the same as the Joint Consultative Committee;

Figure 3.3
Organization of the Five Power Defence Arrangements

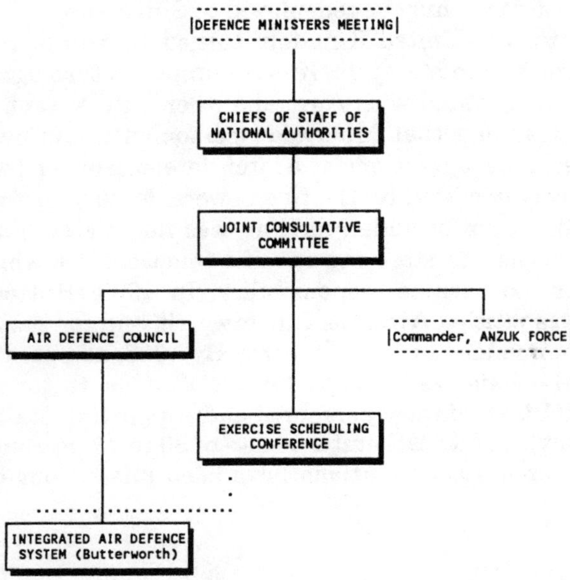

it approves proposed military exercises for the year and allocates funds. IADS is located inside the air force base at Butterworth. The Council supersedes the Air Defence Advisory Working Group, which was formed in 1968.

The Army Advisory Working Group, established in 1968, did not continue beyond 1971. Pulada, the jungle warfare school at Ulu Tiram, Johor Bahru, was Malaysianized in 1971. The Five Power Naval Advisory Working Group was set up in 1968 to coordinate naval components located at Changi Point, Singapore. The Group set up the Maritime Joint Operations Centre for the 1970 military exercises. In 1971, the two advisory working groups were superseded by the Exercise Scheduling Conference, which meets for about a day each year to finalize plans for air, ground, and maritime exercises by the air force, army, and navy, respectively, about two to four years in advance. The Conference is attended by defense advisors and commanders of the three armed services of the participating countries.

As regards infantry contingents, Britain's Far East Command and the Commonwealth Far East Strategic Reserve were phased out in 1971. Reduced to some 7,000 men, the remaining troops of Australia, New Zealand, and the United Kingdom (one battalion each) were transferred to Singapore and placed under the Commander, ANZUK Force, who was responsible to the Chiefs of Staff of the three countries (see Table 3.3). It is rumored that the three British battalions, assigned to Hongkong until 1997, may be redeployed to Singapore.

In 1970, after the United Kingdom turned control of Butterworth Air Force Base over to Malaysia, Kuala Lumpur in turn agreed to have the base jointly operated with Australia when FPDA went into effect, on the understanding that Malaysian personnel would be trained to assume all technical operations at a later date except for IADS, which was to be jointly operated by the five powers. Each year from 1971 to 1987 a memorandum of understanding was negotiated between Australia and Malaysia to state the specific functions for which the two countries were to assume responsibility. In 1980, Butterworth Air Force Base was retitled Air Base Butterworth, and for the first time a Malaysian commander assumed control. By 1988, all operational functions were Malaysianized except for IADS. The Butterworth base houses about 1,500 military personnel and supporting staff (including a rifle company). The IADS unit consists of 30 to 40 persons.

Gradually, foreign contributions have been phased out of most as-

Table 3.3
Five Power Defence Arrangements: External Contributions

Donor	Contribution	Location	Status
Australia	1 infantry battalion	Singapore	withdrawn 1973
	1 rifle company	Butterworth	still present
	1 Mirage squadron	Butterworth	withdrawn 1974
	1 Mirage squadron	Butterworth	replaced 1988
	Mirage detachment	Singapore	replaced 1988
	c.10 F111 aircraft	Butterworth	on rotation since 1984
	10-20 F18 aircraft	Butterworth	on rotation since 1988
	c.3 P3C aircraft	Butterworth	on rotation since 1984
	1 destroyer or frigate	Singapore	withdrawn 1973
	1 submarine	Singapore	on rotation
	IADS contribution	Butterworth	still present
New Zealand	1 infantry battalion	Singapore	withdrawn 1989
	1 frigate	Singapore	withdrawn 1976
	1 helicopter squadron	Singapore	withdrawn 1989
	IADS contribution	Butterworth	still present
United Kingdom	1 infantry battalion	Singapore	withdrawn 1974
	1 frigate	Singapore	withdrawn 1976
	1 submarine	Singapore	on rotation
	1-4 marine reconnaissance aircraft	Singapore	withdrawn 1976
	combat units	Singapore	on visit
	ships	Singapore	on visit
	aircraft	Singapore	on visit
	1 helicopter squadron	Butterworth	withdrawn 1976
	IADS contribution	Butterworth	still present

signments, although technicians from each of the five countries remain to staff IADS. In 1974, all British ground forces were withdrawn from Malaysia and Singapore, and the ANZUK force was terminated. The British frigate, helicopter squadron, and marine reconnaissance aircraft were recalled in 1976, when the rest of the U.K. contribution was placed on indefinite rotation to other ports or bases in the Pacific.

Australia recalled its infantry battalion and naval contingent from Singapore in 1973. One squadron of Mirage fighter jets was withdrawn in 1974. A detachment of Mirages from a second squadron posted at Butterworth continued to rotate to Tengah until 1983, when the venue shifted to Paya Lebar (Singapore's former international airport). Canberra retired its remaining Mirages from Butterworth in March 1988, replacing them with 10 to 20 F18 aircraft to be stationed for 16 weeks each year. Several F111 aircraft have rotated between Butterworth and Darwin in recent years. In 1984, Australia decided to dispatch two to three P3C air force maritime reconnaissance aircraft to Butterworth on a rotating basis as well. Submarine surveillance in Southeast Asian waters continues as before. Since 1988, Australia has maintained 300 to 400 military personnel, with up to 700 dependents, at Butterworth. Malaysia's armed forces increased from 60,000 in 1979 to 113,000 in 1988, and it recently began a substantial modernization of its aircraft.

New Zealand removed its frigate in 1976, but maintained an overseas posting at Singapore until 1989, when Wellington withdrew the New Zealand Force Southeast Asia (NZForsea), consisting of an infantry battalion, three helicopters, and support units, numbering 740 personnel. Three or four New Zealanders remain in Singapore to coordinate training exercises with Malaysian and Singaporean troops.

All five FPDA countries have remained active since 1971. In 1982, it was reported in some circles that Thailand had expressed an interest in joining FPDA. When Brunei became independent in 1985, a similar rumor spread, since Brunei personnel train in all five countries' defense institutions and all five countries attend Brunei's jungle warfare training school. Under Brunei's defense agreement with the United Kingdom, a battalion of Gurkha troops is assigned from Hongkong; this agreement will become obsolete in 1997, when China will assume authority over Hongkong. Were another country to join FPDA, the ministers of the five countries would doubtless have to meet again.

Each country bears the cost of billeting its own troops in Southeast Asia in accordance with the Asian Way principle of equality. The host countries defray travel and per diem expenses for Malaysian and Singaporean troops to train in Australia and New Zealand. Personnel undergoing training under FPDA have expenses defrayed by their own armed service. Foreign forces pay rent for accommodations in Malaysia and Singapore.

The United Kingdom donated nearly a half billion dollars of equipment and facilities when it evacuated former installations in Malaysia and Singapore, first in 1971 and finally in 1976. Wellington's efforts in 1983 and 1984 to obtain some cost sharing from Singapore resulted in a contribution by the latter of $26,000. The New Zealand commitment was approximately $28.6 million in Singapore during 1986, and Australia's expenditure is about twice that amount.

The external powers agreed in 1971 to provide four forms of assistance: training personnel, facilities for training, (including instructional courses abroad), expert advice and assistance in operational and technical matters, and assistance in the supply of military equipment. Navigational aids, surveys, telecommunication systems, and construction of facilities were undertaken as elements of the training programs. Except for an occasional U.K. naval presence in the region, the only British presence today is at the IADS facility.

IADS, the primary multilateral project, consists of a reconnaissance coordination facility based primarily on radar installations operated throughout peninsular Malaya and Singapore. Fighter aircraft are also at the disposal of IADS in case of an intrusion into the region.

Military exercises involve attack and defense maneuvers involving aircraft, antiaircraft batteries, ground-to-air missiles, ships, and troop maneuvers on the ground. The exercises have picked up in tempo and in numbers since 1980. For IADS, major exercises are held twice each year; lesser exercises take place several times annually. Non-IADS air exercises have occurred once each year since 1971, rotating between Malaysian and Singaporean locations. About ten of the Mirage jets have flown to Singapore on a regular basis as a part of the air exercises. Singaporean military aircraft flew to Butterworth for the first time in 1985; the first Malaysian military aircraft visited Singapore in 1986.

In 1972, a naval maritime exercise was held; this practice resumed in 1981 in what is now called the Starfish series. A one-week Starfish series is held each year in the South China Sea, rotating between Malaysian and Singaporean waters. There is joint advance planning. The roles of scheduling officer and task force commander alternate between the Malaysian Fleet Operations Command and the Singaporean Headquarters Fleet Operations Command. About 2,000 personnel, ships, and military aircraft are involved.

An army military exercise (landex) was held in 1975, again in 1980, and has been held annually ever since. The venue rotates among all four countries in the region, though not in any particular order; when they occur in Malaysia or Singapore, they are simulated exercises, with compass and map readings. Although Singapore sends trainees to the jungle warfare school at Pulada, Malaysia, it did not participate in multilateral exercises on Malaysian soil under FPDA until 1985. Malaysian troops have not participated in landex at Singapore thus far. No bilateral exercises are envisaged.

FPDA is integrated with mutual-assistance programs provided by Australia and New Zealand, including bilateral specialist training to the Malaysian and Singaporean armed forces. Instructors at Pulada have been drawn from Australia and New Zealand, and Malaysian instructors have trained personnel in New Zealand. Pulada students also come from Australia and New Zealand. Great Britain does not participate in military training. On-base training takes place at Butterworth and in Singapore.

As FPDA is the successor to AMDA, it continued, in effect, as a supplement to SEATO until the latter's demise in 1977. FPDA was intended to cover only Singapore and the Malay peninsula. The ANZUS pact included Sabah and Sarawak in its scope until these two territories became states in the Federation of Malaysia.

SUMMARY AND CONCLUSIONS

Among the various military arrangements in Asia, the unobtrusive AMDA and FPDA have outlasted SEATO. While the SEATO Council attracted headlines, AMDA and FPDA technical assistance and military exercises proceeded without adverse publicity.

SEATO was set up on a loose basis to provide guarantees to Southeast Asia in general and Indochina in particular, and it was kept apart from arrangements involving Malaya (later Malaysia). Since military exercises were the only continuing projects related to security, SEATO decided to enhance public relations through civilian projects, though some had military implications. The public relations effort failed, however; the word never got out that SEATO was more a civilian than a military organization.

Because of a policy of French military self-reliance under President Charles de Gaulle, France was the first to demur. Pakistan left next, feeling betrayed in its defeat by India during the Bangladesh War of 1971. When SEATO proved to be a paper tiger in Indochina in the mid-1970s, there was much sentiment for abandoning it. Washington found SEATO to be a useful foil in responding to domestic critics of U.S. participation in the Vietnam War; Washington asked Australia to remain in SEATO lest ANZUS be sacked.

Thailand eventually sounded the death knell of SEATO. The student revolution in the fall of 1973 was hostile to SEATO. U.S. forces were removed from northern Thailand at Bangkok's insistence in 1973, but improvements on a major naval base at Sattahip continued. Then, in May 1975, U.S. troops were sent to the Utapao naval base in Thailand en route to rescue the *Mayaguez* crew detained by the new Kampuchean government. Thai leaders seized upon this action, denouncing it as an invasion of Thai sovereignty, demanded a withdrawal of all U.S. forces, an end to U.S. construction of Sattahip, and eventually an abolition of SEATO itself.

AMDA was originally an element in the devolution of colonial control to Malaya. When Malaysia was created, the redrafting of AMDA occurred with just enough publicity to let Indonesia know that a military conflict over Sarawak would find Malaysia defended by a solid phalanx of allies. The peaceful formation of Malaysia, hence, is due in large part to AMDA. Australia and New Zealand premised their AMDA contributions on a solid U.K. presence, so the East-of-Suez policy of 1967 meant that AMDA had become obsolete.

FPDA began as an effort to replace the vacuum left by the departure of British military forces from Southeast Asia. Eventually it was hoped that Malaysia and Singapore would handle their own defenses in view of their interest in the neutralization of Southeast Asia, a policy supported in 1971 by ASEAN. Australia and New Zealand were interested in FPDA because their policies of "forward defense" meant meeting an adversary in a buffer region, rather than fighting on their own soil. The United States was sensitive to the implications of FPDA on SEATO, but the Nixon Doctrine of 1969 was consistent with the aim of FPDA as a transitional arrangement through which countries in Asia would gradually assume control over their own defense.

Great Britain withdrew troops from Malaysia and Singapore in 1974. Australia primarily filled the vacuum, and New Zealand enjoyed Singapore as a foreign posting to provide an attractive incentive to recruitment until increasing costs precluded this arrangement by the end of the 1980s. As Australia and New Zealand began to abandon the concept of forward defense, Malaysia and Singapore were increasingly able to handle various elements of their own defense.

When the armed forces of Vietnam overran Cambodia in 1979, FPDA activities picked up in tempo. Military exercises were revived. By the mid-1980s, Malaysian and Singaporean military personnel and aircraft were even crossing each other's borders, achieving a degree of solidarity only hoped for in 1971 – yet another example of the Asian Way principle of incrementalism. The two countries were fully managing their own military affairs by the end of the 1980s, a tribute to the success of military training over the nearly two decades since FPDA was conceived. IADS at Butterworth is virtually all that remains of daily multilateral cooperation under FPDA today, but the Asian Way spirit of equalitarian cooperation will keep consultative and operational elements of the organization alive for many years to come.

SEATO proved to be a paper tiger that came into conflict with pan-

Asianism and other principles of the Asian Way. The radar system around the Malay peninsula and Singapore provides a realistic project for FPDA, which has embodied the equality principle of the Asian Way and thereby has served to break down barriers between Malaysia and Singapore.

NOTES

1. See Michael Haas, *The Pacific Way: Regional Cooperation in the South Pacific* (New York: Praeger, 1989), chap. 3.

2. For references to SEATO documents, see Michael Haas, *Basic Documents of Asian Regional Organizations* (Dobbs Ferry, NY: Oceana Publications), vol. 5, pp. 112–30. For a bibliography of secondary sources for all the organizations described in this chapter, see pp. 87–111.

3. For references to AMDA documents, see Michael Haas, *Basic Documents of Asian Regional Organizations* (Dobbs Ferry, NY: Oceana Publications), vol. 5, p. 131.

4. For references to FPDA documents, see Michael Haas, *Basic Documents of Asian Regional Organizations* (Dobbs Ferry, NY: Oceana Publications), vol. 5, pp. 131–32.

4 CASTING A WIDE NET (WITH MANY HOLES) TOWARD AFRICA

While conflicts between Western capitalist and Eastern-bloc socialist countries dominated international events after World War II, the economic plight of less developed countries received little attention in the world community. Championing the cause of poorer countries, Indian Prime Minister Jawaharlal Nehru persuaded leaders in many newly independent states that they comprised a Third World with no reason to take sides in the East–West struggle.

To build a nonaligned movement, the leaders of Burma, Ceylon, India, Indonesia, and Pakistan – then known as the Colombo Powers – met together at Colombo, Ceylon, in April 1954, where they agreed to convene a large-scale conference of nonaligned countries. After a preparatory conference in Bogor, Indonesia, the inaugural Conference of Nonaligned Nations convened in May 1955 at Bandung, Indonesia.

The nonaligned movement has two organizational manifestations today. One is the continuing series of conferences in the tradition of the Bandung meeting. A second outcome is the establishment of international organizations to provide self-help in specialized areas. At the crossroads between Africa and Asia, Cairo hosts many of these organizations, most of which are nongovernmental. Two intergovernmental bodies are headquartered in Asia. These are the Asian-African Legal Consultative Committee (AALCC) and the Afro-Asian Rural Reconstruction Organization (AARRO).

ASIAN-AFRICAN LEGAL CONSULTATIVE COMMITTEE (AALCC)[1]

Newly independent countries of Asia participated in United Nations organs during the late 1940s but felt estranged from cold war issues. The International Law Commission (ILC) was no exception. Since international law was originally developed by the former imperial powers, many treaties legitimized unequal treatment by the metropoles in the affairs of former colonies. France, Great Britain, and the United States continued to dominate proceedings of the ILC and other international legal conferences in view of their long tradition of expertise in the field and their highly professional staff work before the meetings. Such countries as India held views differing from those expressed by Western countries on a variety of legal issues; lacking a well-prepared common position, however, Third-World countries tended to vote along with their erstwhile colonial mentors and chief suppliers of foreign aid.

During an international legal conference at New Delhi in 1954, the Chief Justice of Burma suggested holding an Asian legal conference. The idea for sharing legal expertise in the region hit a responsive chord in New Delhi, and Nehru convened an Asian Legal Conference at New Delhi later in 1954 to discuss means for pooling research on legal questions. The representatives in attendance, mostly legal advisers from foreign affairs ministries, agreed in principle to form an Asian Legal Consultative Committee (ALCC). In April 1955, ALCC was the only organization endorsed by the Asian-African Conference at Bandung. Then on November 15, 1956, plenipotentiaries adopted Statutes of the Committee. The inaugural session of the Committee, held at New Delhi during April 1957, was attended by several African countries that were interested in joining. ALCC agreed to enlarge its scope, and at the second session of the Committee in October 1958, the organization became the Asian-African Legal Consultative Committee (AALCC).

Statutes of the Committee specify four major functions. Article 3a authorizes a review of any item to be discussed by ILC or a similar body. Article 3b instructs the Secretariat to disseminate views agreed upon by the Committee. Article 3c encourages countries to put an item on the agenda by preparing memoranda for general discussion. Under Article 3d, matters of common concern can be discussed without prior preparatory work.

The highest organ of AALCC is the Committee (see Fig. 4.1), which meets in annual sessions of about seven to eight days. Sessions are attended by cabinet ministers, attorneys-general, supreme court justices, judges, and ambassadors. The Committee has three subsidiary bodies: the Secretariat and two regional centers for arbitration.

Figure 4.1
Organization of the Asian-African Legal Consultative Committee

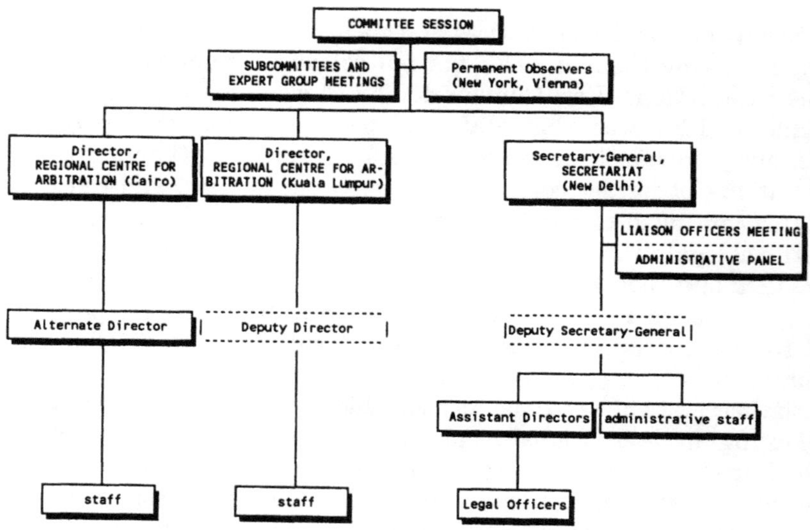

The AALCC had a small coordinating office at New Delhi from 1957 to 1971, when the Secretariat was established. The Secretariat is headed by a Secretary-General and has an administrative side and a legal research side. The Committee also retains a Permanent Observer to the UN in New York and a Permanent Observer to the UN offices in Vienna, where the ILC meets.

Each diplomatic mission of the member countries in New Delhi designates an AALCC Liaison Officer. The Liaison Officers Meeting, which takes place for one day every two months, serves as the channel of communication between the Secretariat and the member governments. An Administrative Panel, a committee of five from the Liaison Officers Meeting, advises the Secretary-General on administrative matters.

The Statutes classify members as Original Members, other full Members, and Associate Members (see Table 4.1). AALCC started with seven members and now has thirty-eight Members and two Associate Members. There are three categories of Observers: nonmember Asian-African states, international organizations with which the AALCC has relations, and non–Asian-African states. Australia and New Zealand have been accorded Permanent Observer Status and can attend sessions of the Committee, its subcommittees, and technical working groups on a regular basis. Each year the Committee prepares a

Table 4.1
Asian-African Legal Consultative Committee: Membership and Assessments

Year Joined	Member Countries	Assessment (1985)[a]
1956	Burma (w 1974)	
	Egypt	$3,500 + 2.5%
	India	3,500 + 6.0
	Indonesia	3,500 + 5.0
	Iraq	3,500 + 5.0
	Japan	3,500 + 30.0
	Sri Lanka	3,500 + .5
	Syria (w 1959, r 1970)	3,500 + .5
1958	Sudan (w 1961, r 1986)	3,500 + .5
1959	Pakistan	3,500 + 2.5
1961	Morocco (w 1964)	
	Thailand	3,500 + 1.5
1963	Ghana	3,500 + 1.5
1968	Jordan	3,500 + .5
1969	Philippines (a, m 1971, w 1985)	
	Sierra Leone	3,500 + .5
1970	Iran	3,500 + 3.5
	Kenya	3,500 + .5
	Kuwait	3,500 + 5.0
	Malaysia	3,500 + 2.5
	Nigeria	3,500 + 5.0
	South Korea (a, m 1973)	3,500 + 3.5
1971	Nepal	3,500 + .5
1972	Mauritius (a, m 1976)	3,500 + .5
1973	Bangladesh	3,500 + .5
	Botswana (a)	1,500
	Gambia	3,500 + .5
	North Korea	3,500 + .5
	Singapore	3,500 + 1.5
	Tanzania	3,500 + .5
1974	Saudi Arabia (a)	1,500
1976	Libya	3,500 + 5.0
	Oman	3,500 + 1.5
	Qatar	3,500 + 2.5
	Somali	3,500 + .5
	Turkey	3,500 + 3.5
	North Yemen	3,500 + .5
	United Arab Emirates	3,500 + 2.5
1979	Ethiopia (a, w 1981)	
	Uganda	3,500 + .5
1980	Cyprus	3,500 + .5
	Mongolia	3,500 + .5
	Senegal	3,500 + .5
1983	Australia (o)	
	China	3,500 + 6.0
	New Zealand (o)	
Totals	42-4=38 Members 2 Associate Members 2 Observers	c. $3,000,000

[a]Consists of a flat rate plus a proportional rate; the latter exceeded 100 percent when China joined in 1983, as AALCC had not yet agreed upon a new set of rates.

Key: a = Associate Member
m = later joined as full Member
o = Permanent Observer status
r = rejoined
w = withdrew

list of invitations to all governments in Asia and Africa except for those to which objections have been raised in the past by members; on this basis, Afghanistan has not been invited since 1978.

Most expenses of the Secretariat, shared by member countries entirely, are paid out of the general budget account (Table 4.1). Associate Members contribute $1,500, full Members an average of $3,500 as a base rate, with the remaining amount proportional to UN contributions. This departure from the Asian Way principle of equality recognized Africa's greater need and limited resources. The Secretary-General and Assistant Directors are seconded by their home governments; their shares are not reflected in the annual budget, which was about $3 million in 1985. Arabic-speaking countries have funded an Arabic budget since 1978 to support language interpretation at meetings and translation of publications. Member countries sometimes provide voluntary contributions for specific projects or purposes. No funds are accepted from outside Africa or Asia.

One activity during the first decade of AALCC (1957–67) was the codification of international law from a Third-World perspective; papers were prepared and discussed on various topics under consideration by the ILC. The second focus was to provide advisory recommendations on specific questions referred to AALCC by various member countries. Eight issues were finalized in the form of reports or statements; draft articles and conventions emerged in seven cases. Some issues were not finalized but were discussed quite thoroughly in accordance with the Asian Way spirit of consensus building.

In the second decade (1967–77), AALCC sought primarily to prepare countries to review issues under discussion at UN conferences, including the Law of the Sea Conference. Details of the archipelagic principle and the concept of exclusive economic zone (EEZ), developed in AALCC discussions, were eventually included in the Law of the Sea Treaty of 1982. AALCC also was concerned with the development of commercial and private international law and influenced the formation of the arbitration rules of the UN Commission on International Trade Law (UNCITRAL), which were adopted in 1976.

When the third decade began, AALCC adopted an Integrated Scheme for Settlement of Disputes, then formed regional centers for arbitration of commercial disputes. In addition, standard commercial contracts and joint-venture agreements were drawn up for the benefit of member countries.

AALCC continues the work of the early decades in regard to codification of international law, advisory recommendations on legal questions, and preparation for UN conferences. Expert group meetings are held on such topics as commodity sales, EEZs, promotion and protection of investments, and shipping. The Secretariat has also sought partners for joint ventures that have financing from UN agencies or the World Bank.

The Secretariat trains legal officers of member countries through periodic seminars. The publications program of AALCC is quite active. One of the earliest compilations was of the constitutions of African and Asian countries. Proceedings of the sessions of the Committee are an excellent resource for international legal scholars.

In 1980, AALCC became the eleventh intergovernmental organization to be accorded Permanent Observer Status by the UN General Assembly. AALCC has submitted major studies assessing the functioning of the UN system in several specific areas.

Regional Centers for Arbitration

Most commercial arbitration in international trade has been referred on an ad hoc basis to institutions in developed countries, where costs are high and the probability of success for Third-World commercial firms is low. Nonetheless, commercial dispute settlement was not discussed by the Committee until 1974. After the UNCITRAL arbitration rules were adopted by the UN General Assembly in 1976, AALCC's Trade Law Sub-Committee discussed the idea of regional arbitration centers, since members wished to ensure that the new rules would be used as much as possible. Plans for regional arbitration centers were approved by the Committee in 1977.

In 1978, regional arbitration centers were formed in Kuala Lumpur and Cairo. Between 1980 and 1983, however, the Cairo center suspended operation because of strained relations between Egypt and other Arab countries following the détente between Egypt and Israel. In 1980, the Nigerian government agreed in principle to set up a regional center for arbitration at Lagos, but preparatory work was suspended due to domestic political uncertainties there. Centers at Lagos, Nairobi, and Tehran are now under consideration.

The Kuala Lumpur facility was established by an exchange of letters between AALCC and the government of Malaysia in 1978, followed by a more formal agreement in 1981. A similar three-year Agreement and Memorandum of Understanding were adopted by AALCC and Egypt in 1979, and were extended in 1983 and 1986.

According to the Administrative Rules of both facilities, the centers have five functions:

(a) promoting international commercial arbitration in the region; (b) coordinating and assisting the activities of existing arbitral institutions particularly among those within the region; (c) rendering assistance in the conduct of *ad hoc* arbitrations particularly those held under the UNCITRAL Arbitration

Rules; (d) assisting in the enforcement of arbitral awards; and (e) providing for arbitration under the auspices of the Centre where appropriate.

Both centers have a Director, appointed by the host country, who is a part-time employee. Although there is a provision for a second-in-command from a nonhost country, only Cairo has filled this position (see Fig. 4.1). Both centers, in consultation with the AALCC Secretary-General, have set up advisory panels to provide advice on promotional operations.

An International Panel of Arbitrators, selected by AALCC, lists some 244 qualified persons available to serve as arbitrators. Neither regional center itself provides any arbitration on its own but instead facilitates arbitration using this panel. The Kuala Lumpur center has entered into agreements with the International Center for Settlement of Investment Disputes (ICSID) and with facilities in Australia, India, Japan, and South Korea. The Cairo center has similar agreements with ICSID and arbitration courts in Australia, Canada, Germany, Jordan, Morocco, Spain, and the United States. Venues for arbitration may vary.

A country desiring arbitration can utilize any facility that it chooses. The use of Arabic at the Cairo center makes the selection more convenient for Arabic-speaking countries, whereas English is used at the Kuala Lumpur center. The arbitration facility may be used by any corporation and may involve firms in countries that are not members of AALCC.

The Malaysian government provided financing of all local costs during the first three years of operation of the Kuala Lumpur center (1978–1981), while the AALCC Secretariat defrayed promotional costs for travel outside Malaysia. This arrangement continued for the next three years; funds were derived from interest drawn from a $200,000 grant from Malaysia in 1981. Since mid-1984, the AALCC Secretariat has also provided a nominal amount. Local costs of the center in Cairo (nearly $250,000) are handled by the Egyptian government, promotional expenses outside Egypt by the AALCC Secretariat. The centers were supposed to be funded jointly by host governments and the AALCC Secretariat only for the first three to six years; thereafter, it was anticipated that the centers would be self-supporting.

AALCC centers impose modest charges for arranging arbitrations, based on actual expenses incurred. Each party pays legal costs for its own attorneys. The fees of arbitrators depend on such factors as the complexity of the case, nature of the dispute, and length of hearings. Parties defray a proportion of administrative charges and arbitrator fees fixed in the arbitral award. Center directors estimate costs, and both parties place deposits in equal amounts as an advance against costs before the arbitration can proceed. If hearings become prolonged, supplementary deposits can be required.

The centers provide facilities for either ad hoc or UNCITRAL-based arbitration. Officially, the regional centers coordinate AALCC's Disputes Settlement System. The Director of each center acts as Appointing Authority under UNCITRAL arbitration rules and can, if the parties agree, do so as well in ad hoc arbitrations. The Appointing Authority selects the sole arbitrator unless the parties agree otherwise. The Cairo center handled its first case in 1980. Kuala Lumpur got its first case in 1986.

Thus far, most of the work of the centers has been promotional; the aim is to encourage more commercial contracts to be drawn up with clauses providing that one of AALCC's regional arbitration centers will be utilized in case of a dispute between the parties. Conferences and seminars are organized to train arbitrators and to disseminate an awareness of the existence of the regional centers. All commercial contracts now drawn up in Malaysia have such a clause; many other countries have encouraged placing similar clauses in new commercial contracts.

The centers are also responsible for facilitating the enforcement of arbitral awards. Under Malaysian law, enforcement proceedings can be instituted before the Malaysian High Court. The centers are pledged to promoting ratification of the UN Convention on the Recognition and Enforcement of Arbitral Awards. So far, ten Asian and Pacific countries are parties to the convention. In 1985, AALCC authorized the centers to expand the scope of their operations to include conciliation.

AFRO-ASIAN RURAL RECONSTRUCTION ORGANIZATION (AARRO)[2]

The aspirations of Third-World countries to become industrial powers have generally been frustrated wherever agricultural workers have tried to produce food either for local markets or for the tables of First-World consumers. The term *rural reconstruction* refers to the mobilization of the rural population to provide food for industrial workers in Third-World cities. As urbanization has outpaced rural development, poorer countries need to coordinate national development through programs of integrated rural development.

In August 1955, Japan sponsored the East Asian Rural Reconstruction Conference to promote the concept of community development in rural areas. Since delegates expressed interest in intergovernmental cooperation on this issue, India convened the first Afro-Asian Rural Reconstruction Conference at New Delhi in 1961. The Food and Agriculture Organization of the United Nations (FAO) had not yet launched any regional projects, so Director General B. R. Sen urged the conference to start an international organization relating to rural reconstruction. Egypt then hosted a follow-up Afro-Asian Rural Reconstruction Conference at Cairo from March 19–31, 1962, when a Constitution for AARRO was adopted.

AARRO's Constitution specifies several functions: promoting cooperative activities; exchange visits of farmers and experts; organizing meetings, seminars, conferences, exhibitions, and fairs; producing literature; initiating studies; and helping members to obtain external financing in the field of rural development (Article I).

The plenary organ of AARRO is the Conference, which meets triennially for weekly sessions (see Fig. 4.2). Between Conferences, an Executive Committee meets for about three days once each year. The Executive Committee consists of the President of the Conference, the two Vice Presidents (one from Africa, the other from Asia), and up to nine additional members, such that the representation is half from each continent. In March 1967, the Executive Committee formed the Sub-Committee of Experts, which screens the work program in two-day meetings held once every three years. In 1970, the Executive Committee established the Liaison Committee to handle questions of policy between Executive Committee meetings; Liaison Committee members are from the diplomatic missions of member countries in New Delhi.

The Executive Committee and Liaison Committee supervise the Secretariat, which opened its doors officially in New Delhi in March 1966. A Secretary-General heads the Secretariat, which is divided between administrative and program staff.

The Executive Committee has authorized four regional offices. The Regional Office for the Middle East at Amman began in 1967 but was dormant from mid-1968 to 1986. The Regional Office for East and Central Africa at Addis Ababa functioned from 1968 to 1973. The Regional Office for the Far East at Seoul has been in operation since 1973. The Regional Office for West Africa at Accra was to start in 1971, but it is still in the planning stage.

There have been two AARRO training centers. In 1967, the Institute for the Development of Agricultural Cooperation in Asia (IDACA) in Tokyo established a special program for AARRO known as the Research and Educational Center for Asia (RECA). In 1970, an Arab Training Centre (ATC) was established at Sidi Bishr, Alexandria, Egypt, by the Egyptian Training Institute for Community Development. Eventually, a French-speaking training center for Africa was envisaged in Morocco. When this failed to become a reality, the Alexandria center was renamed Afro-Arab Training Centre (AATC). RECA still functions, but AATC has ceased to operate.

AARRO has twenty-four full Members and one Associate Member

Figure 4.2
Organization of the Afro-Asian Rural Reconstruction Organization

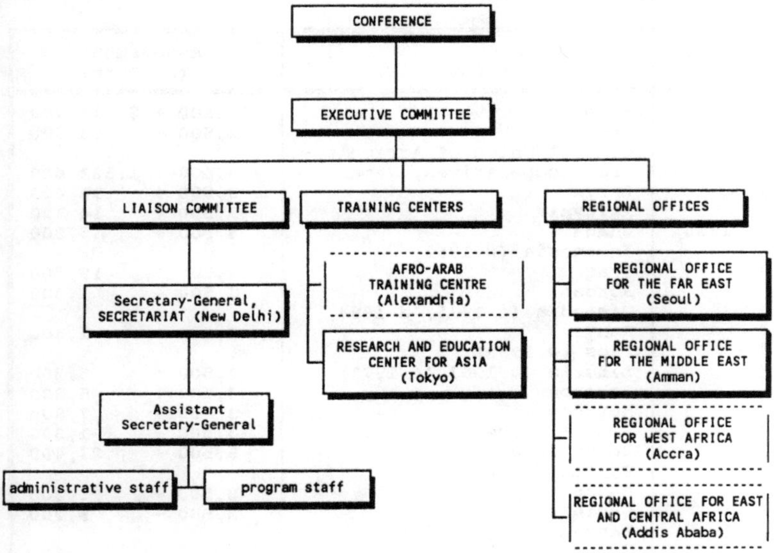

(see Table 4.2). A nongovernmental organization of farmers and rural residents may join as long as its respective government approves. The Central Union of Agricultural Cooperatives thus joined in place of the government of Japan.

Host countries fund the regional offices and training centers. The Secretariat and scholarship fund are defrayed by assessments that depart from the Asian Way principle of equality: each full member pays a flat rate of $3,500 plus ten percent of its current FAO contributions (and an equivalent amount for the Republic of China, which does not belong to FAO) (Table 4.2). In addition, Egypt, Ghana, India, Japan, South Korea, and Taiwan (China) have made additional grants from time to time. In 1983, the Secretariat received $296,000 in member contributions, though by the end of 1983 contributions in arrears totalled about $646,000.

Training is one of the key elements of AARRO. Short-term (three-week) courses are held at RECA. In addition, AARRO helps applicants to receive scholarships for six- to twelve-week instruction at six collaborating institutions: the Council of Agriculture, Taipei; Egyptian International Centre for Agriculture, Cairo; Indian Agricultural Research Institute, New Delhi; National Institute of Small Industry Extension Training, Hyderabad; Punjab Agricultural University, Ludhiana; and

Table 4.2
Afro-Asian Rural Reconstruction Organization: Membership and Assessments

Year Joined	Member Countries	Assessment (c. 1985)
1962	Egypt	$3,500 + $ 11,700
	India	3,500 + 94,900
	Central Union of Agricultural Cooperatives, Japan	3,500 + 1,523,600
	Libya	3,500 + 36,400
	Malaysia	3,500 + 14,300
1963	Ghana	3,500 + 5,200
	Indonesia (w 1969)	
	Iraq	3,500 + 19,500
	Jordan	3,500 + 1,300
	Cambodia (i 1975, d 1984)	
	Kenya	3,500 + 1,300
	Laos (w 1969)	
	Liberia (a 1963, f 1971)	3,500 + 5,200
	Lebanon	3,500 + 5,200
	Morocco	3,500 + 7,800
	Sierra Leone	3,500 + 1,300
	South Korea	3,500 + 23,400
	Sri Lanka (w 1969)	
	Sudan	3,500 + 1,300
	Syria (i)	3,500 + 5,200
	Tanganyika (w 1965)	
	Tunisia (w 1983)	
	Vietnam (i 1975, d 1984)	
	Zanzibar (w 1965)	
1966	Algeria (w 1975)	
1967	Ethiopia	3,500 + 1,300
1968	Central Organization for Rural Cooperatives, Iran (w 1973)	
	Philippines	3,500 + 15,600
	Republic of China	3,500 + c.15,600
1975	Mauritius	3,500 + 1,300
	South Yemen	3,500 + 5,200
1976	Maldives	3,500 + 1,300
	United Arab Emirates	3,500 + 15,600
1978	Oman	3,500 + 1,300
1985	Institute of Rural Development, Kenya (a)	
Totals	34-10=24 Members 1 Associate Member	$84,000 + 1,807,000

Key: a = Associate Member
d = dropped from membership
f = later joined as full Member
i = inactive
w = withdrew

Saemul Undong Headquarters, Seoul. AARRO provides airfare to the training institutions; the institutions provide tuition-free training to a quota of AARRO-sponsored students. Training is provided in animal husbandry, cotton production and processing, farm machinary, integrated rural development, plant protection, rice and vegetable production, rural cooperatives, small-scale agro-industry, and soil erosion and amelioration. There are also ad hoc seminars, international conferences, and technical workshops.

In the late 1970s, Jordan and South Korea operated AARRO pilot projects in community development. Study tours in 1969 and 1970 enabled experts to provide advice in the field; these have recently been revived.

Since 1981, a research program has been launched at the Secretariat. One of the recent projects compares cooperatives and extension services in several countries.

SUMMARY AND CONCLUSIONS

AALCC and AARRO, formally unconnected with the conferences of nonaligned nations, have diverged considerably over the years. While AALCC has remained committed to the principles of nonalignment, AARRO has become popular among many aligned Third-World countries.

AALCC's success is due to the high quality of its legal expertise and its patient efforts to build a Third-World consensus. Countries in Africa lacking cadres of legal scholars to prepare for international legal conferences have turned to AALCC for guidance. AALCC's role at the Law of the Sea Conferences attracted considerable attention from countries outside Africa and Asia, and attendance at Committee sessions grew to include countries outside Africa and Asia. In the field of private international law, the Cairo and Kuala Lumpur facilities have persuaded Third-World corporations and governments to utilize arbitration through UNCITRAL rules.

AARRO, in contrast, was viewed initially as an institution trying to promote India's model of food production, emphasizing market-oriented rural cooperatives, and as an alternative to the more self-reliant approach of the International Cooperative Alliance (ICA). The Indian solution was not regarded as appropriate to African problems, however. FAO, meanwhile, began to establish competing regional projects in Africa and Asia, thereby abandoning its special relationship with AARRO. As AARRO Conferences occur triennially, it was difficult to restructure the organization to play a more useful role, and many countries stopped paying annual assessments in the late 1960s. In Asia, the most active members include Japan, the Republic of China, and the Republic of Korea.

AARRO then tried to work through other organizations. The Cairo and Tokyo training centers put an AARRO label onto national efforts, and the cooperating educational institutions helped to maintain at least a minimally visible program. AARRO had no distinctive operational program of its own up to 1981, when the new Secretary-General urged the Secretariat to pursue basic agricultural economic research on selected topics.

Asian Way principles permeate AALCC more than AARRO. Only AALCC has kept growing. But the logistics of organizations seeking to include Africa and Asia, two continents with markedly different levels of development, provided a strong argument for developing intergovernmental efforts for just one region in later years.

NOTES

1. For references to AALCC documents, see Michael Haas, *Basic Documents of Asian Regional Organizations* (Dobbs Ferry, NY: Oceana Publications), vol. 5, pp. 156-61. For a bibliography of secondary sources, see pp. 154–55.

2. For references to AARRO documents, see Michael Haas, *Basic Documents of Asian Regional Organizations* (Dobbs Ferry, NY: Oceana Publications), vol. 5, pp. 162–70.

5 TOKYO AND SEOUL BID FOR LEADERSHIP

When Allied military occupation of Japan ended in 1955, Tokyo was determined to be a good international neighbor. The peace settlement of 1951 required Japan to pay reparations for 10 years, though mostly on an in-kind basis, since Japan had very little foreign exchange. When reparations ended, Japan had recovered to the point where it could continue to provide assistance as a part of the first UN Development Decade, even providing leadership for regional cooperative efforts. Tokyo's earliest initiatives began in the private sector. The Japan Productivity Center (JPC) first attempted to federate productivity centers in Asia, then the Liberal Democratic Party (LDP) of Japan sought a regional body that would link together parliamentarians. A nongovernmental association was not feasible in either case: since governments established many of the productivity centers, and political parties were fused with governments in the many one-party states throughout Asia, the resulting Asian Productivity Organization (APO) and the Asian Parliamentarians' Union (APU) were intergovernmental.

After the Korean War of 1950–53, South Korea sought membership in a multicountry regional security pact to deter aggression from North Korea. When the United States contributed a large contingent of troops to defend the Republic of Vietnam in 1965, Seoul dispatched volunteers from its army, then issued invitations to a diplomatic conference among many of the non-Communist regimes in Asia and the Pacific. The resulting Asian and Pacific Council (ASPAC) in turn launched several subsidiary bodies, two of which have outlived the Council itself.

The Republic of China, meanwhile, tagged along to make important contributions to ASPAC and APU. This chapter, accordingly, focuses on initiatives from Northeast Asia.

ASIAN PRODUCTIVITY ORGANIZATION (APO)[1]

Japan's sole natural resource is its people. Although devastated by World War II, Japan is an economic superpower today. Among the various explanations for this transformation one factor stands out – the productivity of its workers. A second factor that led to Japan's prosperity is that Japanese corporations have subsidiaries abroad and purchase parts made in other Asian countries, where labor costs are modest, although productivity lags compared to that of Japan. Recognizing the need for increased productivity, JPC was founded in 1955, following the example of the European Productivity Agency (EPA), started two years before. Subsequently, other national productivity organizations (NPOs) were set up in Asia.

Kohei Goshi and Ichiro Oshikawa of JPC felt that a federation of Asian productivity organizations could help NPOs in poorer countries. Accordingly, JPC convened the first Asian Round-Table Productivity Conference during March 1959 with the aid of the Japanese government, hoping to create a nongovernmental organization in the region. Since so many countries in Asia had government-controlled NPOs, when the second Asian Round-Table Productivity Conference met in September 1960, the proposal for an intergovernmental organization was approved, consistent with the Asian Way principle of separating politics from administration. A conference in Manila on April 14, 1961, signed the Convention of the Asian Productivity Organization, which was ratified before the end of the year.

According to the APO Convention, the objective of the organization is "by mutual cooperation, to increase productivity in the countries of Asia" (Article 1). The principal vehicle for meeting this objective is technical assistance.

APO's Secretariat is in Tokyo, with a Secretary-General in charge (see Fig. 5.1). The Governing Body meets for four-day sessions once each year. Each member sends a Director, usually the country's minister of international trade, and an Alternate Director, the head of the country's NPO. A Workshop Meeting of NPO representatives meets about four days each year to scrutinize the draft APO program for the following year and the rolling five-year plan for the organization. The Governing Body usually accepts recommendations from the Workshop Meeting, with consensus building based on the Asian Way.

When APO began, there were three divisions in the Secretariat: the Administrative/Budget Division, the Program Division, and the Infor-

Figure 5.1
Organization of the Asian Productivity Organization

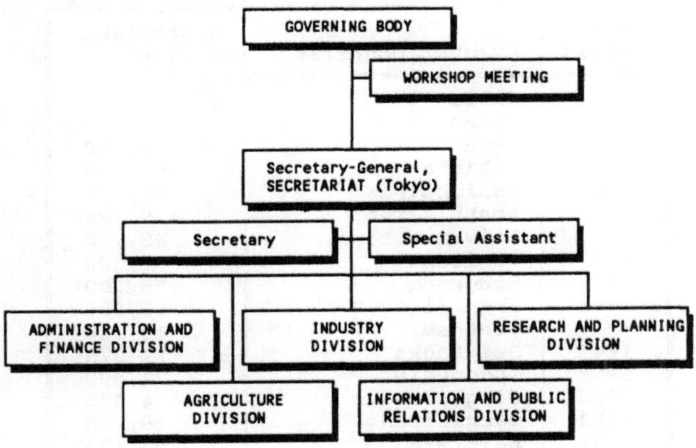

mation Division. The Program Division (now the Industry Division) was responsible for training in the fields of business management and industrial technology. In 1966, the Agriculture Division was set up to service agricultural productivity needs. In 1967, a Regional Information Unit began operations at Manila, in keeping with the Convention's authorization of regional centers on specialized subjects, but this was downgraded to the Production Unit in 1971, with responsibility reduced to printing APO publications. No other efforts were undertaken in regard to APO regional centers. Reorganizations in 1974 and 1986 left APO with five divisions.

Any member of the UN Economic and Social Commission for Asia and the Pacific (ESCAP) is eligible to join APO. There are seventeen members today (see Table 5.1). Although its membership in ESCAP ceased in 1971, Taiwan (China) remains a member in keeping with the Asian Way principle of pan-Asianism. In 1976, APO passed a resolution seeking to attract Pacific island nations; although this was designed to attract Papua New Guinea, Fiji instead joined APO in 1984. Iran indicated an intention to withdraw in 1980 but resumed participation in 1984 after four inactive years. Australia, the Cook Islands, France, the Netherlands, Papua New Guinea, and West Germany have sent observers to APO meetings in recent years.

Expenditures for APO's Secretariat are broken down into administrative expenses and operational expenses. For administrative costs, members pay annual contributions in local currencies based on their gross national income (GNI) (see Table 5.1). Operational costs for projects come from Japan's Ministry of Foreign Affairs and Ministry of

Table 5.1
Asian Productivity Organization: Membership and Assessments

Year Joined	Member Countries	Assessment (1986)
1961	India	$ 326,875
	Japan	1,853,125
	Nepal	5,000
	Pakistan	62,500
	Philippines	38,125
	South Korea	128,125
	Taiwan (China)	88,750
	Thailand	77,000
1963	Hongkong	55,000
1965	Iran (i 1980-83)	295,000
	Vietnam (i 1975-)[a]	13,750
1967	Sri Lanka	11,875
1968	Indonesia	122,500
1970	Singapore	34,375
1982	Bangladesh	26,875
1983	Malaysia	53,125
1984	Fiji	3,125
Totals	17 Members	$6,850,730[b]

[a]Joined as Republic of Vietnam
[b]Including cash grants as well as project grants
Key: i = inactive

International Trade and Industry as well as various external sources. Private-sector firms in each country defray participant costs. APO now sends two technical experts to NPOs each year on six-month assignments to help in program development.

Productivity improvement requires the application of the Asian Way principle of incrementalism. APO activities include research and survey projects, usually followed by conferences or symposia; study missions and technical expert services; and training courses and seminars, with publications for general use. There is a dual emphasis on business administration and production engineering, stressing the training of consultants and trainers for NPOs and similar institutes. APO's activities fulfill five roles: catalyst for multilateral cooperation, information clearinghouse, institution builder, regional adviser, and thinktank for research and evaluation. Most activities focus on institution building.

During the 1960s, APO focused on improving productivity in small- and medium-scale enterprises. Agricultural projects concentrated on better utilization of input materials and on prevention of post-harvest loss and waste of food grains. In the 1970s, APO focused on productivity measurement and analysis, project feasibility, and research on factors that hinder or help productivity. The agriculture program expanded to cover agribusiness management, agricultural chemicals, agricultural diversification, agricultural productivity measurement, changes in food habits, grain marketing, fertilizers, farm mechanization, livestock production and marketing, storage, and food processing. The industry program encompassed automation, computerization, energy conservation, environmental concerns, export marketing, labor-management techniques, quality control, technology transfer, and worker motivation.

In the 1980s, the focus shifted in agriculture to input pricing, biotechnology, construction management, crop insurance and farm credit, development and land-use planning, and feed resources. On the industrial side, emphasis was placed on foreign investment, information technology, management systems and practices to suit different sociocultures, micro–macro linkages, mineral resource assessment, operational productivity measurement and projections, personnel and technology management, plant layout and materials handling, quality control of processed foods, robotics, technology assimilation and adaptation, tourism and hotel management, and treatment of hazardous industrial waste.

ASIAN-PACIFIC PARLIAMENTARIANS' UNION (APPU)[2]

Asian delegates at meetings of the Inter-Parliamentary Union (IPU) had been interacting informally for some time before Japan's foreign ministry began to develop plans for Asian regional cooperation. Members of the Japanese Liberal Democratic Party felt that they should play a role in this venture, based on their contacts with parliamentarians in Asia, and cultivated in part at IPU meetings. Members of the Diet sought a politically oriented body that would unite non-Communist Asia. The Japanese founders, therefore, wanted to exclude Japan's Communist and Socialist parties from representation in the new organization and so considered the possibility of a nongovernmental body.

When Saburo Chiba, longtime colleague of Nobusuke Kishi, learned that Philippine IPU counterparts, especially Senator J. B. Laurel, Jr., and Cornelo Villareal, were enthusiastic about the idea, members of the Diet organized a preliminary meeting in Tokyo in February 1965 with national groups of parliamentarians from Malaysia, South Korea, Taiwan (China), and Thailand. The meeting agreed to call for an Asian Parliamentarians' Union, and the first General Assembly met from November 30 to December 4, 1965, when the Charter for APU was adopted. APU became the Asian-Pacific Parliamentarians' Union (APPU) in 1980, reflecting growth of membership into the South Pacific.

According to the Charter, the aim of APPU is "achieving and preserving freedom and democracy, thereby securing enduring peace and prosperity in Asia and the Pacific" (Article 2). Economic cooperation, exchanges of culture and technology, and discussions on matters affecting peace and security in Asia and the Pacific are the main functions.

The basic unit of APPU is the National Group of Parliamentarians, which is selected by each respective parliament however it chooses (see Fig. 5.2). Each National Group has a National Secretariat, a National Secretary-General, and a President. The General Assembly is the plenary organ of APPU; up to ten representatives from each National Group may attend its annual meetings. The Council, composed of no more than five representatives from each National Group, meets twice each year, once just before the General Assembly. General Assembly meetings last five days; Council sessions are somewhat shorter.

Figure 5.2
Organization of the Asian-Pacific Parliamentarians' Union

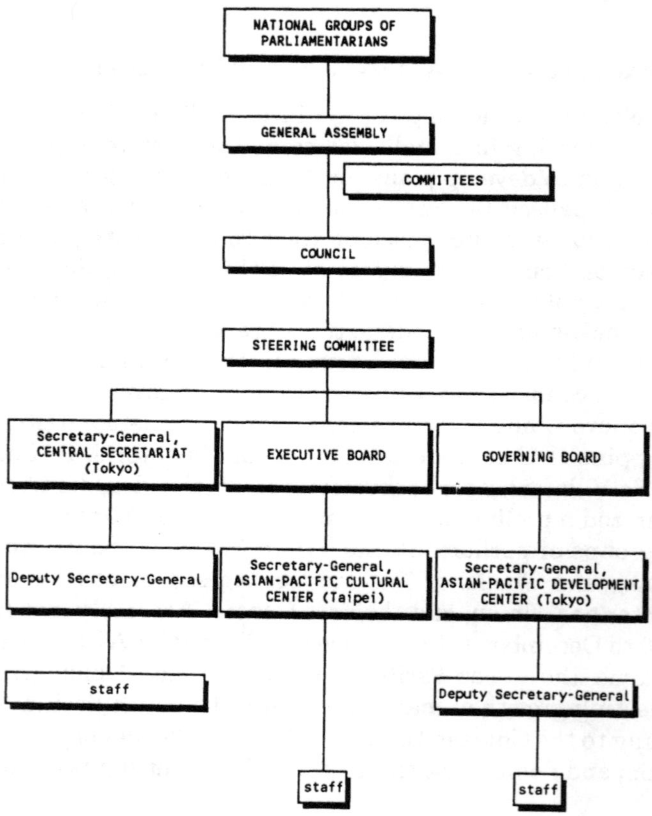

APPU has three subsidiary bodies: the Central Secretariat, the Asian-Pacific Cultural Center (APCC), and the Asian-Pacific Development Center (APDC). In order to coordinate these bodies, a Meeting of Secretaries-General was held in 1972 and thereafter once annually until 1983, when the body became the Steering Committee; meetings are held usually at the time of the General Assembly.

National Groups of Parliamentarians are the official members of APPU, rather than the countries themselves. In countries where there is no separation of powers among various branches of government, the government's chief executive often appoints members of the National Group. The Liberal Democratic party chooses Japan's representatives. In the 1970s, when APPU appeared to be too anti-Communist in orientation to suit the policies of several countries, Malaysia and Indonesia withdrew. Indochinese countries were expelled in 1975. The Philippines sent observers after martial law was declared in 1972; in 1978, when a new interim parliament met, Manila resumed participation, then withdrew in 1984 for lack of funds. In the late 1970s and 1980s, APPU expanded its membership to include ten South Pacific island countries. When Malaysia rejoined in 1984, membership rose to fifteen (see Table 5.2).

Each country's national group defrays expenses of its own participation. Scales of assessments exist for APPU's subsidiary bodies.

The main activity of the General Assembly is the discussion of major political and economic issues of the region. Resolutions are adopted at each session; they usually give instructions to foreign ministries in each country for achieving better relations in the region. The divisive anti-Communist rhetoric of the early years, inconsistent as it was with the Asian Way principle of pan-Asianism, has been toned down.

Central Secretariat

An informal body was established in Tokyo in 1965 to launch APU. By 1970, this body was transformed into a permanent secretariat. In June 1971, this body, named the Central Secretariat, began officially at an office in Tokyo not far from the Diet.

Rules of the Central Secretariat, adopted in 1970, specify four functions: carrying out decisions of the General Assembly and Security Council, acting as an information clearinghouse, maintaining liaison with National Groups of Parliamentarians, and preparing documents for the Union (Article 3). A Secretary-General and Deputy Secretary-General supervise four general service staff.

The Diet financed the provisional headquarters. After the Central Secretariat was formally approved, a funding formula was based on national income figures (see Table 5.3).

Table 5.2
Asian-Pacific Parliamentarians' Union: Membership in the Union and Its Subsidiary Bodies

Year	APPU	APCC[a]	APDC[b]
1965	Japan Philippines (i 1972-78, w 1984) South Korea Taiwan (China) Thailand Laos (d 1975) Malaysia (i 1969, w 1972, r 1984)		
1966	South Vietnam (d 1975)		
1967	Indonesia (w 1974)		
1969			Japan Laos (d 1975) Malaysia (w 1972, r 1984) Philippines (i 1972- 78, w 1984) South Korea South Vietnam (d 1975) Taiwan (China) Thailand
1970	Khmer Republic (d 1975)		
1972			Indonesia (w 1974) Khmer Republic (d 1975)
		Japan Khmer Republic (d 1975) Laos (d 1975) Philippines (i 1972-78, w 1984) South Korea South Vietnam (d 1975) Taiwan (China) Thailand	
1978	Nauru	Nauru	Nauru
1981	Guam (a) Micronesia (a, m 1986) Palau (a) Vanuatu (a, m 1983)	Guam Micronesia Palau Vanuatu	Guam Micronesia Palau Vanuatu
1982	Marshall Islands (a, m 1986) Northern Marianas (a)	Marshall Islands Northern Marianas	Marshall Islands Northern Marianas
1983	Fiji	Fiji	Fiji
1984		Malaysia	
1986	Papua New Guinea Solomon Islands	Papua New Guinea Solomon Islands	Papua New Guinea Solomon Islands
Total	17-5=12 Members 3 Associate Members	19-4=15 Members	20-5=15 Members

[a] Asian-Pacific Cultural Center
[b] Asian-Pacific Development Center

Key: a = Associate Member
d = dropped from membership
i = inactive
m = later joined as full Member
r = rejoined
w = withdrew

Table 5.3
Asian-Pacific Parliamentarians' Union: Assessments[a]

Member Countries	Central Secretariat	APCC	APDC
Fiji	2.5%	1.9%	4.3%
Guam	1.2	1.0	1.7
Japan	72.7	19.3	22.1
Marshall Islands	1.9	1.4	2.6
Micronesia	1.9	1.4	2.6
Nauru	2.5	1.9	4.3
Northern Marianas	1.3	1.0	1.7
Palau	1.9	1.4	2.6
South Korea	3.8	9.6	17.3
Taiwan (China)	3.8	46.6	17.3
Thailand	3.8	9.6	19.0
Vanuatu	2.5	1.9	4.3
Totals (1985)	$90,000	$103,857	$45,000

[a]Due to rounding, columns do not sum exactly to 100 percent.

Asian-Pacific Cultural Center (APCC)

When Kuomintang troops retired to Taiwan after the revolution on the Chinese mainland in 1949, tons of cultural artifacts of Chinese civilization were crated and transported as well. The National Museum in Taipei has a remarkable collection of materials, with only a fraction on display at a time for lack of space. The idea of a cultural center, therefore, appealed to legislators of the Republic of China.

The notion of a cultural center was discussed during the inaugural APU General Assembly in 1965. In 1966, APU set up a Cultural Committee to develop the idea, and APCC began operation at Taipei in late 1972. APCC's Charter endows the organization with a wide variety of functions relating to the study and propagation of Asia's "cultural and ethical heritage" (Article 2).

APCC's headquarters is directed by a Secretary-General, who is nominated by the National Group of the host country and is approved by the Executive Board (see Fig. 5.2). Each National Group of Parliamentarians sends a Member and a Deputy Member to annual one-day Executive Board meetings, provided that they are national legislators.

APCC membership is identical to APPU membership, although this is not required (see Table 5.2). The National Group of Parliamentarians of the Republic of China absorbed costs of the center from 1972 to 1975. In 1976, a cost-sharing formula was negotiated. Members pay 90 percent of the expenses, Associate Members 10 percent; Japan matches the contribution of the Republic of China, and other Asian members pay about half of Japan's contribution (see Table 5.3).

APCC operates four projects. These are *The Asian Culture Quarterly*; annual exhibitions of painting, calligraphy, and photography; Asian and Pacific cultural scholars' conventions; and the International Youth Tour of Taiwan, which visits sites of cultural significance.

Asian-Pacific Development Center (APDC)

APPU was eager to discuss ideas regarding an Asian common market, customs union, or free-trade area, but parliamentarians felt that many expert meetings would have to come first. APDC (the Asian Development Center up to 1980) responded to this need.

An Indonesian proposal for the establishment of a center to investigate problems of development was adopted by the Economic Committee, then accepted by the APU plenary session in 1967. A committee was then formed, and a plan was presented to the General Assembly in 1968, when a Technical Body was set up, with the Philippine Economic Planning Office as the Coordination Center. Experts on the Technical Body drafted a Charter, which was approved by the General Assembly on November 25, 1969. Two months later, APDC began operation at Manila, and in 1972, a second ADC office opened in Saigon.

Martial law was declared in the Philippines at the end of 1972. As the Philippine National Group no longer existed, the headquarters moved to the office of the Central Secretariat at Tokyo in 1973. The Saigon office closed in 1975, when the city was renamed Ho Chi Minh City.

APDC's Charter entrusts APDC with the task of promoting "regional cooperation toward economic and social development" (Article 1). The highest organ, the Governing Board, usually meets once each year in conjunction with the General Assembly (see Fig. 5.2). Each National Group provides a Governor and Alternate Governor for the Governing Board. The Japanese National Group of Parliamentarians appoints the Secretary-General from within its ranks, so APDC, in effect, is a project of the Japanese National Group.

ADC was initially restricted to members of APU (see Table 5.2). In 1983, the Charter was amended to permit nonmember National Groups of Parliamentarians to join APDC, although this has not occurred.

The Philippine National Congress funded the office at Manila. In 1973, the Japanese National Group took over financing. The Republic of Vietnam, meanwhile, defrayed the costs of the office in Saigon from 1972 to 1975. In 1975, a contribution formula was approved by the Governing Board, with Japan paying $25,000 of the expenses and the remaining members, then South Korea, Taiwan (China), and Thailand, paying $10,000 each. APDC now has a biennial budget: Japan's contribution is to fund a conference in even-numbered years; other members are assessed for APDC operating costs, based on their ability to pay (see Table 5.3).

Initially, APDC studies focused on the lending policies of international financial institutions, a proposed Asian payments union, integrated social and economic development, trade policies of the People's Republic of China, functions of Asian international organizations in relation to the UN system, U.S. policy toward China, and a survey of the Khmer Republic's economy. When APDC moved to Tokyo, studies were completed on medium- and small-scale industries in rural areas, land tenure and reform, aquaculture, mineral resources development, supply and demand for food in Asia, housing development, and the role of Japan in the North–South dialog. Since 1978, APDC has hosted biennial week-long Expert Conferences for Economic Development in Asia and the Pacific, while commissioning prefeasibility studies for possible projects of the Association of South East Asian Nations (ASEAN) to be financed by Japan.

ASIAN AND PACIFIC COUNCIL (ASPAC)[3]

The armies of North Korea and South Korea clashed in June 1950, five months after U.S. Secretary of State Dean Acheson declared the area to lie outside of the Pacific "defense perimeter" of the United States. U.S. forces were dispatched along with those from other countries around the world under the UN Command. For many countries, the cause of Korea symbolized the need for collective security, that is, the willingness of all states to aid a small state under unprovoked attack.

As guerrilla operations increased in tempo within South Vietnam in the mid-1960s, the United States sent combat forces to aid the Republic of Vietnam. The Republic of Korea was one of the first to join the United States in the effort, and its troops remained until the peace settlement of 1973. Seoul felt that the South-East Asia Treaty Organization (SEATO), which South Korea was ineligible to join, had failed to prevent the war and that a new organization was needed to stop Communist aggression in Asia.

Seoul believed that an Asian and Pacific treaty organization (APATO) would have deterred both the Korean and Vietnam Wars. Although the Philippines, Republic of China, Republic of Vietnam, and Thailand were interested in an APATO, two countries that sent troops to Vietnam were opposed: Australia and New Zealand. Japan and Malaysia were also against an APATO. With APATO doomed, President Park Chung Hee and Foreign Minister Lee Tong Won unsuccessfully sought a Southeast Asian foreign ministers conference in 1964. As an alternative, Seoul issued invitations to the Ministerial Meeting for Cooperation in the Asian and Pacific Region in June 1966. With 10 countries in attendance, the meeting was the largest diplomatic forum in Asia since the Bandung Conference of 1955. The joint communiqué, known as the

ASPAC Declaration, launched the Asian and Pacific Council, which met annually until 1972, although some of its subsidiary bodies are still in operation.

According to the eighth paragraph of the ASPAC Declaration, the ministers' "urgent need for continuing consultations" aimed at "forging better international understanding, promoting closer and more fruitful regional cooperation and further strengthening Asian and Pacific solidarity." The actual purpose of ASPAC was to fight the cold war.

The annual meeting of foreign ministers, known as the Ministerial Meeting, lasted about three days (see Fig. 5.3). A Standing Committee met for a day each month as a preparatory body for the forthcoming Ministerial Meeting; it was chaired by the foreign minister of the next host country and attended by ambassadors of ASPAC countries assigned to that country.

Seoul proposed that ASPAC have a permanent secretariat, but other countries preferred a more informal arrangement. Each country maintained a National Secretariat, which served as the ASPAC secretariat when the Ministerial Meeting rotated to that country. ASPAC created five autonomous projects in specialized fields (discussed below), only two of which remain today (see Table 5.4).

Figure 5.3
Organization of the Asian and Pacific Council

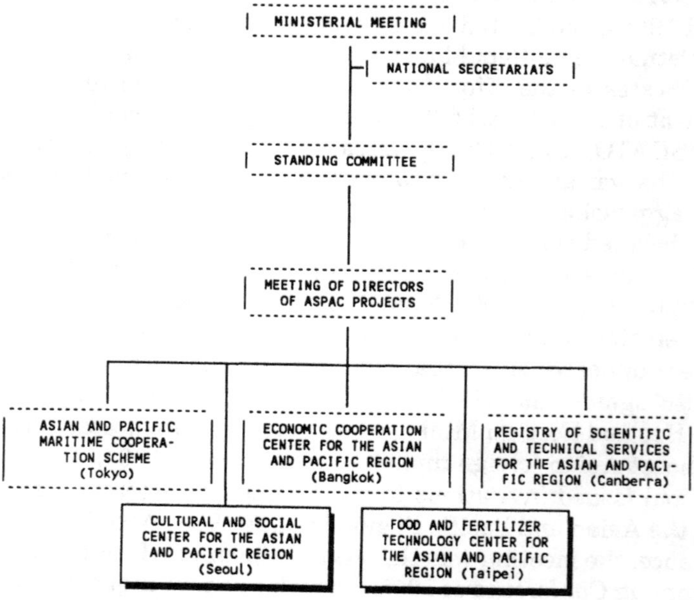

Table 5.4
Asian and Pacific Council: Formation and Termination of Centers

Year	Organization Formed	Organization Terminated
1966	ASPAC	
1968	CULSOCEN	
1970	ECOCEN	
	FFTC	
1971	Registry	
	APMCS	
1972		ASPAC
		APMCS
1974		Registry
1975		ECOCEN
Totals	6 organizations	4 organizations

Nine of the countries at the inaugural meeting in 1966 were considered members. Laos, formally neutralized by the Geneva Conference of 1962, attended Ministerial Meetings as an Observer. Japan invited Indonesia to the Ministerial Meeting in 1969, and the Philippines welcomed both Indonesia and the Khmer Republic in 1971. There was no formal membership provision, so host countries invited "free countries in the Asian and Pacific region," in accordance with the ASPAC Declaration.

One aim advanced by South Korea through ASPAC was to build anti-Communist solidarity, particularly to prevent the People's Republic of China from gaining admission to the United Nations, contrary to the Asian Way principle of pan-Asianism. When the People's Republic of China was seated at the UN in 1971, association with ASPAC was considered anachronistic. After a lukewarm Ministerial Meeting in 1972, it was Thailand's turn to host the 1973 meeting. When Bangkok demurred, Seoul asked Tokyo to convene the next session. Tokyo refused, remembering anti-ASPAC student riots in 1969 that forced Japan to move to Ministerial Meeting from Tokyo to isolated Kawana in order to guarantee security. Since only Korea was willing to host a continued ASPAC, with the expected nonattendance by other countries, no further ASPAC meetings were held, and in time three of ASPAC's five projects folded as well.

Aside from resolutions adopted by the Ministerial Meetings, the main legacy of ASPAC emerged from its autonomous centers (see Fig. 5.3). A Philippine-proposed Food Processing Center came too late, inasmuch as it was first discussed in 1971 and approved only provisionally in 1972.

Host countries for Ministerial Meetings provided secretariat costs. Four centers had their own independent financing formulas, and the

Japanese government defrayed the full cost of the Asian and Pacific Maritime Cooperation Scheme (APMCS).

Cultural and Social Center for the Asian and Pacific Region (CULSOCEN)

In 1966, South Korea and Thailand proposed a center for cultural and social affairs at the inaugural ASPAC Ministerial Meeting. After the Standing Committee studied the feasibility and scope of such a center, the Ministerial Meeting accepted the proposal in 1967 as ASPAC's first project, and the founding agreement was signed during the Ministerial Meeting on August 1, 1968. CULSOCEN's offices opened three months later.

According to the Agreement Establishing the Cultural and Social Center for the Asian and Pacific Region, its aim is to "promote friendly relations and mutual understanding among the peoples of the Asian and Pacific Region through the furtherance of collaboration in cultural and related social fields" (Article II).

CULSOCEN's office is in Seoul (see Fig. 5.4). The Executive Board, composed of the Korean foreign minister and ambassadors (or their alternates) of the ASPAC member countries located in Seoul, met in annual two-day sessions in the early years; today it holds one-day annual meetings. The Director is secretary to the Executive Board. The Working Group consists of the Director of the Cultural Affairs Division of the Korean foreign ministry and officials designated by representatives from embassies of member countries in Seoul; although it

Figure 5.4
Organization of the Cultural and Social Center for the Asian and Pacific Region

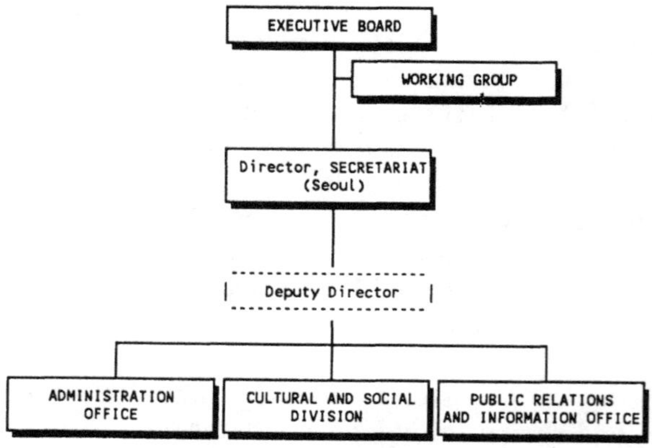

met monthly for one-day sessions in the early period, today it meets once each year just before Executive Board sessions to review administrative and technical details. The operational work is carried out primarily by the Cultural and Social Division.

All ASPAC members joined in 1968 (see Table 5.5). Five countries withdrew in the 1974–76 period; the Philippines pulled out in 1980, when it could no longer afford to pay assessments. Contributions toward operational costs are based roughly on national incomes; the host government defrays administrative expenses (see Table 5.5).

Conferences and seminars have been the major activities of CULSOCEN; about two each year were held from 1969 to 1979 on such themes as audiovisual education, music, museum development, juvenile delinquency, preservation of cultural heritage, rural and urban development, social development, teaching materials, university presses, use of television to promote cultural understanding, and youth and development. Nine ASPAC Fellowship Exchange Program awards have been made annually to artists, cultural experts, educators, journalists, and social scientists in each country for three-month study tours in other member countries. The educational program sponsored booklets for schoolchildren on cultures of the region. The social program funded a few research projects. The annual Asian and Pacific Film Festival has presented documentary and dramatic films to audiences in each of the member countries since 1969. The information clearinghouse program started a literary translation program and a radio and television exchange program, but now its principal project is the *Asian and Pacific Quarterly of Cultural and Social Affairs* and the printing of proceedings of its conferences and seminars.

Food and Fertilizer Technology Center for the Asian and Pacific Region (FFTC)

The island of Taiwan reverted from Japanese control to become an integral part of the Republic of China after World War II. In 1949, many non-Communist refugees left the mainland for Taiwan in the wake of the victory of the revolution led by Mao Tse Tung. Although Taiwan was hardly the most progressive province of China, the island has experienced remarkable economic progress. Since one element in its success is the use of modern farming methods and extension services to bring about a productive food industry, the Republic of China proposed an ASPAC project in the field of agriculture.

The initial ASPAC Declaration called for a study of a commodities and fertilizer bank to cope with periodic shortages of both food and fertilizers in the region at that time. After exploring the idea further, the Republic of China decided that a food and fertilizer technology

Table 5.5
Cultural and Social Center for the Asian and Pacific Region: Membership and Assessments

Year Joined	Member Countries	Assessment (1987)[a]
1968	Australia (w 1974)	
	Japan	20.0%
	Malaysia (w 1974)	
	New Zealand (w 1976)	
	Philippines (w 1980)	
	South Korea	53.4
	South Vietnam (w 1975)	
	Taiwan (China)	26.7
	Thailand (w 1976)	
Totals	9-6=3 Members	$400,000

[a]Due to rounding, the column does not sum exactly to 100 percent.
Key: w = withdrew

center as a major vehicle for information dissemination would be more feasible. In early 1969, an Experts Meeting examined the proposal and made a favorable recommendation, which in turn was refined by the Standing Committee, and the Council adopted the Agreement Establishing a Food and Fertilizer Technology Center for the Asian and Pacific Region on June 11, 1969.

According to the agreement, FFTC's purpose is "to promote, among and in the Members, the exchange and dissemination of technical information and experience on agricultural food production and, in particular, on the use of chemical fertilizers and the adoption of modern farming methods, so as to achieve an increased output and higher incomes for farmers in the Asian and Pacific Region" (Article II).

The Executive Board, the highest organ of FFTC, meets twice each year for a day or two to approve the annual report, audit report, budget, and future work program (see Fig. 5.5). The Board is headed by the Chairman of the Council for Agriculture, Republic of China; other members are the Minister of the Korean Embassy in Taipei and the Chief, Cultural Affairs and Technical Cooperation, Japan Interchange Association, Taipei. Technical supervision is maintained by the Working Group, which consists of the Vice Chairman of the Council of Agriculture; the Deputy Director, Department of East Asian and Pacific Affairs, Ministry of Foreign Affairs, Republic of China; the Counsellor of the Korean Embassy at Taipei; and a representative from the Japan Interchange Association at Taipei. The Working Group meets just before the Executive Board.

All ASPAC members joined FFTC (see Table 5.6). Four countries withdrew from FFTC while establishing relations with the People's

Figure 5.5
Organization of the Food and Fertilizer Technology Center for the Asian and Pacific Region

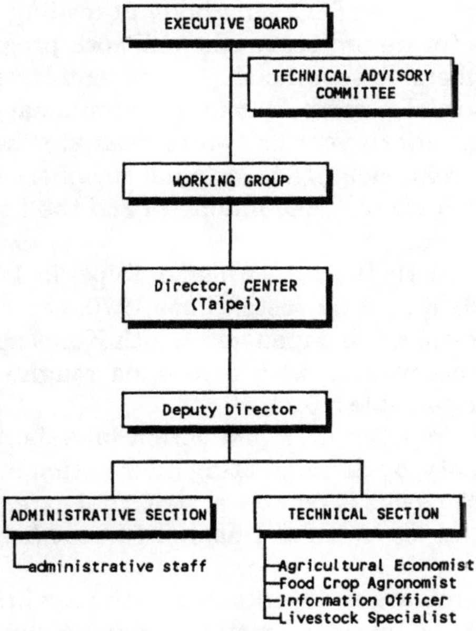

Table 5.6
Food and Fertilizer Technology Center for the Asian and Pacific Region: Membership and Assessments

Year Joined	Member Countries	Assessment (1987)[a]
1970	Australia (w 1975)	
	Japan	17.0%
	Malaysia (w 1973)	
	New Zealand (w 1975)	
	Philippines	
	South Korea	7.3
	South Vietnam (w 1975)	
	Taiwan (China)	75.8
	Thailand	
Totals	9-4=5 Members	$743,800

[a]Due to rounding, the column does sum exactly to 100 percent.
Key: w = withdrew

Republic of China. In 1975, the Philippines and Thailand decided to refrain from attending the Executive Board, although they have not formally withdrawn. In 1976, accordingly, FFTC organized the Technical Advisory Committee (TAC) as a body of leading scientists in the region to discuss future project needs and work programs. While current FFTC members have official governmental representatives on TAC, other experts also serve, but in a personal capacity. TAC holds one-week meetings every year or two to evaluate the work of FFTC. Representatives from each of the original members except Australia and South Vietnam are on TAC; Indonesia and the United States have also been represented.

FFTC began with an Interim Office in Taipei in 1969, with the Republic of China defraying all costs. Since 1970, the host has provided administrative costs, while Japan and South Korea contribute to operational costs in accordance with a formula roughly proportional to national income (see Table 5.6).

FFTC seeks to improve food production in Asia, in terms of both quantity and quality, by disseminating information on modern agricultural methods. The focus is on how agricultural extension workers can transmit results of agricultural research to best help farmers in the field.

About seven seminars and workshops each year bring together crop and soil scientists to exchange results. Training courses and lectures are provided to extension workers and experienced farmers. By 1988, FFTC had conducted 134 seminars, training courses, and workshops, with a total of over 7,000 participants. High priority has been assigned to rice production; in recent years, upland crops, such as cassava, corn, Irish potatoes, soybeans, sweet potatoes, and wheat, have been given attention. Grassland farming and livestock production have also been stressed. Agricultural economics, especially farm management, has been emphasized along with agricultural technology, including farm mechanization, pest and disease control, and post-harvest technology.

Recent training topics have covered agronomy, aquaculture, artificial insemination, hilly land development, multicropping, plant breeding, plant diseases and pests, post-harvest technology, rice production, seed production and plant breeding, and soil and fertilizer management. The focus of training is on problems of institutional support of farming, such as agricultural economics, the extension system, farm cooperatives, and food marketing, as well as on small-scale, "backyard" livestock production, disease control, livestock feeding and management, pastures, and forage.

FFTC operates field demonstrations and field projects in order to attend to the practical needs of farmers. FFTC offers study grants for younger scientists, consultancy grants (in which experts go to developing member countries to provide assistance), thesis awards, and research awards.

Economic Cooperation Center for the Asian and Pacific Region (ECOCEN)

An economic coordination center was proposed in the original ASPAC Declaration. Subsequently, Thailand developed a proposal, which was adopted by the Council on June 19, 1970. ECOCEN opened in Bangkok on April 1, 1971, but closed in 1975.

The Agreement Establishing an Economic Cooperation Center for the Asian and Pacific Region states the purpose of ECOCEN: "to promote closer harmonious economic relations among, and accelerate economic development in member countries . . . and to encourage further economic cooperation, trade and investment among Members for their mutual benefit, bearing in mind the desirability for broader cooperation in the region as a whole" (Article II).

The highest organ of ECOCEN, the Executive Board, met as needed at least once each year and was chaired by the Thai foreign minister (see Fig. 5.6). An Alternate Member Meeting during the year handled more detailed supervision of ECOCEN. The Secretariat was headed by a director, who chaired the Alternate Member Meeting. Initially, ECOCEN assigned junior economists to specific projects. In 1974, ECOCEN set up an Administration Office, a Project Planning and Promotion Office, and a Research and Information Office.

All nine ASPAC countries joined ECOCEN in 1970. Laos attended the inaugural meeting of the Executive Board as an Observer.

Thailand financed ECOCEN from 1971 to 1973, when it operated on a provisional basis. The 1972–73 budget consisted of $37,545 for administrative costs and $82,455 for operational costs. Later budgets were not made public.

ECOCEN had three major activities. First, studies were undertaken to determine which operational projects to sponsor; besides exploring schemes for regional harmonization and trade expansion, commodities were identified for exchange through trade rather than being produced competitively as import substitutes behind protective tariff barriers. Next, meetings and workshops, as identified by the studies, were held to locate executives in private businesses who would support schemes for industrial complementation, payments unions, and free trade areas. ECOCEN succeeded in linking together the Southeast Asian automobile industry on behalf of the proposed industrial complementation project of ASEAN, wherein each country agreed to produce a different automotive part. Meetings of industrial planners and industrial financiers received emphasis as well. The third project was an annual survey

Figure 5.6
Organization of the Economic Cooperation Center for the Asian and Pacific Region

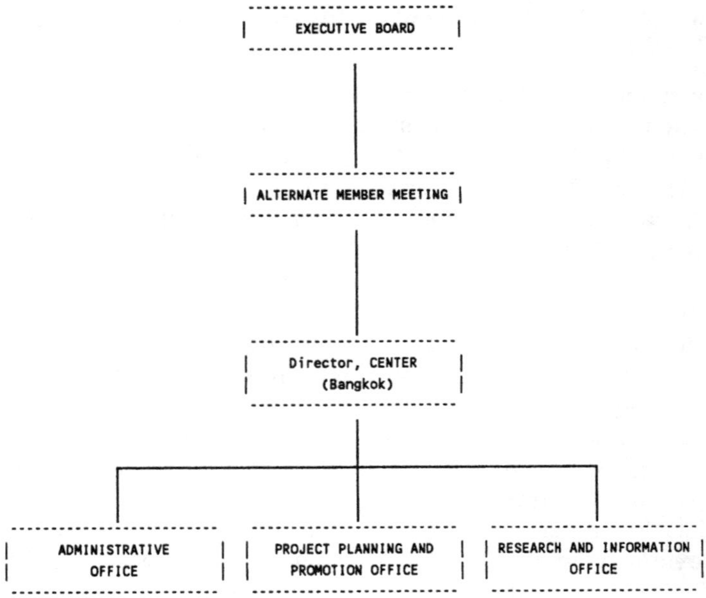

of economic conditions and regional economic cooperation efforts in which ECOCEN served as an information clearinghouse.

In 1975, Thailand decided to shut down ECOCEN. As a legacy of ASPAC, Thai public opinion considered ECOCEN to be as unacceptable as SEATO.

Registry of Scientific and Technical Services for the Asian and Pacific Region

Technical experts abound in the Asian and Pacific region. When countries need consultants, however, they tend to rely on professionals who are integrated into bureaucratic niches. Some of the best experts are not consulted abroad because their own governments do not know of their existence and thus cannot promote their services. The aim of developing an information base of consultants in various fields of expertise motivated the formation of the Registry.

A technical coordination center was one of the schemes approved in principle in the ASPAC Declaration of June 1966. Although the Ministerial Meeting accepted an Australian proposal for a registry of scientific and technical services in July 1967, the project was initially an

Australian effort. In 1968, the Registry opened its doors in Canberra on an interim basis; it became fully operational in 1969, after the Ministerial Meeting opened the Registry for membership in 1971.

According to the Agreement Establishing a Registry of Scientific and Technical Services for the Asian and Pacific Region, the purpose of the Registry was "to develop a central bank of information on the location of scientific and technical expertise within the ASPAC region by collecting information on the activities of organizations concerned with economic development within the ASPAC region and by other means" (Article II).

The Executive Board, consisting of a ministerial-level official from Australia and ambassadors from ASPAC countries posted to Canberra, held an annual regular session to supervise the Registry (see Fig. 5.7). A Working Group of lower-level officials convened between Executive

Figure 5.7
Organization of the Registry of Scientific and Technical Services for the Asian and Pacific Region

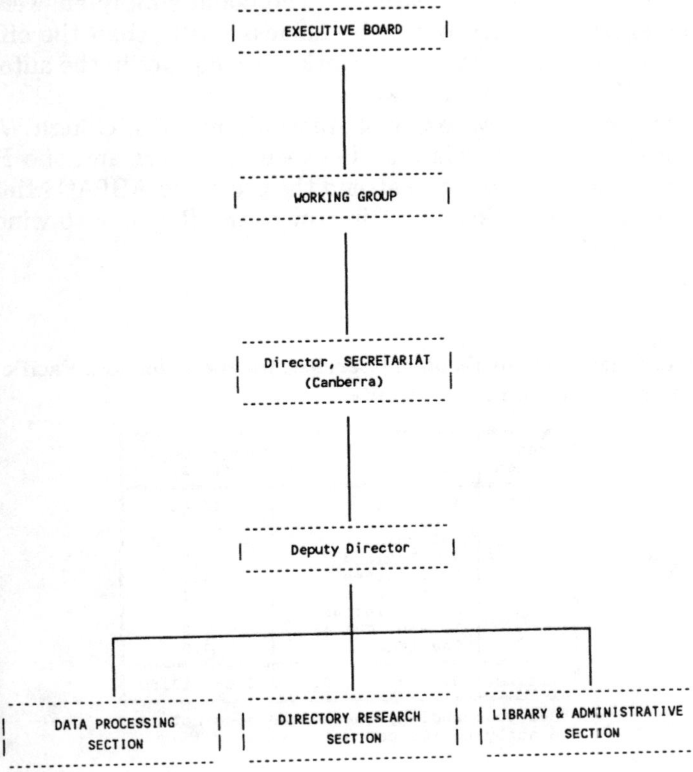

Board meetings. The Director relied on a Technical Advisory Committee to review the proposed work program.

All nine ASPAC countries joined. Australia defrayed all expenses from 1967 to 1971. Thereafter, contributions were received in amounts roughly corresponding to national incomes of the member countries (see Table 5.7).

The main project was the compilation of comprehensive lists (registers) of scientific and technical experts in fields related to economic development. At first, an omnibus register was compiled, but soon this became unwieldy, so specialized registers were drawn up for the fields of animal husbandry, forestry, and forest products. Registers for computer facilities and applications for science and technology, engineering and industrial research groups, food plant industry, soils, and entomology experts were added next. A second project was a quarterly bibliography of pertinent articles in the fields of science and technology. An information storage and retrieval system was developed, as well as an index to selected articles from journals in the Registry's library. An Inquiry Service, consisting of a panel of consultants in various scientific and technical fields, was set up to receive questions and to refer them to experts or researchers who could supply answers. This academic exercise turned out to be far less useful than the efforts of ECOCEN to establish a viable network of executives in the automobile industry of Southeast Asia, however.

On becoming Prime Minister of Australia in 1973, Gough Whitlam took steps to establish relations between Australia and the People's Republic of China. Refusing to attend the projected ASPAC Ministerial Meeting in 1973, he asked the Director of the Registry to wind down operations by 1974.

Table 5.7
Registry of Scientific and Technical Services for the Asian and Pacific Region: Membership and Assessments

Year Joined	Member Countries	Assessment (1972)[a]
1971	Australia	45.6%
	Japan	23.3
	Malaysia	
	New Zealand	8.7
	Philippines	3.9
	South Korea	6.2
	South Vietnam	.8
	Taiwan (China)	7.8
	Thailand	3.9
Totals	defunct in 1974	$156,513.50

[a]Due to rounding, the column does not sum exactly to 100 percent.

Asian and Pacific Maritime Cooperation Scheme (APMCS)

Inasmuch as Japan has no natural resources aside from the productivity of its population, it must rely on imports of all sorts, necessitating a large volume of shipping. Many of the seas beyond Japan are unsafe, however, and ship repair facilities abroad do not always measure up to the standards required to keep commercial vessels moving with minimum delays.

Concerned over oil spills in the age of supertankers, the Japan Association for Preventing Marine Accidents and the Japanese Shipowners' Association formed the Malacca Straits Council (MSC) of Japan in July 1968, then incorporated it as a public corporation in April 1969, hoping to get Indonesia and Malaysia to participate in a joint effort. Japan's foreign minister, accordingly, proposed a maritime cooperation scheme to the Ministerial Meeting in June 1969. After a preparatory Meeting of Experts convened in 1970, the subsequent Ministerial Meeting approved Guiding Principles of the scheme when it met from July 14 to July 16, 1971.

According to the first of the Guiding Principles of the Asian and Pacific Maritime Cooperation Scheme, the aim was "to improve the environment for maritime traffic in the Asian and Pacific region. . . . " The provision went on to specify that APMCS should operate "by promoting regional cooperation for marine rescue operation and by disseminating up to date hydrographic information and data among the Asian and Pacific region interested."

Since the project was to be a cooperative scheme, Japan's foreign ministry provided liaison and coordination, meeting with officials from embassies of the participating countries assigned to Tokyo. Meetings of experts were to work out details of various elements of the scheme and then review operations so that reports could be issued to the ASPAC Standing Committee. In 1970, an experts meeting adopted Principles of the Cooperation for Marine Rescue Operations. A second meeting of experts, held in November 1971, discussed a program on shipbuilding and ship administration.

There was no formal procedure for membership in APMCS. The Guiding Principles opened the scheme to Members and Observers of ASPAC. All nine ASPAC countries, with Indonesia and Laos as Observers, attended the experts meeting in 1971.

Japan paid for the entire cost of coordination. Host countries and home governments of participants were to share training costs.

Japan was to provide training courses for hydrographic surveying and oceanographic observations. Australia, Japan, and New Zealand volunteered to accept trainees in shipbuilding. New Zealand also offered to provide observers and trainees in its search and rescue operations. APMCS was also to operate an information exchange program but collapsed before developing these ideas further.

When Thailand refused to host the ASPAC Ministerial Meeting scheduled for 1973, Japan demurred and decided to abandon APMCS in 1972.

SUMMARY AND CONCLUSIONS

APO began as a technical organization that preferred to be nongovernmental. ASPAC was a rear-guard effort to prevent the People's Republic of China from gaining admission to the United Nations. APU also tried to keep the cold war alive in its early years. When the China seat passed to the mainland in 1971, ASPAC was an anachronism. APU nearly collapsed as well, but survived as APPU, due as much to generous Japanese funding as to its new direction toward the South Pacific. APO, meanwhile, continued to operate with as high a degree of professionalism as before.

APO has continued to flourish on funds from the government of Japan. In Japan, management training programs are often provided as a part of continuing in-service training. APO provides the same opportunity for company executives in countries lacking the resources to upgrade the skills of their middle- and top-level personnel. Corporations headquartered in Japan import parts made elsewhere in Asia, and increased productivity in these companies keeps manufacturing costs down. Companies outside the vertically integrated network of Japanese corporations and suppliers have been able to benefit from APO as well. The chief focus initially was in upgrading business administrative practices, but so many of the companies wanted to learn about technological advances that programs focused on engineering components as well. Agriculture became a new focus so that countries with large rural populations could develop agroindustries.

APU began as an anti-Communist organization and continued as a virtual clone, financed by the Kishi faction of the Liberal Democratic party. Many Asian countries dissociated themselves from the anti-Communist rhetoric. Then Japan made talk about an "Asia/Pacific community" into a reality by approaching parliamentarians in the South Pacific eager to attract Japanese financing for their own economic development. Retitled the Asian-Pacific Parliamentarians' Union, APPU has supported South Pacific island states by calling for an end to French colonial rule and nuclear weapons testing. But APPU survives as a club still dominated by the same Japanese parliamentary faction, able to penetrate more deeply into the informal foreign-policy decision making of a diverse set of countries than Japan's overformal foreign ministry. APPU centers are perhaps too modest to make a significant contribution to the region, but they do demonstrate pan-Asian good will, consistent with the Asian Way.

South Korea's motives in forming ASPAC were all too clear, but only right-wing factions in the various member countries shared its anti-Communist fervor. After the admission of the People's Republic of China to the United Nations in 1971, normalizing relations with China held more promise with new left-wing governments in Australia, New Zealand, and Thailand than did keeping the cold war alive in northeast Asia.

CULSOCEN continues to operate from its office in Seoul, hoping to expand into the South Pacific, but without the resources or strong host-country commitment to do so. CULSOCEN's decline appears to be due to the fact that South Korea was generous as long as its own foreign-policy goals were supported, but, when the situation reversed, Seoul's support faded. CULSOCEN's program has been more ambitious than that of APPU's Asian-Pacific Cultural Center, but now the two are equally inconsequential without competing, awaiting a possible merger.

With the increasing isolation of the Republic of China, FFTC was one of Taipei's vehicles for maintaining international contacts. FFTC's host government has been as supportive as the organization's Directors have been imaginative in ensuring that the Center conducts worthwhile activities, and by 1988 FFTC was reviving projects that had once been abandoned.

When ECOCEN began, Southeast Asian countries were dissatisfied with work at the UN's ECAFE (now ESCAP), which then was oriented toward the perspectives of India and Japan. ECOCEN followed up a study financed by the UN Development Program (UNDP) for ASEAN, completed in 1972, by encouraging automotive parts manufacturers to form an ASEAN industry club; by 1980, long after ECOCEN was shut down, a complementation package was negotiated within the industry, although ASEAN awaits funding to integrate the scheme. Similar industry clubs were planned, in keeping with the Asian Way principle of building consensus among key leaders in the region. ECOCEN did not see many of its bold ideas come to fruition, since the Thai public could not tolerate anything connected to ASPAC after 1973.

The Registry offered to store information, only to fall victim to a new Australian foreign policy. Technical assistance expertise still relies primarily on governmental nominees.

Corporate interests in Japan pushed APMCS with particular reference to the Malacca and Singapore straits, as well as waters adjacent to the South China Sea. Indonesia, interested enough to attend the first meeting of experts, insisted that the archipelagic principle be recognized: Jakarta required ships passing through its various straits to acknowledge Indonesian sovereignty over waters that Japan preferred to consider as international. A search and rescue operation was not a matter of controversy, and shipbuilding was another APMCS function that steered clear of the sensitivities of Indonesia and its close partner, Malaysia, which was an initial ASPAC member. APMCS training in hydrographic surveying was in connection with an ongoing project in the Malacca Strait. Japan hoped that APMCS might influence the traffic separation scheme that Indonesia and Malaysia were developing for the Malacca Strait, but both countries were eager to exclude Japan from any such role, as we discover in Chapter 8.

Thus, APO most embodies the Asian Way, ASPAC the least. APPU's survival can be traced to a shift from the narrow pursuits of cold-war diplomacy to a greater appreciation of the principles of the Asian Way. Japan's bid for leadership succeeded to the extent that Tokyo went along with the Asian Way. The Republic of Korea used ASPAC to advance its own foreign policy, contrary to the Asian Way. The Republic of China was grateful for international contacts through all three bodies. Northeast Asia, in balance, did not constitute the dynamic part of Asia with regard to regional cooperation. That honor fell to Southeast Asia, as we shall see in Chapters 6, 7, and 8.

NOTES

1. For references to APO documents, see Michael Haas, *Basic Documents of Asian Regional Organizations* (Dobbs Ferry, NY: Oceana Publications), vol. 5, pp. 220–56. For a bibliography of secondary sources, see pp. 217–19.

2. For references to APPU documents, see Michael Haas, *Basic Documents of Asian Regional Organizations* (Dobbs Ferry, NY: Oceana Publications), vol. 5, pp. 387–95. For a bibliography of secondary sources, see p. 386.

3. For references to ASPAC documents, see Michael Haas, *Basic Documents of Asian Regional Organizations* (Dobbs, Ferry, NY: Oceana Publications), vol. 5, pp. 462–91. For a bibliography of secondary sources, see pp. 456–61.

6 WHEN JAPAN LISTENS, WHO TALKS IN SOUTHEAST ASIA?

Japan's first efforts at regional cooperation, the Asian Productivity Organization (APO) and the Asian-Pacific Parliamentarians' Union (APPU), were initiatives from the private sector. The success of both organizations spurred the Japanese government to take bolder action. Inasmuch as any plans for regional cooperation hatched in Tokyo were bound to recall the infamous prewar Greater East Asia Co-Prosperity Sphere, the Ministry of Foreign Affairs proposed the Ministerial Conference for the Economic Development of Southeast Asia (SEAMCED) as an opportunity for Southeast Asian countries to tell Japan what they needed.

MINISTERIAL CONFERENCE FOR THE ECONOMIC DEVELOPMENT OF SOUTHEAST ASIA (SEAMCED)[1]

Takeo Miki, named Foreign Minister in 1964, launched a new era of internationalism in Japanese foreign policy, carrying out Prime Minister Eisaku Sato's policy of "Asian diplomacy." Miki felt that the best way to overcome the odium surrounding the Co-Prosperity Sphere and similar ideas was to encourage countries to make their own demands upon Japan, rather than the other way around.

Clearing his ideas with the United States beforehand, Miki convened the inaugural Ministerial Conference for the Economic Development of Southeast Asia in Tokyo on April 6–7, 1966. As the meeting began, Miki announced that Japan would increase foreign economic aid to 1 percent of its GNP by 1968. Countries were urged to present proposals for regional cooperative efforts at SEAMCED each year. Japan, in turn, would provide equipment, finances, and personnel for each project.

No formal set of purposes was ever stated for the series of conferences. The joint communiqué from the inaugural meeting identified two aims: "promoting the economic development of Southeast Asian countries, and . . . bringing about prosperity and stability in Asia." SEAMCED was similar to the Colombo Plan Consultative Committee in having recipient countries seek funds. Unlike the Colombo Plan, however, the projects had to be multilateral, and Japan was the only donor country involved. In time, SEAMCED spawned five regional organizations (see Table 6.1).

Heads of economic planning, finance, and trade ministries attended SEAMCED conferences for about three days each year. A Thai proposal in 1973 for a central office was not approved. The host country instead provided the conference secretariat. A Joint Working Committee set the agenda (see Fig. 6.1).

Six countries joined Japan at the first conference in 1966, and five who joined later brought the total to twelve countries (see Table 6.2). India, Pakistan, Sri Lanka, and the United States sent Observers, but were from outside Southeast Asia and hence did not join. Each year there were country reports, ad hoc Working Group reports on proposed regional projects, and annual reports from SEAMCED-endorsed organizations.

Five organizations, described below, were approved by SEAMCED. A Southeast Asian Medical and Health Organization (SEAMHO) was proposed, and an Interim Secretariat was set up at Jakarta in 1971 for

Table 6.1
Ministerial Conference for the Economic Development of Southeast Asia: Formation and Termination of Subsidiary Bodies

Year Joined	Organization Formed	Organization Terminated
1966	SEAMCED	
1967	SEAFDEC: MFRD	
	TD	
	COORDCOM	
1970	IGCC	
1971	SGATAR	
1972	SEAPCENTRE	
1973	SEAFDEC: AQD	
	SEATAC[a]	
1975		SEAMCED
1978		SEAPCENTRE
1982		IGCC
Totals	7 organizations	3 organizations

[a]COORDCOM became an organ of SEATAC in 1973.

Figure 6.1
Organization of the Ministerial Conference for the Economic Development of Southeast Asia

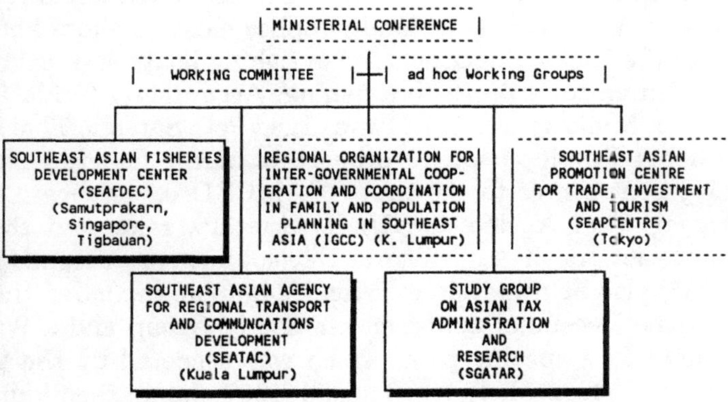

what was called the Regional Project on Public Health and Pesticide Control, but the idea of SEAMHO did not strike a responsive chord elsewhere. A Southeast Asian Medical Information Center (SEAMIC) was eventually set up in Tokyo on a nongovernmental basis, without membership involving other countries. Vietnam proposed a Southeast Asian College of Engineering in 1972, but Bangkok was already the site for the Asian Institute of Technology (AIT).

Table 6.2
Ministerial Conference for the Economic Development of Southeast Asia: Membership

Year Joined	Member Countries
1966	Japan Laos Malaysia Philippines Singapore South Vietnam Thailand
1967	Indonesia
1968	Australia (o, m 1973) New Zealand (o, m 1973)
1971	Khmer Republic
1973	Burma, 1973
Totals	defunct in 1975

Key: m = later joined as full Member
o = Observer

SOUTHEAST ASIAN FISHERIES DEVELOPMENT CENTER (SEAFDEC)[2]

Although seafood constitutes nearly 90 percent of the animal protein in the diets of Asian countries, and supplies close to shore had been dwindling in the 1960s, Southeast Asian fishing boats and technology were still oriented toward offshore fishing. Accordingly, Prida Karnasut of the Thai Ministry of Agriculture urged Pote Sarasin, Thai Minister of National Development, to propose a marine fisheries research and development center to the first SEAMCED conference; Chakratong Tongyai, Thai Agriculture Undersecretary, reiterated the idea at the Southeast Asian Agricultural Development Conference in December 1966, also held in Tokyo. When Singapore seconded the Thai proposal at the December conference, a Study Group and a Working Party formulated a specific plan, which was accepted by the second SEAMCED conference, held April 26–28, 1967. Japan then joined the Working Party, which drafted a treaty that was signed on December 28, 1967. The organization began in March 1968 for an initial ten-year period, and in 1978 SEAFDEC was continued indefinitely beyond its trial period.

According to the Agreement Establishing the Southeast Asian Fisheries Development Center, the purpose of SEAFDEC is "to contribute to the promotion of the fisheries development in Southeast Asia" (Article 1). There are six tasks:

> (i) to train fisheries technicians of the Southeast Asian countries; (ii) to study such fisheries techniques as are suited to the fisheries in Southeast Asia; (iii) to develop fishing grounds and to conduct investigation of fisheries resources and research in fisheries oceanography in Southeast Asia; (iv) to collect and analyze information related to the fisheries in Southeast Asia; (v) to provide the Members with the results of studies and researches by the Center and other information and (vi) to handle other matters. (Article 1)

SEAFDEC's Council meets for five days each year (see Fig. 6.2). There are three Departments.

The founding agreement did not specify the location for SEAFDEC's Secretariat. After SEAFDEC began, the Council decided to fuse the Secretariat with the Training Department. Initially, the Secretariat was in Bangkok. In 1973, when facilities for a permanent site were completed, the Secretariat moved to Samutprakarn, south of Bangkok on the Gulf of Siam. A Bangkok office was established again in 1981, this time as a Liaison Office to serve both the Training Department and the Secretariat. The head of the Secretariat, the Secretary-General, is also Chief of the Training Department; the Deputy Chief of the Training Department is Deputy Secretary-General (see Fig. 6.3).

Figure 6.2
Organization of the Southeast Asian Fisheries Development Center

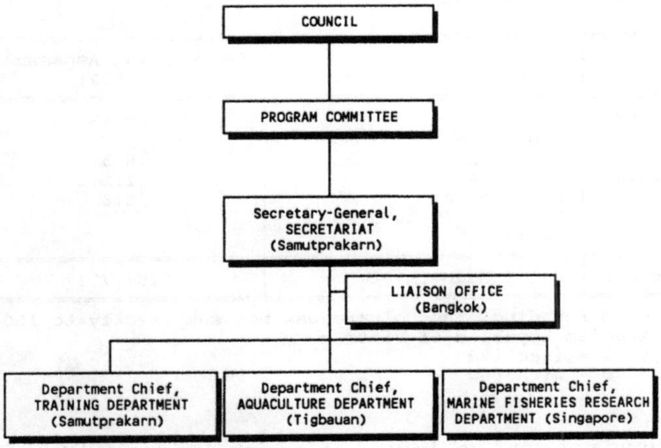

Each Department is headed by a Department Chief, who is a national from the host country. In 1976 and 1977, the three Department Chiefs and Deputy Chiefs formed an Interdepartmental Consultative Meeting, which was superseded in 1978 by the Program Committee, composed of Chiefs, Deputy Chiefs, and representatives of each member country. The Program Committee meets for four days each summer to prepare for the fall Council meeting.

All twelve members of SEAMCED were invited to sign SEAFDEC's founding agreement, and six did so (see Table 6.3). Vietnam was inactive after 1975, and in 1980 Hanoi stated that it considered that the SEAFDEC membership of the Republic of Vietnam had ended in 1975, when the Republic of Vietnam ceased to exist. The Khmer Republic and Laos sent Observers to the Council meeting in 1973; successor

Figure 6.3
Organization of SEAFDEC: Secretariat

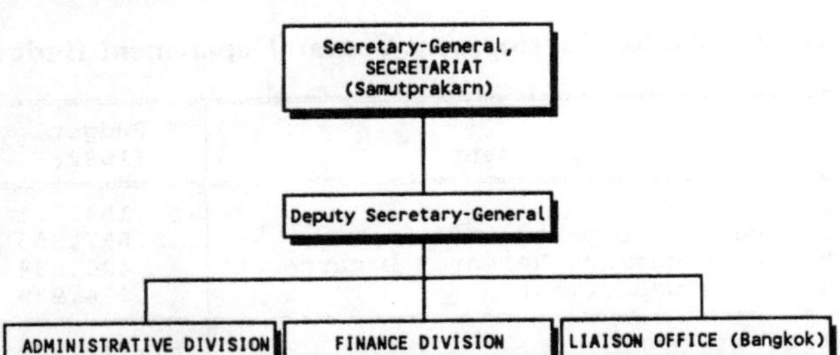

Table 6.3
Southeast Asian Fisheries Development Center: Membership and Secretariat Assessments

Year Joined	Member Countries	Secretariat Assessment (1982)[a]
1967	Japan	86.8%
	Singapore	
	Thailand	6.3
1968	Malaysia	1.2
	Philippines	5.8
	Vietnam (i 1975-79, w 1980)[b]	
Totals	6-1=5 Members	$154,771

[a]Due to rounding, the column does not sum exactly to 100 percent.
[b]Joined as Republic of Vietnam
Key: i = inactive
w = withdrew

regimes have not done so. Indonesia, which decided not to join in view of independent funding for fisheries projects from UN agencies, attended as an Observer in 1974, 1982, and 1984. Trainees at SEAFDEC projects, in keeping with the pan-Asian principle of the Asian Way, have come from Bangladesh, Brunei, Burma, China, Hongkong, India, Indonesia, Maldives, Pakistan, Sri Lanka, Taiwan (China), as well as from the Solomon Islands and various African and Latin American countries.

Japan is the primary source of funds for the Secretariat (see Table 6.3). Host countries for each Department, including the Secretariat, defray all capital and most administrative costs. Japan provides a Deputy Chief and some other professional staff to each Department; it has donated training ships and a research vessel to the Departments in Thailand and Singapore, respectively, along with ship repair services. Of the three Departments, the Aquaculture Department (AQD) has by far the largest budget (see Table 6.4).

The Secretariat serves as an information clearinghouse on fisheries

Table 6.4
Southeast Asian Fisheries Development Center: Department Budgets

Department	Budget (1982)
Secretariat	$ 154,771
Aquaculture Department	5,617,355
Marine Fisheries Research Department	420,934
Training Department	924,939
Total	$7,117,999

development. The Liaison Office assembles and distributes SEAFDEC publications, including proceedings of meetings and technical publications.

Each Department originally had a basic Plan of Operation and a Working Program. Subsequently modified, the Departments now operate on the basis of three-year plans.

Training Department (TD)

The earliest idea was for SEAFDEC to train fishing personnel in the use of oceangoing ships to catch fish in waters farther from shore than had been customary in Southeast Asia. The original Plan of Operation and Program of Work of the Training Department (TD), adopted by the inaugural SEAFDEC Council in March 1968, specified two major functions: "(i) to train fisheries technicians of the Southeast Asian countries in various aspects of modern marine fisheries, engineering, and navigation technique; (ii) to make studies on such types of fishing gears and methods suited to the fishes in Southeast Asia. . . . "

In November 1980, the Plan of Operation shifted attention from deep-sea fishing to coastal and small-scale fisheries; research was broadened to include "studies on fisheries resources and fishing grounds, fishing gear and craft improvement, as well as on statistics and socioeconomic aspects related to marine capture fisheries, in order to facilitate the management and rational use of the fisheries resources in Southeast Asian waters." Navigation and craft improvement research were dropped from the Plan of Operation in 1983.

TD operated out of Bangkok until 1973, when it moved to Samutprakarn. TD has four divisions and shares the Liaison Office with the Secretariat of SEAFDEC (see Fig. 6.4). The Department originally had a training vessel, *Paknam*, a steel-stern trawler. A fiberglass

Figure 6.4
Organization of SEAFDEC: Training Department

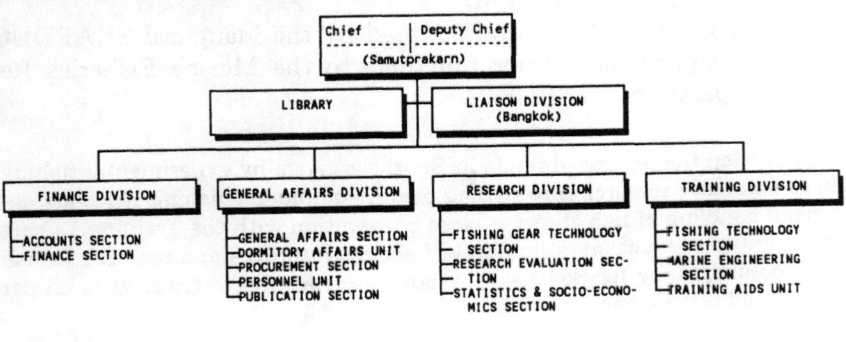

purse seiner, the *Platoo*, and a wooden trawler, the *Plalung*, were acquired to handle new activities closer to shore in 1980 and 1982, respectively.

TD began by offering a course in fishing-gear technology and navigation, followed by a second course in marine engineering and refrigeration, both involving operations in the deep sea. Classes run for eighteen months, with about twenty-five students; training includes classroom and shipboard training, with a segment of instruction in Japan. Trainees, nominated by member countries, receive SEAFDEC fellowships. Some students specialize in fishing technology, others in marine engineering, but all learn about fishing operations, navigation, and marine engineering. In 1977, TD training expanded to include small-scale coastal fisheries training, including short-term training and demonstration courses for local fishing personnel, fishery extension officers, and university students. Some 1,676 participants had been trained by 1987.

In 1978, TD took over a project that was once a focus of the Marine Fisheries Research Department: stock-assessment studies to find new fishing grounds in the region. Since 1983, TD has provided on-the-job research training in stock assessment, fishery oceanography, and fishing-gear development. In 1988, TD embarked on a study of artificial reefs as a means for conserving and developing coastal fishing resources.

Marine Fisheries Research Department (MFRD)

The original idea for SEAFDEC focused on training. Although the harvesting of fish from the sea is essential to provide food, fishing personnel need to know where to go, and the harvest must be transported to a market for sale. When Singapore proposed a research institution, the momentum for SEAFDEC was established. After Japan agreed to donate a research vessel and a Plan of Operation was adopted, the research department was incorporated into the proposal presented to SEAFDEC in 1967.

The 1968 Plan of Operation adopted by the inaugural SEAFDEC Council assigned four major functions to the Marine Fisheries Research Department (MFRD):

> (i) to develop the fishing grounds in Southeast Asia by experimental fishing; (ii) to carry out research into fishing gears, equipment, fishing methods and general handling of fish at sea in close cooperation with the Training Department; (iii) to conduct investigation of fisheries resources and research in fisheries oceanography for Southeast Asian countries; (iv) to train research personnel and technicians.

In 1976, a new function was added: "to conduct research and development of fishery post-harvest technology." The Plan of Operation adopted in 1980 revised priorities as follows:

> (i) to promote, undertake and coordinate research on post-harvest technology, directed towards maximal utilization of available fish resources, and to further the development of the fish processing industry in the region; (ii) to examine the problems related to the handling, preservation, and quality control of fish and fish products, and to recommend measures to upgrade the quality of fish and fish products in the region; (iii) to establish an effective system for the smooth transfer of post-harvest technology to the region through workshops, training programs, publications, etc.; (iv) to facilitate the activities of the Aquaculture Substation in Singapore.

The Aquaculture Substation, a unit of SEAFDEC's Aquaculture Department, was abolished in 1987.

MFRD is located at Changi Point, Singapore (see Fig. 6.5). Facilities were ready in February 1970.

Primary research was conducted aboard the *Changi* until 1975, when Burma seized the *Changi*. Rangoon alleged that the ship was illegally inside its territorial waters; though the crew was released seventy-eight days later, the ship was confiscated and eventually repainted and converted into a Burmese fishing vessel. Thereafter, MFRD chartered ships or shared the use of ships with other agencies (including TD's *Paknam*) until 1980, when MFRD was reorganized to reflect its new mandate in post-harvest technology.

Initially, MFRD conducted deep-sea voyages, using vertical handline and trawl fishing in search of new fishing grounds. The research involved fisheries resources evaluation and oceanographic studies. Da-

Figure 6.5
Organization of SEAFDEC: Marine Fisheries Research Department

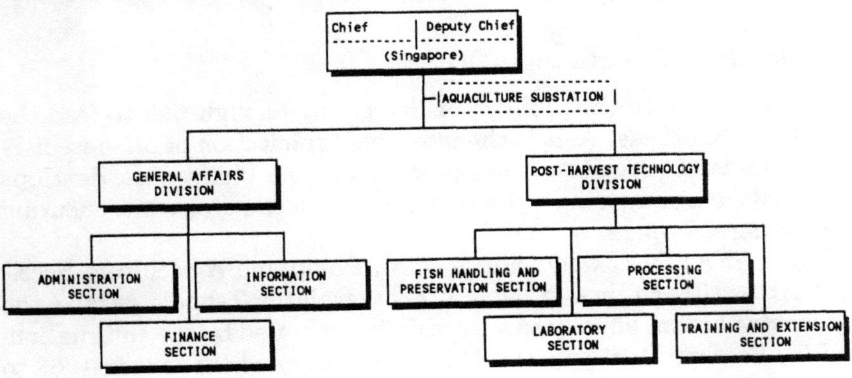

ta were collected on the size, composition, growth, feeding habits, fecundity, ecology, and taxonomy of fish, their eggs, and larvae. By 1975, there were forty-one cruises, covering nearly 120,000 square miles, taking 495 days, with 1,003 trawl hauls, and catching about 223 metric tons of fish. In addition, oceanographic studies took place at 522 stations on the temperature, currents, and chemical, physical, and biological properties of the ocean at various depths; sources of nutrients were located in various parts of the seas, and MFRD prepared oceanographic atlases.

After the *Changi* was seized, MFRD considered new options. Since it had found no new fishing grounds, its fisheries research program was transferred in 1980 to the Training Department. In 1976, MFRD focused on fish utilization, that is, on post-harvest technology problems. Currently, MFRD is developing marketable products that use fish normally considered to be unpalatable by the consumer: rather than throwing away so-called "trash fish," the aim is to develop fishcake, fishball, and other fish jelly and nonjelly products. A second project focus is on fish preservation: methods of freezing and icing are being tested to extend the shelf life of warm-water fish species. Icing has been more successful in some cases than freezing, which is more costly and often makes fish less flavorful and nutritious.

From 1968 to 1974, some twenty-four trainees were annually enrolled in a one-year course on marine fisheries research; participants wrote research papers on their work during the year. In 1976, research fellowships were available for trained researchers. Because MFRD has a mission of disseminating information on new products and new methods for handling fish, extension activities have increased in recent years. Beginning in 1980, two- to four-day demonstration and practice sessions have been available for food processors; on-site visits to fish factories have also been undertaken. In addition, two-week training courses for fishery technicians and extension workers have been held since 1983. Up to 1988, MFRD had trained 281 fishing personnel.

Aquaculture Department (AQD)

One approach to the problem of harvesting enough fish to feed the peoples of Southeast Asia is the intensive exploitation of offshore fishing grounds. Aquaculture, long practiced in the Philippines, develops fishponds, catching a limited number of fish in one area while ensuring restocking elsewhere.

While SEAFDEC was being formed, Philippine Agriculture Secretary Arturo Tanco thought that a "blue revolution" should parallel the "green revolution" already so successfully promoted by the International Rice Research Institute (IRRI). Tanco presented the idea in 1968 to

SEAMCED, which in turn referred the proposal to SEAFDEC. After funding arrangements were agreed upon, the Council approved the Aquaculture Department (AQD) by a resolution adopted during a meeting of the Council in July 1973, rather than by a revision of the founding agreement.

The Council then approved AQD's initial Plan of Operation and Program of Work, specifying three major functions:

> (i) to promote, undertake and coordinate research which is necessary for the development of the aquaculture industry in the region, (ii) to train experts in aquaculture at various levels, from the researcher level down to the technician level, (iii) to arrange for the exchange and dissemination of knowledge and information in the field of aquaculture and related activities to meet the needs of member-countries.

AQD's headquarters is at Tigbauan, about fifteen miles southwest of Iloilo City, Panay Island, Philippines (see Fig. 6.6). AQD operates several research facilities: the main station at Tigbauan; a brackishwater station at Leganes, Iloilo; a freshwater station at Tapao Point, Binangonan, Rizal; and a substation for finfish broodstock development at Igang, Nueva Valencia, Guimaras Island. Other substations were set up, but were eventually phased out when specific projects were completed. In 1986, AQD was reorganized into the Administration, Finance, Information, Research, and Training divisions. Liaison Offices operate in Iloilo (for research and training) and Mandaluyong, Metro Manila (for external affairs).

Initially, half of AQD's funds were from Japan, the other half came from the Philippine government. Japan currently provides one-twelfth of the Philippine contribution, mostly in the form of personnel, supplies, and training scholarships. External support comes from sources in Australia, Belgium, Canada, Denmark, France, New Zealand, Sweden, the United Kingdom, and the United States. In 1983, the Food and Agriculture Organization of the United Nations (FAO) identified

Figure 6.6
Organization of SEAFDEC: Aquaculture Department

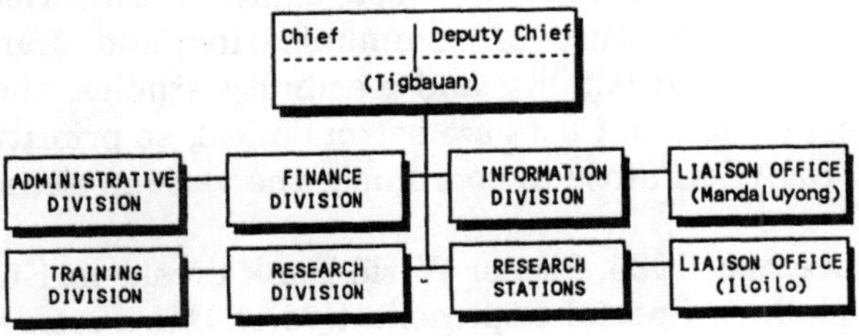

AQD as the Regional Lead Center in the Philippines for FAO's Network of Aquaculture Centers in Asia (NACA).

Research concentrates on three aquatic groups: crustaceans (crabs, prawns, shrimps); finfishes (carp, groupers, milkfish, seabass, siganids, tilapia); and mollusks (mussels, oysters) and seaweeds. Activities focus on producing adequate supplies of quality seeds through hormone injections; improving culture techniques (including water quality management); formulating low-cost feeds and natural propagation techniques; identifying diseases, pests, and predators; improving the design of aquaculture facilities; socioeconomics of aquaculture; aquatic pollution; and improvement of stocks for aquaculture through genetic selection. AQD looks at the culture of economically important species in the region, and takes pride in the fact that the number of fish species in the region has increased from thirty-seven in 1969 to fifty in 1986.

AQD regularly offers six courses for trainees, ranging from three to eight weeks in duration: aquaculture for social scientists, brackishwater pond culture, hatchery of marine finfishes, prawn hatchery and nursery operations, freshwater aquaculture, and sanitation and culture techniques for tropical bivalves. The aim is to gather, process, and disseminate knowledge in order to ensure effective transfer of aquaculture technologies to fish farmers and other technical experts. Internship training is also available on disease diagnosis, feed formulation, and plankton culture; practicum training exists for undergraduate studies in biology and fisheries. By 1988, some 2,181 persons had been trained. AQD also provides technical assistance. Technology verification projects test potential aquaculture techniques in different sites to facilitate adoption by the private sector. In addition to AQD's main task of fish stock development, in 1988 new programs in post-harvest technology were approved.

SOUTHEAST ASIAN AGENCY FOR REGIONAL TRANSPORT AND COMMUNICATIONS DEVELOPMENT (SEATAC)[3]

A major impediment to economic development and regional cooperation within Southeast Asia has been the lack of adequate communication and transportation links between adjacent countries. Development of an infrastructure of communication and transportation facilities requires prefeasibility and feasibility studies, then funding, and finally construction. Costs are astronomical, so priorities must be determined. SEATAC arose to coordinate the various elements in this process.

During November 1965, former World Bank President Eugene Black visited Bangkok as Special Representative of U.S. President Lyndon

Johnson to finalize arrangements for the Asian Development Bank (ADB). Malaysian Deputy Prime Minister Tun Abdul Razak then approached Black to discuss possible funding for a transportation and communication development project. Black encouraged Razak to proceed, and the need for improved regional transport facilities received favorable mention at the inaugural SEAMCED conference. While issuing invitations for a Conference of Southeast Asian Officials on Transport and Communications in Kuala Lumpur for September 1967, Razak convened a Pre-Conference Planning Group to visit countries in the region during June and July 1967, in order to canvass sentiment for the project and to solicit proposals for the meeting.

The Kuala Lumpur conference discussed ninety-five proposals for sums totaling about $1 billion to be completed from 1970 to 1990. To establish priorities, the delegates formed the Coordinating Committee of Southeast Asian Senior Officials on Transport and Communications (COORDCOM). One month after COORDCOM's first meeting, held in March 1968, SEAMCED endorsed COORDCOM and supported the latter's request for ADB to do a comprehensive study of fundable transport and communications projects in Southeast Asia. When ADB's regional transport survey was released in early 1972, a Ministerial Conference on the Development of Transport and Communications in Southeast Asia met in Kuala Lumpur in May 1972 to evaluate the survey. The ministers agreed that COORDCOM should continue as an organ of a new organization, the Southeast Asian Agency for Regional Transport and Communications Development (SEATAC). SEATAC offices opened in Kuala Lumpur in January 1973.

COORDCOM discussed a Draft Charter for SEATAC in 1973. Since differences of opinion on the draft were irreconcilable, a Draft Inter-Governmental Operational Agreement for Southeast Asian Cooperation in Regional Transport and Communications Development was adopted by COORDCOM on December 7, 1974, subject to approval by a second Ministerial Conference. That conference, scheduled for 1975, was called off when regimes of the three Indochinese members of SEATAC changed. Since SEATAC had many confidential papers relating to Cambodia, Laos, and Vietnam, it preferred to await the resumed participation by the three countries. Because Indochina has not returned to SEATAC meetings, no such Ministerial Meeting has been held, and the Draft Agreement serves as an informal set of terms of reference for SEATAC, in keeping with the Asian Way principle of consensus building.

According to the Draft Agreement, SEATAC's purpose is "to contribute to the acceleration of the development of transport and communications of member countries and thereby assist in the promotion of economic cooperation and development" (Article 1). The principal function is "to promote the implementation of projects, programs and policies" (Article 2).

SEATAC's plenary organ, the Ministerial Conference, met only in 1972, though the Draft Agreement prescribes biennial meetings (see Fig. 6.7). COORDCOM met about twice each year from 1968 to 1974, when it was temporarily superseded by Informal Consultative Meetings (ICMs), attended by the same officials, until the organizational basis for SEATAC could be clarified. In December 1978, COORDCOM resumed four-day meetings on an annual basis, preceded by ICMs of equal duration but with more technical experts in attendance.

An Interim Secretariat for COORDCOM was established in 1967 in Kuala Lumpur. In 1972, the Ministerial Conference upgraded the body to a Secretariat for SEATAC, starting 1973, when the Interim Director became the Director of the Secretariat.

Figure 6.7
Organization of the Southeast Asian Agency for Regional Transport and Communications Development

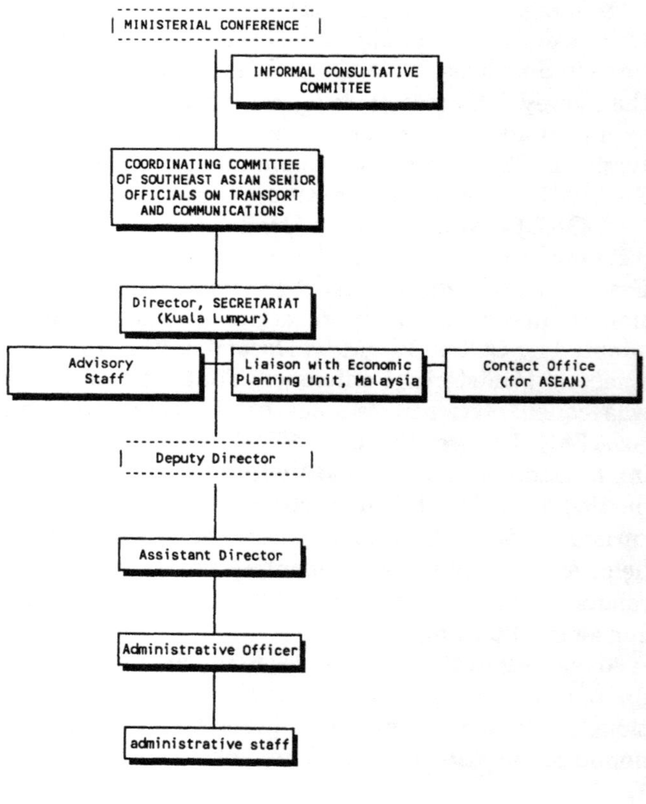

Besides a Deputy Director there were three Assistant Directors in the original structure—for administration, economics, and engineering. Currently, there is only an Assistant Director. In 1982, experts were recruited from donor countries in the fields of economics, maritime safety, and shipping and ports to serve as an advisory staff, functioning in a consultative capacity; there were five foreign experts as recently as 1985.

No formal procedure for SEATAC membership has been adopted, since the Draft Agreement has never been formalized. Seven countries signed the Agreement to Finance the Interim Secretariat to COORDCOM in 1971 (see Table 6.5). The Khmer Republic sent an Observer in 1971, then joined in 1972. Singapore, an original member, became satisfied with its own level of transport and communications development and withdrew in 1973. Indochinese countries have been inactive since 1975. Brunei, an Observer at COORDCOM meetings up to 1971, opted out of ADB's regional transport survey and failed to participate in COORDCOM thereafter.

Malaysia absorbed costs of the Interim Secretariat up to 1971, when SEATAC member countries agreed to match a U.S. Agency for International Development (USAID) grant on an equal basis; the Khmer Republic and Laos were exempt from payment due to their greater needs. Since 1974, Secretariat costs have been apportioned on the scale used by the Southeast Asian Ministers of Education Secretariat (SEAMES), which in turn is based on relative ADB subscriptions (see Table 6.5). Costs of feasibility and prefeasibility studies are primarily borne by external sources.

COORDCOM meetings instruct the Secretariat to commission and monitor prefeasibility studies, which identify specific projects, and feasibility studies, which evaluate economic benefits, costs, and technical obstacles to projects identified for possible implementation in the field of transport and communications.

When the Asia-Pacific Telecommunity (APT) was founded in the mid-1970s, SEATAC decided to focus on transportation projects alone. Projects now cover water transport (channel dredging, joint shipping services, maritime safety, port and ferry development and management, river transport, shipping technology), air transport (freight services, passenger traffic, pooling arrangements), land transportation (coastal shipping, feeder roads for rural areas, road safety, urban transport), and tourism (ferry services, multimode network, wildlife conservation) projects.

SEATAC has sponsored eight seminars on urban transport problems, some of which led to later comprehensive studies. There have been ten training courses on maritime transport management, mostly dealing with roll-on roll-off ferry/terminals service.

Table 6.5
Southeast Asian Agency for Regional Transport and Communications Development: Membership and Assessments

Year Joined	Member Countries	Assessment (1984)
1971	Indonesia	29.0%
	Laos (i 1975-)	
	Malaysia	22.7
	Philippines	24.8
	Singapore (w 1973)	
	Thailand	23.5
	Vietnam (i 1975-)[a]	
1972	Cambodia (i 1975-)[b]	
Total	8-1=7 Members	$157,436

[a]Joined as Republic of Vietnam
[b]Joined as the Khmer Republic
Key: i = inactive
w = withdrew

By 1985, some fifty-four projects had been completed, thirteen were ongoing, and twenty-two were at the proposal stage. Among these eighty-nine projects, twenty-six have involved a single country, and the rest have been drawn up for two or more member countries.

As SEAMCED ceased to meet and SEATAC membership declined, SEATAC found itself in closer touch with ASEAN's Committee on Transportation and Communications (COTAC); a COTAC Contact Officer has been part of SEATAC's structure. One of SEATAC's largest projects is a study of the possibility of an ASEAN shipping line to provide an alternative to the high-cost shipping cartel known as the Far Eastern Freight Conference (FEFC), an arrangement under which shipping companies operating between the region and either Europe or North America fix freight rates. This project is opposed by Singapore but remains a concern of SEATAC until a specific proposal can be developed to meet Singapore's objectives, in keeping with the Asian Way principle of consensus building.

REGIONAL ORGANIZATION FOR INTER-GOVERNMENTAL COOPERATION AND COORDINATION IN FAMILY AND POPULATION PLANNING IN SOUTHEAST ASIA (IGCC)[4]

When population grows faster than national income, the per-capita gains due to economic development are erased. Since some Southeast Asian countries have extraordinarily high birthrates, a program focusing on family and population planning seemed an essential feature of an overall development strategy for the region.

Dissatisfied with the proliferation of UN programs related to family and population, Khir Johari, head of Malaysia's National Family Planning Board, sounded out the views of Southeast Asian countries in early 1970 on the possibility of a project in this field. He then hosted the Southeast Asia Ministerial Conference on Family and Population Planning in Kuala Lumpur on October 22–24, 1970, where it was agreed that an Inter-Governmental Coordinating Committee (IGCC) and an Interim Secretariat should be established for a period of three years to design and execute a program. IGCC held its inaugural meeting in Kuala Lumpur in April 1971, and SEAMCED approved IGCC during the following month. Initially, the organization was called Inter-Governmental Coordinating Committee, Southeast Asia Regional Cooperation in Family and Population Planning. In 1973, it was renamed the Regional Organization for Inter-Governmental Cooperation and Coordination in Family and Population Planning in Southeast Asia. The IGCC acronym survived the renaming, but the organization folded in 1982.

The joint communiqué of the 1970 Southeast Asia Ministerial Conference on Family and Population Planning set initial terms of reference for the organization. Although IGCC's Meeting of Senior Government Officials (SGO) approved a Charter in October 1976, it was neither adopted by a Ministerial Meeting nor ratified by the member countries; nevertheless, it became an informal guideline for IGCC.

According to the proposed Charter, the main objective was "to promote cooperation and coordination among Southeast Asian countries in the field of Population and Family Planning in order to achieve an improved standard of living in the Region through a balanced economic and population growth." The same document stated that the main function of the organization was "to promote . . . joint regional projects and programs of mutual benefit concerning Population and Family Planning," with an emphasis on "(i) training of medical, paramedical and other personnel, (ii) information, education and communication, (iii) medical/clinical services."

The highest organ was the Ministerial Conference, composed of ministers of health or social welfare; it met only in 1970 and 1973 (see Fig. 6.8). A Council of Ministers was to be established, according to the proposed Charter. In 1970, the Ministerial Conference set up the IGCC as a panel of heads of national population and family planning boards to screen proposed projects. IGCC met from 1971 to 1973, and in 1972 IGCC convened the semiannual meeting of SGO to review the feasibility of proposed programs. SGO, in turn, convened Expert Working Groups to look at technical aspects. Advisory Group meetings, consist-

Figure 6.8
Organization of the Regional Organization for Inter-Governmental Cooperation and Coordination in Family and Population Planning in Southeast Asia

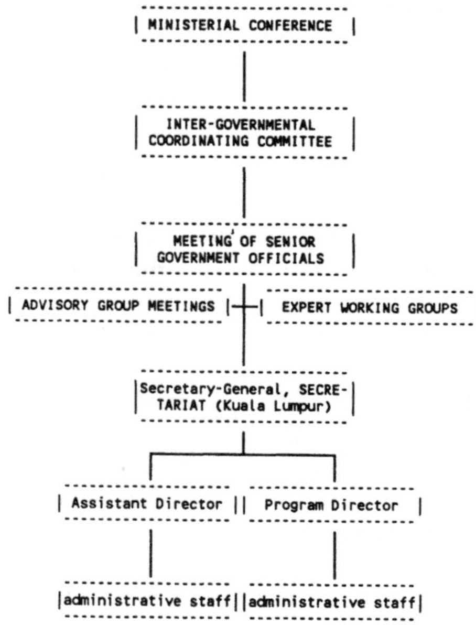

ing of representatives from agencies providing funds or personnel to support the projects, examined administrative and budgetary elements.

Since the Indochinese countries failed to attend after 1973, no further Ministerial Conferences or IGCC meetings were held. SGO continued to meet twice yearly, assisted by meetings of the Expert Working Groups and the Advisory Group.

The Interim Secretariat, established in Kuala Lumpur in 1971, was headed by a Secretary-General. The Secretariat became permanent in 1973. A Program Director handled projects in public health fields, while an Assistant Director coordinated projects on social science subjects and served as the administrative coordinator of the organization. As IGCC approved individual projects, ad hoc steering committees coordinated details involving donor agencies, experts, and government agencies represented at the meetings.

There was no formal procedure for membership. The Ministerial Meeting of 1970 and the inaugural IGCC meeting in 1971 were attended by seven countries, which were assumed to be the initial members (see Table 6.6). Later in 1971, Laos and Nepal indicated interest and were accepted as new members.

USAID supported Secretariat costs from 1971 to 1973. Thereafter, each country made voluntary contributions for administrative costs of the Secretariat (Table 6.6), while donor agencies defrayed operational projects.

The main activities of IGCC were seminars, which brought together experts and government officials; about three occurred each year, with recommendations emerging as the final product of the meetings. In the early years, the emphasis was on inventories of the key components of population and family planning programs. Conferences were held on administration, evaluation, information and education, logistics and supply, services, and training. Thereafter, the meetings identified individual problems within each general area.

IGCC organized two training courses and a study tour. It established an information center, with a network of communication on recent developments in the field of family and population planning. An educational consultant developed a curriculum for adult education. A marketing consultant researched motivational efforts required for successful population and family planning programs. National training programs were undertaken for the three Indochinese countries, which lacked national family planning programs, while key personnel from other IGCC countries received training to upgrade their skills.

In the 1980s, USAID was no longer interested in funding population and family planning programs, and IGCC was dissolved in 1982. Population and family planning programs in the region are now financed by Australia within the framework of ASEAN.

Table 6.6
Regional Organization for Inter-Governmental Cooperation and Coordination in Family and Population Planning in Southeast Asia: Membership and Assessments

Year Joined	Member Countries	Assessment (1976)
1971	Indonesia	$ 20,000
	Khmer Republic (i 1975-)	
	Laos (i 1975-)	
	Malaysia	30,000
	Nepal	1,000
	Philippines	20,000
	Singapore	20,000
	Thailand	20,000
	Vietnam (i 1975-)[a]	
Totals	defunct in 1982	$111,000

[a]Joined as Republic of Vietnam
Key: i = inactive

STUDY GROUP ON ASIAN TAX ADMINISTRATION AND RESEARCH (SGATAR)[5]

Economic development requires modern tax systems that can provide proper revenue and investment incentives. In Southeast Asia, tax systems have been Western transplants, favoring the interests of former colonial powers and present multinational corporations. The result is a poor revenue yield, inequitable distribution of income, and inefficient administrative practices.

In 1968, Angel Yoingco, Executive Director of the Joint Legislative-Executive Tax Commission of the Philippines (now the National Tax Research Center), attended a meeting of the Inter-American Center of Tax Administrators. Upon his return, he proposed a similar organization for Asia to Eduardo Romualdez, Philippine Secretary of Finance, whose successor, Cesar Virata, agreed to present the proposal to SEAMCED in 1970. Initially, the idea was for an Asian Center for Tax Administration and Research (ACTAR) to act as a clearinghouse for information exchange. An initial meeting of the Study Group on Asian Tax Administration and Research (SGATAR) was held in Manila in February 1971, when consideration was given formally to the idea of ACTAR. While the foreign minister of Japan was willing to consider the proposal, Japan's finance minister demurred. Singapore stated that the proposal needed more work. In accordance with the Asian Way principle that the goal of information exchange transcends the particular organizational methods of implementation, SEAMCED agreed that SGATAR should meet annually to exchange views on tax matters, while further consideration was given to the ACTAR proposal. In 1974, the Philippines felt that it had no alternative but to withdraw the ACTAR proposal. Yearly meetings of SGATAR, nonetheless, continue today.

There is no formal enumeration of objectives, although the "purposes and benefits" of SGATAR were spelled out in the 1974 meeting, as follows: "(a) exchange of information, (b) discuss problems and possible solutions, (c) keep abreast of new tax legislation developments in the other countries, (d) sharing of experiences, (e) discussion on topics at the annual Meetings."

The principal organ is the annual Meeting, which lasts five to six days (see Fig. 6.9). The host country provides a Secretariat and Secretary-General for the meeting. Most SGATAR committees provide routine services for the conference, but the Committee on SGATAR Project has responsibility for determining priorities of new joint projects and makes recommendations for research studies to the annual Meeting. The Philippine National Tax Research Center coordinates most

Figure 6.9
Organization of the Study Group on Asian Tax Administration and Research

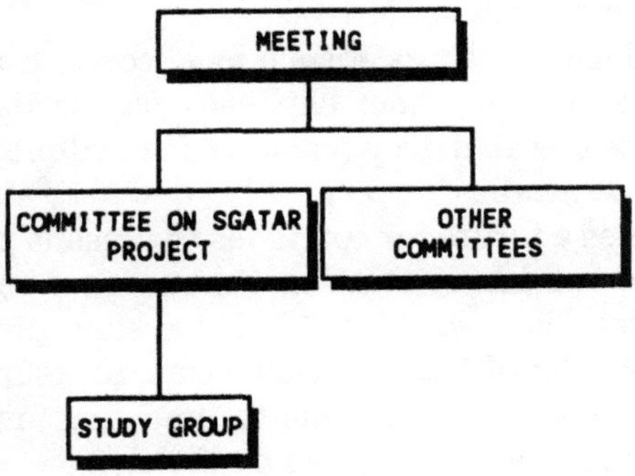

studies; each country designates a researcher to complete its portion of a study.

Initially, SGATAR membership was open only to countries attending SEAMCED. Eight countries joined SGATAR simply by attending its initial meeting in 1971 (see Table 6.7). Burma and the Khmer Republic joined in 1973, Australia and New Zealand in 1974. Indochinese coun-

Table 6.7
Study Group on Asian Tax Administration and Research: Membership

Year Joined	Member Countries
1971	Indonesia Japan Laos (i 1973-) Malaysia Philippines Singapore Thailand Vietnam (i 1973-)[a]
1973	Burma Cambodia (o 1972, i 1973-)[b] Burma
1974	Australia New Zealand
1981	South Korea
Totals	13 Members

[a]Joined as Republic of Vietnam
[b]Joined as Khmer Republic
Key: i = inactive
o = Observer

tries have been inactive since 1973. Since SEAMCED held its last meeting in 1974, the informal membership requirement was waived to permit South Korea to join in 1981.

Hosts for SGATAR meetings absorb local costs. Each country pays for transportation and per diem expenses for its participation. The Philippines volunteered to defray an ACTAR headquarters, and it usually funds SGATAR studies.

SGATAR provides a forum for countries to present papers on various subjects related to tax administration. About three topics are selected at each meeting for discussion. In 1984, for example, the topics concerned computerization of tax administration, measures for improving voluntary compliance in tax payments, and training programs and personnel management systems for tax officials.

Eight joint research projects have been completed thus far: a glossary of tax terms, a study of tax systems, a history of SGATAR, a survey of tax administration procedures, a survey of property valuation, a survey of income taxation, a survey of laws and practices on sales taxation, and a survey of fiscal incentive systems. Two projects are ongoing, one on tax avoidance and evasion, the second on direct and indirect taxation. The joint projects result in publications available for public distribution, but annual SGATAR proceedings are confidential.

In 1982, the Asian-Pacific Tax and Investment Research Center (APTIRC), a regional clone of the International Bureau of Fiscal Documentation (IBFD) at Amsterdam, was set up in Singapore. APTIRC, which has held annual Asia-Pacific Tax Conferences since 1983, is a nongovernmental international organization engaging in research and documentation on investments and international taxation; it provides assistance to accountants, attorneys, banks, corporations, and governments in the region. Angel Q. Yoingco, a founder of SGATAR, chairs the Board of Governors of APTIRC, but otherwise the two bodies are distinct.

SOUTHEAST ASIAN PROMOTION CENTRE FOR TRADE, INVESTMENT AND TOURISM (SEAPCENTRE)[6]

When SEAMCED first met, one of the most serious obstacles to development in Southeast Asia was the lack of capital. With insufficient foreign exchange to purchase industrial machinery, three obvious avenues were to increase exports, to attract investment, and to lure tourists.

A proposal for economic development promotion centers in each Southeast Asian country was presented to SEAMCED in 1969. After follow-up meetings in 1969 and 1970, Japan came out in favor of one institution. A Southeast Asian Promotion Centre for Trade, Investment and Tourism (SEAPCENTRE) proposal was then approved by SEAMCED during December 1972.

SEAMCED adopted the agreement establishing SEAPCENTRE on January 20, 1972. In 1973, SEAPCENTRE opened in Tokyo for a five-year trial period; it was extended to the end of 1978, when it closed down.

According to the founding agreement, the aim of SEAPCENTRE was threefold: "(i) to promote exports from Southeast Asian countries, (ii) to accelerate the inflow of investments to the region (iii) and to increase tourist traffic to and through the region" (Article 1). SEAPCENTRE was authorized to undertake a wide variety of activities, including expositions, trade fairs, exhibitions, publicity programs, data collection, research, information dissemination, and "to exercise its good offices in facilitating technical cooperation related to trade, investment and tourism" (Article 2).

The plenary organ was the Council (see Fig. 6.10), consisting of a Director and Alternate Director from each member country. A Standing Committee, composed of representatives from the embassies of

Figure 6.10
Organization of the Southeast Asian Promotion Centre for Trade, Investment and Tourism

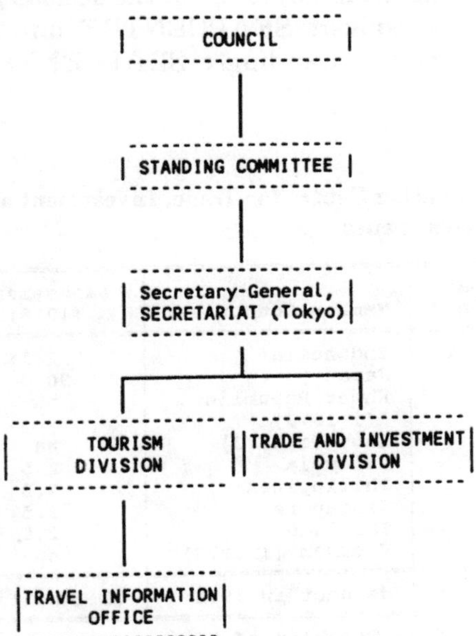

member countries assigned to Tokyo, with a representative from Japan's Ministry of International Trade and Industry, met approximately one day per month. The Secretariat was in Toranomon, Tokyo, with a Travel Information Office across town in Yurakucho.

Nine countries signed the agreement establishing SEAPCENTRE in 1972 (see Table 6.8). Japan contributed 90 percent of the total budget; the member countries shared the rest on an equal basis (Table 6.8). Trade and investment missions to Southeast Asia were funded on the basis of a one-fourth contribution by Japan, three-fourths by the countries visited.

The Trade and Investment Division held yearly conferences, exhibitions, investment promotion missions, market surveys, seminars, trade missions (product finding and purchasing missions), and provided an inquiry and consulting service. The Tourism Division provided displays, investment promotion activities (conferences, market surveys, missions, seminars), publicity (meetings with tourism organizations, publications, travel documentaries, and similar visual aids), survey teams for countries requiring technical assistance, surveys of visitor satisfaction, training programs, and served as an intermediary between travel agencies in Japan and Southeast Asian tourist destinations.

SEAPCENTRE reported to SEAMCED during its first two years. After 1975, SEAPCENTRE consisted of Japan and the five countries of ASEAN. When Prime Minister Takeo Fukuda pledged greater interest in supporting ASEAN in 1977, one of the actions giving substance to his pledge was to convert SEAPCENTRE into a project of the ASEAN-Japan Dialogue. Accordingly, SEAPCENTRE was, in effect,

Table 6.8
Southeast Asian Promotion Centre for Trade, Investment and Tourism: Membership and Assessments

Year Joined	Member Countries	Assessment (1978)
1972	Indonesia	2.5%
	Japan	90.0
	Khmer Republic (i 1973)	na
	Laos (i 1973)	na
	Malaysia	2.5
	Philippines	2.5
	Singapore	2.5
	Thailand	2.5
	Vietnam (i 1973)[a]	na
Totals	defunct in 1978	$1.1 million

[a]Joined as Republic of Vietnam.
Key: na = not assessed

renamed the ASEAN Trade, Investment and Tourism Promotion Centre, and the staff moved to a display center in Ikebukuro, Tokyo. In June 1983, Japan set up a fund to support similar functions in the region at the ASEAN Secretariat in Jakarta under the title Japan-ASEAN Cooperation Promotion Program (JACPP). Once again, we can see the Asian Way principle of separating a goal from the organizational form of attaining that goal.

SUMMARY AND CONCLUSIONS

Japan's invitation to have countries in Southeast Asia propose projects was premised on the desire of Tokyo to seem helpful, not domineering, in accordance with the equality principle of the Asian Way. Japan was not prepared to fund every proposal, however, so Southeast Asian countries turned SEAMCED around and asked Japan where it was willing to commit resources.

SEAFDEC was a prescient effort, inasmuch as within a decade, provisions of the Law of the Sea Treaty had established 200-mile exclusive economic zones (EEZs) that closed the South China Sea and adjacent areas to unrestricted Japanese fishing. Fishing boats indigenous to Southeast Asia long operated close to shore, many fishing grounds were unexplored, and aquaculture was just beginning to become a science in the mid-1960s. Tokyo supplied the knowledge and resources so that Southeast Asian fisheries personnel could expand their capabilities, at the same time as the increased harvest derived from Southeast Asia meant lower prices on seafood in Japan. Conflict resulted between deep-sea fishing and near-shore fishing, when the indigenous fishing industry suffered as big boats with expensive equipment exploited fishing resources. Meanwhile, no new fishing grounds were discovered, a fact that was realized after Burma seized a SEAFDEC research vessel. The emphasis shifted to near-shore fishing at AQD and TD, while MFRD tried to find ways to make new types of fishcake for Japanese and Southeast Asian consumers and discovered how long various species could be kept fresh and nutritious by placing them on beds of ice in supermarkets. Although AQD went through a period of change in leadership in the early 1980s, when irregularities were found in the account books of the organization, the region is able to attribute much of its doubling in fish harvesting from 1967 to 1985 to the new and successful technology of AQD. The conflict between small-scale and deep-sea fishing remains, however. In 1988, Malaysia proposed to host a fourth center, to be called the Marine Fisheries Resource Development and Management Department, attesting to the continuing vitality of SEAFDEC.

SEATAC began with the aim of moving projects in telecommunications and transportation from the proposal stage to completion, but its role narrowed when APT was formed, permitting SEATAC to focus more on transportation systems. Air transport was so profitable that SEATAC shepherding was unnecessary. Land transport is less important in Southeast Asia than sea transport, so the development of an ASEAN shipping line was pursued through feasibility studies. SEATAC approved two alternative routes in 1985, but more port calls are needed before the shipping line can be considered economically profitable. Since much trade in the region goes to Singapore for reshipment, Singapore opposes an ASEAN shipping line: it might lose business. Ultimately, the region may have its own shipping line to take its products to First-World countries, where most of the traffic goes at present, but the matter has been deferred in accordance with the Asian Way principle of consensus building so as not to antagonize Singapore. SEATAC has instead pursued an intensification of transportation networks inside each of the countries.

The key to population and family planning in Southeast Asia is the use of contraceptives, something resisted by men and expensive for women. UN agencies did not want to deal with this problem, so IGCC pursued action-oriented efforts. After an early IGCC survey of needs, projects were articulated to specifics. In the 1980s, the United States opposed such efforts, however, and IGCC was a casualty not only of this turnabout but also of its own success in generating practical projects that did not need to be repeated. Technical assistance in population planning became an ASEAN project with Australian funding by 1980.

Japan's finance minister objected to SGATAR, fearing that Southeast Asian countries would discourage investment through new taxes on multinational corporations. SGATAR became a forum for tax administrators and researchers on less controversial topics, though it has discussed tax evasion by foreign corporations at recent meetings. The ACTAR proposal was for seminars, an exchange program, and more venturesome studies. Nevertheless, SGATAR is useful as it now functions, enabling officials to share experience and information relating to tax administration. APTIRC could readily serve as SGATAR's secretariat, but SGATAR proceedings are considered too sensitive to warrant public release, so an informal body is more practical in any case.

SEAPCENTRE could not break down all barriers to trade, investment, and tourism involving Southeast Asia. In regard to trade, Japan continued to import raw materials and parts from small manufacturing firms in Southeast Asia; little progress occurred in efforts of Southeast Asian textile manufacturers to gain entry into the lucrative Japanese market. Investment capital from Japan continued to flow to countries with yen deficits, but to industries largely designed to contribute parts for assembly into manufactured products in Japan. Japanese tourists began to travel to Southeast Asia in greater numbers, though often in prepaid package tours through Tokyo travel agencies to Japanese-owned hotels. In 1978, SEAPCENTRE was converted into a Japanese institution, subject to review at meetings of the ASEAN-Japan Dialogue.

SEAMCED proved useful. Southeast Asians did not instruct Japan on how to spend its money, however. Contrary to the Asian Way principle of equality, SEAMCED placed Japan in the role of an elder brother, with Southeast Asians as younger brothers. SEAMCED's subsidiary bodies redressed the imbalance. Meanwhile, Southeast Asian countries set up their own organization in 1967, one year after SEAMCED began, calling their effort ASEAN. This latter organization is analyzed in the chapter that follows.

NOTES

1. For references to SEAMCED documents, see Michael Haas, *Basic Documents of Asian Regional Organizations* (Dobbs Ferry, NY: Oceana Publications, 1979), vol. 6, pp. 501–503. For a bibliography of secondary sources for all the organizations described in this chapter, see pp. 497–503.
2. For references to SEAFDEC documents, see Michael Haas, *Basic Documents of Asian Regional Organizations* (Dobbs Ferry, NY: Oceana Publications, 1979), vol. 6, pp. 504–17.
3. For references to SEATAC documents, see Michael Haas, *Basic Documents of Asian Regional Organizations* (Dobbs Ferry, NY: Oceana Publications, 1979), vol. 6, pp. 518–25.
4. For references to IGCC documents, see Michael Haas, *Basic Documents of Asian Regional Organizations* (Dobbs Ferry, NY: Oceana Publications, 1979), vol. 6, pp. 526–32.
5. For references to SGATAR documents, see Michael Haas, *Basic Documents of Asian Regional Organizations* (Dobbs Ferry, NY: Oceana Publications, 1979), vol. 6, pp. 534–35.
6. For references to SEAPCENTRE documents, see Michael Haas, *Basic Documents of Asian Regional Organizations* (Dobbs Ferry, NY: Oceana Publications, 1979), vol. 6, p. 533.

7 *ASEAN: A SPIRIT OF COOPERATION TO BE EMULATED*

The first use of the term *Southeast Asia* occurred when British Prime Minister Winston Churchill and U.S. President Franklin Roosevelt set up the South-East Asia Command (SEAC) at the Quebec Conference of August 1943. With Lord Mountbatten as Supreme Allied Commander, the aim of SEAC was to coordinate the recapture of Burma and Malaya from Japan. SEAC allocated food supplies and transported coal and freight for civilian as well as military purposes in an effort that integrated countries of the region for the first time.

In March 1946, when the Supreme Allied Command was abolished, Lord Killearn was assigned as Special Commissioner in South East Asia to take over the civilian functions of the command, including settling postwar problems in Indonesia, alleviating food shortages, and advising London on problems of foreign affairs in the region. The Special Commission, which he headed, had representation from British Borneo, Burma, Ceylon, Hongkong, Indochina, Indonesia, and Malaya. In May 1946, Malcom McDonald was appointed Governor-General of Malayan and Borneo Territories, with broad powers to coordinate policies relating to the independent sultanates of Borneo and Malaya as well as the colony of Singapore. Both Killearn and McDonald had headquarters in Singapore. In August 1946, Killearn established an Economic Organization to handle economic reconstruction, and monthly Liaison Meetings of the organization's Economic Department involved other countries in the region as well. The posts of Governor-General and Special Commissioner merged in May 1948, when McDonald became Commissioner General for the United Kingdom in South East Asia.

When the Labour party came to power in London in 1946, it proceeded to grant independence to most of Britain's colonies. After a White Paper of January 1946 proposed a union of the Malay sultanates, the Union of Malaya was established in April 1946, and the British urged the rest of Malaya to form a federation to supersede the Union. The Federation of Malaya was established on February 1, 1948, with Singapore excluded from its scope.

Meanwhile, although left-wing elements in France wanted a federated Indochina to replace French rule as World War II ended, French Premier Georges Bidault insisted on the maintenance of French sovereignty. The result was Ho Chi Minh's war of independence within Vietnam. In 1947, Ho Chi Minh called for a Southeast Asia League to replace colonial rule in the region.

During World War II, Japan ceded occupied territories of France, then ruled nominally by the Vichy government, to Thailand. After the war, France wanted the territories back. Thailand proposed economic concessions in exchange for a return of the territories during the Franco-Siamese Conciliation Commission, which met in July 1947 in Washington to settle the claims. The French delegate, in response, mooted the idea of a Southeast Asian union to be called the Consultative Committee for Economic and Cultural Relations of Southeast Asian Nations. Although the idea was acceptable to Thailand, Paris vetoed the idea, as it presumed that Cambodia and Laos would soon be independent and would serve, along with France, on the Commission.

In July 1947, a meeting of Southeast Asia Countries' Representatives denounced colonial policies in the region. In September 1947, the same group called for a Southeast Asia Federation. Both declarations fell on deaf ears, however.

The first effective step in building a subregional community in Southeast Asia came fourteen years later, when Malaya, the Philippines, and Thailand formed the Association of Southeast Asia (ASA) in 1961. ASA had some problems, described below in more detail, and a loose consultative arrangement involving Malaysia, the Philippines, and Indonesia was formed under the name Mushawarah Maphilindo in 1963. Maphilindo, in turn, was a nonstarter. In 1967, the Association of South East Asian Nations (ASEAN) was launched.

ASEAN is the most successful Asian political regional organization to date. Other organizations have flattered it by putting "ASEAN" in their titles. Although most of the latter efforts have been nongovernmental, two are intergovernmental: the ASEAN Inter-Parliamentary Organization (AIPO) and the Meeting of the Chiefs of National Police of the ASEAN Countries (known as ASEANAPOL).

This chapter reviews all five organizations. ASA and Maphilindo give information on the immediate antecedents of ASEAN; AIPO and

ASEANAPOL demonstrate how ASEAN has inspired other efforts throughout Asia.

ASSOCIATION OF SOUTHEAST ASIA (ASA)[1]

Malaya's full independence came in 1957. Tunku Abdul Rahman, Malaya's first prime minister, did not want to join the South-East Asia Treaty Organization (SEATO), since he could rely on the Anglo-Malayan Defence Agreement (AMDA). Believing that peace with neighboring countries could be brought about through collective economic and social projects in the region, he proposed a Southeast Asian Friendship and Economic Treaty (SEAFET).

In January 1959, the Tunku visited Philippine President Carlos Garcia, who was enthusiastic about the idea of a new intergovernmental organization among Southeast Asian countries. In March 1959, the Tunku prepared a draft SEAFET. During July 1959, Thai Foreign Minister Thanat Khoman circulated a proposal for a Southeast Asia Community Organization (SEACOR) to all capitals in the region except Hanoi. In October 1959, the Tunku solicited comments on SEAFET, suggesting a summit conference at Kuala Lumpur in early 1960 to discuss the proposal. When the Philippines, South Vietnam, and Thailand responded favorably, Garcia suggested a preliminary meeting of lower-level representatives instead. Thanat then drafted a compromise plan for an Association of South-East Asian States (ASAS) for circulation in early 1960. The foreign ministers of Malaya, the Philippines, and Thailand then met in Kuala Lumpur in February 1961, agreeing in principle to set up a new organization; each country then drafted proposals. In June 1960, working groups from the three countries formed the Joint Working Party, which prepared the agenda for a second foreign ministers' meeting, hosted by Thanat from July 31 to August 1, 1961. On the first day of the meeting, the three issued a joint communiqué, known as the Bangkok Declaration. The Association of Southeast Asia had begun.

According to the Bangkok Declaration, the main purpose of ASA was "to establish an effective machinery for friendly consultations, collaboration and mutual assistance in the economic, social, cultural, scientific and administrative fields." Cooperation was envisaged in "economic, cultural, educational and scientific fields," including "the promotion of Southeast Asian Studies," with a view to establishing "machinery for fruitful collaboration in the utilization of their respective natural resources, the development of their agriculture and industry, the expansion of their trade, the improvement of their transport and communication facilities, and generally raising the living standards of their peoples." Although the Philippines wanted to draft an ASA constitution, the other two countries demurred.

The conference of foreign ministers, known as the Ministerial Meeting, was ASA's major organ (see Fig. 7.1). Meetings lasted from three to five days in length; they rotated among the member countries during 1961, 1962, 1963, then resumed in 1966 and 1967.

Between Ministerial Meetings, the Standing Committee met for one day each month to carry out the work of ASA. The Standing Committee was chaired by the foreign minister of the country designated to host the next Ministerial Meeting; ambassadors of the two countries assigned to the host country served on the Standing Committee.

A Joint Working Party met about a month before the Ministerial Meeting to fix the agenda. Ad hoc committees existed in several specialized fields. In 1963, the ministers formed three Permanent Committees; each member country then chaired one of the committees.

Each country established an ASA National Secretariat, including a National ASA Secretary-General, to coordinate activities. National Secretariats serviced the committees and Ministerial Meetings.

Malaya felt that the cohesion of the three countries augured well for ASA but that other countries, such as South Vietnam, might taint the organization ideologically (see Table 7.1). Although Saigon wanted to join, ASA agreed not to expand until results emerged, following the Asian Way principle of incrementalism. Indonesia, feeling that ASA was too pro-West, refused to join ASA. Singapore became independent of the Malaysian Federation in 1965, but by then ASA was on hold.

In 1961, the United Kingdom announced its intention to permit Malaya to include Sabah, Sarawak, and Singapore. Soon after, the Philip-

Figure 7.1
Organization of the Association of Southeast Asia

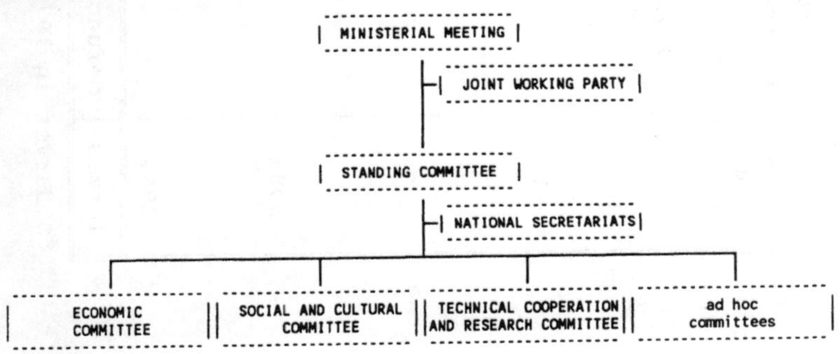

Table 7.1
Association of South East Asian Nations and Related Organizations: Membership

Year	ASA	Maphilindo	ASEAN	AIPO	ASEANAPOL
1961	Malaya Philippines Thailand				
1963		Indonesia Malaysia Philippines			
1967			Indonesia Malaysia Philippines Singapore Thailand		
1977				Indonesia Malaysia Philippines Singapore Thailand	
1981					Indonesia Malaysia Philippines Singapore Thailand
1984			Brunei[a]	Brunei[a]	Brunei
Totals	defunct in 1967	defunct in 1963	6 Members	6 Members	6 Members

[a]Observer in 1973

pine Congress issued a resolution laying claim to Sabah. Malaysia severed ties with the Philippines, and after twice postponing the 1962 Ministerial Meeting, there were no Ministerial Meetings until 1966; projects continued on a bilateral Malaysia–Thai and Philippine–Thai basis until 1966, following the Asian Way principle of Asian solutions to Asian problems.

The 1962 ASA Ministerial Meeting agreed that each country would set aside $1 million of its national budget as a contribution to an ASA Fund. The amounts were callable, similar to callable contributions to the World Bank, to pay for the expenses of approved projects; contributions were the same for the three countries, reflecting the Asian Way principle of equality.

Although ASA provided an opportunity for the three countries to discuss foreign-policy issues and to develop common positions, this was not the main content of Ministerial Meeting joint communiqués, which reviewed proposed and completed technical projects. The Asian Way principle of separating politics from administration was observed.

The earliest projects were in the field of education, including exchanges of experts, research fellows, social workers, women leaders, youth leaders, and radio programs. The Philippines offered university scholarships, study tours were sponsored by Malaysia, and Thailand agreed to take similar measures. Dance and cultural troupes visited the member countries; art exhibitions and sporting events were also held. Malayan Airways and Thai Airways began pooling arrangements, and a through-train service from Bangkok to Kuala Lumpur started as an ASA project. Studies on closer economic cooperation and other proposals remained at the project identification stage.

By 1966, ASA earmarked five projects for external financial aid, but multilateral funding never materialized. Informal ASA voting blocs formed at UN conferences, where the three countries lobbied to make the discussion more attuned to Third-World concerns, inasmuch as the Bangkok Declaration stated that ASA was to help other organizations to be more effective.

MAPHILINDO[2]

There were several British colonial entities in Southeast Asia: the Straits Settlements (Labuan, Malacca, Penang, and Singapore), the four Federated Malay States of central Malaya, the five Unfederated Malay States in northern and southern Malaya, and British Borneo (Brunei, Sabah, and Sarawak). In 1945, Malacca and Penang joined the nine Malay states to form the Malayan Union, which in 1948 became the Federation of Malaya.

Full independence came to Malaya in 1957. After discussions with leaders in the Borneo colonies, Kuala Lumpur and Singapore, London announced its intention in November 1961 to give Brunei, Labuan, Sabah, Sarawak, and Singapore to Malaya as of 1963 to form the Federation of Malaysia. Jakarta, however, perceived the addition of North Borneo (called Kalimantan in Indonesia) to be an act of "neocolonialism." In the Philippines, the proposed annexation of Sabah raised objections because the territory had once been a part of the Sulu sultanate, which also included Mindanao and the Sulu archipelago. Indonesia rushed troops to the borders of Malaysia, and the Philippine Congress passed a resolution condemning the annexation.

In 1962, Philippine President Diosdado Macapagal, who feared the consequences of deteriorating relations among neighboring countries in the region, conceived of the idea of a loose confederation of all Malay peoples in Borneo, Indonesia, Malaya, and the Philippines. This Macapagal plan for a joint consultative arrangement, in accordance with the Asian Way principle of consensus decision making, was to be called the Confederation of Nations of Malay Origin. After a brief discussion during the March 1963 annual session of the UN Economic Commission for Asia and the Far East (ECAFE) among Indonesian Foreign Minister Subandrio, Malaysian Deputy Prime Minister Abdul Razak, and Philippine Vice President (and Foreign Minister) Emmanuel Pelaez, Thai Foreign Minister Thanat urged Malaysia's Prime Minister Rahman to attend the twice-postponed ASA Ministerial Meeting in order to meet President Macapagal in early April 1963. Macapagal proposed to meet Indonesian President Sukarno, but Rahman insisted on a three-power conference in mid-April 1963 to be attended by the foreign ministers' principal assistants. When no results came from this lower-level meeting, Rahman invited Sukarno to Kuala Lumpur, where the Macapagal plan was discussed and an invitation was extended for a meeting of the three foreign ministers in Manila to discuss the plan. After the foreign ministers approved the main thrust of the Macapagal plan in a document known as the Manila Accord on June 11, 1963, the three heads of government confirmed the arrangement on August 4, 1963, issuing the Manila Declaration for an organization called Mushawarah Maphilindo. The consultative framework established thereby is available for further implementation at any time, but no organization per se has ever been set up.

According to the third paragraph of the Manila Accord, "the three countries share a primary responsibility for the maintenance of the stability and security of the area from subversion in any form of manifestation in order to preserve their respective national identities, and to ensure the peaceful development of their respective countries and of the region. . . . " The Manila Declaration reaffirmed these principles and pledged a commitment to

[1] the principle of equal rights and self-determination of peoples, . . . [2] the common interest of their countries, to maintain fraternal relations, to strengthen cooperation among their peoples in the economic, social, and cultural fields in order to promote economic progress and social well-being in the region, and to put an end to the exploitation of man by man and of one nation by another, . . . [3] the common struggle against colonialism and imperialism in all their forms and manifestations and for the eradication of the vestiges thereof in the region in particular and the world in general, . . . [and 4] a new and better world based on national freedom, social justice, and lasting peace.

Under Mushawarah Maphilindo (loosely translated as Maphilindo Council), the Conference of Foreign Ministers was subsidiary to the Summit Conference (see Fig. 7.2). Both organs were to meet at least once each year. Further machinery "for frequent and regular consultation" was to be defined later, according to the Manila Accord, but would be "at all levels . . . in dealing with common problems of security, stability, economic, social and cultural development." Each country was to set up its own national secretariat until a central secretariat was established. The three heads of government did not meet again until 1977. The occasion, not specifically identified as a Maphilindo activity, was the day following the meeting of heads of government of ASEAN in Kuala Lumpur in August 1977. The purpose of the meeting was to negotiate a border crossing and border patrol agreement between Malaysia and the Philippines; Indonesia served as a mediator.

Figure 7.2
Organization of Maphilindo

The three countries involved in Maphilindo were Indonesia, Malaysia, and the Philippines (see Table 7.1). Although references were made to the Federation of Malaysia in the text of the Manila Declaration (but not the Manila Accord), the representative from Kuala Lumpur was identified as the "Prime Minister of the Federation of Malaya."

The meetings sought to build a framework for resolving disputes involving territories that Malaya wished to include in Malaysia. The Manila Accord accepted the authority of the UN Secretary-General as an impartial agent to determine the wishes of the peoples of the Borneo territories, with the proviso that the Philippines would utilize peaceful means through international law to resolve its claim; this included the possibility of submitting the dispute to an international tribunal and refraining from military actions. The three countries agreed to allow the UN Secretary-General to administer a plebiscite in Labuan, Sabah, and Sarawak, with the three affected governments sending observer teams. The three heads of government also agreed that foreign bases were temporary in nature and would not be used to subvert each other. A UN plebiscite was held, and Malaya followed the wishes of the inhabitants and annexed Labuan, Sabah, Sarawak, and Singapore to become Malaysia on August 31, 1963. At the last minute, Brunei decided to remain under the British flag for another 20 years. Malaysia repudiated Maphilindo in June 1966.

ASSOCIATION OF SOUTH EAST ASIAN NATIONS (ASEAN)[3]

Sukarno, having agreed to Maphilindo, would not join ASA. Indonesia continued as a leader of the nonaligned nations. Singapore, meanwhile, was expelled from the newly formed Malaysia in 1965, so it was also outside of ASA. In early 1966, Sukarno's government fell, however, and General Suharto became the new President of Indonesia. Adam Malik, named Foreign Minister, formulated a new foreign policy for Indonesia more in keeping with Asian Way principles.

In July 1967, one month before the scheduled ASA Ministerial Meeting, Malik went to Bangkok to discuss with Thai Foreign Minister Thanat the possibility of a new regional organization. Thanat was enthusiastic about Malik's idea for an Association of South East Asian Nations, and a joint Indonesian-Thai draft emerged, based in part on elements of ASA. The two then invited foreign ministers of Malaysia, the Philippines, and Singapore to Bangsaen, a Thai seaside resort, for informal discussions. When the five reached an agreement, they drove to Bangkok, rewrote the Indonesian-Thai draft, and issued what is now known as the ASEAN Declaration on August 8, 1967. The ASA Council, scheduled for the same month, was never held. ASEAN is often considered to have superseded ASA, but the newer organization assumed an independent character of its own.

The most basic agreements of ASEAN, the Declaration of ASEAN Concord and the Treaty of Amity and Cooperation in Southeast Asia, were adopted nine years later by the first Meeting of Heads of Government of ASEAN in Bali on February 24, 1976.

The ASEAN Declaration was largely a carbon copy of the ASA Declaration. The Declaration of ASEAN Concord, which only refers to ASEAN in its title, states as its purpose "to promote perpetual peace, everlasting amity and cooperation among their peoples which would contribute to their strength, solidarity and closer relationship" (Article 1). The Treaty of Amity and Cooperation in Southeast Asia makes reference to ASEAN as an organization and stipulates a detailed program of action. The preamble provides two overriding aims: (1) "to promote peace, progress, prosperity and the welfare of the peoples of member states" and (2) "to consolidate the achievements of ASEAN and expand ASEAN cooperation in the economic, social, cultural and political fields. . . . "

Organization

ASEAN is a multilevel organization that needs to be described in detail in order to be appreciated (see Fig. 7.3). Meetings of Heads of Government (summit meetings) first occurred in 1976 and 1977. After 1977, Malaysian leaders refused to attend a summit in Manila, the next host country by ASEAN's rule of alphabetical rotation of meetings, until the Philippines agreed to renounce its claim to Sabah. The new Philippine constitution, ratified in February 1987, removed this barrier, and the third Summit Meeting was held in December 1987.

The ASEAN treaty establishes a High Council of ministerial-level officials for the pacific settlement of disputes. This body has never met.

Since 1967, however, the plenary body has been the Annual Ministerial Meeting (AMM) of the foreign ministers (see Fig. 7.4). ASEAN foreign ministers meet as needed throughout the year, sometimes in

Figure 7.3
Organization of the Association of South East Asian Nations

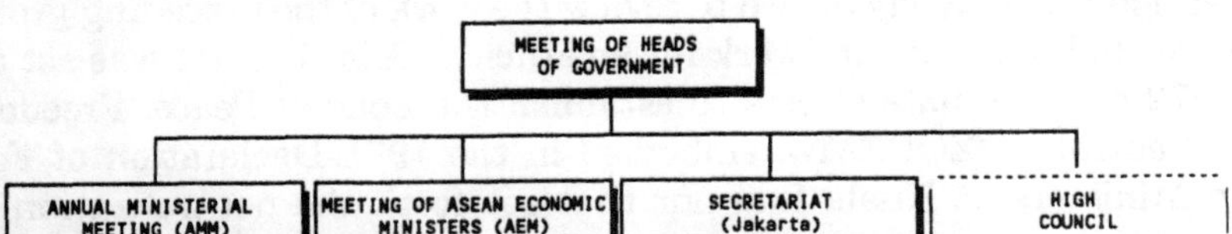

Figure 7.4
Organization of ASEAN: Foreign Ministers' Side

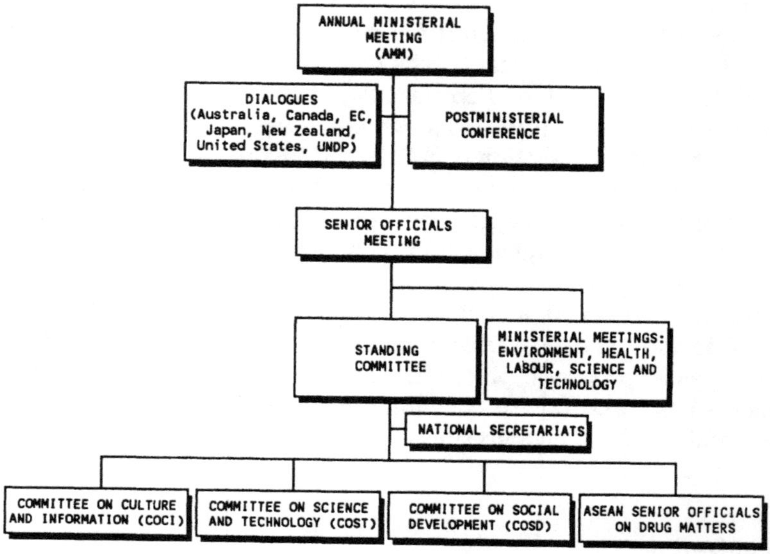

what is called Extraordinary ASEAN Meetings and sometimes bilaterally, but only one such meeting is the focal point for ASEAN. All decisions are based on the Asian Way principle of unanimous consensus.

A Standing Committee meets bimonthly between annual sessions of the foreign ministers' meeting. The Standing Committee is chaired by the foreign minister of the country to host the next annual AMM and includes ambassadors from ASEAN countries posted to that country. The Standing Committee coordinates the organization and compiles an annual report on the work of the organization.

In preparation for the AMM each year, there is a sequence of meetings, starting with the Preparatory Meeting of ASEAN Directors-General (heads of ASEAN National Secretariats), proceeding to the Standing Committee meeting, then a Senior Officials Meeting (SOM) of undersecretaries of foreign affairs, and finally the AMM itself. Each lower body takes a day or two to review the work of the preceding group in order to lay the groundwork for an efficient AMM. SOM was set up in 1972 to coordinate efforts to establish the Zone of Peace, Freedom and Neutrality (ZOPFAN), embodied in the 1971 Declaration of Foreign Ministers at Kuala Lumpur that set forth the neutralization of

Southeast Asia as ASEAN's principal political goal. SOM now reviews all diplomatic action taken to implement proposals emerging from the Standing Committee's annual report, meeting as often as four times each year for two-day sessions.

In 1977, ASEAN foreign ministers met with major external donors, known as Dialogue partners, to review cooperative programs. Meetings have been held since that time with the following regular Dialogue partners: Australia, Canada, European Community (EC), Japan, New Zealand, UN Development Program (UNDP), and the United States. Starting in 1984, Postministerial Conferences (PMCs), consisting of all ASEAN foreign ministers and the foreign ministers of all Dialogue partners (except for EC), have been held on the day after the AMM; individual Dialogues (including EC) then take place on the final day.

ASEAN countries were not content to allow external corporations and Chinese merchants to continue to eclipse the potential for indigenous capitalism in Southeast Asia. In 1969, ASEAN asked the United Nations to survey prospects for regional economic cooperation. By 1975, a meeting of ASEAN Economic and Planning Ministers convened, initially to review findings from the resulting UN study. The ASEAN Economic Ministers (AEM), as the body is now known, have met on an annual or biannual basis ever since, preceded by Senior Economic Officials Meetings to coordinate input from the various ministries involved (see Fig. 7.5).

Originally, the AMM set up ad hoc and Permanent Committees, with undersecretary representation, in specialized areas to encourage cooperation involving other ministries. Because so many committees found themselves reporting both to AMM and AEM, the Kuala Lumpur summit of 1977 rationalized the structure. Four permanent bodies now report to AMM (see Fig. 7.4) and five to AEM (see Fig. 7.5) through the Standing Committee. To direct some of AEM's committees, there are three ministerial bodies, most of which meet at irregular intervals: the Economic Ministers on Agriculture and Forestry, Economic Ministers on Energy Cooperation, and Economic Ministers on Industry.

Preparatory bodies of senior civil servants from relevant ministries precede committee meetings. Committee chairs rotate alphabetically among member countries. In 1987–88, for example, the Permanent Committees were supported by twenty-three subcommittees and twenty-seven expert working groups. Some 179 meetings and project activities took place during 1987–88, according to the *Annual Report of the ASEAN Standing Committee.*

Other ministerial meetings have occurred apart from the AEM and AMM. These include ASEAN ministers of education; environment;

Figure 7.5
Organization of ASEAN: Economic Ministers' Side

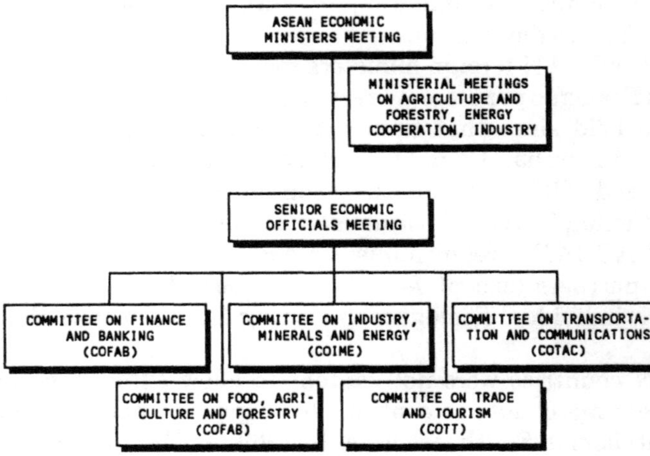

health; information; justice, law, and attorneys-general; labor; science and technology; and social welfare. Of these bodies, only the labor ministers have met on a regular basis.

Originally, there was no central Secretariat. Each country maintained its own National Secretariat, which served as the ASEAN Secretariat when that country hosted the AMM. In 1973, AMM agreed to have a Secretariat; Jakarta was selected as the site in 1976. A Secretary-General heads the Secretariat (see Fig. 7.6). There are three Bureaus (Economic Bureau, Science and Technology Bureau, and Socio-Cultural Affairs Bureau), an Administrative Office, a Public Infor-

Figure 7.6
Organization of ASEAN: Secretariat

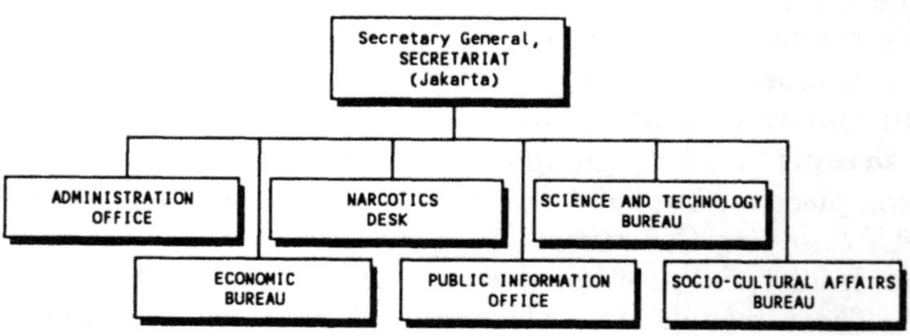

mation Office, and, since 1981, a Narcotics Desk. Secretariat personnel primarily service meetings of ministers and committees.

National Secretariats continue, inasmuch as they coordinate Committee projects in each country; they are headed by National Directors-General. The National Secretariat hosting the AMM provides the conference secretariat; the same arrangement applies to other meetings.

Membership

ASEAN began with five members (see Table 7.1). After serving as an Observer at AMMs in 1982 and 1983, Brunei joined in 1984. Other countries have been Observers at AMM sessions: Fiji (1985), Khmer Republic (1971, 1973, 1974), Laos (1969, 1971, 1973, 1974), Papua New Guinea (1976, 1978–present), and South Vietnam (1969, 1971). AMM has invited Prince Norodom Sihanouk as the representative of Cambodia in recent years.

Papua New Guinea, which is not interested in joining ASEAN as a full member, was admitted to Observer status in three permanent committees in 1986: Committee on Food, Agriculture and Forestry (COFAF), Committee on Social Development (COSD), and Committee on Science and Technology (COST). In June 1987, AMM agreed to accept Papua New Guinea's application to sign the Treaty of Amity and Cooperation, which is open, as well, to all countries in Southeast Asia. Papua New Guinea signed in September 1987.

In the early years, ASEAN hoped that Burma would eventually participate, while resisting overtures from Indochina on the grounds that the problems of Indochina could be best handled through ASEAN after military hostilities ceased. Since 1975, there has been little interest in admitting Indochinese countries, though Vietnam stated its readiness to join in 1979, and again in 1988 and 1989. Malaysia responded in 1989 that there is a possibility of accepting Vietnam into ASEAN if it renounces the use of force to invade other countries; Indonesia and the Philippines have suggested that Vietnam could do so by signing the ASEAN treaty. In 1981, Sri Lanka was reported to have submitted a formal application for membership. ASEAN countries believe that they have enough difficulties perfecting their relationship among themselves without adding additional countries as members.

Dialogue partner relationships evolved from foreign aid programs; they identify needs of ASEAN countries and review progress. Each Dialogue is handled by an ASEAN Coordinating Country, which rotates alphabetically at two- to three-year intervals. Dialogue meetings convene once each year at the Deputy-Secretary level between each Dialogue partner and ASEAN countries to review annual reports. Dialogue meetings rotate between the donor and ASEAN Coordinating Country. Since three Dialogue partners (Canada, EC, and New Zealand) have established detailed cooperative agreements with ASEAN countries, their Joint Cooperative Consultative Meetings take place at the ambassadorial level about four times each year, usually in conjunction with Standing Committee meetings. In addition, senior civil service officials from ASEAN countries meet experts from the cooperative programs and their respective projects, such as the ASEAN Food Handling Bureau; at these meetings there is a review of technical progress. Other meetings of various sorts occur throughout the year with Dialogue partners. Regular ministerial-level meetings have been held only with EC and Japan. Individual ASEAN projects are negotiated and administered through the National Secretariat in the country in which they are located, though they report to the Standing Committee through the appropriate Permanent Committee.

In 1980, ASEAN foreign ministers met with India, but only for a single meeting, as New Delhi later recognized the new Cambodian regime established when Vietnamese troops drove the Pol Pot regime out of Phnom Penh. In recent years, the Republic of Korea has sought to establish a dialog with ASEAN, but no action has been taken by ASEAN to pursue this possibility. Indonesia was ASEAN's "interlocutor" with Vietnam until 1988; Malaysia has served in the same capacity vis-à-vis Arab countries.

Funding

In 1969, an ASEAN Fund was approved, consisting of $1 million set aside each year in the national accounts of the member countries, intended for nonpersonnel items. The exact amount spent was not made public, but the expenditures were quite modest; there is a Joint Management Committee for each project. The six National Secretariats follow the same general procedures. There are now two additional sources of funds. The Secretariat in Jakarta has a budget of its own, to which ASEAN member countries contribute an equal share (see Table 7.2). ASEAN funding is also available from the Dialogue partners.

The Secretariat administers three special funds set up by former Japanese prime ministers. In 1977, Takeo Fukuda promised a Japanese donation of up to $1 billion to ASEAN. Known as the Fukuda Fund, some $20 million was placed in the custody of the Secretariat in 1979. Although the fund was initially designed to finance proposed

Table 7.2
Association of South East Asian Nations: Secretariat Assessments

Member Country	Assessment (1984)[a]
Brunei	16.7%
Indonesia	16.7
Malaysia	16.7
Philippines	16.7
Singapore	16.7
Thailand	16.7
Total	$1,800,000

[a]Due to rounding, the column does not sum exactly to 100 percent.

ASEAN Industrial Projects (AIPs), these projects were not developed as quickly as had been hoped, so the Fukuda Fund has become the Cultural Fund; interest from the fund supports projects in each ASEAN country, as approved by the Committee on Culture and Information (COCI), subject to review by the Standing Committee, which authorizes transfers of money from the ASEAN Secretariat to the member countries. An annual meeting of the Advisory Group of the ASEAN Cultural Fund examines how the fund's portfolio is managed.

In 1980, Japan began the first of 10 annual contributions to the Japan Scholarship Fund for ASEAN Youth. This donation is known as the Ohira Fund after Prime Minister Masayoshi Ohira. Each country, Brunei excepted, designates a Coordinating Agency to award annual amounts of $200,000 for scholarships at Japanese institutions of higher learning.

The Suzuki Fund, named in honor of Japanese Prime Minister Zenko Suzuki, assists human resources development. Launched in 1984, funds from the ASEAN-Pacific Cooperation in Human Resources Development (APC-HRD) Project assist governmental productivity and vocational training centers. Each participating ASEAN country designates a national center to receive the funds. Japan pledged 5 billion yen (then about $25 million), with matching amounts from all Dialogue partner countries.

In 1983, the Japan-ASEAN Cooperation Promotion Program (JACPP) Fund was established to facilitate Japanese economic cooperation, investment and trade promotion, and transfer of technology between ASEAN countries and Japan. ASEAN's Secretary-General chairs the committee managing the fund; other members are representatives from Indonesia's ASEAN National Secretariat and the embassies of ASEAN countries and Japan posted to Jakarta.

In 1988, Tokyo established the ASEAN-Japan Development Fund and the Japan-ASEAN Comprehensive Exchange Program. The former consists of $2 billion in investment capital for the private sector. The latter promotes exchanges in a variety of fields between ASEAN countries and Japan.

Whereas Japan uses the lump-sum method of allocation to ASEAN, other donors finance technical assistance projects on an individual basis. Recent allocations are as follows (in equivalent U.S. dollars): Australia, $7.9 million (1986); Canada, $14.3 million (1986); EC, $37.6 million (1984); New Zealand, $1.3 million (1987); UNDP, $1.5 million (1986); and the United States, $4.1 million (1986).

Projects

One of the most important aspects of ASEAN is to provide a forum in which to discuss various topics. While informal discussion on political matters has led to bold declarations, many decisions are kept quiet and unofficial; subsequently a portion of these discussions will be given an ASEAN label. ZOPFAN, for example, has been accepted in principle by China, the Commonwealth, all three Indochinese countries, the Nonaligned Nations Conference, the United States, and the Soviet Union. When Vietnamese troops entered Cambodia in 1978, AMM strenuously sought the removal of Vietnam's forces through annual ASEAN resolutions, and ASEAN persuaded the UN General Assembly to adopt similar resolutions each year. In 1987, Indonesia persuaded ASEAN countries to agree in principle to a Southeast Asian Nuclear Weapon Free Zone (SEANWFZ) as a component of ZOPFAN. The Philippine constitution of 1987 declared the country to be nuclear-free, a step in the direction of SEANWFZ, but Soviet bases in Vietnam and U.S. bases in the Philippines keep ZOPFAN from becoming a reality. In these cases, the Asian Way principle of consensus decision making has kept ASEAN together.

Initially, the Standing Committee compiled a set of projects recommended by the various ad hoc and Permanent Committees, leaving matters of implementation mostly to the National Secretariats. Some of the early projects, such as an ASEAN tourism survey, were defrayed from the ASEAN Fund, but most recommendations were for projects to receive funding from UN agencies. Due to increased financial support from ASEAN's Dialogue partners after the summit conferences of 1976 and 1977 and the formation of the Secretariat at Jakarta, myriad ASEAN projects exist today.

The Dialogues involve three facets. One element is an effort by the Trade Preferences Negotiating Group (TPNG), a subcommittee of the Committee on Trade and Tourism (COTT), to obtain more favorable terms for entry into the markets of external countries. The second element consists of technical-assistance programs of various sorts. The third element is a more general, usually informal, discussion on matters of international politics, such as the Cambodian War.

Concerning TPNG, ASEAN countries have sought preferential rates as an economic unit in the generalized system of preferences (GSP) of each Dialogue partner country. Negotiations are at various stages with each external country, but most countries have accepted the common rule of origin (CRO) principle for exports that involve up to 50 percent of ASEAN-country raw materials. Australia modified its GSP in 1986 to set up a uniform 5 percent margin of preference (MOP) for all items from developing countries. In 1974, EC allowed certain products to be imported under its GSP from Singapore, provided that the products came from other ASEAN countries; in 1975, the CRO principle was applied to ASEAN as a whole. Japan's GSP, the least generous among the Dialogue partners, has improved in recent years. New Zealand offers a 20 percent MOP for about 1,000 items; Brunei and Singapore, with per-capita incomes more than 80 percent of New Zealand's, are outside the GSP, though Wellington has set up special MOPs for a few Singapore products and allows imports of Brunei oil on a duty-free basis. In 1982, the United States proposed an ASEAN–US free trade area. Since this might flood ASEAN countries with U.S. products, a so-called ASEAN–US Initiative is now under negotiation. Meanwhile, the United States has about 2,800 items on its GSP list for duty-free treatment, with ASEAN considered as a unit for purposes of its CRO requirements; affluent Singapore is excluded. TPNG also negotiates with the Far Eastern Freight Conference (FEFC) to lower freight rates.

The Committee on Finance and Banking (COFAB) administers projects in the fields of banking, customs, insurance, investment, and tax administration. In 1979, COFAB approved the ASEAN Finance Corporation (AFC), a private-sector firm incorporated in Singapore. AFC began in 1981 with $100 million in equity capital pledged by 140 banks in all ASEAN countries. Funding was based on equal monetary commitments from all ASEAN countries except Brunei to provide investment capital for ASEAN commercial projects. Up to 1986, AFC had participated in loans to two governmental joint ventures and fourteen joint ventures in the private sector, with AFC funds matched by non-ASEAN countries.

In 1983, the ASEAN Bankers Acceptance (ABA) scheme, another private-sector project, began on a trial basis between Indonesia and Thailand, using AFC starting capital of $6 million. The facility, which used local currency to purchase products from another ASEAN country for 30 days, was not successful because the market was too small to be priced competitively, and cut-rate equivalents were available from New York banks. The ASEAN Reinsurance Pool, launched by the Singapore Reinsurance Corporation in 1982, was superseded in 1988 by the $3 million nongovernmental ASEAN Reinsurance Corporation.

COFAB's most significant project is the ASEAN Swap Arrangement, begun in 1977. Under this arrangement, each country provides a credit line for use in case of short-term liquidity problems. When the arrangement began, $20 million was set aside in each ASEAN central bank. If an ASEAN country encountered a foreign-exchange cash flow shortfall, it could swap up to $40 million for domestic currency for three months, with an extension of credit for another three months. In 1978, the total set aside was raised to $40 million per country, and in 1982, the maximum line of credit increased to $80 million. Each central bank, except for Brunei, acts on behalf of the government or responds to applications from commercial banks inside its borders to use the arrangement. The standard fee is the interbank rate (mean of buying and selling rates) for the initial swap, with forward rates calculated using the Eurodollar rate quoted by the Bank for International Settlements (BIS). The initial swap is effected through a spot sale of U.S. dollars against the domestic currency of the borrowing participant, followed by a forward purchase by the same participant until the line of credit is settled.

The Committee on Food, Agriculture and Forestry (COFAF) sponsors projects related to food, agriculture, forestry, livestock, and fisheries. In 1977, ASEAN rice-exporting countries (principally Thailand) agreed to give one another the right of first refusal on stocks in case of emergency, and nearly one million tons were traded. Under the ASEAN Food Security Reserve scheme, some 53,000 metric tons of rice are now maintained in national stocks; a country in surplus sells to a country with a shortfall at preferential rates. External donors support projects in agricultural development planning, food handling, forest tree improvement, pesticide management, plant quarantine training and timber technology, all of which operate at various sites throughout the region.

The Committee on Industry, Minerals and Energy (COIME) has pursued projects in the fields of mining exploration and mine safety, energy and coal cooperation, and support for small- and medium-sized industries. COIME's primary responsibility for many years has been the development of ASEAN Industrial Projects (AIPs). Five AIPs were initially approved for the establishment of new industries for the region, with each country pledged to buy shares of equity capital. Only the urea projects of Indonesia and Malaysia are operational, although a

Board of Directors is now meeting to implement the Copper Fabrication Project in the Philippines. AIPs require the host country to acquire 60 percent equity, and a minimum of 1 percent of the shares is held by each of the remaining countries. Shares may be held by government agencies or private businesses approved by governments in each country. The board of directors of each AIP primarily consists of nationals of ASEAN member states. Each AIP may secure loans to complete facilities; the original Fukuda Fund is still available in principle. The Indonesian project has an equity of $93.9 million; Malaysia, the Philippines, and Thailand pledged shares of 13 percent each (Brunei was exempted from participation). A similar arrangement exists for the Malaysian AIP.

Because AIPs involve heavy capital investment in major industrial enterprises, the lack of immediate results was a source of some frustration within ASEAN. A second type of project was then pursued. Known as ASEAN Industrial Complementation (AIC) projects, the idea was for one country to specialize in producing a part for a larger product that was assembled by companies in the private sector. AIC products would then be manufactured exclusively for two to three years, with preferential access to the markets of ASEAN countries. The initiative was left entirely to ASEAN industry clubs, which were to notify COIME of agreements. The only approved package, for motor vehicles, came onstream in 1982 because several automotive parts plants already existed on an exclusive basis in the region; implementation time, thus, was nil. In 1983, additional products deepened the package of automotive parts. Although, by 1986, trade in the first set of products exceeded $1 million, primarily in the sale of V-belts, the second set was shelved, as the three-year exclusive production element was not much of an inducement.

While AIPs require participation by each ASEAN government on a massive scale, the AIC concept showed that the private sector in at least one area was willing to forge ahead if left unencumbered, as long as there were governmental incentives. Accordingly, a scheme of ASEAN Industrial Joint Ventures (AIJVs) started in 1983. When prospective joint-venture partners find each other, and their respective governments grant preferential market access (scheme participation) for the finished products, pledges for equity participation are obtained, and AIJVs are first approved by COIME, then by AEM. Financing of AIJVs is more flexible than for AIPs. Non-ASEAN investors may own up to 90 percent of AIJV stock. A pre-approved list of 106 products is now being reviewed so that AIJVs will not need formal approval through a complicated process of ASEAN committee meetings. There are fifteen approved items on the list so far.

COIME is also responsible for the Emergency Petroleum Sharing

Scheme, which began on a trial basis in 1977 and was officially adopted in 1986. Countries with an oversupply sell to countries with an undersupply under the scheme. No preferential rates are involved; terms are negotiated bilaterally.

The Committee on Trade and Tourism (COTT) is responsible for the highly publicized Preferential Trading Arrangements (PTA), under which four ASEAN countries have agreed to ease trade barriers among themselves; Brunei and Singapore are excluded, and some exceptions from the various requirements are granted to Indonesia and the Philippines. In the first round of TPNG negotiations after the PTA agreement was signed in 1977, some seventy-one items were accepted for tariff-free entry. Subsequently, the list expanded until 14,462 items were on the list in 1988, with MOPs ranging from 20 to 25 percent, and a CRO of at least 50 percent (35 percent in some cases), with about 5,000 items on an exclusion list. In 1987, AEM agreed to a five-year plan in which the exclusion lists would be reduced to account for no more than 10 percent of all products imported from other ASEAN countries, with the CRO decreased from 50 to 35 percent. In addition, all items included within PTA would increase to 50 percent MOPs, with the items removed from the exclusion lists accorded a minimum of 25 percent MOPs. The current aim is to increase ASEAN trade so that the percent covered by PTA will increase from the present 5 percent to a goal of 50 percent.

In 1980, TPNG sought across-the-board tariff reductions for all products traded at a value up to $50,000 per year; this ceiling was raised each year until it reached $10 million in 1984, with a flat 25 percent tariff reduction for items above that amount, though the exclusion list still applies. Impatient with progress, the Philippines and Singapore agreed to bilateral tariff reductions, starting with 10 percent cuts for 1,758 products in 1977. AIC, AIP, and AIJV products are accorded virtually duty-free entry into ASEAN markets.

Yet another approach under PTA is the sectoral method, approved in 1983. Under this approach, 50 percent MOPs are granted in specific economic sectors without an import-value limit. Sectors identified thus far are cement, chemicals, food, rubber products, and textiles. In 1986, AEM approved the concept of an ASEAN Preferential Tariff Quota Scheme under which tariffs would be lowered bilaterally for products excluded from the PTA until volumes reached a ceiling, when higher tariffs would be charged. Both schemes were frozen in 1987, when AEM decided to deepen provisions of the existing PTA.

Since import licensing and unstandardized trade nomenclature are among several nontariff trade barriers (NTBs) that prevent full implementation of PTA, AEM agreed in 1987 to freeze all NTBs at the present levels. Negotiations for rollbacks in NTBs are in progress.

In 1986, AEM approved an arrangement to shortlist ASEAN construction contractors for projects financed by the Asian Development Bank (ADB) and the World Bank. Under this scheme, only one ASEAN firm will be nominated to bid when there are several prequalified contractors. Both banks have new provisions to prefer local contractors even when their bids for projects are slightly higher than outside firms.

COTT also integrates ASEAN policy in regard to entry into the markets of developed countries and toward worldwide negotiations under the General Agreement on Trade and Tariffs (GATT). COTT has presented ASEAN views on negotiations for the multifiber arrangements (MFA) and to the economic summit of the seven industrialized countries.

COTT supports tourism promotion projects, including participation in tourist fairs and forums. In 1985, COTT approved an ASEAN Tourism and Information Centre for Kuala Lumpur; the office was to open in 1989.

Projects of the Committee on Transportation and Communications (COTAC), which outnumber those of the other Committees, are in the fields of civil aviation, land transportation, postal services and telecommunications, and shipping and ports. Integrated work programs have developed in all four fields.

In civil aviation, the ASEAN circle trip fare, as well as search and rescue activities involving aircraft and ships, date back to 1972. COTAC has sought to protect ASEAN stopovers on long-distance air travel involving Australia and Hongkong, on the one hand, and European destinations, on the other hand. ASEAN pressure for improved air-traffic services resulted in a new air route, approved by the International Civil Aviation Organization (ICAO) in 1985, which has eased congestion and limited delays at four of the principal ASEAN airports.

COTAC's land transportation efforts have sought to develop ferry links across various international waterways, harmonizing and standardizing driving regulations, and developing rail transport and internal waterways. Training courses, conferences, and studies have been the principal projects. Domestic driving licenses are now reciprocally accepted by the other ASEAN countries.

COTAC is responsible for the ASEAN regional satellite and ASEAN submarine cable projects; the former uses the Indonesian domestic satellite, the latter is completed but will be upgraded to an optical-fiber system in the 1990s. In 1986, the ASEAN Cableship Private Ltd. was incorporated in Singapore to handle maintenance of the submarine cable. In addition, COTAC has developed a television exchange program and a framework for avoiding radio-frequency jamming at border areas. Postal cooperation has involved exchanges and training of postal officials as well as letter-writing contests and stamp exhibitions; a second-class airmail rate has been accepted bilaterally between some ASEAN countries.

COTAC's shipping and ports program has helped to develop fully containerized ports through various training programs. An ASEAN liner service is under study through SEATAC.

The Committee on Culture and Information (COCI) handles projects in four major media: visual arts; performing arts; literary works and ASEAN studies; and communication media. Projects include exhibitions and festivals.

The Committee on Social Development (COSD) has five subsidiary bodies to supervise projects on health and nutrition, labor affairs, population, women's programs, and youth programs. Most projects involve research and training.

The ASEAN Senior Officials on Drug Matters (ASOD) coordinates cooperation in substance abuse and narcotics control. In 1980, four facilities began: the Training Center for Drug Enforcement Officers (Chiang Mai); the Training Center for Preventive Drug Education (Quezon City); the Training Center for Law Enforcement (Bangkok); and the Training Centre for Treatment and Rehabilitation (Kuala Lumpur).

The Committee on Science and Technology (COST) is responsible for projects in food development, energy and natural resources development, manufacturing industry development, and science and technology infrastructure. Most activities involve applied research. Its publication, the *Journal of Science and Technology,* began in 1984.

Many projects designate a particular country as the lead country or establish centers of excellence in one or more of the member countries. For this reason, most ASEAN projects operate outside the Secretariat, and some are run by the National Secretariats apart from the various committees. In 1973, for example, the Singapore ASEAN Secretariat set up an ASEAN training awards program in which students from other ASEAN countries pursue courses of study at Singapore educational and training institutions with costs absorbed by the Singapore ASEAN national budget. By 1986, some 700 trainees had taken advantage of this program, which offered 123 courses of study.

Influence on Other Organizations

ASEAN has served as a forum to plan joint policies with regard to other international organizations. The International Labor Organization (ILO), for example, has supported the ASEAN Labor Ministers' Meeting since 1984 for the ASEAN Program on Industrial Relations and Labor Studies (APIRLAS), which consists of about two symposia and six study teams each year.

Within Asia, ASEAN served as the catalyst for the formation of other organizations. Many nongovernmental organizations have taken on an ASEAN label; most are not connected with ASEAN, but some are formally affiliated. The procedure for obtaining recognition is to apply to the Secretariat, which has the power to designate an organization as an Affiliated Organization. An Affiliated Organization can then display the ASEAN logo, use Secretariat facilities for meetings, and submit proposals to the appropriate ASEAN committee, which in turn can facilitate external funding. Thus far, thirty-one organizations have been so designated. ASEAN has encouraged fifteen industry clubs to pursue plans for the AICs.

Business executives in external countries have organized various meetings with their ASEAN counterparts over the years. These include the ASEAN–Australia Business Council, ASEAN–Canada Business Council, ASEAN–EC Business Council, ASEAN–United States Business Council, and many others.

Two related intergovernmental organizations are outside the framework of ASEAN. Although the ASEAN Inter-Parliamentary Organization (AIPO) and the Meeting of the Chiefs of National Police of ASEAN Countries (ASEANAPOL) have asked ASEAN to be recognized as a part of the formal structure of the organization, they remain institutionally separate.

ASEAN INTER-PARLIAMENTARY ORGANIZATION (AIPO)[4]

Each year ASEAN legislators attend meetings of the Inter-Parliamentary Union (IPU). For many years ASEAN parliamentarians met together informally at IPU meetings. During August 1973, Malaysian legislators went to Indonesia in the first of a series of bilateral exchange visits, and the idea for an ASEAN parliamentary organization grew out of these visits. Indonesia hosted an ASEAN Inter-Parliamentary Meeting on January 8–11, 1975. An ASEAN Inter-Parliamentary Conference was then held during August 1975, but there was no legislature in the Philippines, which was under martial law. Shortly after an interim Philippine legislature was formed, a meeting convened in Manila on September 2, 1977, when Statutes of the ASEAN Inter-Parliamentary Organization were adopted. Known as the Manila Declaration, the Statutes state four aims of the organization:

(1) to promote closer inter-parliamentary cooperation among the parliaments

of ASEAN member countries and closer contacts and understanding among their members; (2) to facilitate the achievement of the goal of . . . ASEAN; (3) to study, discuss and suggest solutions to problems of common interest; (4) to keep all the AIPO member Parliaments informed of steps taken and progress achieved by each Parliament in realization of the aims and purposes of the AIPO (Article 2).

The General Assembly, the plenary organ, meets each year for about a week (see Fig. 7.7). AIPO limits attendance to fifteen members from each national parliament. The Working Committee meets twice each year in the same country as the forthcoming General Assembly; no more than five parliamentarians are chosen by each country to serve on the body. A Working Committee sets the agenda for the General Assembly, makes recommendations, and drafts resolutions for the consideration of the General Assembly.

Indonesia, the Philippines, and Thailand have offered to provide a central office. For the present, the host country for the General Assembly establishes a secretariat; the Speaker of the host parliament is the President of the General Assembly, and the host country selects a nonparliamentarian to be the Secretary-General for that year.

Inasmuch as the organization is an outgrowth of ASEAN, the same countries are members (see Table 7.1). After sending an Observer to the General Assembly in 1983, Brunei joined in 1984, though it is unable to participate in full since it does not have a legislature. Parliaments hosting the General Assembly may invite observers from countries that enjoy diplomatic recognition by all six ASEAN countries. Observers thus far have come from Australia, Canada, Japan, and South Korea. AIPO meeting expenses are borne by the host parliament. National parliaments defray expenses for their own delegates.

The EC Parliament is a formal Dialogue partner with AIPO, an arrangement established in 1979. Special AIPO sessions with the EC

Figure 7.7
Organization of the ASEAN Inter-Parliamentary Organization

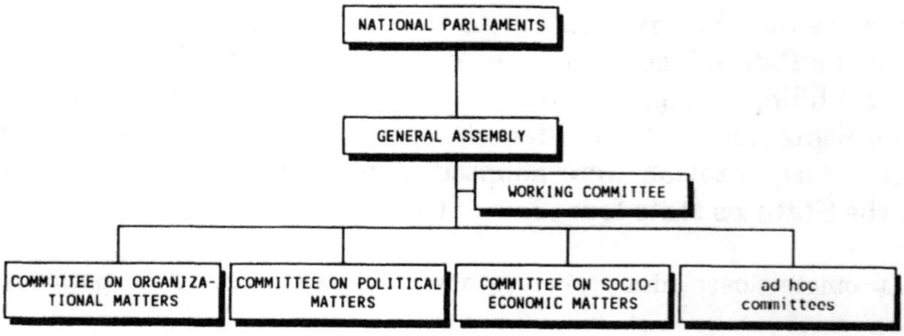

Parliament occur annually, alternating between Strasbourg and the venue of AIPO's General Assembly. A Panel Dialogue took place with members of Japan's Diet for the first time in 1984.

The main task of AIPO is to facilitate the implementation of ASEAN decisions into the law of the member countries, but discussions sometimes cover other topics. AIPO's Committee on Organizational Matters handles exchange visits of parliamentarians, and has supported conferences and study tours on population, resources, and development. Exchange visits have been conducted with parliamentarians from Australia, Canada, the EC, Japan, and South Korea. The Committee on Political Matters has commented on problems in Afghanistan, Cambodia, and Palestine. The Committee on Socio-Economic Matters has urged tighter enforcement of drug-traffic laws, rural youth training, programs for the elderly, dialogues on resources and population problems, greater access to markets in the EC, more intra-ASEAN trade, tourism development, wildlife and environmental protection, and studies of labor resources in the region.

MEETING OF THE CHIEFS OF NATIONAL POLICE OF THE ASEAN COUNTRIES (ASEANAPOL)[5]

Criminal activity, particularly in regard to narcotics traffic, is not merely a national or bilateral problem. Drug merchants, for example, go from one country to a second country to drop merchandise for reshipment to a third country. For many years, Asian chiefs of police have met informally at meetings of the International Association of Chiefs of Police (IACP) and of the International Criminal Police Organization (INTERPOL), but the critical needs of the region required more direct contact than through yearly conferences in distant capitals.

A series of bilateral arrangements, notably between Indonesia and the Philippines, had been operating prior to the 1980s, when the use of countries as transit points for drug traffic became more prevalent. Accordingly, Lieutenant General Fidel Ramos, Director General of the Integrated National Police of the Philippines, invited chiefs of police of the other ASEAN countries to a conference in Manila during October 1981 to discuss measures for improved regional cooperation in regard to law enforcement and crime control. The meeting approved the formation of ASEANAPOL.

The Joint Statement of October 23, 1981, established four terms of reference for ASEANAPOL:

(1) to enhance the law and order situation within each ASEAN country in cooperation with each other; (2) to foster the advancement and professional

development of persons working in the field of law enforcement and the maintenance of peace and order; (3) to foster the development of new and innovative techniques of police administration/management particularly in regard to the problems of preventing and controlling crime, maintaining order and, above all, securing justice for both the victim and the criminals; and (4) to increase public understanding of and community interest in policies and programs related to law enforcement and the other aspects of the criminal justice system.

Police chiefs are the principal delegates at the annual three-day ASEANAPOL Meeting (see Fig. 7.8). Senior officers in each delegation present country papers on specific topics in committee meetings between the opening and closing sessions. In 1985, three commissions discussed proposed collaborative arrangements of various sorts. There is no permanent central office, so each host country provides secretariat functions until the next host country forms the new sessional secretariat.

Membership parallels ASEAN (see Table 7.1). The Royal Papua New Guinea Constabulary has applied for Observer status; ASEANAPOL has deferred consideration.

There is no ASEANAPOL budget. The host country defrays secretariat costs. Each national police force pays the costs for its own participants in the annual meeting.

ASEANAPOL has reviewed the following topics over the years: counterfeiting, criminal aspects of local Communist insurgency and subversion, drug abuse and narcotics, joint border crossing and patrols, regional cooperation in crime control, refugees, and terrorism. ASEANAPOL has also discussed the establishment of information and personnel exchanges, study tours, and training programs. Information about national programs is shared, and bilateral arrangements continue.

At an informal level, the personal familiarity among those in attendance serves to facilitate effective and rapid collaborative action whenever crime crosses international borders, demonstrating the vitality of

Figure 7.8
Organization of the Meeting of the Chiefs of National Police of the ASEAN Countries

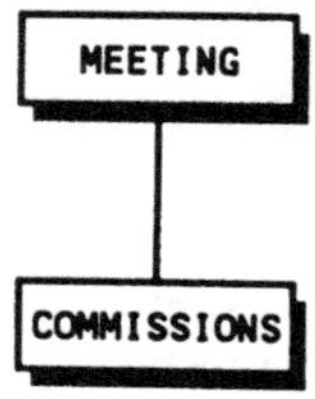

the Asian Way principle of pan-Asianism. ASEANAPOL has agreed to the exchange of information among its law enforcement officials on counterfeiting, credit card fraud, fake cashing of travelers' checks, firearms smuggling and trafficking, flight of criminals from arrest or prosecution, and illicit drug trafficking as well as assistance in investigations of such illegal activities when they cross the borders of member countries. In addition, the police chiefs have agreed in principle to extradite fugitives from justice.

SUMMARY AND CONCLUSIONS

ASA provided a structure and a framework for cooperation along entirely new lines. This type of organization did not need a budget, a headquarters, or outside funds to function. Although ASA was short-lived, ASEAN copied its example, and ASA foreign ministers agreed to continue their projects as ASEAN projects thereafter.

Maphilindo never advanced, since Malaya was intent on becoming Malaysia. In accordance with UN plebiscites, Indonesia gave up all claims to Sabah and Sarawak by 1967, when ASEAN began. The Philippine claim to Sabah was formally abandoned in 1987, when it adopted a new constitution.

Comments on ASEAN have filled more editorial columns than all other regional organizations in Asia combined. It is difficult to add to the chorus, as other voices are already so deafening. We must regard ASEAN as a modest undertaking initially. In the early years, there was no Secretariat, and the program of activities was hardly impressive. One presumptuous early observer urged ASEAN to take over the role of the former South-East Asia Treaty Organization (SEATO);[6] ASEAN leaders reacted with extreme displeasure to this suggestion, as Indonesia's initiative was in the spirit of the nonaligned movement, and the ASEAN Treaty of Amity and Cooperation specifically excludes military projects from its scope.

Nonetheless, outside influences have been important to ASEAN. The victory of socialist regimes in Indochina in 1975 triggered the Summit Conferences of 1976 and 1977, when ASEAN was revitalized. A Secretariat was then approved, and the committee structure was reorganized. ASEAN, once a project largely of the foreign ministries, became a multiministry effort. A study on possible economic measures for regional cooperation by a UN study team became a guidebook for the ASEAN Economic Ministers, to whom most of the ASEAN committees reported after 1977. Australia, Canada, the EC, Japan, New Zealand, and the United States then realized that their aid programs could be marketed as ASEAN projects more effectively than as isolated bilateral efforts. When the Cambodian War began in 1978, the foreign ministers pressured Vietnam to leave defenseless Cambodians to rule by the genocidal Pol Pot clique. ASEAN then designed a Coalition Government of Democratic Kampuchea (CGDK) so that Sihanouk could represent Cambodia in various international organs. The foreign ministers generated various peace plans, all of which were rejected by the Indochinese foreign ministers, who responded with counterproposals of their own. Indonesian diplomacy then led to an initial conference in Bogor during July 1988, in which the ASEAN states, contending Cambodian factions, Laos, and Vietnam initiated a peace process. Thus, ASEAN remains an organization with economic plans and diplomatic initiatives.

ASEAN has forged a unity out of countries that were once suspicious of each other. Its meetings are warm, consensus emerges through sophisticated diplomacy, and its statements have clout. ASEAN countries vote together as a bloc in almost every international forum. The term *ASEAN* has become a household word all over the world of international politics. Aid programs to the region and trade policies must take all the countries as a unit into account. The term *ASEAN* has been used so widely that it has become a catchphrase to refer to the six member countries without regard for the specific organization, leading to confusion in many quarters about the nature of ASEAN. Accordingly, the analysis above is based on the official record of ASEAN as an intergovernmental organization. ASEAN is an organization, after all, not a mystical concatenation of six countries, as many journalists and scholars mistakenly report.

What are the accomplishments of ASEAN in retrospect? On the political front, ASEAN should be noted more for ZOPFAN and SEANWFZ than for the checkered pressures associated with the Cambodian War, in which ASEAN abandoned the pan-Asian spirit of the Asian Way from 1978 to 1988. On the economic side, the increase in technical assistance to ASEAN is substantial. External countries realize that funds have a greater impact when distributed to a coordinated group of countries than when duplicated in bilateral aid projects. In negotiations for greater access to markets in donor countries, ASEAN has had considerable difficulty along with all Third-World countries, which generally lack leverage; by keeping negotiations on a regular basis, incremental gains have occurred, but without fanfare.

ASEAN's self-help projects in the economic realm are notable – truly Asian solutions to Asian problems. The modest but useful monetary swap arrangement and the rice and petroleum emergency programs have never received the favorable comment that they deserve. The industrial complementation scheme, industrial projects, and joint-venture projects have been highly touted as providing opportunities for the region to gain new industries in one country without having to spend vast sums on facilities that might eventually be duplicated in another member country. But implementation of these schemes was delayed for over a decade because governments encouraged undercapitalized, indigenous industries to compete with multinational corporations. Moreover, such countries as Indonesia, the Philippines, and Thailand are large enough in population to have industries of their own in nearly every economic sector; in the long run, they do not need to pool resources to opt for regionally based industries, unlike the fate of impoverished African countries or ministates in the Caribbean and South Pacific. Most AIPs were nonstarters, since they could not get external financing, with foreign control limited to no more than 49 percent of their assets. While the AIPs appeared to be bogged down, AICs were pursued. An automotive complementation package was agreed upon, but when several countries were attracted by immediate joint-venture prospects in the private sector with Japanese financing and technology, and preferential AIC market access was only to last at best for three years, AICs were shelved. At this point ASEAN hit upon the flexibility of AIJVs, in which two or three countries are free to negotiate as much as 60 percent private-sector participation. In 1987, Japan's ASEAN development fund promised $2 billion to support AIJVs and other private-sector loans. AIJVs, as a result, can move as rapidly down the pipeline today as private-sector interests permit.

An ASEAN customs union or common market is a long way off. Although PTA would wreak very little havoc if it were in full operation, there is little incentive to use a MOP of 25 percent on a 40 percent item (to derive a mere 10 percent tariff reduction), for example. Singapore has opted for free trade with or without ASEAN, the Philippines has long supported a common market, but Brunei, Indonesia, and Thailand feel that they need more time to develop infant industries. Even this reluctance appears now to be crumbling: voices of caution are being upstaged by a younger generation of economists, who favor a more intense ASEAN economic community, basing their judgment on solid economic considerations. Most ASEAN countries prefer to sell to the First World to obtain foreign exchange, and most of their trade is of this sort, so the reluctance to increase intra-ASEAN trade is understandable. Even so, intra-Asean trade has skyrocketed: only one-tenth in 1967, it comprises nearly one-fourth of the trade volume of ASEAN countries, mostly due to sales of food and petroleum.[7] The spirit of ASEAN cooperation, based as it is on Asian Way consensus building, has worked to promote increased trade where complicated negotiations have dithered. The goal by 1992 is to have half of all member country trade under PTA. NTBs, subject to a standstill in 1987, are to be rolled back as well.

The ASEAN "we-feeling," unmatched elsewhere around the Third

World, expects peace and uses peaceful methods to resolve conflicts. ASEAN's example leads the way for other groups of countries in the world.

AIPO, similar to the Asian-Pacific Parliamentarians' Union (APPU) in several ways, limits its attention primarily to issues in Southeast Asia. Since chief executives appoint so many of the delegates, we may view AIPO as a kind of end-run by the heads of state around foreign ministers, who dominate ASEAN. Thus, AIPO is a club for parliamentarians who seek to goad the foreign ministries.

Crime crosses international borders. Cooperation in pursuing criminals requires officials in different countries to know each other personally. ASEANAPOL makes for more efficient police activities and enables technicians to discuss more efficient methods of crime control, while higher-level officials develop working relationships that transcend national parochialisms.

In all, ASEAN is the most impressive regional organization in Asia today. The thesis that regional cooperation has been ASEANized is presented in Chapter 14.

NOTES

1. For references to ASA documents, see Michael Haas, *Basic Documents of Asian Regional Organizations* (Dobbs Ferry, NY: Oceana Publications, 1979), vol. 6, pp. 287–88. For a bibliography of secondary sources on all organizations described in this chapter, see pp. 246–86.

2. For references to Maphilindo documents, see Michael Haas, *Basic Documents of Asian Regional Organizations* (Dobbs Ferry, NY: Oceana Publications, 1979), vol. 6, p. 289.

3. For references to ASEAN documents, see Michael Haas, *Basic Documents of Asian Regional Organizations* (Dobbs Ferry, NY: Oceana Publications, 1979), vol. 6, pp. 290–300.

4. For references to AIPO documents, see ASEAN Inter-Parliamentary Organization, *First General Assembly: Joint Communiqué* (Jakarta, January 8–11, 1975) and later communiqués issued by AIPO countries each year in alphabetical rotation.

5. For references to ASEANAPOL documents, see national police organizations in ASEAN member countries. Proceedings are confidential.

6. Bernard K. Gordon, *The Dimensions of Conflict in Southeast Asia* (Englewood Cliffs, NJ: Prentice-Hall, 1966). The farewell address of the final SGATO Secretary-General, as noted in Chapter 3, was pointedly ignored.

7. One-fifth of ASEAN trade is with EC, another fifth with Japan, and yet another fifth with the United States.

8 CLONES OF ASEAN IN SOUTHEAST ASIA

Four organizations in Southeast Asia resulted neither from the Ministerial Conference for the Economic Development of Southeast Asia (SEAMCED) nor the Association of South East Asian Nations (ASEAN). The most prominent is the Southeast Asian Ministers of Education Organization (SEAMEO). A related effort is the now-defunct Regional Institute of Higher Education and Development (RIHED). The Tripartite Council (TC), composed of three ASEAN members, is a consultative arrangement related to maritime traffic in the straits of Malacca and Singapore. These three largely have ASEAN country membership. The fourth organization, the Conference of the Foreign Ministers of Kampuchea, Laos, and Vietnam, has emulated ASEAN in many ways.

SOUTHEAST ASIAN MINISTERS OF EDUCATION ORGANIZATION (SEAMEO)[1]

Economic development requires human capital, so the shift from agriculture to industry means that workers must be trained for new occupations. Therefore, the role of education is central to development. About one-third of the national budgets within Southeast Asia is devoted to education, and the populations are eager for education to advance themselves. No single country has the expertise to modernize its own educational system in all fields required for development, however, so centers of excellence with programs of training and research in particular fields underlie the logic of SEAMEO.

During 1965, the U.S. military contribution to Vietnam escalated considerably. To balance the military aid effort, President Lyndon Johnson pledged $1 billion to support efforts toward regional development and dispatched former World Bank President Eugene Black to Southeast Asia as his Special Representative. Meanwhile, in November 1965, Johnson announced support for programs in international education.

The UN Educational, Scientific, and Cultural Organization (UNESCO), having held an initial Conference of Asian Ministers of Education and Ministers Responsible for Economic Planning in 1957, decided to reconvene the conference in November 1965. Inasmuch as the agenda was set months before the latest U.S. initiatives, the Thai Minister of Education invited Southeast Asian delegates to stay after the meeting to discuss possibilities for regional cooperation. This meeting was the first of what later was called the Southeast Asian Ministers of Education Council (SEAMEC). SEAMEC met with Black, who was enthusiastic about the concept of a regional education organization; after he returned to Washington, the U.S. Agency for International Development (USAID) made plans to finance the ideas of SEAMEC.

An Interim Secretariat, called the Southeast Asian Ministers of Education Secretariat (SEAMES), was set up within the Thai ministry of education in early 1966 to develop and coordinate proposals for regional centers. An initial SEAMES discussion paper listed fifteen possible projects. Teams of experts from the various Southeast Asian countries refined the ideas and submitted them to a technical workshop during July 1966. A select committee of undersecretaries of education screened the proposals in October, and in November 1966 SEAMEC endorsed the concept of an organization composed of at least four centers of excellence in various fields of education in accordance with the Asian Way principle of Asian solutions to Asian problems.

At the third SEAMEC conference, held in Singapore on February 6–8, 1968, a Charter was signed. The new body was named the Southeast Asian Ministers of Education Organization (SEAMEO).

The Charter states that the purpose of the organization is "to promote cooperation . . . through education, science and culture in order to further respect for justice, for the rule of law and for the human rights and fundamental freedoms which are the birthrights of the peoples of the world" (Article 1). Four functions are specified:

(a) collaborate in the work of advancing the mutual knowledge and understanding of the peoples in Southeast Asia as well as the rest of the world; (b) promote and collaborate . . . in joint projects and programs of mutual benefit concerning education, science and culture and assist the members in the development of educational activities; (c) maintain, increase and diffuse knowledge; (d) assist in articulating education to the economic and social goals in the individual member States. (Article 1)

SEAMEC, the plenary organ of SEAMEO, has annual meetings lasting about five days, although it has occasional extraordinary sessions (see Fig. 8.1). SEAMEC decides matters of general policy, appoints the SEAMES Director, approves the budget for SEAMES, and receives annual reports from the various SEAMEO centers and projects.

In order to screen technical issues on SEAMEC's agenda, a Project Directors/High Officials Meeting (PDM) was held from 1967 to 1977. The "high officials" were mostly education undersecretaries. In 1978, the High Officials Meeting (HOM) superseded the PDM; it holds annual week-long sessions. In 1971, after SEAMEC met, the Center Directors Meeting (CDM) was first held to resolve problems of implementation and coordination.

SEAMES became an independent office in 1968 and moved to the Darakarn Building in Bangkok. SEAMES's Director has a major responsibility in fund-raising (see Fig. 8.2). In 1972, the position of Deputy Director was added, primarily to assist in administrative coordination.

Since SEAMES has ex officio membership in SEAMEC, and the SEAMES Director is an ex officio member of the governing boards of all centers and projects, SEAMES staff–mostly from the Program Division–attend the CDM, the HOM, and meetings of Governing Boards of the various regional centers.

Figure 8.1
Organization of the Southeast Asian Ministers of Education Organization

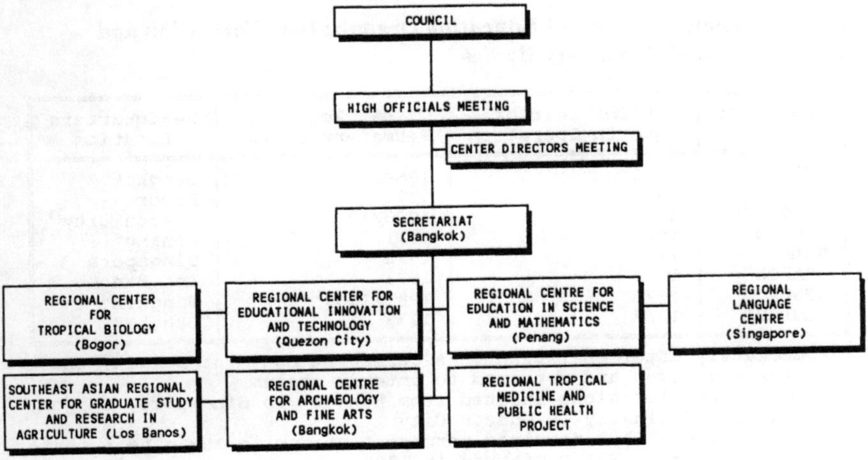

Figure 8.2
Organization of the Southeast Asian Ministers of Education Secretariat

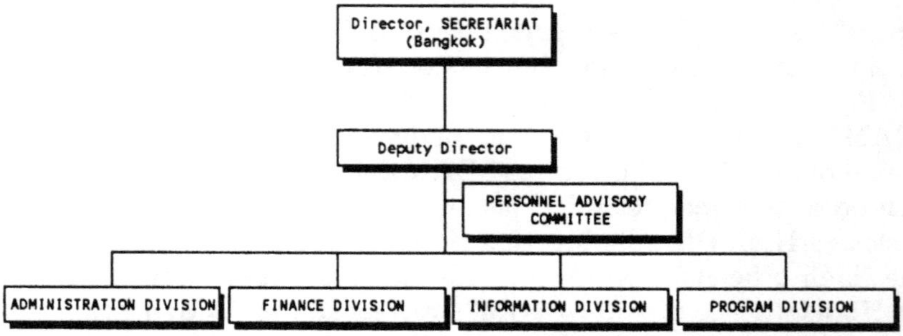

SEAMEO's six centers and one project, described below, are distributed among the member countries on the basis of the Asian Way principle of equality. Each center and project began on an interim basis, then acquired permanent status when SEAMEC approved its initial Enabling Instrument (see Table 8.1).

The countries involved in the first SEAMEC subsequently joined in 1968 (see Table 8.2). Two countries joined later – the Khmer Republic in 1971 and Brunei in 1984. SEAMEO liaison with each member country operates through National Committees of experts. National Centers host seminars and provide liaison with each SEAMEO regional center.

Associate Membership, designed in 1972 to attract Japan to participate, encouraged Australia, Canada, France, and New Zealand to join.

Table 8.1
Southeast Asian Ministers of Education Organization: Formation and Transformation of Subsidiary Bodies

Center or Project	First Year of Interim Operation	Year Acquired Permanent Status	Headquarters Location
SEAMES	1966	1968	Bangkok
BIOTROP	1968	1973	Bogor
INNOTECH	1970	1975/1980[a]	Quezon City[b]
RECSAM	1968	1971	Penang
RELC	1968	1972	Singapore
SEARCA	1967	1971	Los Banos
SPAFA	1978	1981/1987[c]	Bangkok[d]
TROPMED	1967	1973	Bangkok

[a]Immediately after operating on a permanent basis at Saigon, the Center was moved and returned to interim status
[b]Headquarters locations shifted from Bangkok to Singapore, Saigon, Bangkok, and finally to Quezon City
[c]As a Project, SPAFA acquired permanent status in 1981; as a center, permanent status was conferred in 1987
[d]On an interim basis an office opened in Phnom Penh briefly in 1975

Table 8.2
Southeast Asian Ministers of Education Organization: Membership and SEAMES Assessments

Year Joined	Member Countries	Assessment (1985)
1968	Indonesia	25.00%
	Laos (i 1975-)	0.22
	Malaysia	19.51
	Philippines	21.39
	Singapore	8.84
	Thailand	20.28
	Vietnam (i 1975-79, w 1980)[a]	
1971	Cambodia (i 1975-80)[b]	0.82
1973	Australia (a)	
1974	France (a)	
	New Zealand (a)	
1984	Association of Canadian Community Colleges (aa)	
	Brunei	3.94
1988	Canada (a)	
Totals	9-1=8 Members 4 Associate Members 1 Affiliate Member	$362,421

[a]Joined as Republic of Vietnam
[b]Joined as Khmer Republic
Key: a = Associate Member
aa = Affiliate Member
i = inactive
w = withdrew

Affiliate Membership, established in 1983, attracted the Association of Canadian Community Colleges (ACCC).

The Khmer Republic (later named Democratic Kampuchea), Laos, and South Vietnam were inactive after 1975. SEAMEC decided in 1976 no new members could join until at least one of these states resumed participation. In 1980, the Embassy of Vietnam in Manila sent a representative to the Governing Board of the Southeast Asian Regional Center for Graduate Study and Research in Agriculture (SEARCA); when he encountered a representative of Democratic Kampuchea (the Pol Pot regime just driven out of Phnom Penh by the Vietnamese army) at the meeting, the result was that Vietnam withdrew from SEAMEO. The Coalition Government of Democratic Kampuchea (CGDK) has represented Cambodia since 1982.

Members are eligible to participate in the various centers and projects, though they do not always do so. Singapore first participated in SEARCA in 1974, and it withdrew from the Regional Tropical Medicine and Public Health Project (TROPMED) in 1976. Brunei has not yet fully participated in all SEAMEO programs. Nonmember countries have also participated. Japan and West Germany have been Observers at SEAMEC. Some Regional Center for Tropical Biology (BIOTROP) courses have been held in Japan. Regional Center for Educational Innovation and Technology (INNOTECH) projects have had sites in Bangladesh, Liberia, and Jamaica. TROPMED conferences have been convened in Japan and South Korea. Participants have come from many non-SEAMEO countries in accordance with the Asian Way principle of pan-Asianism.

Budgets have four categories: Capital Funds (for buildings), Operating Funds (for staff and administrative services), Special Funds (for participants), and Other Funds (for externally funded research projects and expert assistance). Initial Capital Costs for SEAMES were from Thai sources. The Ford Foundation defrayed half of the start-up Operating Costs, with a matching amount from member countries. Contributions of members, based on relative capital subscriptions to the Asian Development Bank (ADB), support Operating Costs (Table 8.2). Inactive Cambodia and Laos are currently exempted from contributions. Thailand makes additional donations from interest on bank deposits. Neither Associate nor Affiliate Members contribute to the SEAMES budget; they provide Other Funds for research and training at the centers and projects. China, Japan, the Netherlands, the United Kingdom, the United States, and West Germany also donate Other Funds.

USAID provided matching amounts for each center through three phases of development: project development planning, interim operation, and the first five years of permanent operation. Host countries are now primarily responsible for financing SEAMEO centers and projects. SEAMEO is one of the best financed Asian regional organizations today (see Table 8.3). The organization's assets were $32.29 million as of mid-1986. Capital assets are estimated at $24.12 million.

In 1971, an effort was made to establish a SEAMEO Endowment Fund and a SEAMEO Educational Development Fund (SEDF) to support Special Funds. In 1973, SEAMEO Educational Development bonds were offered for sale, but only two countries subscribed. By the end of the 1970s, SEAMES consolidated the Laotian and Thai bond sales into SEDF, which in 1984–85 had $369,079.

Out of the dozen or so proposals presented to SEAMEC in 1966 and 1967, five regional centers and one regional project were approved (see Table 8.1). The SEAMEO Centre for Archaeology and Fine Arts (SPAFA) started as the second Regional Project in 1978, then became the sixth Regional Center in 1986, and was given permanent status in 1987. In 1988, Brunei offered to host a seventh Regional Center, to focus on vocational education; this proposal is under study.

Each center and project integrates three activities: personnel development (training, exchange of experts, and study visits), research and

Table 8.3
Southeast Asian Ministers of Education Organization: Budgets of Subsidiary Bodies

Center or Project	Budget (1985)
SEAMES	$ 362,421
BIOTROP	1,107,440
INNOTECH	3,495,158
RECSAM	1,312,014
RELC	1,926,720
SEARCA	1,289,309
SPAFA	238,687
TROPMED	6,295,513[a]
Totals	$16,027,262

[a]Includes National Centers

development (from applied research to the development of curriculum materials), and information dissemination (mainly publications). SEAMES also provides funds for staff development (supporting SEAMEO professionals who study at institutions of Associate Members to upgrade their skills and enrich their experiences).

In 1985, SEAMES's Program Division began to coordinate the Pilot Project on Integrated Community-Based Human Resources Development by forming development service teams from some of SEAMEO's 13,000 graduates, who in turn drew up development programs at specific sites. SEAMEO centers in each country select pilot sites, mostly in rural areas; community centers are then developed as focal points for integrating developmental activities.

SEAMEO Regional Center for Tropical Biology (BIOTROP)

Environmental problems in Southeast Asia are a function of natural disasters, soil erosion, pestilence, and pollution, as well as the lack of adequate electrical power, irrigation, flood control, and other facilities. Timber exploited from forests can cause soil erosion and pollution of streams; an ecosystem of animals and plants can be lost thereby. The objective of BIOTROP is to work toward the solution of biologically rooted impediments to development and environmental imbalances caused by careless practices in the pursuit of economic development.

Established by SEAMEC on February 6, 1968, as the Regional Center for Training, Research and Post-Graduate Study in Tropical Biology, BIOTROP's name changed in 1969 to the Regional Center for Tropical Biology. Originally, it was hoped that BIOTROP would be fused with a national facility, and BIOTROP was initially grafted onto the

National Biological Institute at Bogor on the grounds of the botanic gardens not far from the Agriculture University of Indonesia. When this arrangement did not work out, the Asian Way principle of separating politics from implementation meant that in 1972 BIOTROP became independent and moved to Tajur, Bogor.

According to its Enabling Instrument, BIOTROP is "to assist the Member States to identify biological problems the solution of which will enhance economic development in their respective countries" (Section II). But the emphasis is more on biology than on economics.

BIOTROP is supervised by a Governing Board (an Advisory Council until 1971), which meets for five-day sessions each year (see Fig. 8.3). The Director is aided by a Deputy Director for Administration and Finance and a Deputy Director for Programs.

The Tropical Aquatic Biology Program looks at problems of pollution in coral reefs, mangroves, and open waters. The Tropical Forest Biology Program assesses how to repair damage on ecosystems due to excessive logging. The Tropical Agricultural Pest Biology Program determines how best to control insects, rodents, and weeds that are responsible for the transmission of diseases to animals, crops, and humans. Research consists of surveys of field conditions and experimental testing. Each research program has training courses, from six weeks to ten months, and sponsors conferences and seminars. There is one major scientific meeting each year.

SEAMEO Regional Center for Educational Innovation and Technology (INNOTECH)

Educational systems in Southeast Asia in the 1960s still followed traditional approaches. Western notions of the "educated gentleman" informed the role of schools in colonial administrations. Since a generalist is neither an entrepreneur nor a technical specialist, two roles needed in developing countries, exigencies of development were often at odds with bureaucrats in ministries of education. Meanwhile, Southeast Asian countries were unable to afford the conventional model of education from developed countries in which students sit at desks in classrooms, have textbooks and various supplies, and use a library in each school. As an Asian solution to an Asian problem, INNOTECH was set up to expose educational administrators and technologists to new possibilities in adapting education to demands for economic and social development, using a systems approach in training a cadre of educational administrators and specialists to restructure educational systems in Southeast Asia in order to serve the needs of the next generation better.

In 1967, SEAMEC advocated combining separate proposals for a

Figure 8.3
Organization of the SEAMEO Regional Center for Tropical Biology

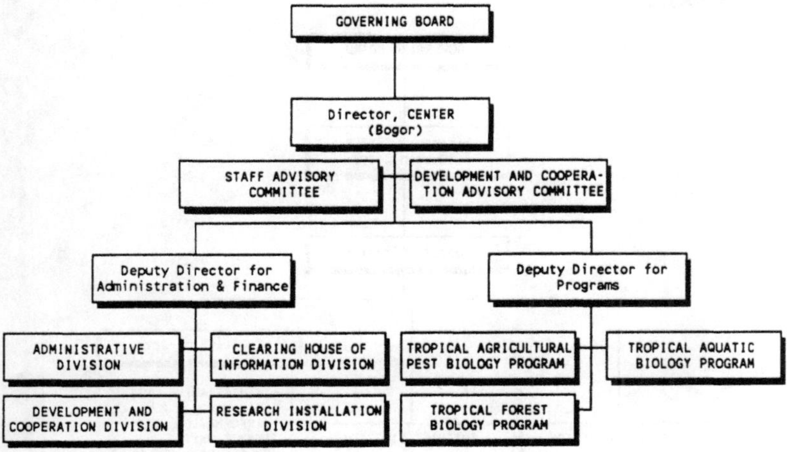

book development center, an educational radio and television institute, and an audiovisual education center into a single facility. Following a Specialists Meeting on Educational Innovation and Technology in Pago Pago, American Samoa, during 1968, Vietnam drafted a proposal, and SEAMEC approved the organization's framework in January 1970. INNOTECH's Enabling Instrument, adopted on February 7, 1975, states two objectives: to "help solve common problems in the Region and assist Member States in the identification of solutions to their individual educational problems" (Section II).

INNOTECH began operation with an interim office in Bangkok because Saigon was preparing a host facility in early 1970. In August 1970, INNOTECH moved to Singapore until the permanent facilities in Vietnam were ready for occupancy. In 1973, INNOTECH moved to Saigon, but in 1975, the political situation was in flux, so the center returned to Bangkok. In 1976, the Philippines offered a new home for INNOTECH, and in 1980, SEAMEC decided to make the Philippines the permanent host country.

INNOTECH is under the supervision of a Governing Board, which meets for four days each year (see Fig. 8.4). Starting in 1981, biennial seminars of experts have reviewed the work program. INNOTECH is administered by a Director. The Deputy Director supervises the Research Division and the Training Division. The Assistant Director manages six support units.

Initially, INNOTECH operated one-month seminars for senior officials from ministries of education and three-month training courses

Figure 8.4
Organization of the SEAMEO Regional Center for Educational Innovation and Technology

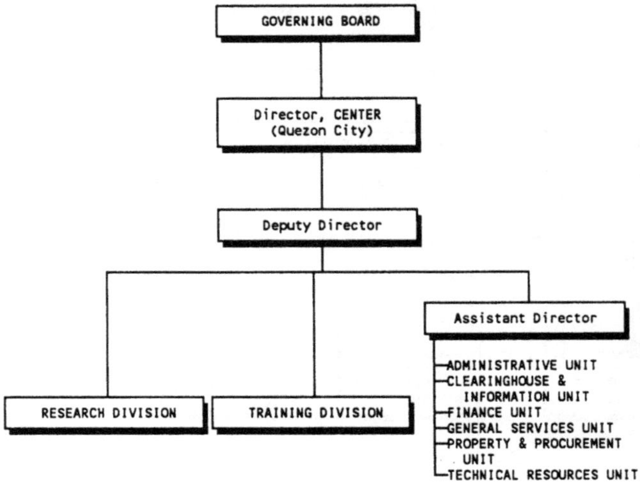

for educational managers; these were shortened by 1973. The courses seek to produce educational researchers who can plan, develop, disseminate, evaluate, implement, and manage innovative research projects.

The SEAMEO Nonformal Education Project (SNEP), operated by SEAMES from 1978 to 1983, consisted of training courses, research projects, regional seminars, personnel exchanges, and an information clearinghouse, with special emphasis on upgrading the quality of rural extension workers and vocational education trainers. The venues of each activity varied, and all SEAMEO centers handled local coordination except for INNOTECH. In 1983, in accordance with the Asian Way principle of incrementalism, SNEP activities became an INNOTECH project.

Several INNOTECH research projects have now concluded. Project Progress, the first, identified objectives at the primary level throughout the region. Project Action then surveyed means to achieve the objectives specified in Project Progress. Project Clear launched the information clearinghouse activities of INNOTECH, which involves a library, publications program, and the production of slide-tape learning resources.

Project IMPACT (Instructional Management by Parents, Community and Teachers), Project CB-BLP (Community-Based Basic Learning

Packages), and Project RIT (Reduced Instructional Time) came next. Project NTR of T (Nontraditional Roles of Teachers) developed teacher preparation packages for several nontraditional school approaches and now includes case studies for indigenous learning systems. Project DELSILIFE (Development of a Learning System for the Improvement of Life) developed a coordinated educational intervention system to improve the quality of life of the rural poor through practical learning programs. The project Using Indigenous Learning Systems to Improve the Quality of Education in Deprived Communities began in 1984. The Test Development Program, which ran from 1980 to 1982, designed tests as evaluation instruments to measure the effectiveness of previous INNOTECH research projects. The project was so successful that INNOTECH set up an Evaluation Unit, with its main project now called Test-Based Instructional Program for Basic Education.

INNOTECH is one of sixty Associate Centers in Asia that form the Asian Program of Educational Innovation for Development (APEID), a project organized by the Bangkok regional office of UNESCO. The other SEAMEO center that belongs to the APEID network is RECSAM.

SEAMEO Regional Centre for Education in Science and Mathematics (RECSAM)

Most Southeast Asian countries are abundant in natural resources, including coconuts, palm oil, rubber, timber, and tin; but these commodities are usually extracted as primary products and shipped to First-World countries for processing and finishing. Southeast Asia then imports the manufactured goods at higher prices than the primary products, due to the value added in the First World. Although Third-World countries want to process and finish their own primary products, they lack the trained personnel for the task. Education in basic science and mathematics, therefore, is essential to bring about a shift from primary to secondary industry in Southeast Asia. RECSAM, accordingly, was proposed by Malaysia at the second SEAMEC conference in 1966, then approved in February 1968. According to RECSAM's Enabling Instrument, adopted in 1971, the purpose of the center is "to assist the Member States to improve the teaching of Science and Mathematics" (Section II).

RECSAM is located in Glugor, Penang, at one end of the Malayan Teacher's College, near the Universiti Sains Malaysia. The Governing Board meets once each year for about four days. The Board appoints the Director, who heads RECSAM (see Fig. 8.5). There are two Deputy Directors, who each supervise two Assistant Directors.

Figure 8.5
Organization of the SEAMEO Regional Centre for Education in Science and Mathematics

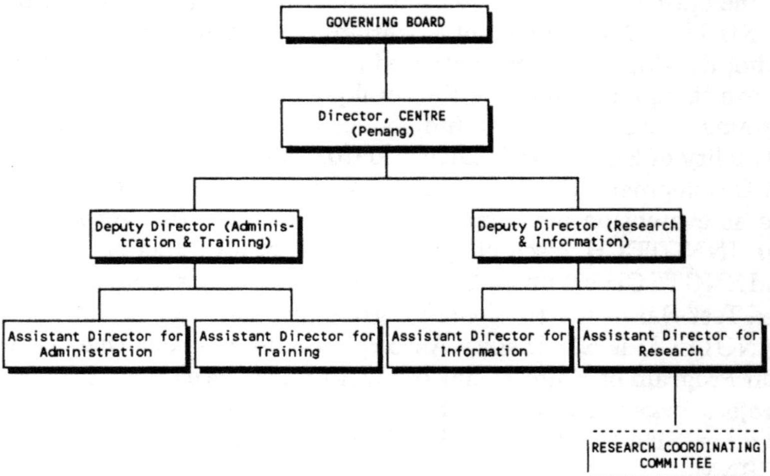

RECSAM offers three types of courses. Research and development courses focus on classroom activities and developing learning modules and equipment. Training courses have been held on audiovisual hardware and software. Diploma courses involve research projects at a field site and are for intensive study over a six-month period on teaching approaches and strategies; on learning evaluation, measurement, and remediation; and on educational technology and vocational education.

Initially, the Southeast Asian Science and Mathematics Experiment (SEASAME) brought together a science teaching prototype that combined conceptual, process, and systems approaches. SEASAME has been field tested and adopted, with appropriate modifications, in various locations. In 1985, RECSAM encouraged its course participants to embark on action research projects, focusing mostly on how to ensure that science and mathematics teaching will have the greatest impact on students and on society. The specific areas of focus are on mastery of classroom teaching, the role of calculators and computers, the use of science learning in everyday life, and on the development of scientific attitudes.

RECSAM has also conducted about four one-week conferences, seminars, and workshops each year. The publications program converts the various project results into instructional materials, reference guides, technical reports, and training manuals. In addition, RECSAM publishes the semiannual *Journal of Science and Mathematics Education in Southeast Asia.*

SEAMEO Regional Language Centre (RELC)

Literacy must increase for a country to develop economically and socially. Southeast Asian countries have a variety of tongues; each ethnic group in multiracial societies of the region has a different language, and there are problems in developing national languages. RELC exists to service these kinds of problems and needs.

Although initially called the Regional English Language Centre, with a mandate to improve the teaching of English as a second or foreign language, RELC dropped the word "English" from its name in 1977, retaining the original acronym, RELC. According to the Enabling Instrument, approved on January 27, 1972, RELC's aim is "to assist the Member States to improve the teaching of English and other languages" (Section II), so the retitling was an Asian solution to an Asian problem that had been anticipated in the first place, and RELC now promotes effective teaching of national and international languages.

The Governing Board meets for about three days each year. The Director and Deputy Director divide the work into three sets of tasks: academic and professional services, administrative services, and special services, which in turn are supervised by several committees (see Fig. 8.6).

After a decade of upgrading skills of English-language teachers in the region, RELC began to issue Diplomas for advanced training in linguistics. In 1982, RELC began a course program of up to two years leading to the Ph.D. in Applied Linguistics. The National University of Singapore was to confer the M.A. and Ph.D. degrees, but in 1987 the Advanced Diploma and Ph.D. programs were discontinued; the remaining M.A. program is only for sponsored or private candidates. RELC now offers a Diploma in Applied Linguistics and a Diploma in Teaching of English to Speakers of Other Languages.

RELC has a Language Teaching Institute for those seeking to improve their English-language abilities. The program is run independently and is not integrated into RELC's SEAMEO projects.

RELC has organized colloquia, forums, public lectures, and staff seminars over the years. Each year a regional seminar devotes major attention to problems, solutions, and strategies for implementing language policies in the countries of the region. RELC is also a center for research activity, including staff research, student research, and research by distinguished scholars. The *RELC Journal* is a major journal in the field of applied linguistics.

Figure 8.6
Organization of the SEAMEO Regional Language Centre

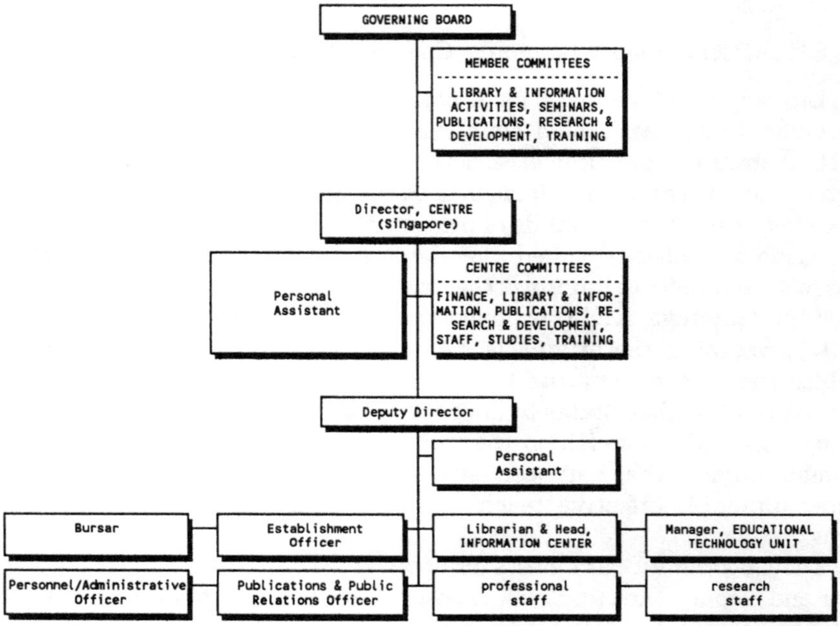

SEAMEO Southeast Asian Regional Center for Graduate Study and Research in Agriculture (SEARCA)

Some 70 percent of Southeast Asian workers depend on agriculture for their livelihood, although agriculture constitutes from 30 to 60 percent of the GNP of these countries, according to the Asian Agriculture Survey of the ADB. Many peasants are undernourished, so agricultural productivity is an important priority for social progress. Farmers need to be better informed on modern farming methods, and the food must have adequate nutritional content.

SEARCA emerged from a Philippine initiative. The Agricultural Advisory Council (AAC) approved the idea of SEARCA in June 1967, an Interim Project Office was at the Los Banos campus of the University of the Philippines in July 1967 and SEAMEC conferred permanent status to SEARCA in January 1971.

The Enabling Instrument, adopted on January 25, 1973, states that SEARCA is "to provide . . . high-quality graduate education and training in agriculture, promote, undertake and coordinate research programs related to the needs and problems of the region, and disseminate the findings of agricultural research and experimentation" (Article I).

ACC, renamed the Agricultural Governing Board in 1971 and the Governing Board in 1977, meets once each year for a three-day session (see Fig. 8.7). The Executive Committee meets every so often to approve personnel appointments and other matters that require immediate decisions while the Governing Board is not in session.

A Director heads the center. Deputy Directors are in charge of administrative services and graduate education and training. The Director has direct responsibility for research and development and special projects.

The Special Projects Division handles an ongoing project, the Agricultural Information Network for Southeast Asia (AgInfoNet-SEA), related computer services, and any short-term projects that may arise. AgInfoNet-SEA organizes, stores, retrieves, and exchanges information about published and unpublished studies on research in agribusiness, biotechnology in agriculture, farming systems, integrated pest management, post-harvest technology, and research and extension management.

In 1969, subcenters were proposed for each member country. The

Figure 8.7
Organization of the SEAMEO Southeast Asian Regional Center for Graduate Study and Research in Agriculture

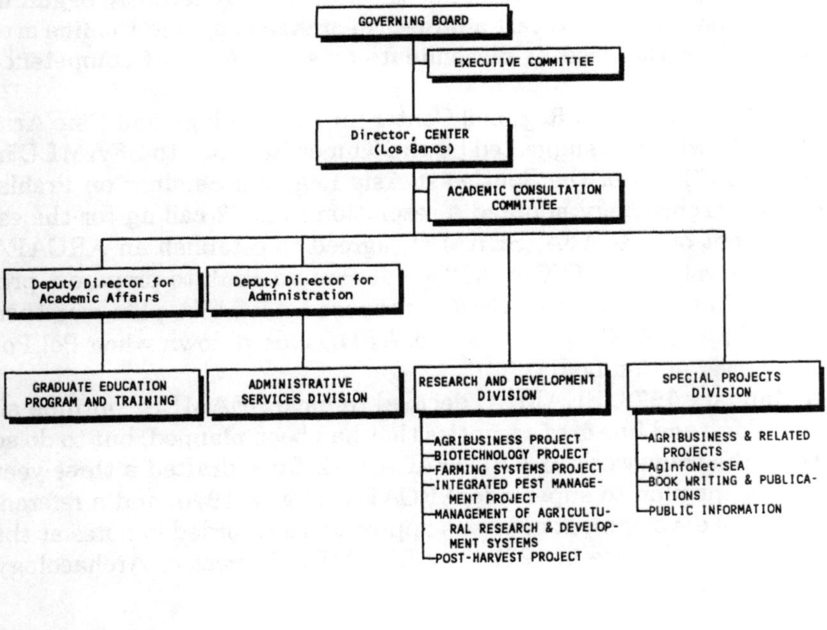

Philippines and Thailand were in favor of the idea, and Vietnam offered to sponsor a tropical veterinary science subcenter, but the other countries demurred, and the idea was dropped in accordance with the Asian Way principle of consensus decision making.

SEARCA has established several extension sites, called Social Laboratories. In earlier years, these were at various locations in the Philippines; SEARCA phased out its participation as the communities developed. Currently, Nakorn Si Thammarat Agricultural College operates six sites in southern Thailand under the framework of SEARCA.

SEARCA provides scholarships for M.S. and Ph.D. candidates. Most degrees have been awarded by the University of the Philippines at Los Banos, although, since 1981, scholarships have been offered at Central Luzon State University, the Philippines; Kasetsart University, Thailand; and Universiti Pertanian, Malaysia. In 1988, SEARCA began to organize a consortium of sixty-nine universities so that a graduate student enrolled in one institution can have access to courses at other institutions, thereby rationalizing exchange and visiting professorship arrangements. There are also short courses, and about six seminars and workshops per year. SEARCA has completed more than fifty research and development projects.

SEAMEO Regional Centre for Archaeology and Fine Arts (SPAFA)

The civilizations of Southeast Asia are quite fascinating, but work to collect artifacts from the ground or the sea has only recently begun in earnest. The decision to start a project in archaeology and the fine arts was based on the need to disseminate existing levels of competence more widely.

The idea of an Asian Regional Center for Archaeology and Fine Arts (ARCAFA) was first suggested by the Khmer Republic to SEAMEC in January 1971. After the Southeast Asia Regional Seminar on Prehistory and Archaeology adopted a resolution in 1972 calling for the establishment of ARCAFA, SEAMEC agreed to establish an ARCAFA Project Development Office (APDO) at Phnom Penh to prepare a program for implementation. APDO's proposed ARCAFA plan was then endorsed by SEAMEO in 1975, but APDO closed down when Pol Pot seized power in Cambodia.

In January 1976, SEAMEC decided to have SEAMES continue all archaeology and fine arts activities that had been planned, but to do so outside the framework of ARCAFA. A task force drafted a three-year development plan to supersede ARCAFA later in 1976, and a referendum on the development plan was approved, as recorded in notes at the SEAMEC conference in 1977. The SEAMEO Project in Archaeology and Fine Arts (SPAFA) then began in 1978 for a three-year period, with a possibility of renewal thereafter.

In early 1981, SPAFA acquired status as a permanent project, based on a development plan for 1981–86. When Thailand decided to provide a permanent home for the project, further programming arose, and in 1985 SEAMEC approved in principle the establishment of the SEAMEO Centre for Archaeology and Fine Arts (still called SPAFA due to the familiarity of the acronym over many years). The Asian Way principle of incrementalism had paid off.

The initial Enabling Instrument, approved by SEAMEC in January 1979, was revised in January 1986. The principal objective is "to advance mutual knowledge and understanding among the countries of Southeast Asia through regional programs in archaeology and fine arts" [Article II(4)].

SPAFA began with a Coordinating Unit, headed by a Coordinator, under a Governing Board. Three Sub-Centers were grafted onto national programs: the Sub-Center for Underwater Archaeology (Bangkok), Sub-Center for the Restoration and Preservation of Ancient Monuments (Borobudur), and the Sub-Center for Prehistory (Manila). In 1981, the structure expanded somewhat, with each country having an archaeological and a fine arts component. Jakarta picked up the Sub-Center for Archaeological Research (superseding the Borobudur facility) and the Sub-Center for the Performing Arts, Quezon City added the Sub-Center for Fine Arts, and the Thai Sub-Center included both archaeology and fine arts in one facility.

SPAFA today has a Director, Deputy Director, and three divisions (see Fig. 8.8). SPAFA, which started at the SEAMES office, is now at the new Thai cultural center in Bangkok.

Although ARCAFA anticipated participation from all SEAMEO member countries in principle, SPAFA originally did not. Only Indonesia, the Philippines, and Thailand sponsored Sub-Centers; Malaysia sent participants to many SPAFA seminars, training programs, and workshops, and in 1981 the Sarawak Museum in Kuching offered a workshop on ceramics. As a regional center, SPAFA is now open to all SEAMEO countries.

Participating member countries defrayed about half of SPAFA's expenses from 1978 to 1981; the UN Development Program (UNDP) defrayed the other half. Participating member countries then shared overhead expenses, with contributions from several sources. Japan donated funds to build the new Thai cultural center. SEAMEO countries are responsible for the remaining costs of SPAFA.

SPAFA has provided training in the conservation and restoration of monuments and artifacts, preservation of traditional performing arts, identification and dating of pottery and other artifacts, and programs

Figure 8.8
Organization of the SEAMEO Regional Centre for Archaeology and Fine Arts

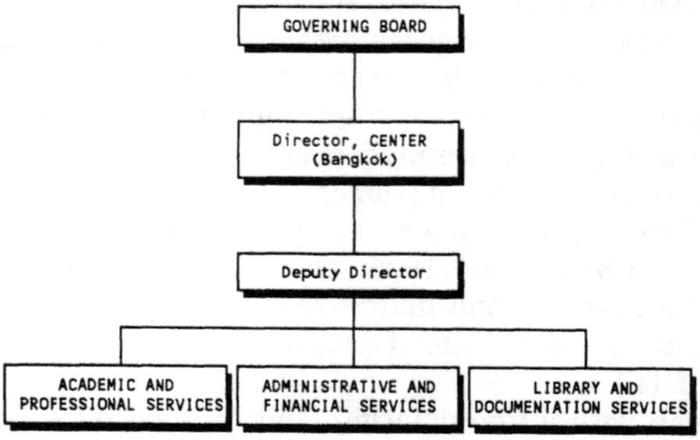

for music and visual arts for elementary and secondary teachers as well as for extension education.

SEAMEO Regional Tropical Medicine and Public Health Project (TROPMED)

Southeast Asia is plagued with endemic tropical diseases in rural areas and a shortage of trained physicians, public health officials, and medical scientists on the spot to deal with these problems. As economic and social development proceeds, more people can afford adequate medical care, and better public health facilities can be constructed, but the number of personnel to meet the challenge is less than it could be. In times past, medical students too often went to the First World for study and remained there, not returning to their country of origin; some returned but were not trained to treat tropical diseases or preferred to remain in cities. Appropriate expertise exists throughout the region but it is scattered about, not found in a single institution. Accordingly, a project was needed to pool existing resources in order to increase the number of trained personnel in several specialized areas at the various national medical centers rather than at one single institution, yet another Asian solution to an Asian problem.

After SEAMEC's first meeting in 1965, task forces went to Malaysia, the Philippines, Thailand, and Vietnam to determine the feasibility of a project linking national centers for tropical medicine in SEAMEO countries. In September 1966, SEAMEO approved the idea, and a Central Coordinating Board (CCB) was established in 1967. Each SEAMEO country then developed a five-year development plan by

August 1969, identifying an existing governmental institution as its TROPMED National Center.

The Enabling Instrument, adopted by SEAMEC on January 25, 1973, endows TROPMED with the following aim: "prevention, control, and eradication of the tropical endemic and environmental diseases so as to improve the health and standards of living of the peoples of Southeast Asia" (Section II). To accomplish this objective, TROPMED has two functions: "to promote cooperation in postgraduate training and teaching as well as research work in the field of Tropical Medicine and Public Health."

The Governing Board replaced CCB as the highest organ of TROPMED in 1973 (see Fig. 8.9). Each participating country's minister of education appoints a representative to the board, which has an annual four-day session. The Central Office of TROPMED, adjacent to the Thai National Center in Bangkok, is headed by a Project Coordinator and has a Technical Assistant, who is in charge of publications and arranges conferences and seminars, and an Administrative Officer, who handles the work associated with selection of trainees and fellowship recipients. Each participating country, in turn, has a TROPMED National Committee to oversee its own contribution to TROPMED from its National Center.

Figure 8.9
Organization of the SEAMEO Regional Tropical Medicine and Public Health Project

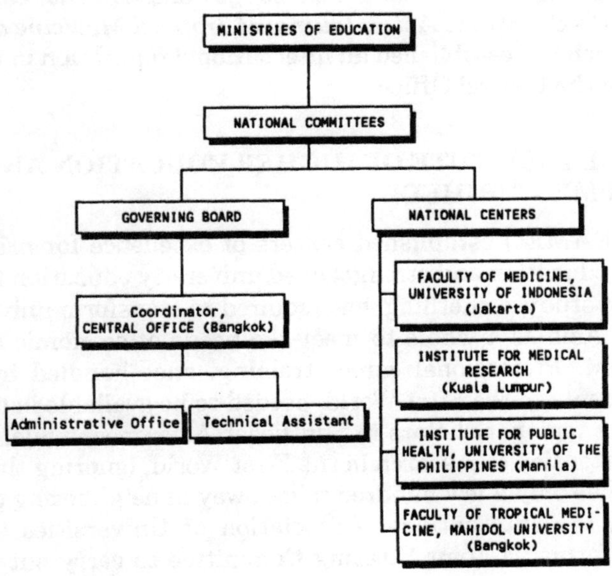

Capital costs for the Central Office are entirely the responsibility of Thailand, which houses the Central Office. For Operating Funds, participating countries make equal contributions to the Central Office. Each National Center has a separate budget for its own national activities, some of which are part of the TROPMED program.

Each TROPMED National Center selected at least one specialization. Originally, these were the following: nutrition and radio isotopes (Indonesia); environmental sanitation, venereal disease (Khmer Republic); public health and helminthology (Laos); applied parasitology and entomology, medical laboratory technology (Malaysia); rural public health (Philippines); occupational health, urban public health (Singapore); general and clinical tropical medicine and pediatrics (Thailand). When Singapore withdrew in 1976, the Philippines picked up occupational health and Thailand absorbed urban public health. In 1976, the Philippines also took over Vietnam's program in medical microbiology.

Each National Center provides courses of study from six months to three years in each of these fields of study. The degrees range from diplomas to M.S., M.P.H., and M.D. degrees. TROPMED provides research grants to upgrade skills among younger scientists in the region. Each National Center focuses on research projects related to its primary specialization. Through mid-1982, over 400 research projects had been conducted under TROPMED auspices.

The Central Office has no say over the staffing, syllabi, or research at the various National Centers; it administers the scholarship program, organizes at least one regional seminar and one technical meeting each year, and arranges for personnel exchanges and external consultants. TROPMED's *Southeast Asian Journal of Tropical Medicine and Public Health*, which has established an international reputation in its field, is a project of the Central Office.

REGIONAL INSTITUTE OF HIGHER EDUCATION AND DEVELOPMENT (RIHED)[2]

While SEAMEO established centers of excellence for primary and secondary education and strengthened university education in particular fields of study, something was required to transform universities in Southeast Asia as a whole to meet the needs of economic and social development. Professional career training, once handled by sending bright students to the First World, needed to be available in the universities of the region. Scholars in Southeast Asia, meanwhile, were paying more attention to research in the First World, ignoring the possibilities available only a few hundred miles away in neighboring countries.

In 1959, the International Association of Universities (IAU) and UNESCO formed a Joint Steering Committee to carry out collaborative efforts as a follow-up to the Conference of Asian Ministers of Education and Ministers Responsible for Economic Planning, held two years earlier. With Ford Foundation funding, the Joint Steering Committee commissioned a comprehensive analysis of the role of universities in promoting development within Southeast Asia. In 1965, the study was endorsed by IAU, SEAMEC, and UNESCO. The 1966 SEAMEC conference considered the proposal for a center for inter-university cooperation, but action was deferred indefinitely.

In 1968, the Joint Steering Committee, deciding to bypass SEAMEO, set up a Preparatory Commission that canvassed governments and universities on a draft scheme for inter-university cooperation. In 1969, a conference of Southeast Asian governments and universities convened in Singapore and accepted the proposal in principle.

RIHED's two basic documents were adopted in April 1970 during a meeting of the Interim Committee of Management, held in Singapore. They were the Memorandum of Association and the Articles of Association, which established RIHED as a Singapore corporation. According to the third article of the Memorandum of Association, the objective of RIHED was "to stimulate and facilitate cooperation among the universities and the Governments of the countries in Southeast Asia and to enhance the contributions of higher education to the social and economic development of the countries of the region and of the region as a whole."

RIHED was supervised by a Governing Board, which elected an Executive Committee and a Finance Committee to handle business between annual one-day sessions (see Fig. 8.10). The Executive Committee prepared the agenda for the Governing Board, and the Finance Committee fixed budgetary allotments; they met twice each year for about one day.

The Institute was at Singapore. In 1972, RIHED began three research surveys, and the Director hired three Project Directors, each with one Senior Research Fellow. In 1973, each project added a Junior Research Fellow. Member governments nominated a Country Collaborator for each project. After outside funding ended in 1976, several reorganizations occurred. The position of Deputy Director was added to aid in coordinating research, while the original Library and Documentation Office continued. In view of financial irregularities discovered in 1984 and a lack of direction in the organization, RIHED shut down in 1985.

The initial 1969 conference involved nine countries, but only seven became members in 1971 (see Table 8.4). Burma and the Philippines decided not to join, although the latter participated in several projects in accordance with the Asian Way principle of pan-Asianism.

Four agencies, accorded nonvoting membership, sat on RIHED's ori-

Figure 8.10
Organization of the Regional Institute of Higher Education and Development

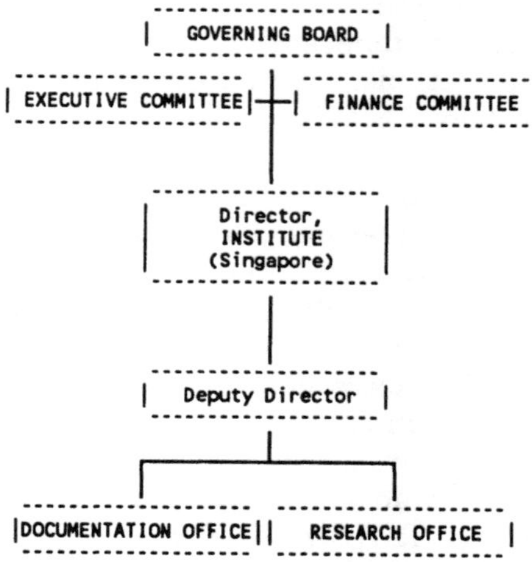

ginal Governing Board: the Association of Southeast Asian Institutions of Higher Learning (ASAIHL), IAU, SEAMEO, and UNESCO. As contributors, the Ford Foundation and USAID participated along with these organizations until 1976; even after both terminated funding to RIHED, the Ford Foundation continued to attend, although USAID did not.

In August 1983, Singapore gave notice of its intention to withdraw from RIHED. Since Singapore was the host government for the Institute, the organization either had to secure a new host government or

Table 8.4
Regional Institute of Higher Education and Development: Membership and Assessments

Year Joined	Member Countries	Assessment (1982)
1971	Indonesia	34.4%
	Cambodia (i 1975-)[a]	
	Laos (i 1975-)	
	Malaysia	27.6
	Singapore	6.8
	Thailand	31.2
	Vietnam (i 1975-)[b]	
Totals	defunct in 1985	$322,861

[a]Joined as the Khmer Republic
[b]Joined as Republic of Vietnam
Key: i = inactive

had to be absorbed into SEAMEO. SEAMEO demurred, and RIHED no longer exists.

When RIHED began, the Ford Foundation and USAID contributed equal amounts to the organization, providing about three-fourths of the total budget requirements. In 1976, these two sources ended, and UNESCO became the largest outside contributor, at about 15 percent of RIHED's budget. Member countries provided overhead expenses for RIHED, based on SEAMES's scale of assessments (see Table 8.4). Singapore provided rental and secretarial services as an in-kind contribution. After 1976, project funding came from sources in Canada, Singapore, and West Germany as well as the International Labor Organization (ILO), UN Economic and Social Commission for Asia and the Pacific (ESCAP), and UNESCO.

RIHED completed sixteen studies up to 1984; a few additional studies were finalized in 1985. Country collaborators wrote chapters, leaving project coordination to RIHED.

RIHED held twenty-six conferences related to the research projects; national seminars were later held to follow-up the regional conferences. RIHED also provided two- to three-week training courses for middle- and upper-level management of university administrative personnel.

The work was considered finished by 1985, since many of its recommendations had been implemented. The Asian Way principle of separating goals from bureaucracies enabled RIHED to experience a decent burial.

TRIPARTITE COUNCIL (TC)[3]

Maritime traffic has been subject to many hazards between the Indian and Pacific oceans through the Malacca and Singapore straits, which measure only three miles in width at their narrowest point and have many crosscurrents, reefs, and rocks, and have a depth of only 2.5 fathoms at a dangerous shoal near the middle. Traversed by more than 100 ships per day, only the Dover Strait has more maritime traffic. Foreign powers have used the seas to send invading forces. Pirates and smugglers have operated outside the framework of international law. Supertankers have brought a risk of oil spills. Maritime safety has been a concern as traffic has increased, and during the 1970s there were from 62 to 126 collisions per year. The Malacca Strait also has important fishing grounds, and ferryboats transport persons and goods across the channel.

In 1949, the International Court of Justice (ICJ) ruled that the Corfu Strait was an international waterway, with the right of "innocent passage" because it connects two parts of the high seas. The Convention on the Territorial Sea and Contiguous Zone of 1958 defined the rights of "innocent passage" and "transit passage," but it was not ratified by Indonesia and it did not anticipate the era of supertankers and massive oil spills. Meanwhile, in December 1957, Indonesia asserted the archipelagic principle that waters up to twelve miles surrounding its islands were territorial, so innocent passage would be granted only in cases where its sovereignty and security were not violated, a position based in part on the ICJ's decision in the Anglo-Norwegian Fisheries Case of 1951. Military vessels, for example, were not considered to engage in innocent passage.

Deliberations at the UN Law of the Sea Conferences after 1958 raised the question of sovereignty over straits once thought to be international waterways. In July 1962, Indonesia further clarified its position by requiring advance notice for foreign warships traversing Indonesian waters except where they followed prescribed sea lanes.

In March 1967, Indonesia and Malaysia signed an agreement for joint action against piracy in the seas north of the island of Kalimantan (Borneo). Shortly after a British hydrographic survey reported in 1967 that maps of the Malacca Strait were deficient, a supertanker scraped bottom, and in early 1968, another ship was grounded just outside Singapore harbor. Fears of oil spills loomed large. As Japanese supertankers were the primary threat to the Malacca and Singapore straits, the three coastal countries agreed to conduct several hydrographic surveys, the first of which was contracted to Japan early in 1969.

Concerned with matters of safety, the Japan Association for Preventing Marine Accidents and the Japanese Shipowners' Association formed the Malacca Straits Council of Japan (MSC) in July 1968, then incorporated MSC as a public corporation in April 1969. After a preliminary survey in early 1969 by a Japanese ship, with full cooperation from the three coastal countries and including the formation of a Straits of Malacca Survey Committee, four Japanese destroyers arrived in the strait on a training mission in October 1969, and the chief of the Japanese naval staff noted that British forces were to be withdrawn within a year or two in the region. MSC then approached Indonesia, Malaysia, and Singapore in January 1970 to establish a four-power survey project, with Japan as an equal partner, that would undertake a thorough hydrographic survey, with an internationally managed traffic separation scheme as an eventual goal.

These Japanese initiatives, contrary to the Asian Way principle of equality, prompted Indonesia and Malaysia to consider a formal declaration that the Malacca Strait was a territorial waterway. The first appearance of a Soviet naval flotilla in the Indian Ocean in March 1968, the proclamation of the Nixon Doctrine in July 1969 regarding U.S. withdrawal from the region, and the major British military departure from Southeast Asia expected by December 1971 also had an impact. In 1970, Indonesia and Malaysia signed a treaty declaring the Malacca Strait to be a territorial waterway. In April 1971, Jakarta asserted that all alien vessels in its waters needed prior permits from either the Ministry of Communications or the Ministry of Defense, the former for civilian ships, the latter for military ships.

In early October 1971, ministers of communication of Indonesia and Singapore, the Indonesian ambassador to Singapore, the Singapore defense minister, and the acting foreign minister of Singapore met in Singapore. One week later Indonesia's ambassadors to Malaysia and Singapore met in Kuala Lumpur with three Malaysian officials: the minister of communications, attorney general, and the deputy secretary-general of foreign affairs. The three foreign ministers next met in Kuala Lumpur in November 1971 to approve Japan's proposed hydrographic survey and to set up a Tripartite Council (TC) as a coordinating body to oversee maritime safety – and the survey – through the Malacca and Singapore straits. In March 1973, Tengku Razaleigh Hamzah, then President of the Associated Malay Chambers of Commerce of Malaysia, proposed a Malacca Strait Authority (MSA) to collect tolls, but this idea never got off the ground.

According to the joint statement issued on November 16, 1971, cooperation involved concern for one single issue, namely, safety of navigation. A joint statement issued on February 19, 1975, formalized the aims of the organization to be twofold: "to protect the coastal states from damages resulting from oil pollution . . . [and] the need to maximize the safety of navigation in the Straits of Malacca and Singapore. . . ."

Although Indonesia and Malaysia declared the Malacca Strait to be a territorial waterway, Singapore dissented, since its port would benefit financially from more traffic. This difference of opinion is noted in the joint declaration, but in accordance with the Asian Way principle of consensus building, the goal shared in common was not torpedoed by the matter in dispute.

In April 1972, Indonesia and Malaysia declared that the Malacca Strait was no longer open to military ships or to tankers with 200,000 tons or more of cargo. Such vessels would have to go through either the Flores, Lombok, or Makassar straits, which the two countries agreed to consider Indonesian territorial waters. Indonesia claimed the right to search any ship and to object to arms being carried to an unfriendly country. Inasmuch as such a policy was to add about forty hours to the normal voyage of supertankers from the Middle East to Japan, Japanese interests feared still more restrictions and pressured their government to do whatever could be done to make passage through the Malacca Strait more navigable.

Although the three countries endorsed the idea of a Traffic Separation Scheme (TSS) in April 1973, and hydrographic surveys were completed by 1974, there appeared to be no urgency to sign or implement such an agreement until January 1975, when the supertanker *Showa Maru* spilled a cargo of oil in the Malacca Strait, prompting the TC joint statement on February 19, 1975, which further formalized the organization. TC then adopted the Indonesia-Malaysia-Singapore Traffic Separation Scheme Rules and Recommendations, also known as the Tripartite Agreement on the Safety of Navigation in the Straits of Malacca and Singapore, on February 24, 1977. In November 1977, the Senior Officials Meeting drafted a report for presentation to the International Maritime Consultative Organization (IMCO, now the International Maritime Organization, or IMO), which in November 1979 endorsed TSS with some modifications. TSS became operational on May 1, 1981.

The Tripartite Council, the highest organ of the organization (see Fig. 8.11), consists of the three countries' foreign ministers or their deputies and meets at least once each year. In February 1975, the TC set up the Council for the Safety of Navigation and the Control of Marine Pollution in the Straits of Malacca and Singapore, known as the Council of Ministers; this body meets once each year and is composed of transport ministers. In addition, a Senior Officials Meeting (SOM) assists the Council and monitors ad hoc expert groups; SOM meets for one day at least twice each year.

The three countries remain involved (see Table 8.5). Japan originally hoped for a four-country organization. In October 1966, Thailand ex-

Figure 8.11
Organization of the Tripartite Council

Table 8.5
Tripartite Council: Membership

Year Joined	Member Countries
1971	Indonesia Malaysia Singapore
Total	3 Members

tended the limits of its territorial waters to 12 miles and thus fronts on the Malacca Strait at a point where the width is about 200 miles. In 1973, Thailand concluded agreements with Indonesia and Malaysia in regard to its continental shelf boundaries in the strait. The only sea access between Thailand's east and west coasts is through the straits of Malacca and Singapore, so Bangkok has an interest in the organization but has not supported the positions of Indonesia and Malaysia. Indeed, Japan has approached Thailand from time to time on the possibility of constructing a canal or pipeline across the Kra isthmus to bypass the Malacca and Singapore straits.

The three TC countries finance their own portions of the cooperative efforts. There is no central budget, though a revolving fund for antipollution activities has been considered.

Although Razaleigh's proposal for toll charges was turned down, heavy users of the straits nevertheless defray costs of making the waterways navigable. Great Britain and Japan have borne the full cost of hydrographic surveys.

Japan signed agreements in 1969, 1972, and 1981 to provide technical assistance concerning the Malacca and Singapore straits; some $24.1 million was spent. (The alternative of rerouting cargo through the Lombok Strait would have cost each tanker about $1 million per year.) Japan also paid damages for the *Showa Maru* oil spill.

TC's main project is the TSS, which involves three waterways: the Malacca Strait, the Eastern Singapore Strait, and the Western Singapore Strait. Vessels proceeding through the waterways must have at least 3.5 meters of under-keel clearance at all times; those with draughts of 15 meters and above must go through a designated deep water route, where no passing is allowed, and all other vessels must keep out of this area. The maximum speed is twelve knots during passage through critical areas. There is a reporting procedure for large vessels, navigational aids, and tidal charts.

The TSS could not begin until hydrographic surveys were completed.

After preliminary British and Japanese surveys were completed in the late 1960s, Japan agreed to provide a hydrographic survey, which began in 1972 and concluded in 1974, producing common datum charts and tidal and currents studies. In May 1981, Japan signed an agreement with the three countries to provide assistance in regard to dredging, navigational aids, and surveying of the waterways covered by the TSS.

Marine pollution is another project area. The three countries are now formulating a joint policy on the subject.

CONFERENCE OF THE FOREIGN MINISTERS OF KAMPUCHEA, LAOS, AND VIETNAM[4]

In 1947, the Vietminh, that is, Vietnamese loyal to the forces of Ho Chi Minh, proposed a Southeast Asia League as an organization to build solidarity against continued colonial rule in the region. In response, later the same year, the idea of a Pan Southeast Asian Union was mooted by the French delegate to the Franco-Siamese Conciliation Committee as a channel for French aid to Indochina, which was still under French rule. In September 1947, a meeting of Southeast Asia Countries' Representatives, having denounced colonialism in the region, proposed a Southeast Asia federation. The next initiative came from Cambodian Prince Norodom Sihanouk. Having been deposed in 1970, the prince fled to Beijing, where a Three Peoples Conference was held later the same year, and Sihanouk met representatives from China and North Vietnam. As these proposals were clearly for propaganda purposes, the ideas were not pursued.

In 1975, indigenous forces in Indochina, led by Communist parties, came to power. North and South Vietnam were officially unified on July 2, 1976. The Democratic Kampuchea regime of Pol Pot, eventually allied with China, began to pursue irredentist ambitions toward the southern part of Vietnam. In response to threats and a dozen or so border incursions by Democratic Kampuchea, Vietnam launched a preemptive attack against Pol Pot's Khmer Rouge army in December 1978. Within a month, the Khmer Rouge had been driven out of most of Cambodia, and a regime more friendly toward Vietnam began to operate in Phnom Penh under the name People's Republic of Kampuchea (PRK).

On the occasion of the first anniversary of the overthrow of Pol Pot, Vietnam's Foreign Minister Nguyen Duy Thinh convened a meeting of the foreign ministers of the three Indochinese countries in Phnom Penh on January 5, 1980. The first meeting was called the "Vietnamese, Kampuchea and Lao Foreign Ministers' Conference," but the second meeting was called the "Conference of Foreign Ministers of Kampuchea, Laos, and Vietnam." In 1985, Vietnam's Foreign Minister Nguyen

Co Thach referred to the meetings as "Conferences of the Foreign Ministers of the Three Indochinese Countries."

In February 1983, the heads of state of Kampuchea, Laos, and Vietnam held a summit conference in Vientiane; they appeared to charge the Ministerial Conference with the following tasks:

> (1) promote mutual solidarity and cooperation, to assist one another in national edification and defense . . . ; (2) continuously strengthen solidarity and cooperation . . . through negotiations . . . ; (3) develop long term cooperation and mutual assistance among two or three parties in all fields . . . ; (4) strengthen solidarity among the three peoples against any maneuver of division by enemies and any manifestation of big power chauvinism and narrow-minded nationalism, constantly educate the three countries' peoples on the traditional friendship and special relationship among them, as well as against any activity susceptible of harming their friendship.

Subsequently, the foreign ministers continued to meet for two days twice each year, alternating their venues among the three countries (see Fig. 8.12). At the 1986 conference, regular meetings were discontinued. The next meetings were in July 1988 and April 1989. Only one Summit Conference has taken place.

Figure 8.12
Organization of the Conference of the Foreign Ministers of Kampuchea, Laos, and Vietnam

After the 1983 summit, each country set up a Commission for Economic and Cultural Cooperation "to promote economic cooperation and coordination of national plans for economic development." The structure was dismantled in 1989. Important members of each country's Communist party Central Committee served on the commissions, which had consultative powers. Thus, Hanoi had a Vietnam Committee for Economic and Cultural Cooperation with Kampuchea and Laos; Kampuchea and Laos had similar bodies. Starting in July 1983, heads of the commissions met in two-day sessions twice each year under the title of Session of the Lao, Vietnamese, and Kampuchean Commissions for Economic and Cultural Cooperation. Bilateral meetings occurred sporadically throughout the year, and trilateral meetings of other ministerial-level officials were also held; the latter included the civil aviation, communication, state banking, trade, and transport ministers. Trilateral commissions among the three countries were to be established whenever feasible in such fields as culture, economics, sports, science, and technology. Although Vietnam wanted to set up a formal secretariat, Kampuchea and Laos demurred, and Hanoi withdrew its suggestion in accordance with the Asian Way principles of equality and consensus in decision making.

There is no formal membership aspect to the conferences (see Table 8.6). Each country defrays its own costs of participation, though Vietnam usually provides the personnel and other costs for bilateral and trilateral cooperative projects.

The foreign ministers have issued detailed communiqués that state the positions of the three countries on many subjects, although in more detail regarding the Cambodian War, since ASEAN repeatedly called for Vietnamese troops to leave even if Pol Pot forces were to retake control. During the 1983 summit conference, Vietnam announced that military units would be withdrawn from Kampuchea by 1990. The

Table 8.6
Conference of the Foreign Ministers of Kampuchea, Laos, and Vietnam: Membership

Year Joined	Member Countries
1980	Kampuchea[a] Laos Vietnam
Totals	3 Members

[a]Renamed Cambodia in 1989

three countries first met ASEAN countries at Jakarta in July 1988 to embark on a peace process. The three countries have also indicated an interest in supporting ASEAN's Zone of Peace, Freedom and Neutrality (ZOPFAN).

The cooperation commissions agreed in principle on major guidelines for an economic, cultural, scientific, and technical cooperation program. Projects involved highway improvement, irrigation, a petroleum pipeline, and duty-free trade cooperation. Integration of the three economies was once a goal, and Laos and Vietnam began coordinating their state plans, but there was progress only in trade cooperation. Measures for political integration are not involved, as Vietnam repeatedly assured Kampuchea and Laos that it did not intend to establish hegemony over Indochina in any form. Economic cooperation was abandoned in 1988, amid plans to open all three countries to foreign investment and capitalist reforms. Vietnam, meanwhile, indicated in 1988 that it was again interested in joining ASEAN, a development that would cause the three-power organization to become obsolete.

SUMMARY AND CONCLUSIONS

SEAMEO, one of the most professionally competent regional organizations in Asia, enjoys a surplus of applicants at its centers, and external funds support participants from countries around the world. BIOTROP has tackled the immense problem of restoring ecosystems damaged by careless exploitation of natural resources. INNOTECH leads the way in systems approaches to educational administration. RECSAM seeks to upgrade education in science and mathematics so that Southeast Asia will develop its own cadre of scientists and engineers in due course. RELC has transformed language instruction methods into language learning approaches. SEARCA is a major center for agricultural research. SPAFA's efforts to preserve and restore the cultural heritage of the region have answered a need identified for several decades. TROPMED enables physicians to train in Southeast Asia, with tropical diseases in the forefront.

There is a significant gap in SEAMEO coverage, however. The lack of understanding among the masses on matters of economics, government, history, law, psychology, and sociology is quite evident within Southeast Asia. Some government leaders even admit that their country is not ready for democracy because their citizens are not properly educated regarding the responsibilities and rights accorded free peoples, although SEAMEO's Charter directs the organization "to further respect for . . . fundamental freedoms."

When RIHED began in the mid-1960s, the universities in its member countries were far too traditional and needed to be attuned to problems of economic and social development. By the mid-1980s, new orientations pervaded most universities in the region, and a new generation of vigorous and well-trained business and professional leaders emerged. RIHED may have succeeded so well that it was no longer needed.

Appalled by the prospect of Japan's corporations appearing to dictate what should be done to make the Malacca Strait more navigable for Japanese commercial ships, Indonesia and Malaysia first made it clear that the strait was not an international waterway. They would allow Japan to undertake a hydrographic survey only on two conditions – that Tokyo would first recognize that foreign vessels had to obtain permission to be in waters once viewed as international and that there would be no four-power regime to supervise a traffic separation scheme. Japan rerouted its largest supertankers through the Lombok and Makassar straits in the interest of safety, thereby depriving Singapore of considerable business. Although Singapore opposed mandatory regional pilotage and toll collection, it could do nothing about waters that were outside its jurisdiction. Joint action was exigent, nonetheless. Instead of a strong strait authority, a Tripartite Council formed as a coordinating body.

The three Indochinese countries achieved national liberation in 1975 after a long and bitter struggle, but their resources for postwar reconstruction were minimal. Vietnam provides leadership to the three-country foreign ministers conference, since its resource base is larger. The conference has all but accepted ZOPFAN, but diplomatic wrangling with ASEAN continued so long as ASEAN sought to keep Pol Pot forces active in Cambodia, contrary to the overwhelming wishes of the Khmer people. Cooperative efforts led to integrated economic planning but without much benefit. The conference's success lies in the inability of ASEAN to isolate any of the three countries. ASEAN, forced to deal with Indochina as a bloc, now faces an era when the benefits of cooperation with Indochina will propel all Southeast Asia into a community more in keeping with Asian Way principles. In 1989, Vietnam asked Thailand to coordinate a regional consultative body linking ASEAN and Indochina, and the PRK changed its name back to Cambodia.

When the Indochinese countries left SEAMEO and RIHED, the two bodies became ASEAN clones. When they return and the Indochinese foreign ministers' conference folds, ASEAN will be at a crossroads.

NOTES

1. For references to SEAMEO documents, see Michael Haas, *Basic Documents of Asian Regional Organizations* (Dobbs Ferry, NY: Oceana Publica-

tions), vol. 7, pp. 28–118. For a bibliography of secondary sources, see pp. 25–27.

2. For references to RIHED documents, see Michael Haas, *Basic Documents of Asian Regional Organizations* (Dobbs Ferry, NY: Oceana Publications), vol. 7, pp. 119–23.

3. For references to TC documents, see Ministry of Foreign Affairs, "Straits of Malacca and Singapore – Joint Statement," *Foreign Affairs Malaysia* (November 1971):53–54 and later statements issued by this publication.

4. For references to documents of the Conference of the Foreign Ministers of Kampuchea, Laos, and Vietnam, see Information and Press Department, Ministry of Foreign Affairs, Socialist Republic of Vietnam, *Conferences of Foreign Ministers of Vietnam, Laos and Kampuchea* (Hanoi: Ministry of Foreign Affairs, 1981) and later compilations of communiqués issued by this source.

9 MULTILATERAL MONEY MANAGEMENT IN ASIA

Although the Asian Development Bank (ADB) employs more staff than any other regional organization in Asia (some 600 persons), it has many members outside Asia, and voting power is in the hands of developed countries. ADB provides loans and technical assistance of various sorts, but it does not offer training to personnel of commercial banks. Training is the raison d'être of the organization of Central Banks of Southeast Asia, Australia and New Zealand (SEANZA), which existed before ADB, and one of the functions of the South-east Asian Central Banks Group (SEACEN). ADB finances foreign-exchange costs of development projects, but it does little to stop the outflow of foreign exchange to commercial centers in the First World. The latter task is the aim of the Asian Clearing Union (ACU), which helps central banks to exchange local currencies for intraregional trade, and the Asian Reinsurance Corporation (Asian Re), which underwrites local insurance companies in the region. These five organizations are reviewed in this chapter.

CENTRAL BANKS OF SOUTHEAST ASIA, AUSTRALIA AND NEW ZEALAND (SEANZA)[1]

Initial efforts to provide capital aid to the developing countries of Asia proved difficult in part because central banks of Asian countries lacked trained personnel. There was also a need for trained middle-level personnel.

Governors of the reserve banks of Australia, India, New Zealand, Pakistan, and Sri Lanka met with other Commonwealth central bank governors on a regular basis after World War II. Although the Bank of England provided training for Commonwealth central bankers, the content of the courses bore little relevance to problems of mid-management central banking in Asia. After a meeting of Commonwealth central bank governors at London in early 1956, Governor H. C. Coombs of Australia's Reserve Bank proposed the idea of a more relevant course for the region to his colleagues from India and Pakistan. Coombs next consulted with C. F. Cobbold, Governor of the Bank of England, who approved of the idea of an experimental course for the central banks of Southeast Asia, Australia, and New Zealand in October 1956. In 1957, a Council of central bank governors for the region convened in Sydney to organize an initial banking course, to be held in the same city later the same year. The Council and course were held again at Sydney in 1958. The name SEANZA subsequently was applied to the informal arrangement.

The main purpose of SEANZA, according to J. B. Nairn, Deputy Secretary of the Reserve Bank of Australia, is "to promote cooperation among the member central banks and to foster the professional development of younger central bank executives."[2] No specific document establishes SEANZA on a formal basis. Informality was thought most likely to promote the spirit of equality so important to the Asian Way.

The Council of Governors, the major organ of SEANZA (see Fig. 9.1), meets once each year for two days. During years when training courses are held, the governors open the courses officially, then reconvene in the final week for a Governors' Symposium; in alternate years, they meet to approve the agenda for the next courses. Before the Council meeting, a two-day Advisors Meeting prepares details of the course syllabus for approval by the governors.

Economists and others who lecture at SEANZA courses are called Directors, those taking the course are Participants. Although the course syllabus is similar from year to year, some Directors meet to design specifics of the next course so that the Advisors Meeting can focus on general aspects. The Directing Staff, which also serves as advisers to course participants, reports on each course to the Council. The Directing Staff usually consists of one member from either Australia or New Zealand (in rotation), two Directors from the previous host countries, two Directors from future host countries, and one or two others invited by the Council. The governor of the host bank is the President of the Course. The Director of Studies of the Course is usually the host governor's chief economic adviser.

For a central bank to join SEANZA, it must pledge to host a course at some time in the future, a recognition of the Asian Way principle of equality. All seventeen member banks have done so (see Table 9.1). In the Asian Way spirit of pan-Asianism, other countries have participat-

Figure 9.1
Organization of the Central Banks of Southeast Asia, Australia and New Zealand

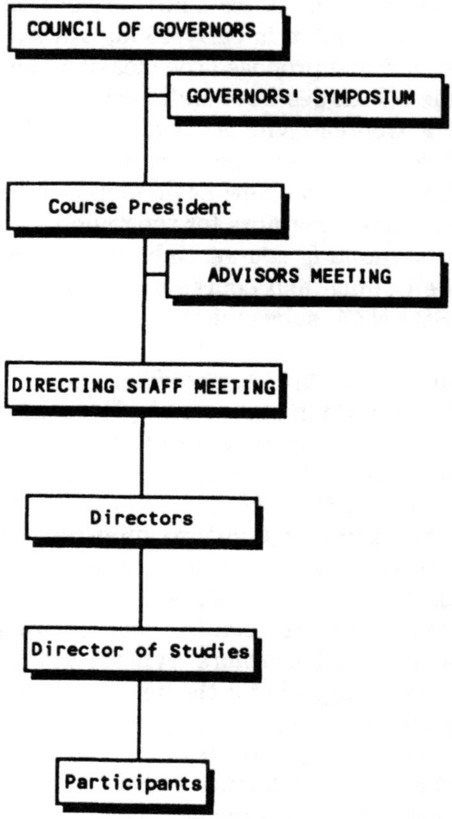

ed, including Burma, Cambodia, Canada, Fiji, France, Ghana, Italy, Jamaica, Luxembourg, Mauritius, the Netherlands, Nigeria, Rhodesia, Sierra Leone, the Solomon Islands, South Africa, the United Kingdom, the United States, Vietnam, West Germany, and Western Samoa. Belgium and Laos have been invited but have not yet attended.

Originally, the host country paid local costs for the course. Developing-country members were hesitant to serve as hosts for this reason. In 1980, effective 1985, the Council of Governors agreed that each country should defray per diem expenses and airfare for its own Directors and Participants. Member countries provide instructors, although they have also come from various international organizations and the Bank of England.

The main activity of SEANZA, the biennial two-month course, covers all aspects of banking. Governors' symposia and council meetings also discuss a wide range of topics on national and international banking. SEANZA facilitates bilateral exchanges and secondments of personnel from one member bank to another; these last from three to six months and are usually hosted by the Reserve Bank of Australia.

ASIAN DEVELOPMENT BANK (ADB)[3]

The World Bank, founded in 1944 as the International Bank for Reconstruction and Development (IBRD), initially aided in Europe's postwar reconstruction. Although the World Bank Group expanded to include the private-sector-oriented International Finance Corporation (IFC) in 1956 and the International Development Association (IDA) in 1960, it was slow to focus on problems of developing countries.

Discussions at the UN Economic Commission for Asia and the Far East (ECAFE, now ESCAP) began to conceive of the possibility of an Asian development bank as early as 1954. By 1958, a scheme for such a bank was discussed in various circles in Tokyo as well.

Table 9.1
Central Banks of Southeast Asia, Australia and New Zealand: Membership

Year Joined	Member Countries
1956	Australia
	India
	New Zealand
	Pakistan
	Sri Lanka[a]
1959	Japan
1963	Philippines
1964	Malaysia
1965	Thailand
1966	Iran
	South Korea
1967	Indonesia
1971	Nepal
	Singapore
1975	Bangladesh
1984	Papua New Guinea
1987	China
Total	17 Members

[a]Joined as Ceylon

The formation of the Inter-American Development Bank (IADB) served as a catalyst to ADB in 1959, when Ceylon's Prime Minister Solomon Bandaranaike proposed the idea of such a bank, an idea that was echoed three years later by C. Longanthan, a banker from Ceylon. In January 1963, Paul Sithi-Amnui, a Thai banker, proposed a regional bank at ECAFE's Intra-Regional Trade Promotion Talks, and ECAFE approved the idea in principle in March 1964. After U.S. President Lyndon Johnson dispatched former World Bank President Eugene Black to identify projects involving regional cooperation that might receive U.S. support in 1965, both Japan and the United States offered initial subscriptions of $200 million to ADB, thereby ensuring that the bank would attract capital from outside the region. ECAFE then drafted a charter, which was signed at a conference of plenipotentiaries immediately after ECAFE's annual session at the end of 1965. ADB opened its doors in 1966.

According to the Agreement Establishing the Asian Development Bank, adopted in Manila on December 4, 1965, there are two aims: "to foster economic growth and cooperation in the region of Asia and the Far East . . . and to contribute to the acceleration of the process of economic development of the developing member countries in the region, collectively and individually" (Article 1). ADB has six functions:

> (i) to promote investment in the region of public and private capital for development purposes; (ii) to utilize the resources at its disposal . . . , giving priority to . . . projects and programs which will contribute most effectively to the harmonious economic growth of the region as a whole, and having special regard to the needs of the smaller or less developed member countries in the region; (iii) to meet requests from members in the region to assist them in the coordination of their development policies and plans with a view to achieving better utilization of their resources, making their economies more complementary, and promoting the orderly expansion of their foreign trade, in particular, intraregional trade; (iv) to provide technical assistance for the preparation, financing and execution of development projects and programs, including the formulation of specific project proposals; (v) to cooperate . . . with public international organizations and other international institutions, as well as national entities whether public or private, which are concerned with the investment of development funds in the region, and to interest such institutions and entities in new opportunities for investment and assistance; and (vi) to undertake such other activities and provide such other services as may advance its purpose. (Article 2)

Each member country has a seat on the Board of Governors, which has an Annual Meeting of about two days (see Fig. 9.2). Every two years the Governors elect members of the Board of Directors, which meets at least once each week.

Figure 9.2
Organization of the Asian Development Bank

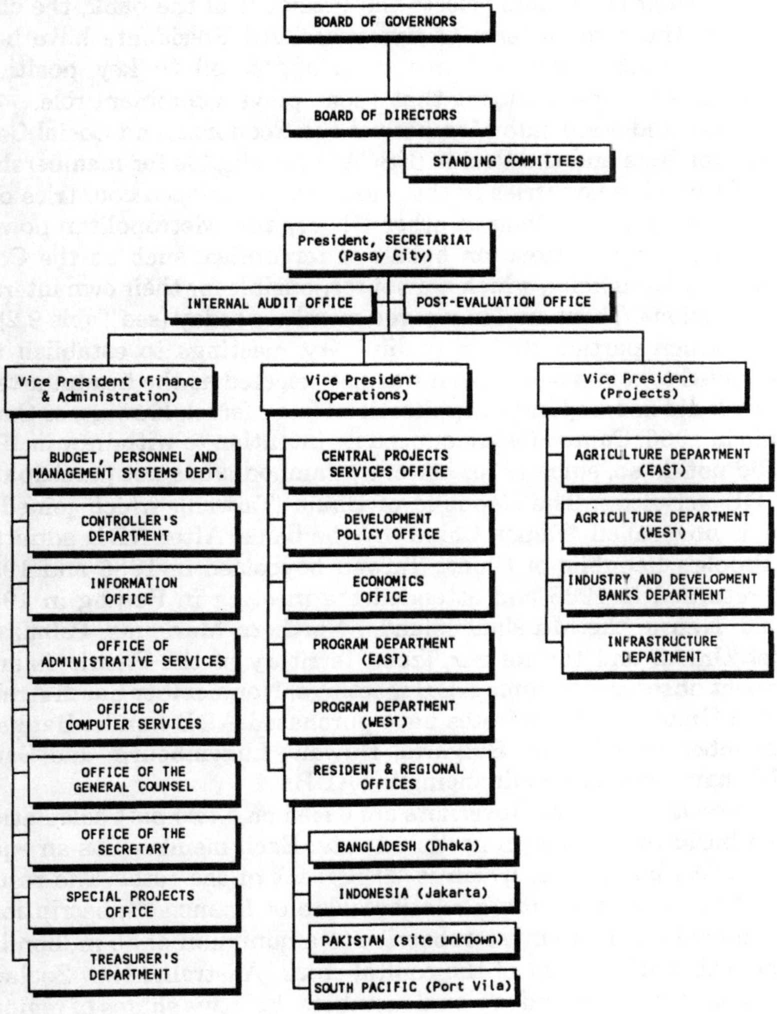

The Secretariat of ADB is in the Philippines. Originally scattered in various office buildings in Makati, the headquarters moved to Pasay City in October 1972. New facilities are to be occupied at nearby Mandaluyong by 1989. From 1971 to 1974, ADB's Office of Financial Advisor had an office in Zurich, and the Information Office assigned a representative to Zurich in 1973 and 1974. In 1982, a Bangladesh Resident Office in Dhaka opened. The South Pacific Resident Office in Port

Vila, Vanuatu, opened its doors in July 1984. A Jakarta office began in July 1987, and an office in Pakistan was approved in 1989.

The Board of Governors selects the President of the bank, the chief executive officer, for a term of five years. All Presidents have been Japanese. Other Japanese have been appointed to key positions throughout the bank, ensuring that Japan plays a dominant role.

Members and Associate Members of the Economic and Social Commission for Asia and the Pacific (ESCAP) are eligible for membership, as are developing countries in the region and developed countries outside the region that belong to other UN organs. Metropolitan powers must submit applications on behalf of territories, such as the Cook Islands and Hongkong, which are not responsible for their own international relations. There are forty-seven members today (see Table 9.2).

Iran, which participated in preliminary meetings to establish the bank, failed to join when Tehran was not selected as the headquarters. The bank did not respond to applications from Israel, Kuwait, or Saudi Arabia in 1966. Cambodia announced its intention to withdraw in 1967 but did not do so; since 1975, however, Cambodia has not participated in ADB activities. The Republic of China (Taiwan), which joined in 1966, is now called "Taipei, China" by the bank. After ADB admitted the People's Republic of China, Taiwan boycotted in 1986 and 1987, then returned in 1988 and attended the meeting in Beijing in 1989. Brunei, Nauru, the Marshall Islands, Northern Marianas, Palau, the Soviet Union, and the former Trust Territory of the Pacific Islands have sent observers to some ADB meetings. Nonmember Saudi Arabia and the United Arab Emirates have purchased ADB bonds. Banks in nonmember Abu Dhabi, Bulgaria, Kuwait, Luxembourg, and Saudi Arabia have arranged co-financing for ADB.

Votes on the Board of Governors are based on a two-part calculation, with a basic vote and a proportional vote. Each member has an equal share of the basic vote, which is 20 percent of the total. The rest is proportionate to a country's relative share of financial subscriptions. Nonregional members must subscribe to a minimum of $5 million but no more than 40 percent of the capital stock. Australia, New Zealand, and Japan are considered regional members. Relative shares of regional members are based on a formula that uses export volume, gross domestic product per capita, and tax revenues. There have been increases in shares on several occasions. The total votes in 1987 were 2,006,253 shares (see Table 9.2).

Due to the weighted-vote formula, representation on the Board of Directors is usually determined through pooling of votes by relatively stable blocs of countries. In 1987, Australia, Canada, China, France, India, Japan, Pakistan, South Korea, Thailand, the United Kingdom, and the United States had seats. Countries in each bloc rotate Director

Table 9.2
Asian Development Bank: Membership and Subscriptions

Year Joined	Member Countries	Subscription (1987)
1966	Afghanistan	0.485%
	Australia	5.528
	Austria	0.726
	Belguim	0.726
	Cambodia (i 1975-)	0.469
	Canada	5.038
	Denmark	0.726
	Finland	0.726
	India	6.008
	Indonesia	5.228
	Italy	2.019
	Japan	12.432
	Laos	0.438
	Malaysia	2.827
	Nepal	0.555
	Netherlands	1.330
	New Zealand	1.780
	Norway	0.726
	Pakistan	2.346
	Philippines	2.527
	Singapore	0.726
	South Korea	4.868
	Sri Lanka	0.937
	Sweden	0.546
	Switzerland	0.940
	Taiwan (China)	1.386
	Thailand	1.626
	United Kingdom	2.226
	United States	12.260
	Vietnam[a]	0.726
	West Germany	4.240
	Western Samoa	0.428
1969	Hongkong	0.906
1970	Fiji	0.485
	France	2.478
1971	Papua New Guinea	0.508
1972	Tonga	0.429
1973	Bangladesh	1.326
	Burma	0.906
	Solomon Islands	0.431
1974	Kiribati[b]	0.429
1976	Cook Islands	0.428
1978	Maldives	0.429
1981	Vanuatu	0.431
1982	Bhutan	0.431
1986	China	6.108
	Spain	0.726
Totals	47 Members	2,006,253 shares

[a]Joined as Republic of Vietnam
[b]Joined as Gilbert and Ellice Islands
Key: i = inactive

and Alternate Director seats at one- or two-year intervals, and Directors can split votes to represent the wishes of each country.

There are five sources of ADB funds: member subscriptions, sales of bonds, loan repayments, co-financing, and income from service fees and bank deposits. All sources are used for loans, although income is partly used to service borrowings and to defray administrative expenses. The bank has attracted about $1.50 from external sources to every $1.00 raised from its members. Bond sales grossed $8 billion by 1987. Through 1987, some 242 loans involved co-financing (from both commercial lenders and international organizations); the ratio of ADB to non-ADB funds was $8.8 billion to $6.3 billion.

When ADB began, total member subscriptions amounted to $1 billion. If countries join or want to buy more stock, a special increase is authorized. Accordingly, authorized capital stock by 1987 was nearly $23 billion. Shares are equal to the International Monetary Fund's (IMF) special drawing rights (SDR) units, which were about $1.30 in 1988.

Out of the total subscriptions, each country transfers a certain percentage to ADB, while the rest is on call in the country's central bank in the form of a promissory note in local currency. Since 1976, the ratio of U.S. dollars to local currency has been 10 : 90. About 40 percent of the bank's liquidity is in yen.

By the end of 1987, there had been 474 Ordinary Loans ("hard" loans at commercial rates) for about $14.7 billion. Local cost financing had been approved for about 40 percent of these projects, but for less than 10 percent of the total amount. All developing countries in Asia are eligible for loans except for Afghanistan, Cambodia, and Vietnam, because they constitute risks as long as they have troops in active combat.

Contributions have been earmarked into several Special Funds accounts that provide "soft" loans (at nominal rates of interest) and technical assistance. The Technical Assistance Special Fund (TASF) began in 1967. In 1968, Japan started the Agricultural Special Fund (ASF) and the Multi-Purpose Special Fund (MPSF), but in 1973 the latter absorbed the former. The Asian Development Fund (ADF) began in 1974. MPSF closed in 1980, and its funds were transferred to ADF. A Japan Special Fund (JSF) started in 1989, with an initial amount of $35.4 million for untied technical assistance grants and private-sector equity investments to assist in human resource development, industrialization, natural resource development, and technology transfer. By the end of 1987, ADB had provided 400 soft loans amounting to $7.1 billion and 1,440 technical assistance projects totaling $1.7 billion.

There are four types of technical assistance, which may use either hard or soft funds. Financial aid may enable a country to apply for a loan (Project Preparation Assistance) or to remove bottlenecks in project completion (Project Completion Assistance). Advisory Technical Assistance enables a country to develop national development plans or sector strategies. Regional Activities support conferences, studies, or projects of other international organizations.

ADB income comes from service fees on loans and investments ($614.7 million and $354.2 million, respectively, in 1987). Interest varies with world market conditions; rates are set semiannually by adding a spread (0.4 percent effective January 1989) to the average cost of outstanding bank bonds. During the first half of 1989, hard loans to governments bore interest at their lowest rate ever – 6.42 percent per year (0.5 percent for administrative costs), with a maturity period of from ten to thirty years and a two- to seven-year grace period. In 1986, the bank first approved loans to the private sector without government guarantees; interest is 1.0 to 1.5 percent above the prevailing rates to governments. Soft loans have a 1.0 percent service charge; repayment is over forty years, with a ten-year grace period. "Blend" loans (soft and hard loan components) have a thirty-five-year term at 1.0 percent. The commitment charge, about 0.5 percent per year on the first three years of undisbursed portions of hard loans and 1.0 percent thereafter, goes into the bank's Special Reserve; in 1987, this amount was about $177 million. Income, after being subtracted from interest payments on bonds, services to members, and administrative expenses, goes into the Ordinary Reserve, which was $1.6 billion by the end of 1987.

ADB invests unused reserve funds mostly in securities issued or guaranteed by member governments and obligations of other multilateral development banks. The remainder is left in time deposits of member country banks and the Bank for International Settlements (BIS). By the end of 1987, the yield of investments was 8.1 percent.

Internal administrative expenses of the bank consist of personnel, office equipment, supplies, and travel. In 1987, expenses totaled $89.5 million.

Loan applications go through several stages of processing. The first step is project identification. Rolling three-year plans exist for each developing member country. If a proposed loan is part of the plan, it can proceed immediately to project evaluation; if not, project preparation is required, consisting of a feasibility study, a fact-finding mission, an appraisal mission, and project evaluation in the form of reports. Various criteria are applied to the proposed project, including economic viability, financial soundness, institutional efficiency, and technical elements, and then a final appraisal report is issued. JSF was established in part to circumvent lengthy loan processing. If a project is suitable, negotiations are undertaken between the country applying and the bank. Once approved by the Board of Directors, project administration begins: preparatory work starts, funds are disbursed for project implementation, and review missions monitor progress. When the project ends, the loan account is closed, and postevaluation is undertaken.

For each project segment, contract bids are tendered. Almost one-fourth of procurement contracts go to Japan, and the United States receives about one-fifth of consulting services. Since many developing countries want their own contractors to play a role, in 1986 ADB adopted a domestic-preference scheme for procurement: the margin of preference for domestic contractors starts at 7.5 percent and goes up to 15 percent for domestic suppliers; no more than half of these contracts may be subcontracted to foreign firms.

Until 1987, ADB supported four types of training: general training, project-related training under bank loans, training for institution building under technical-assistance grants, and on-the-job training in the bank itself. The Japan scholarship program, set up in 1988, finances students from developing member countries in development-related fields. The training is primarily for institutions other than banks.

Since 1983, ADB has financed equity activities, under which private corporations and development-finance institutions may apply to receive investments in share capital, an activity similar to the World Bank's IFC. Under this arrangement, either there is a direct ADB investment or credit is extended. By 1987, there were nineteen such projects, totaling $38 million. The Asian Development Equity Fund (ADEF), launched in 1988, is a facility with $5 million from ADB, $80 million from stock sold in Japan, and most of the remaining $15 million provided by underwriters in Europe. Equity investments are often made on the condition that the receiving country will ease foreign-investor profit repatriation and capital-gains tax regulations.

Under pressure from the United Kingdom and the United States to provide more assistance to the private sector, a proposal for an Asian Finance and Investment Corporation (AFIC) is now under study. AFIC would be an ADB counterpart to the World Bank's IFC.

In 1979, the bank began to report on activities designed to assist special groups, when it indicated that it was undertaking special projects to benefit the poor. Environmental concerns and assistance to the private sector were the subject of attention in 1981 for the first time, and initial projects directed toward women's enterprises were reported in 1983. These new directions came in response to continuing criticism that ADB activities benefit those in the region who are already well off. As a bank, ADB has routinely based loans on the ability to pay back the amount provided. Other considerations, such as the specific benefits to ordinary people, have been given scant attention. In view of its control by First-World countries, ADB observes few Asian Way principles.

SOUTH-EAST ASIAN CENTRAL BANKS GROUP (SEACEN)[4]

While SEANZA courses have been useful, no joint research was possible through the framework of that organization. As a result of the consideration given by many central banks in the 1960s to such important innovations as the formation of ADB and proposals for payments unions, SEACEN emerged.

Central bank governors of Malaysia and Thailand, in private discussion during a meeting of SEANZA's Council of Governors in 1965, decided that a somewhat more flexible and frequent arrangement would serve additional needs of the region. Accordingly, Puey Ungphakorn, Bank of Thailand Governor, convened the first Conference of Governors of the Southeast Asian Central Banks (later hyphenated as South-east) in Bangkok in early 1966. In 1970, SEACEN's Conference of Governors received a report from one of its technical committees recommending the establishment of a training center in Malaysia and a research center in the Philippines. In 1971, SEACEN's first training course began at the training center for Malaysia's central bank. Although SEACEN approved a research center in principle, the Asian Way principle of separating political objectives from administrative implementation meant that the conference would have to agree to consolidate the two proposed centers into one structure and to accept the offer of Malaysia to locate the new facility at Petaling Jaya, which it did in 1975. In 1977, the SEACEN Research and Training Centre, known as SEACEN Centre, opened its doors alongside the National Training Centre for Bank Negara Malaysia, the country's central bank.

SEACEN as a whole has no formal charter. After the Research and Training Centre had been operating five years, legal agreements were drawn up to ensure that the work of the center would be insulated from political control by other governmental ministries, and the center became a nonprofit Malaysian corporation on January 27, 1982. SEACEN's Conference of Governors accepted the Memorandum of Association and Articles of Association ten days later. According to the third article of the Memorandum of Association of SEACEN Centre, its purposes are "to promote a better understanding of financial, monetary, banking and economic development matters . . . and to stimulate and facilitate cooperation . . . in the area of research and training." These aims describe SEACEN as a whole.

The Conference of Governors, composed of central bank governors, meets for two days each year (see Fig. 9.3). The conference set up technical committees to study specific questions in the early years; SEACEN Centre now plays this role.

From 1977 to 1982, the Conference of Governors was the supervising

Figure 9.3
Organization of the South-east Asian Central Banks Group

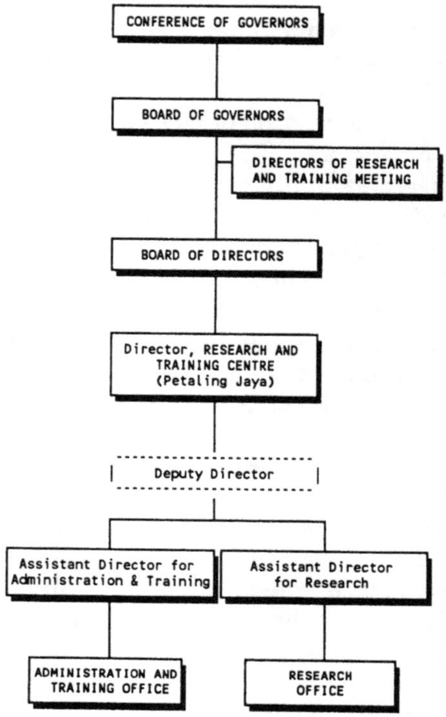

organ for the Research and Training Centre. The Memorandum of Association set up a Board of Governors for SEACEN Centre, consisting of heads of member central banks that choose to participate in the center. The Articles of Association also set up a Board of Directors for SEACEN Centre as a Malaysian corporation, chaired by the Governor of Bank Negara Malaysia; other members are the Deputy Governor of Bank Negara Malaysia and the Director of SEACEN Centre, a nonvoting secretary to the board. The Board of Governors meets for an afternoon session on the final day of the Conference of Governors each year. The Board of Directors meets twice yearly for one-day sessions. Each year a three-day meeting of directors of research and training of participating central banks convenes to decide which research projects and training courses are to be recommended to the Conference of Governors for the work program.

A Director heads SEACEN Centre. There are two Assistant Directors – one for Administration and Training, the other for Research.

Five countries attended the inaugural meeting of SEACEN. Since there is no formal membership provision, attendance is the only indication of membership. Ten countries now belong (see Table 9.3). Vietnam was inactive from 1975 to 1980, when it resumed participation in the Conference of Governors by sending an Observer; it has continued to do so each year since 1983.

Membership on the Board of Governors differs from membership in SEACEN as a whole. Burma was invited but failed to send a representative to the Board of Governors in 1982; although not a signatory to the 1982 agreements, it is considered to be a member both of SEACEN and of SEACEN Centre. Cambodia and Vietnam have chosen not to participate in SEACEN Centre and sit on neither the Board of Directors nor the Board of Governors of SEACEN Centre.

In 1984, the budget of SEACEN was $487,000, excluding the donation by Malaysia for the physical facilities of SEACEN Centre. The funding formula is in two parts (see Table 9.3). Half of the expenses are shared equally by all participating countries; the other half is proportionate to each country's relative shares of SDRs.

A primary goal of the early conferences was to provide a forum to discuss international financial problems. Training activities began in 1972. Training courses on inspection and supervision of financial institutions and national economic management occur at regular intervals. The remaining courses have mostly been held only once or twice, covering such topics as balance of payments, financial analysis, foreign-exchange policies, management of branch banks, and small-sector

Table 9.3
South-east Asian Central Banks Group: Membership and Assessments for SEACEN Centre

Year Joined	Member Countries	Assessment (1984)[a]
1966	Malaysia	17.2%
	Philippines	15.2
	Sri Lanka	11.2
	Thailand	14.2
	Vietnam (i 1975-79)[b,c]	na
1967	Indonesia	25.6
	Nepal	7.8
	Singapore	8.8
1969	Cambodia (i 1975-)[c]	na
1975	Burma	7.6
Total	10 Members	$487,000

[a]Due to rounding, the column does not sum exactly to 100 percent.
[b]Joined as Republic of Vietnam
[c]Not a member of boards supervising SEACEN Centre
Key: i = inactive
na = not assessed

financing. Each year there are about four training courses, which last forty days. SEACEN Centre conducts training through seminars, mostly three days in length. Directors of supervision have met almost every year since 1980. Seminars have treated such topics as adjustment policies in an unbalanced world economy, balance of payments, coordination of fiscal and monetary policy, country risk, fiscal disequilibrium, identification and treatment of problem financial institutions, interest rates, personnel development, the unorganized money market, and stabilization of commodity prices and export earnings.

SEACEN research, such as the annual report on economic conditions in SEACEN countries, is presented to the conference each year. The center also prepares in-house project research and coordinates collaborative efforts among experts in the region.

ASIAN CLEARING UNION (ACU)[5]

John Maynard Keynes proposed an international clearing union to the world monetary conferences in 1943, recommending that credit replace gold and foreign exchange as the basis for international finance. Although his proposals were not accepted when the World Bank was formed, they awaited a new era to come to fruition.

Although Third-World countries might achieve some economic growth if they were to trade with one another in the same manner as do the countries of Europe, one fundamental barrier to such trade is that purchases must be made either in the local currency of the developing countries or in currencies with a high degree of international convertibility, such as the U.S. dollar. Because local currencies are infrequently used, Third-World trade requires an importing country to convert its currency into U.S. dollars in order to pay them to an exporting country, which in turn changes U.S. dollars into local currency to pay employees for the work involved in manufacturing the product. For each conversion from one currency to another a bank charges a fee. As a result, there is very little Third-World trade. It is more profitable for Third-World countries to deal directly with First-World trading partners so long as there is no mechanism, such as a payments union, for exchanging one Third-World currency for another with greater ease.

The idea of a payments union emerged at a session of ECAFE in 1963. By 1967, Iran and Pakistan formed a payments union as a project of Regional Cooperation for Development (RCD), an organization also linked with Turkey. Further ECAFE efforts resulted by April 1971 in a Preparatory Committee for the Establishment of an Asian Clearing Union, and the Agreement Establishing the Asian Clearing Union was presented to ECAFE's session in April 1973. ACU started in November 1975.

The founding agreement sets forth three purposes of ACU:

(a) to provide a facility to settle, on a multilateral basis, payments for current international transactions among the territories of participants; (b) to promote the use of participants' currencies in current transactions between their respective territories and thereby effect economies in the use of the participants' exchange reserves; and (c) to promote monetary cooperation among the participants and closer relations among the banking systems in their territories and thereby contribute to the expansion of trade and economic activity among the countries of the ECAFE region. (Article II)

The headquarters (Agent Bank) is at the offices of Iran's central bank in Tehran. Central bank governors of ACU serve on the Board of Directors (see Fig. 9.4). Member central banks, in turn, designate an officer-in-charge to handle ACU business as individual transactions occur. A General Manager handles operations, assisted by a Deputy General Manager, an accountant, a clerk, a typist, and two other general services staff members, all employees of the Iranian government on full-time special assignment for ACU.

The idea of an Asian clearing union envisaged membership by all or most Asian countries. India's role as a de facto balancer of payments in South Asia, unique among Asia's subregions, ensured that South Asian countries would carefully consider the idea of the union. India

Figure 9.4
Organization of the Asian Clearing Union

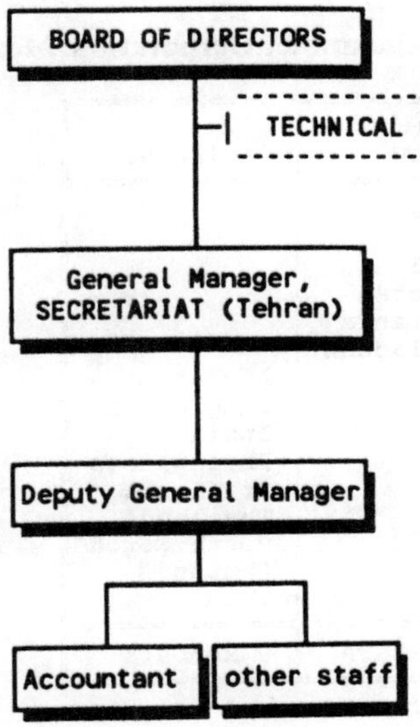

and six adjacent countries became the sole members of ACU (see Table 9.4). Although Cambodia, Laos, and Vietnam participated in the preparatory meeting in 1973, they did not sign the agreement. The Association of South East Asian Nations (ASEAN), meanwhile, formed its own payments union in 1977. In 1982, the governor of Iran's central bank visited Singapore, Malaysia, and Thailand to discuss their willingness to join ACU. Meanwhile, RCD collapsed in 1979.

Under ACU, the Agent Bank in Tehran converts currencies into Asian monetary units (AMUs) until a settlement clears on the final day of February, April, June, August, October, and December of each year. AMUs are equal to SDRs. Net savings to member countries average 0.2 percent of each transaction: this is the difference between the buying and selling rates at most commercial banks. Currently, if lines of credit are exceeded in sixty days, an interest charge is applied as part of the terms of settlement. The interest is BIS's closing rate for sixty days of Eurodollar deposits.

Originally, there was some reluctance to use ACU facilities, which are voluntary. India was the largest user, and Bangladesh, Burma, and Nepal transacted only nominal amounts; only about five percent of intraregional trade was involved. The Asian Way principle of incrementalism then took over. In 1983, Iran decided to route all eligible transactions through ACU, India followed suit in 1984, and the other countries decided in principle to do so in the future. As a result, in 1987, ACU reported 484 million AMU transactions, more than three times the figure for 1980. Out of the total transactions through ACU, about 63

Table 9.4
Asian Clearing Union and Asian Reinsurance Corporation: Membership

Year Joined	ACU	Asian Re
1974[a]	India Iran Nepal Pakistan Sri Lanka	
1975	Bangladesh	
1977	Burma	Afghanistan Bangladesh India Philippines Sri Lanka Thailand
1978		South Korea
1979		Bhutan China
Totals	7 Members	9 Members

[a]Dates of ratification

percent were settled in 1987 in foreign exchange, and the rest were cleared inside the system; this was almost the reverse of the 1982 percentages. Transactions through ACU account for almost half of total trade among the member countries.

Petroleum and petroleum products were originally excluded from ACU, since large oil companies have intercompany account clearance so that exports and imports often do not involve the receipt and payment of foreign exchange. Since 1985, oil and gas payments have been eligible for settlement though ACU. Currently, the UN Conference on Trade and Development (UNCTAD) is designing a reserve fund and a swap arrangement in the framework of ACU.

ASIAN REINSURANCE CORPORATION (Asian Re)[6]

Businesses require insurance against fires and other casualties. As industry and trade grow in the developing countries of Asia, the need for insurance multiplies. National insurance companies generally begin with a small capital base and have to reinsure their policies; in addition, the insurance business requires technical expertise for determining rates and terms as well as for dealing with claims. Both the capital for reinsurance and the expertise in the industry are primarily in developed countries, so the foreign exchange sought by local corporations to enhance national development drains away through the purchases of First-World insurance or reinsurance.

In the early 1970s, UNCTAD began to study the problem of loss of foreign exchange due to insurance premiums paid by the Third World, recommending the establishment of exchanges, pools, and national and regional reinsurance corporations. One estimate, based on figures compiled by UNCTAD, was that in the mid-1970s nine developing countries in Asia were averaging a loss of $20 million in foreign exchange per year due to reinsurance. This proved to be an underestimate, since more than half of the total reinsurance business in Southeast Asia (about $30 million) was in the reinsurance companies of Japan, the United Kingdom, and the United States in the mid-1980s, according to the Singapore Reinsurance Corporation. While life insurance premiums in Japan sum to 290 percent of the country's GNP, the corresponding figure for all of Asia is only 25 percent. The aim of the Asian Reinsurance Corporation, thus, is to develop a strong insurance industry throughout Asia by providing reinsurance and technical training for the region.

One reinsurance pool already existed in the region. Members of the East Asian Insurance Congress (EAIC)–consisting of government and private insurance corporations from Hongkong, Indonesia, Japan, Malaysia, Singapore, South Korea, Taiwan (China), and Thailand–established an Asian Reinsurance Pool on a voluntary basis. Although the African Development Bank (AfDB) had developed plans for an African reinsurance corporation, ADB was not interested in such a plan for Asia. Control of the African institution was largely in the hands of countries of that region, whereas Japan, a First-World country with a strong reinsurance industry, plays a pivotal role in ADB.

ESCAP and UNCTAD then convened the first Round-Table Meeting on Asian Reinsurance Cooperation in October 1974, which in turn set up a preparatory committee to develop a scheme for an Asian reinsurance corporation. The founding agreement was open for signature in April 1977, and Asian Re began on March 31, 1978.

According to the Preamble and Decision of the Agreement Establishing the Asian Reinsurance Corporation, Asian Re has four functions:

> 1. . . . operate as a professional reinsurer accepting business from the insurance markets . . . and retroced[ing] its surpluses after net retention with priority given to the national insurance and reinsurance markets of the member States, 2. . . . invest a sizeable proportion of its funds within the region, provided that such investments meet with the requirements of sound insurance techniques, 3. . . . serve as a regional center for the collection of insurance information and the development of expertise in insurance and reinsurance . . . , 4. . . . provide technical assistance to the national insurance markets of the member States.

The Council of Members, the ministerial-level governing body (see Fig. 9.5), meets at least once each year, initially for two-day sessions. The Management Board meets between Council sessions as often as needed; these occurred quarterly in the early years, but they are more frequent at present. The Management Board consists of the Chairman and Vice-Chairman of the Council as well as the General Manager and Assistant General Manager of the Corporation.

Any developing member country of ESCAP may join Asian Re by signing the founding agreement, depositing subscriptions for shares within six months of signing, and by ratifying the agreement. Nine members have joined thus far (see Table 9.4). Iran, the first country to sign the agreement, failed to deposit its instrument of accession with ESCAP, and thus did not become a member. In accordance with the Asian Way principle of pan-Asianism, Indonesia, Malaysia, Pakistan, and Singapore have placed business with Asian Re but have not joined. Four other countries attended preliminary meetings but have not yet participated: Fiji, Hongkong, Trust Territory of the Pacific Islands, and Western Samoa.

The authorized capital of Asian Re is $15 million, divided into 15,000 shares of $1,000 each. Each member must subscribe and pay $500,000

Figure 9.5
Organization of the Asian Reinsurance Corporation

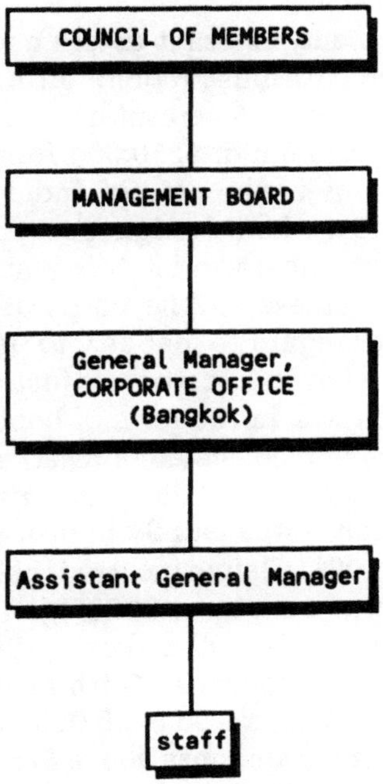

(500 shares), so the current nine members make up a total of $4.5 million in assets (paid-in capital). Until 1983, half of a country's shares could be paid in local currency (100 percent in the case of Afghanistan, Bangladesh, and Bhutan, designated as Least Developed Countries), provided that it was convertible and remittable whenever needed by the corporation. However, exchange losses were too great to permit this provision to continue, so the subscribed capital is now in U.S. dollars for all countries. Although individual governments pay for shares, one national institution may be permitted by that government to participate in purchasing a portion of the country's capital stock allotment. All amounts must be placed in demand deposits under the Asian Re name in a national banking institution.

Funds on deposit with Asian Re may be in the form of bonds or cash deposits. Interest on bonds will accrue to the corporation, as will the amount of premiums paid by insurance companies to Asian Re for reinsurance; this income, all exempt from local taxation, can be invested inside or outside the same country or paid out in the form of dividends to the country. So far, although investment has been occurring, Asian Re has paid no dividends; up to 60 percent of profits can be paid out as dividends. Originally, at least 10 percent of the profits were to go into reserve until the reserve was as large as the operating capital; this limit has not yet been reached.

Each member government, unless it enters a reservation when signing the founding agreement, must require all national insurance and reinsurance institutions to cede 5 percent of all outward treaty reinsurance to Asian Re (or a premium of $250,000 from these treaties, when this is a lesser amount, as in the case of India, the Philippines, and South Korea). In countries where foreign insurance firms use external reinsurance, Asian Re members must bring about a commensurate contribution of their business to the corporation. No country has signed a reservation with regard to inability to pay cessions.

By the end of 1985, Asian Re assets were just over $9.8 million. Out of this total, $6.7 million was in the form of bonds, cash deposits, and accrued interest; $2.4 million consisted of reserves held by ceding companies; $0.7 million were amounts due from insurers and reinsurers; and the value of the balance was largely in office equipment. Management expenses were $81,008. Claims incurred, net of reinsurances, were $2.5 million, and there was a net loss of $267,412 in 1985 due in part to the declining value of the U.S. dollar. The corporation held 508 contracts, mostly from member countries, with an estimated premium of $7.6 million. Contracts cannot exceed $250,000, although Asian Re can secure joint underwriting for amounts above $150,000.

Asian Re maintains portfolios for fire, marine hull business, cargo and combined marine, aviation, and miscellaneous, engineering, and combined portfolios. During 1983, an aviation portfolio was phased out, and Asian Re commenced underwriting a book of facultative business.

Training activities include seminars for insurance managers and courses for insurance underwriters. Asian Re staff have been lecturers at various conferences in the region. Meetings of experts have been convened, and Asian Re experts have provided technical assistance in various fields, including marine cargo underwriting and crop insurance.

SUMMARY AND CONCLUSIONS

ADB, with all the resources at its disposal, is criticized for its allocations. In order to ensure that loans will be completed and repaid, only a small portion of its activities have involved the least-developed countries, which have the greatest need.

One reason a country applies for a loan could be that a commercial firm is considering foreign investment, but there is an insufficient source of electric power, too few roads on which to haul commodities to port, inadequate port facilities, and the like. The loan, then, provides the infrastructure that the corporation requires. As soon as a project is completed, the corporation derives its profit, while the cost of the loan is passed on to the indigenous population through increased taxation, higher rates for electricity, and other devices that favor the elites over the masses. Presumably, new jobs for the people add to their income so that they can afford higher taxes. Such calculations are in exact terms for the corporation and the government, but the ordinary person's plight is not noticed. When the scenario of economic gain for all goes awry, the ordinary people are the ones who suffer, but the bank is paid back.

While loans have tended to focus on particular projects as isolated efforts, many countries structure their economies so that a small elite gains benefits, leaving the people to suffer whatever consequences might ensue. Some critics have sought to persuade the bank to undertake policy-oriented loans—that is, to tie the granting of a loan to changes in policies that eliminate corruption and overconcentration of resources in the hands of noncompetitive corporate giants. As many as one-third of the loan projects have been approved, former ADB officials have alleged, on noneconomic grounds. At best, the loans often reward government ministers who are making domestically unpopular but economically necessary decisions. In other cases, it is alleged, the payoff is to a particular corporation (writing the specifications so that only one firm can do the job), with a side payment to the government minister who agrees to the terms of an unneeded project, such as the dredging of a harbor into which no ships have ever or will ever sail.

Continued increases in capital have been voted over the years, although nearly half of the capital is unused; inasmuch as the increases require more capital commitments from developing countries, the developing countries are thus compelled to make loan applications so that their funds will be put to some use. This leaves bank lenders in the role of promoting increased lending for its own sake, according to many critics. The activity of the bank must be of use to someone or it would not continue, so cynics who have no sophistication on economic matters point to overpaid janitors, secretaries, and officials at the bank.

How can ADB respond to all these criticisms? There are two levels of analysis: the project level and the impact on a country as a whole. ADB's rolling three-year plans for individual countries, sometimes combined with econometric models, are not part of the public record, so we are unable to see precisely in which direction the bank is going—and why. We can either rely on flowery statements or look at the record.

Difficult as it is to document how much of an impact an individual project can have on a country as a whole, ADB has only recently begun to report how projects enhance the living standards of ordinary people.

Agriculture is the largest sector aided by the bank, accounting for about one-third of all loans, and ADB's agriculture policy appears to put large-scale infrastructure in place, the beneficiaries for which will be corporate farmers. Developing countries want to manufacture their own automobiles, elevators, refrigerators, and stereos. The paucity of loans to industry suggests that ADB wants the developing member countries of Asia to produce raw materials but not to process or manufacture from their own natural resources except to make parts for assembly into products finished in the First World. Countries in ASEAN, as a result, have tried to develop their own regional industrial policies for lack of interest from ADB. Although ADB has made some effort to respond to these criticisms, many observers insist that there will have to be major changes in policies lest the bank lose credibility in the years ahead.

While SEANZA developed highly professional training courses, the development needs of the countries of Southeast Asia required a more politically sensitive body to conduct technical research, and SEACEN was the result. In more recent years, SEACEN's training program has expanded, and its research has been more technical because ASEAN's Committee on Finance and Banking (COFAB) now does research on the more politically oriented issues.

Iran, somewhat chagrined that the headquarters of ADB was not located at Tehran, where it could mobilize capital from countries of Western Asia, was quick to assume leadership in ACU. While the Shah was still in power, ACU was seen as an element of prestige but not taken seriously by those in charge. After the establishment of the Islamic Republic of Iran, with its emphasis on self-reliance by Third-World countries, ACU flowered. An UNCTAD study and exemplary diplomacy by Tehran spread the word that ACU would benefit all. The first breakthrough came when Iran decided in 1983 to clear all of its relevant transactions through ACU; when India followed suit in 1984, and all gas and oil transactions came under ACU in 1985, the facility was assured of success. ACU's aim is to encourage intraregional trade by making it more profitable. Prospects for this development depend on the advance of such organizations as the Bangkok Agreement – a preferential trading agreement involving Bangladesh, India, South Korea, and Sri Lanka that is described in Chapter 13. ACU is now studying the feasibility of adding a reserve fund and a swap arrangement to its activities, although the Bank of India is opposed, since it already plays this role for ACU members.

Asian Re doubled its assets in its first decade of operation. The risks are considerable, and the elimination of insurance for aviation is due to the frequency of airline disasters. Although one ESCAP official estimated in 1978 that within a decade Asian Re might have $25 billion in assets and could be self-financing, current assets are just short of $10 million. Asian Re has operated at a loss for more than one year in the 1980s, a difficult decade for all international businesses. Premium rates have increased, since Asian Re follows market rates set by Lloyd's of London and professional reinsurers in the First World, and business has slowed. The need to improve the technical skills of national insurance companies prompted Asian Re to provide technical assistance to the region.

In 1982, insurance companies in ASEAN started a reinsurance pool, which was upgraded to the ASEAN Reinsurance Corporation by 1988. While the premiums of Asian Re were about $7.6 million at the end of 1985, the ASEAN Reinsurance Corporation started with $3 million, compared to the $28.7 million in underwriting by the private sector in the six ASEAN countries and about $700 million in reinsurance premiums estimated by Asian Re in all Asian countries.

The tension between ADB and the rest of the organizations in this chapter highlights a central fact. The use of Asian Way principles has propelled the other organizations forward, while ADB has become increasingly controversial.

NOTES

1. For references to SEANZA documents, see Michael Haas, *Basic Documents of Asian Regional Organizations* (Dobbs Ferry, NY: Oceana Publications, 1979), vol. 6, pp. 43–44. For a bibliography of secondary sources for all the organizations described in this chapter, see pp. 15–27.
2. Personal correspondence, December 16, 1987.
3. For references to ADB documents, see Michael Haas, *Basic Documents of Asian Regional Organizations* (Dobbs Ferry, NY: Oceana Publications, 1979), vol. 6, pp. 28–42.
4. For references to SEACEN documents, see Michael Haas, *Basic Documents of Asian Regional Organizations* (Dobbs Ferry, NY: Oceana Publications, 1979), vol. 6, pp. 43–47.
5. For references to ACU documents, see Michael Haas, *Basic Documents of Asian Regional Organizations* (Dobbs Ferry, NY: Oceana Publications, 1979), vol. 6, p. 48.
6. For references to Asian Re documents, see Michael Haas, *Basic Documents of Asian Regional Organizations* (Dobbs Ferry, NY: Oceana Publications, 1979), vol. 6, pp. 49–50.

10 GETTING THE WORD OUT IN ASIA

Modern societies require a continuous, efficient, inexpensive, and speedy flow of information. In the 1960s, mail in Asia flowed unpredictably, radio and television were poorly developed, and telephone connections had low fidelity and thus low frequency. Efforts to upgrade the communication systems in Asia have been undertaken by the Asian-Pacific Postal Union (APPU), Asia-Pacific Institute for Broadcasting Development (AIBD), and the Asia-Pacific Telecommunity (APT).

ASIAN-PACIFIC POSTAL UNION (APPU)[1]

Foundation, Organization, and Membership

Starting in the 1950s, the Universal Postal Union (UPU) began to encourage the formation of "restricted postal unions" in various parts of the world to promote better services and programs in one region that would be inappropriate for another. APPU traces its origin to a visit in 1959 of Korean Postmaster-General Shin Duck Lee to his counterpart in the Philippines, Enrico Palomar, concerning the possible formation of an Asian bloc within UPU, an idea that developed into the concept of a restricted postal union. Subsequently, the Manila Postal Conference of 1961 adopted an agreement to form the Asian-Oceanic Postal Union (AOPU). By 1962, although only four countries had ratified the agreement, a Central Office opened in Manila. When the number of ratifications was sufficient, the new organization was officially activated on July 1, 1966. The change in name to APPU in 1981 confirmed that the new states of "Oceania" recognize themselves as "Pacific" island nations.

Each Congress of APPU adopts a new Asian-Pacific Postal Convention. According to the Convention of 1981, the purpose of the Union is to "extend, facilitate and improve the postal relations between the member-countries and promote cooperation in the field of the postal services" [Article I(2)].

APPU's Congress, the plenary organ of APPU, consists of postmasters-general from the member countries; it meets for about two weeks every five years (see Fig. 10.1). Between Congresses APPU is managed by the Executive Council, which meets for about one week each year, with deputy postmasters-general in attendance.

The Central Office is managed by the Director, who is Postmaster-General of the Philippines. The Assistant Director does most of the administrative work, assisted by two secretaries.

There are twenty member countries (see Table 10.1). In 1974, when the People's Republic of China considered joining, AOPU suspended the Republic of China, following a similar development in UPU. The

Figure 10.1
Organization of the Asian-Pacific Postal Union

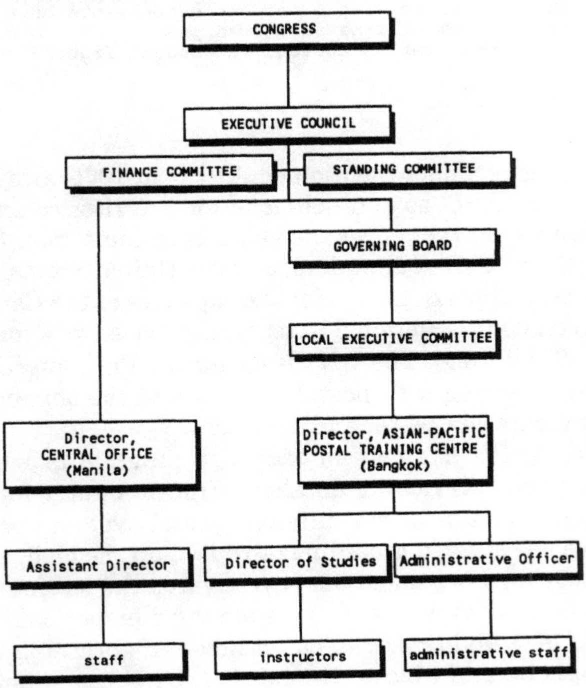

Table 10.1
Asian-Pacific Postal Union: Membership, Assessments for the Central Office, and Cost Sharing for the Asian-Pacific Postal Training Centre

Year Joined	Member Countries	CO Assessment (1983)	APPTC Cost Sharing (1984)[a]
1962	Philippines	$1,641.04	60%
	South Korea	2,461.56	10
	Taiwan (s 1974)		
	Thailand	1,641.04	37
1968	Japan	4,102.60	
	Laos	1,641.04	
1969	Australia	4,102.60	
1970	Indonesia	2,461.56	33
	New Zealand	4,102.60	
1973	India	4,102.60	0
1975	China	4,102.60	
1976	Bangladesh	2,461.56	0
	Malaysia	1,641.04	40
	Papua New Guinea	1,641.04	0
1977	Pakistan	2,461.56	50
1979	Sri Lanka	2,461.56	0
1981	Singapore	1,641.04	
1982	Maldives	1,641.04	0
	Nepal	1,641.04	0
1983	Bhutan	1,641.04	0
1985	Nauru[b]		0
Totals	21-1=20 Members	$47,590.16	$429,575

[a]Figures represent the percentage of costs paid by the country for its students; countries with 0 percent assessments have their costs provided in the form of free scholarships
[b]Assessment was the same as Bhutan, but budget figures for 1985 are unavailable
Key: s = suspended

People's Republic of China then joined APPU in 1975. Only members of UPU can join APPU, so non-self-governing territories are ineligible for membership. Observers over the years have come from Hongkong, Iran, Portugal, the United Kingdom, and the United States.

Each member's apportionment for the expenses of the Central Office (CO) is based on its international letter traffic, based on a formula used by UPU (see Table 10.1). The UN Development Program (UNDP) has funded projects dealing with postal training and the ongoing effort to set up a documentation center and data bank.

Since 1964, APPU has had an exchange program in which postal officials visit postal services in another member country for up to one month in order to learn how a different postal system operates. The Central Office has studied procedures to speed up the mail, such as the return of empty mail bags, and has investigated the feasibility of abolishing internal air conveyance charges among member countries. Currently, APPU is studying how to assist non-self-governing territories, such as Hongkong and Macao. In addition, UPU has supplied an expert to set up a postal documentation study center, who is studying delivery time between member countries to determine procedures for speeding up the mail.

Asian-Pacific Postal Training Centre (APPTC)

Postal training in the region mainly focuses on the lower levels of operation, as countries prepare newly recruited personnel to handle the rising need for mail services. Higher-level officials, meanwhile, had been receiving training at schools located in developed countries at considerable expense, leaving middle-level personnel without a facility to upgrade their skills until they moved to higher levels of management responsibility. After collaborating with AOPU in holding training seminars for senior postal officials in 1969 and 1970, UPU set up the Asian-Oceanic Postal Training School (AOPTS) in Bangkok in 1970 with UNDP funding. UNDP set up a Governing Board in 1968 to start planning, and the school began operation in 1970. In 1975, AOPTS became a part of APPU, and in 1981 its name changed to Asian-Pacific Postal Training Centre.

The Governing Board consists of one representative from each contributing and participating postal administration and the Chairman of the APPU Executive Council (see Fig. 10.1). The Director of the APPU Central Office, the Economic and Social Commission for Asia and the Pacific (ESCAP), UNDP, and UPU are Observers on the Governing Board. The Governing Board meets each year in conjunction with the annual APPU Executive Council. General Regulations for AOPTS were first adopted by the Governing Board in 1977.

Originally, there was an Executive Committee for AOPTS, composed of representatives from the diplomatic missions of each participating country assigned to Bangkok. This Local Executive Committee, restructured since AOPTS was absorbed by APPU, now brings together the Director General of the Thai Post and Telegraph Department, the APPTC Director, and APPTC's Director of Studies. It meets for one day every two months, although officially meetings are supposed to be held only twice each year.

The center was next to the Bangkok central post office up to 1979, when it moved to the site of the Thai national postal training center adjacent to the Laksi post office, Bangkok. The Governing Board selects the Director, Director of Studies, and the instructors. The Local Executive Committee appoints the Administrative Officer, and the Director recruits general service staff.

Three types of countries are involved in APPTC training: APPU member countries that finance their own students, APPU and non-APPU countries that send students with fellowship support, and

APPU member countries that provide cash or in-kind contributions. Australia, Japan, New Zealand, and India have been donors. Except for Australia and New Zealand, all APPU members have sent students to APPTC. Laos has been inactive in recent years.

Up to 1975, UNDP and UPU defrayed two-thirds of AOPTS costs, with the balance paid by the participating countries. Currently UNDP and UPU provide only about one-eighth of the total, with the donor and participating countries supplying funds for instruction and administration, respectively (see Table 10.1). APPTC also trains personnel from nonmember countries: nonmember Brunei defrays the cost of its trainees, and the rest receive scholarships from Australia, Japan, UNDP, or UPU.

There are eight regular training courses each year. The core course for mid-management personnel, the postal management course, has been run since 1969. In 1975, an instructor training course was added to provide a vehicle for training instructors from the national postal training schools; in the same year, the mail routing and circulation course and the postal statistics course were initiated. In 1976, the audit and inspection of post offices course began, and the international postal services course started in 1979. Two new courses began in 1981: the postal financial management course and the postal planning and development course.

Initially, instructors at AOPTS were from outside the region; in 1987, the faculty were from Indonesia, Pakistan, the Philippines, South Korea, and Thailand. Consultants from India and Japan serviced specific courses.

Much of the course content is of a practical nature, following the Asian Way principle of Asian solutions to Asian problems, and involves problem-solving activities in the classroom and in the field. Students collect data of various sorts and write reports on their individual efforts. As a result, the center has gradually developed a data bank of statistics for the region to augment its collection of library resources for trainees.

ASIA-PACIFIC INSTITUTE FOR BROADCASTING DEVELOPMENT (AIBD)[2]

Radio and television are the principal media through which the public now learns about the world. Developing countries, with particular needs to inform citizens of changes in their countries, want to present a coherent alternative to the canned programming that can so easily be purchased from developed countries. The idea of AIBD is to develop more expertise for employees of national broadcasting industries.

In 1964, a nongovernmental organization, the Asian Broadcasting

Union (ABU), was formed in Tokyo for radio and television professionals in the region. ABU approached the UN Educational, Scientific, and Cultural Organization (UNESCO) for funds to upgrade skills of broadcasters in the region. When UNESCO held a Meeting on Radio and Television in the Service of Development in 1966, participants asked UNESCO to survey training needs. In 1967, UNESCO commissioned such a study, using funds from UNDP. The report, presented at a meeting in Kuala Lumpur sponsored by UNESCO in 1968, estimated that 20,000 of the 35,000 broadcasting employees of the region needed professional training, and a regional training center was proposed.

Malaysia was seeking at that time to establish a national training center. UNDP indicated that it would not support a regional institution to train broadcasting personnel, but that it would finance a Malaysian facility that might be transformed into a regional center when it had perfected its program. Accordingly, in 1976, UNDP funded the National Broadcasting Centre of Malaysia, now the Institut Penyiaran Tun Abdul Razak (IPTAR). Although primarily focusing on Malaysia, experimental regional training was financed by ABU, UNDP, and UNESCO from 1972 to 1975. After a project document and draft agreement for an Asian Institute for Broadcasting Development circulated for endorsement by various member countries in 1975, and UNESCO was favorable toward expanding the scope of IPTAR, two Inter-Governmental Meetings were held in 1977. In August, at the second meeting, the proposed name was changed to Asia-Pacific Institute for Broadcasting Development (though the acronym AIBD was retained), and the agreement was accepted.

The Agreement Establishing the Asia-Pacific Institute for Broadcasting Development specifies four objectives:

> (a) to assist countries members of the Institute . . . to improve the professional capability of their broadcasting systems, through systematic training and research programs consistent with their national development goals; (b) to orient the work of broadcasting organizations and practitioners in member countries towards educational and development goals; (c) to evolve methods, techniques and material resources which will allow them to operate more effectively to these ends; and (d) to create a network of collaborating institutions in the field of broadcasting development, training and research. (Article 3)

The Governing Council, AIBD's plenary organ (see Fig. 10.2), meets for five-day sessions once each year. Eleven countries sit on the Governing Council; one represents Malaysia, the host country, and the rest are elected by postal vote. ABU, the International Telecommunication Union (ITU), UNDP, and UNESCO are nonvoting members. The Governing Council selects the Director of the Institute, who serves as

Figure 10.2
Organization of the Asia-Pacific Institute for Broadcasting Development

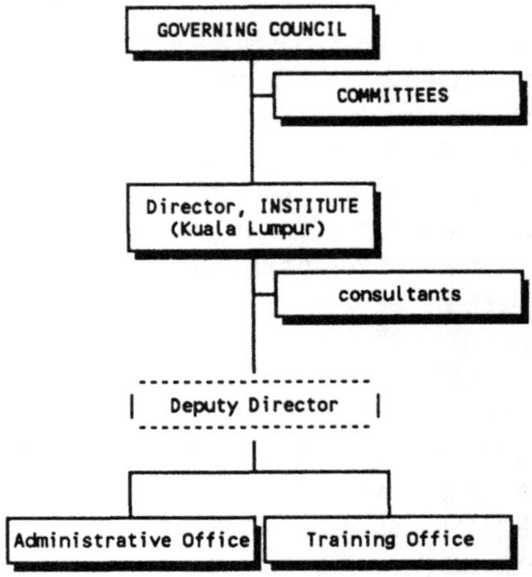

Secretary to the Council. Representatives of the Governing Council tend to be heads of national radio and television broadcasting institutions rather than government ministers. A proposed meeting of ministers of media has not yet occurred.

In 1982, the Governing Council set up a committee with at least four country representatives, the AIBD Director, and other experts in order to review various matters concerned with the Institute in more depth; the committee meets twice a year—two days before the Governing Council and one day after the ABU General Assembly. In 1984, the Governing Council set up a committee to assist in implementing projects funded by the Association of South East Asian Nations (ASEAN). The headquarters of AIBD is at IPTAR in Kuala Lumpur.

Members of ESCAP can join AIBD. Some twenty-eight countries participated in IPTAR training, whereas sixteen have joined AIBD (see Table 10.2). Australia, France, and Japan, which attended the first Inter-Governmental Meeting in 1977, did not join. Among the countries trained from 1972 to 1976, the following have yet to join: Burma, Cambodia, the Cook Islands, Gilbert and Ellice Islands (now Kiribati and Tuvalu), Hongkong, Laos, New Hebrides (now Vanuatu), the Solomon Islands, Tonga, Trust Territory of the Pacific Islands, and Western Samoa. Nonmember countries participating in AIBD training courses are Australia, Bhutan, Brunei, China, the Cook Islands, Kiribati, Nauru, New Caledonia, Niue, the Solomon Islands, Tonga, Trust Territory of the Pacific Islands, Tuvalu, Vanuatu, and Western Samoa.

Trainees have also come from outside the region, including Belgium, Canada, Chile, Egypt, Ethiopia, France, Germany, Iraq, Jamaica, Jordan, Mauritius, Oman, Qatar, the Soviet Union, Sweden, Turkey, the United Kingdom, the United States, and Yemen. Consultancy missions have visited most member countries; one has gone to Macao.

There is no fixed amount for member contributions, based on the Asian Way principle of equality of nations without hierarchy. Members are urged to provide a percentage of the national budget spent on broadcasting to defray personnel costs of the Institute. Each country buys at least one subscription and may subscribe to two or more units as it wishes (see Table 10.2). Since 1985, the minimum subscription has been $750.

There have been more than 300 training courses so far, focusing on audience research and program evaluation, broadcast management, engineering operations, film, news and current affairs, programming and production, resource center development, training materials development, training methodology, and applications of broadcasting in such areas as consumer affairs, education, environment, population planning, and rural development. There are three types of courses – regional, subregional, and in-country – at an approximate ratio of 30 : 20 : 50. Senior- and middle-level personnel take the regional and subregional courses; in-country courses are for lower-level staff. Fellowships support those at the regional training courses, whether in Kuala Lumpur

Table 10.2
Asia-Pacific Institute for Broadcasting Development:
Membership and Contributions

Year Joined	Member Countries	Contribution (1984)
1977	Bangladesh	$ 3,672
	India	22,073
	Indonesia	7,360
	Iran	920
	Malaysia	24,000
	Philippines	2,760
	Sri Lanka	19,369
	Thailand	2,300
1978	Afghanistan	460
	Fiji	460
	Pakistan	3,102
	Papua New Guinea	14,378
	South Korea	7,820
	Vietnam	4,397
1980	Nepal	460
1982	Singapore	3,680
Totals	16 Members	$117,211[a]

[a]Excludes external sources

or elsewhere. In-country training is financed by the country requesting such services; AIBD provides the instructors.

AIBD also sponsors meetings, seminars, and workshops each year to enhance an understanding of newer trends. The Institute has also produced about a dozen publications on various aspects of broadcasting and materials for the various courses. AIBD provides consultancy and advisory services, in which experts aid a particular country. Research has included a study on the international flow of television news and programs.

ASIA-PACIFIC TELECOMMUNITY (APT)[3]

Since much business crosses national boundaries, the lack of reliable and speedy mail service means that other alternatives must be utilized. Most business communication, even inside the borders of developing Asian countries, depends on sophisticated satellite-based technologies for the transfer of information. APT was designed to fill these needs.

The idea of an Asian telecommunity received formal endorsement at the annual session of the UN Economic Commission for Asia and the Far East (ECAFE, now ESCAP) in 1968. A joint ECAFE-ITU Unit was set up to develop an Asian Telecommunication Network (ATN), and by 1970 a dozen countries accepted a plan of operation. With funding from ADB and the World Bank for the construction of cables and other facets of telecommunication systems, construction for ATN began in the 1970s.

Meanwhile, ITU adopted the International Telecommunication Convention of 1973, one provision of which called for regional telecommunication unions. ESCAP (as ECAFE was renamed), accordingly, organized an expert group meeting in October 1975 to draw up a constitution for such a body. The group broadened the scope to an Asia-Pacific Telecommunity, and the resulting Constitution was open for signature at ESCAP's annual session in March 1976. By 1979, the required number of countries ratified, including Thailand, which offered to host the organization.

APT's Constitution lists five objectives:

> (a) to correlate the planning, programming and development within the region of intra-regional and international telecommunication networks to meet immediate and future requirements; (b) to promote the implementation of all agreed networks; (c) to assist the development within the region of the national components of an efficient regional and international telecommunication network; (d) to foster coordination within the region of technical standards and routing plans for intra-regional and international traffic; (e) to seek the adoption of efficient operating methods in regional telecommunication services. (Article 2)

APT's General Assembly occurs once every three years for eleven-day sessions concurrently with the meeting of the Management Committee, a body that meets each year for about a week (see Fig. 10.3). Each year a Working Group of representatives from all member countries reviews various technical reports in order to prepare for the meeting of the Management Committee. The Finance and Program committees screen proposals from the Management Committee, especially the three-year work program. The Consultative Committee coordinates activities with other international organizations, especially ITU.

The Secretariat is at Bangkok. The Executive Director and one or more Deputy Executive Directors are appointed by the Management Committee. The Administrative Office services the organization. The Project Office directs research and technical assistance efforts. The Program Officer handles training.

Any state in the Asian and Pacific region that belongs to the UN or ESCAP is eligible for full membership. Associate Memberships are for Associate Members of ESCAP. Affiliate Memberships are for agencies or companies that operate international telecommunication services; they must be nominated by a Member or Associate Member. Most members joined in 1979 (see Table 10.3). Brunei is arranging to become a full Member. Indonesia was at the General Assembly in 1984; Cambodia and Laos are the only other countries originally involved in ATN that have not joined.

Figure 10.3
Organization of the Asia-Pacific Telecommunity

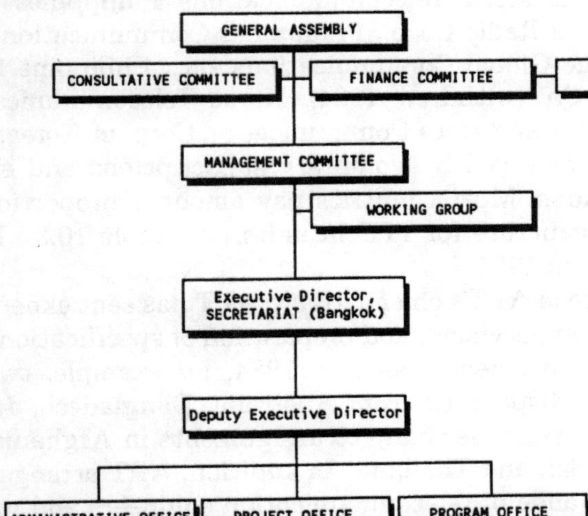

Table 10.3
Asia-Pacific Telecommunity: Membership and Assessments

Year Joined	Member Countries	Units Pledged (1985-87)
1979	Afghanistan	
	Australia	20
	Bangladesh	2
	Burma	1
	China	10
	Hongkong (a)	4
	India	4
	Japan	40
	Malaysia	4
	Nauru	1
	Nepal	.5
	Pakistan (w 1981)	
	Philippines	2
	Singapore	2
	South Korea	10
	Sri Lanka	1
	Thailand	4
	Vietnam (w 1984)	
1980	Brunei (a)	2
	Iran	1
	Maldives	.5
Totals	19-2=17 Members 2 Associate Members	$436,000

Key: a = Associate Member
w = withdrew

Most Affiliate Members also joined in 1979. They include Cable & Wireless Ltd. (Hongkong), Hongkong Telephone Co. Ltd., Kokusai Denshin Denwa Co. Ltd. (withdrew 1984), Nippon Telegraph & Telephone Public Corp., Eastern Telecommunications Philippines Inc., Globe MacKay Cable & Radio Corp., Philippines Communication Satellite Corp., Philippine Global Communications Inc., Philippine Long Distance Telephone Co. (withdrew 1984), Korea Telecommunication Authority (joined 1982), and Data Communication Corp. of Korea.

APT expenses are defrayed by voluntary subscriptions and extra-budgetary contributions. Most countries pay amounts proportionate to the contribution structure for ITU in units (see Table 10.3). Each unit value was $4,000 in 1985.

Technical assistance is APT's chief activity. APT has sent experts to assist in engineering, supervision, and preparation of specifications for development and improvement plans. In 1984, for example, twenty expert missions were dispatched from Australia, Bangladesh, India, Japan, Malaysia, and West Germany to assignments in Afghanistan, Maldives, Nauru, Nepal, and Thailand. In addition, APT arranges for the training and exchange of telecommunication engineers and managerial personnel; training is held at centers in Australia, Hongkong,

India, Japan, Singapore, South Korea, the United Kingdom, and the United States. In 1984, for example, some sixty-eight persons were trained. At least one expert seminar has been held each year.

Highest priority goes to implementation and installation of ongoing network projects; compatible signaling systems and improvements in the quality of service are given particular stress. Rural telecommunications development receives emphasis, along with the development of new technologies related to communication satellites, computer communications, and fiber-optic cables. APT has also sought to promote intraregional rate reductions and to ease unintentional radio frequency jamming through better radio frequency management at the borders of member countries.

Although APT envisaged cables across borders of member countries, the reduced cost of communication satellites brought ATN into existence sooner than expected. The Asian Way principle of agreeing to long-term goals before embarking on implementation strategies paid off.

SUMMARY AND CONCLUSIONS

APPU is a forum where problems can be aired and information about innovations can be diffused. Mail rates have come down within the region, but mail flow is still slow. Although training through APPTC has been very professional, the Secretariat's exchange program has served as more of a well-deserved holiday for selected senior officials.

In many parts of Asia, mail bags for letters from point A to point B are not transmitted until they first fill up; subsequently, these mail bags stay at point B, awaiting mail to make a return trip; for less frequent destinations, this means intolerable delays. As a result, many businesses rely on cables, facsimile, or telex. Other problems of mail delivery, including pilferage, require national programs. APPU, thus, does what it can in the face of incredible constraints.

Since mail service is unpredictable in Asia, and telex traffic is one-way communication, the business of the region requires telephonic communication. Most telephone systems in the early 1970s still linked former colonies with their erstwhile metropoles, and antiquated systems of low fidelity were primarily in use in the region. APT hence began with the objective of establishing new telephone linkages throughout the region. As the cost of satellite communications fell in the 1980s, the aims of APT were achieved far sooner than anyone anticipated. Intranational telecommunication systems in the developing countries of Asia, however, urgently need modernization. Indonesia, which does not belong to APT, has its own communication satellite for both interisland and external use, but internal traffic is still unsatisfactory. The needs of internal development, thus, appear far costlier to fulfill than those of international telecommunication.

The UNESCO study's original estimate was that 20,000 of the 35,000 employees in Asian broadcasting needed training in several fields. The numbers have increased greatly in recent years, and technology has developed even more rapidly. AIBD training of key personnel has sought a multiplier effect on the industry, and the results have been impressive. Programming over Asian television has improved considerably over the years; more high-quality indigenous programming is evident. A nagging question is whether improved professionalism in broadcasting has been used to control populations or whether new, well-presented ideas have provided an image of horizons that can serve to liberate the listening and viewing public. No easy answer to this question is, of course, available, but the aim at AIBD is to create a professional spirit that will serve as a counterweight to misuses of the media.

NOTES

1. For references to APPU documents, see Michael Haas, *Basic Documents of Asian Regional Organizations* (Dobbs Ferry, NY: Oceana Publications), vol. 5, pp. 314–17. For a bibliography of secondary sources, see pp. 312–13.
2. For references to AIBD documents, see Michael Haas, *Basic Documents of Asian Regional Organizations* (Dobbs Ferry, NY: Oceana Publications), vol. 5, p. 318.
3. For references to APT documents, see Michael Haas, *Basic Documents of Asian Regional Organizations* (Dobbs Ferry, NY: Oceana Publications), vol. 5, pp. 319–20.

11 THE "OPECIZATION" OF ASIA

The doubling of oil prices in 1973 by Arab member countries of the Organization of Petroleum Exporting Countries (OPEC) focused attention on communities of countries producing commodities involved in world trade. Before 1973, however, groups of countries had already formed in Asia for commodities that were even more precarious than oil. The Asian Coconut Community (ACC) emerged first, later becoming the Asian and Pacific Coconut Community (APCC). The Association of Natural Rubber Producing Countries (ANRPC) was next, followed by the Asian Vegetable Research and Development Center (AVRDC), the Pepper Community (PC, later IPC for International Pepper Community), and the Asian Rice Trade Fund (ARTF). After 1973, came the Southeast Asia Tin Research and Development Centre (SEATRAD Centre), the Association of Tin Producing Countries (ATPC), and three looser arrangements – the Government Consultation Among Jute Producing Countries (GCJPC), the Intergovernmental Consultative Forum of Developing Tropical Timber Producing/Exporting Countries (ICFDTTP/EC), and the Regional Consultative Group on Silk (RCGS).

Nonetheless, OPEC's example changed the direction of most Asian commodity communities. After the UN General Assembly endorsed the New International Economic Order (NIEO) in 1974, and the UN Conference on Trade and Development (UNCTAD) adopted the Integrated Program for Commodities in 1976, some eighteen primary products were identified for IPC negotiations with the aim of improving the terms of trade for Third-World countries through consumer–producer agreements. A Common Fund, approved in 1980, was to have two components. One was to be a $470 million account that would finance buffer stocks to stabilize earnings of Third-World countries and purchase prices of First-World countries. The second component, an account of about $250 million, was to finance research and development projects, marketing schemes, and assistance in the transportation of commodities so that the Third World would be able to process, manufacture, and sell more of the finished goods now produced from their own natural resources. Although consumer–producer agreements were eventually negotiated for certain commodities, the Common Fund did not have enough support for the decade that followed, so buffer stocks were included in the consumer–producer agreements at terms that could be vetoed by the First World.

ASIAN AND PACIFIC COCONUT COMMUNITY (APCC)[1]

Asian and Pacific countries account for about 90 percent of the world's exports of coconut products. In the Philippines, the coconut industry employs about one-third of the workforce. After World War II, various substitutes (corn, other vegetable oils, and synthetic products) jeopardized the coconut industry. In 1963, the Philippine-Indonesian Coconut Commission (PICC) was set up to promote the industry. After the UN Economic Commission for Asia and the Far East (ECAFE, now ESCAP) adopted a commodity approach in 1966, a major study predicted dire prospects for the industry. In October and November 1968, ECAFE convened two intergovernmental consultations, and the Agreement Establishing the Asian Coconut Community was adopted on December 12, 1968, coming into force in mid-1969. In 1975, with the addition of new countries from Pacific islands, the name changed to Asian and Pacific Coconut Community (APCC).

The founding Agreement states the functions of APCC as "to promote, coordinate and harmonize all activities of the coconut industry with a view to achieving the maximum economic development of the industry" (Article 3). A detailed set of activities is then outlined in regard to problems of production, processing, marketing, and research.

The plenary organ, the Session of the Community, meets for about four days each year; it is attended mainly by ministers of trade (see Fig. 11.1). The Secretariat, temporarily at ECAFE in 1969 before moving to Jakarta in 1971, has an Executive Director and about six administrative support-staff personnel. Although the original intention was to have formal divisions, the professional staff consists of various short-term experts, funded by the UN Development Program (UNDP).

In 1973, ACC convened a Permanent Coconut Production and Productivity Panel (Cocopep) to review technoeconomic matters concerning coconut production and research before the annual Session convened. Since expertise in other areas was needed as well, a UN

Figure 11.1
Organization of the Asian and Pacific Coconut Community

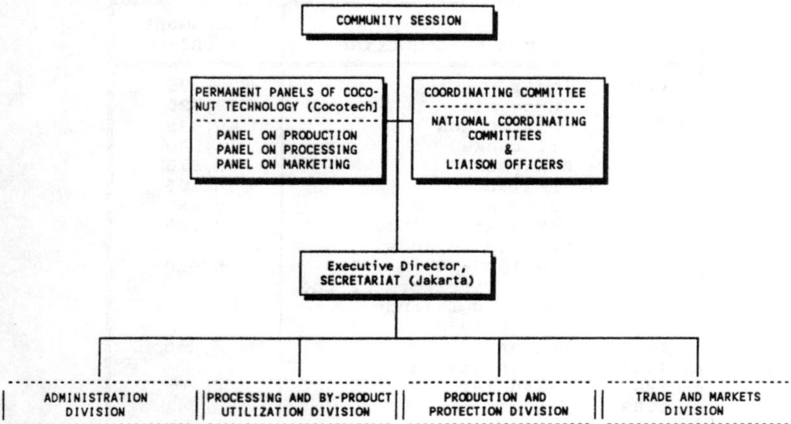

Industrial Development Organization (UNIDO) consultant asked ACC to extend Cocopep's scope to cover marketing and processing. In 1974, ACC formed three panels – production, processing, and marketing – to supersede Cocopep under the title Permanent Panels of Coconut Technology (Cocotech). Cocotech meets once annually to discuss priorities for the next APCC session.

Each country designates a national liaison agency for contact with the Secretariat. In 1974, ACC set up a Coordinating Committee, consisting of national liaison officers, to prepare for the Session meeting; this body no longer meets, but national liaison officers and participants on the three Cocotech panels now comprise each country's National Coordinating Committee.

ACC began with four members in 1969 (see Table 11.1). When ACC identified palm oil as within its scope, consistent with the Asian Way principle of pan-Asianism, Malaysia and Thailand joined. In 1971, the Pacific Islands Producers Association (PIPA), an intergovernmental organization in the South Pacific, expressed an interest in joining the Community, but ACC instead welcomed Western Samoa as a PIPA representative, and later members have primarily come from the South Pacific. Associate Members of the UN's Economic and Social Commission for Asia and the Pacific (ESCAP) join APCC as Associate Members. Since 1976, nonmembers of ESCAP have been eligible to join.

Administrative expenses are defrayed by member assessments, which are determined by a three-part formula that blends the Asian Way principle of equality with estimates of benefits derived from APCC: half is shared equally by all members, one-fourth is proportion-

Table 11.1
Asian and Pacific Coconut Community: Membership and Assessments

Year Joined	Member Countries	Assessment (1983)
1969	India	$20,275
	Indonesia	28,725
	Philippines	40,995
	Sri Lanka	14,100
1971	Malaysia	9,810
	Thailand	16,105
	Western Samoa	5,650
1975	Papua New Guinea	8,120
	Solomon Islands (a 1975-78, m 1978)	5,910
	Trust Territory of the Pacific Islands (a, e 1980)	
1980	Vanuatu, 1980	6,040
1982	Micronesia (a)	
1984	Palau (a)	
1989	Fiji	
Totals	11-1=10 Members 2 Associate Members	$155,730

Key: a = Associate Member
e = membership expired when Trust status ended
m = later joined as full Member

al to shares of coconut production, and one-fourth is based on relative percentages in the monetary value of coconut exports (see Table 11.1). Projects are supported largely by UN agencies; most of some $2 million in aid has gone for personnel provided by UNIDO.

In regard to production, APCC has completed studies on constraints in the uses of high-yielding coconut varieties by smallholders, a socio-economic survey of small-scale coconut growers, a survey of coconut extension services, a draft model program for replanting and rehabilitation of smallholder coconut farms, and studies on water conservation, as well as workshops on phytosanitary regulations, intercropping, coconut statistics, and coconut information. APCC countries then agreed to a common set of production objectives and guidelines for maximizing unit returns on coconut products.

In the area of processing, APCC established a consultancy service and a registry of processing techniques, then sponsored a survey of processing facilities, studies on coconut cream processing, agro-based manufacturing of coconut products, and evaluations of copra crushing techniques, as well as workshops on processing techniques, including coconut wood technology and utilization.

In regard to marketing, APCC has completed studies on remunerative price levels, supply and consumption patterns, copra price stabilization schemes, compensatory payment arrangements, supply management, export restrictions on copra supply, use of vegetable oilseeds and oils, markets for palm kernel oil, shipping problems and freight rates, uniform standards and quality of coconut products, and measures opposing tax proposals of the European Community (EC). APCC holds seminars on markets for coconut products and has established a coconut market research and market information service. Although coconuts were included in UNCTAD's IPC, coconut producers in the Caribbean have not cooperated with APCC. Meanwhile, technological improvements in Asia and the Pacific have put the industry on its feet.

ASSOCIATION OF NATURAL RUBBER PRODUCING COUNTRIES (ANRPC)[2]

Interest in a natural rubber agency began after World War I, when most of the rubber-producing countries were European colonies. In 1934, an International Natural Rubber Agreement (INRA) was reached, but the era of the Great Depression and World War II deprived the agreement of any substantive meaning. Before the war, the United States built up an immense strategic stockpile of natural rubber, thereby ensuring a glut of the commodity after the war. In September 1944, the International Rubber Study Group (IRSG) was formed in London to review problems of production and manufacturing, as well as uses of crude, reclaimed, and synthetic rubber. IRSG in due course expanded to include thirty importer and producer countries.

The IRSG Assembly was scheduled to meet in late October 1967 to discuss methods for stabilizing prices, which had fallen to the lowest level in two decades. Malaysian rubber producers insisted that something drastic was needed, so the Malaysian government convened a meeting of interested producer countries in Kuala Lumpur at the end of October. Thailand proposed formalizing the group, and the countries agreed to a constitution for the new organization, ANRPC, in a meeting in Kuala Lumpur from October 14 to 16, 1970.

The constitution lists three aims: "(a) to bring about coordination in the production and marketing of natural rubber; (b) to promote technical cooperation amongst Members; (c) to bring about fair and stable prices for natural rubber" (Article 4).

The Assembly, the plenary organ, has annual two-day sessions (see Fig. 11.2). An Executive Committee, consisting of one senior official from each country, meets for two days each year to supervise the Secretariat, which is located in Kuala Lumpur and is headed by a Secretary-General.

Figure 11.2
Organization of the Association of Natural Rubber Producing Countries

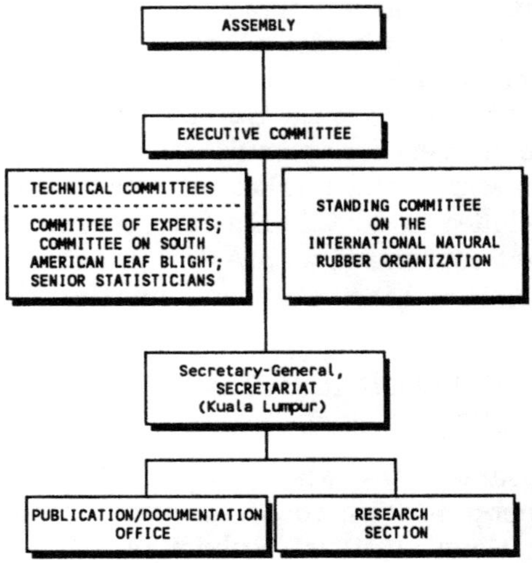

Six countries agreed to the ANRPC Constitution in 1971 (see Table 11.2). India and Papua New Guinea joined four years later. In 1975 and 1976, Vietnam was inactive and failed to pay its required assessment, so it was suspended from ANRPC in 1977. Vietnam returned to membership in 1979 but again failed to provide assessments in 1982 and 1983, so it withdrew in 1984.

Table 11.2
Association of Natural Rubber Producing Countries: Membership and Assessments

Year Joined	Member Countries	Assessment (1984)[a]
1971	Indonesia	$5,000 + 22.7%
	Malaysia	5,000 + 37.6
	Singapore	5,000 + 10.9
	Sri Lanka	5,000 + 5.6
	Thailand	5,000 + 14.3
	Vietnam[b] (s 1977-78, w 1984)	
1975	India	5,000 + 6.2
	Papua New Guinea	5,000 + 2.8
Totals	8-1=7 Members	$196,920

[a]Due to rounding, the column does not sum exactly to 100 percent.
[b]Joined as Republic of Vietnam
Key: s = suspended
w = withdrew

ANRPC Assembly decisions are by a majority vote of members, provided that at least half of the total annual members' production is in the majority, a unique method for ensuring that the Asian Way principle of consensus building will be observed. Since Singapore produces no natural rubber but instead re-exports natural rubber shipped to it by adjacent countries, its voting share is determined through negotiation; in 1984 Singapore's votes were 10.9 percent of the total.

Each member contributes a basic subscription of $5,000 per year. If budget estimates exceed this sum, members pay an amount proportional to their relative share of annual natural rubber production (see Table 11.2). Singapore's contribution percentage equals its voting weight.

The Rubber Research Institute of Malaysia (RRIM) provides information and training for personnel from member countries. In 1971, the International Rubber Research and Development Board (IRRDB) in London identified RRIM as the world regulatory authority for all germplasm of natural rubber, then in 1974 ANRPC and IRRDB set up a joint multilateral clone exchange program. ANRPC's Technical Committee on South American Leaf Blight seeks to prevent this disease from reaching Asia.

Concerning production, ANRPC has encouraged replanting with the newer high-yielding varieties of natural rubber, encouraging productivity rather than expansion in acreage. In the field of processing, ANRPC negotiations pressured Japan to include a minimum percentage of natural rubber in manufacturing synthetic rubber products.

ANRPC has made considerable headway in regard to marketing. In 1970, ANRPC agreed to a joint marketing system that had a goal of 42 percent of the world rubber market by 1999; by 1980, such systems were in place in Indonesia, Malaysia, and Singapore. In 1976, ANRPC agreed to the International Natural Rubber Agreement on Price Stabilization, under which each country has an export entitlement equal to its approximate current share of world production (Indonesia, 29.41 percent; Malaysia, 52.45 percent; Sri Lanka, 5.42 percent; Thailand, 12.72 percent); this agreement led to the first postwar INRA in 1979.

A world shortage in natural rubber developed by the mid-1980s, as orders for latex condoms and gloves soared due to the increase in cases of acquired immune deficiency disease (AIDS). ANRPC schemes for market rationalization became obsolete, as supply could hardly keep up with demand. In 1988, natural rubber prices were $1.20 per kilogram, above the INRA ceiling of $0.94. The U.S. decision not to sell its estimated stockpile of 360,000 tons enables ANRPC countries to benefit from this windfall.

ASIAN VEGETABLE RESEARCH AND DEVELOPMENT CENTER (AVRDC)[3]

Although two-thirds of the workers in Asia are employed in agriculture, many countries import food and have problems of malnutrition. Whereas such basic sources of carbohydrates as rice and wheat are widely available in Asia, deficiencies in vitamins and minerals require increased vegetable production. Before the 1970s, Asian vegetable crops grew mainly in the temperate highlands with small populations because the yield in the heavily populated lowlands was only one-third as much per unit cultivated due to the hazards of hot and humid climates.

In 1948, the Republic of China (Taiwan) and the United States agreed to establish the Sino-American Joint Commission on Rural Reconstruction (JCRR) to develop agriculture in Taiwan. JCRR's success led in 1960 to the establishment of the International Rice Research Institute (IRRI) in Los Banos, the Philippines, to bring the "green revolution" to the basic food staple in Asia; the so-called miracle rice proved to have a high yield potential on a per-acre basis. In 1963, Frank Parker, an official of the U.S. Agency for International Development (USAID), proposed a research institute to develop high-protein, mineral- and vitamin-rich vegetable foods in Asia's lowland tropics. After exploratory efforts of various sorts, AVRDC began on May 22, 1971, when a Memorandum of Understanding was adopted in a meeting in Taipei. The Republic of China donated 116 hectares at the site of the former Tso Chia farm of the Taiwan Sugar Corporation in Shanhua, Tainan, where construction of facilities began in January 1972. Robert Chandler was the first Director in July 1972, one month after he retired as IRRI Director.

According to the founding Charter, AVRDC has three objectives:

> 1. to conduct research on production and marketing programs and to assist participating countries in developing their own adaptive research programs, 2. to carry out training in production and marketing programs and to assist participating countries in developing more efficient training and marketing programs, 3. to develop and provide basic information on improved production and marketing for use in extension services in participating countries. [Article III(1)]

The Board of Directors meets once each year for sessions of about three days (see Fig. 11.3). The Charter envisaged a Technical Advisory Group to oversee the center, but this body never met. In 1979, the Charter was amended to add up to eight experts to the Board as technical experts; currently four serve in this capacity, as the regular members tend to be experts rather than ministers of agriculture.

The Center began with a Director as the head. In 1983, this position

Figure 11.3
Organization of the Asian Vegetable Research and Development Center

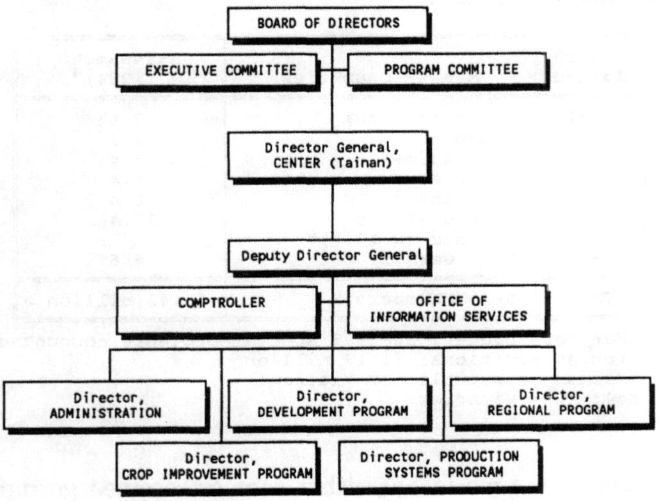

was retitled Director General. In 1986, there was a reorganization, establishing three programs. The Crop Improvement Program handles horticultural and legume development. The Development Program coordinates cooperative programs, training, and the Tropical Vegetable Information Service (TVIS). The Production Systems Program is in charge of crop management, cropping systems, economics and social sciences, nutrition, and on-station testing.

In 1975, AVRDC set up subcenters in Suweon, South Korea, and Los Banos, the Philippines. These cooperative programs provided sites for retesting vegetable varieties and other projects first developed in Shanhua. The two facilities were absorbed by national programs in due course but were retained as cooperative projects, as noted below. For countries that have difficulties with access to Taiwan, AVRDC set up the Thailand Outreach Program (TOP) in 1981 to offer germplasm exchange, training, and other services. In 1987, a site was selected in Niger for a vitamin A garden program to service African nations.

Seven countries were initial members (see Table 11.3). The Asian Development Bank (ADB) and West Germany also joined, as there is a provision for contributing countries and organizations to become members if approved by the Board of Directors. ADB made its final annual regular contribution to AVRDC in 1975, although it still assists specific projects. Vietnam likewise ceased to participate in 1975, although some of its agencies receive germplasm from AVRDC today. Virtually

Table 11.3
Asian Vegetable Research and Development Center: Membership and Assessments

Year Joined	Member Countries	Assessment (1984)[a]
1972	China (Taiwan)	37.6%
	Japan	12.1
	Philippines	5.4
	South Korea	5.4
	Thailand	5.4
	United States	27.4
	Vietnam (w 1975)[b]	
1981	West Germany	6.6
Total	8-1=7 Members	$3.43 million

[a]For core budget; in 1985 special projects accounted for an additional $1.47 million
[b]Joined as Republic of Vietnam
Key: w = withdrew

every country in the world has either sent or received germplasm in connection with AVRDC programs.

Director Chandler insisted upon a large initial investment, so AVRDC began with a $7.5 million budget commitment for the first five years, from 1971 to 1975. The United States agreed to provide 40 percent, with the Republic of China's 30 percent to be matched by other sources. After 1975, when members scaled down their contributions, the budget was divided into two parts: a core budget and a special projects fund. Members defray the core budget primarily; project support comes from several sources. The Republic of China's portion has been provided by such sources as the Taiwan Canner's Association. In contrast with the 1970s, budgets in the 1980s have been increasing steadily. Since 1985, core support has placed more burden on the host government (see Table 11.3).

The principal aim of AVRDC is to develop new, high-yielding varieties of vegetables that will have improved mineral, protein, and vitamin content yet will be tolerant to heat and resistant to diseases, insect pests, and mold in the lowland tropics, where they can be used as quick-growing crops between rice-planting seasons. AVRDC collected some 25,000 varieties of Chinese cabbage, mungbeans, soybeans, sweet potatoes, tomatoes, and white potatoes to crossbreed in the early years, seeking hybrids with the desired characteristics. AVRDC has distributed cultivars and seed packets of the resulting new varieties for retesting elsewhere. When the International Potato Center (CIP) in Peru assumed responsibility for tropical white potato breeding in 1978, AVRDC turned over its white potato germplasm to the local Taiwan

Agricultural Research Institute. In 1986, AVRDC selected the sweet and chili pepper as the newest crop for improvement.

A training program began in 1974. Research internships are available for younger scientists to organize research projects relevant to the needs of their home countries for five- to six-month assignments. Research facilities are available for M.S. and Ph.D. candidates to pursue thesis or dissertation projects; the subject of the research is integrated with an AVRDC research project for a 6- to 18-month period. In previous years, research fellowships were awarded to recent Ph.D.s and experienced M.S.s or Ph.D.s so that they could upgrade their skills through collaborative work over one to two years. In addition, AVRDC has a five-month production training program, a summer student training program, and special-purpose training assignments; these provide practical field experience. In each case, a senior AVRDC scientist works alongside a trainee.

AVRDC concentrates on basic (upstream) research, but it assists participating countries with applied (downstream) research. Cooperative projects, the successor to the subcenter concept, exist in Indonesia, Malaysia, the Philippines, South Korea, Taiwan, and Thailand. In these countries, the trials of AVRDC varieties are a direct part of the Center's research program. Collaborating organizations in these and other countries engage in nursery trials, participate in germplasm and information exchange, and supply trainees to AVRDC. The genetic resources and seed laboratory receives germplasm and distributes seeds. In 1986, some 3,471 new accessions were received for the six principal crops, and 34,682 seed packets were distributed to ninety-nine countries, including the People's Republic of China (through TOP), consistent with the pan-Asian principle of the Asian Way.

In 1981, AVRDC began a garden program, an effort to provide rural and urban poor with a means to grow vegetables on a smaller, yet adequate scale in terms of nutritional needs, using schools as sites and thereby encouraging students to bring the idea home. The vitamin A garden program, established in 1987, serves African countries, where vitamin A deficiency is a problem.

INTERNATIONAL PEPPER COMMUNITY (IPC)[4]

There are two varieties of peppers. Some are consumed whole: these are the green and red varieties under development at AVRDC. Pepper pods, which are black, red, or white when desiccated and reduced to a powder, are used as seasonings; these are of concern to IPC. In both cases, the problem is underproduction.

Before World War II, Indonesia was the world's largest pepper-producing country, accounting for more than 80 percent of the world's black and white pepper. By the late 1960s, diseases and pests and the emergence of new pepper-producing countries caused a drastic decline in market share, and by the 1980s Indonesia accounted for only about one-fourth of world pepper trade, although Asia still accounts for three-fourths of world production. Indonesia was clearly in need of assistance.

UNIDO, aware of problems of the Indonesian pepper industry, sponsored informal pepper talks in Jakarta during July 1970. Subsequently, UNIDO asked ECAFE to convene Inter-Governmental Consultations of Regional Cooperation in Pepper in Asia during early 1971; a proposal for a pepper community was endorsed at the meeting. Delegates called the organization the Pepper Community (PC), leaving the door open to Brazil and Malagasy.

After the founding agreement was adopted at an inaugural PC meeting on August 31, 1972, countries were slow in ratifying. Because only India, Indonesia, and Malaysia joined, the organization remained at a preliminary stage, with an Interim Secretariat at ECAFE. After PC Sessions in 1972 and 1973, no meeting was convened until 1975. Indonesia anticipated that UNIDO would fund a pepper processing research and product development center in exchange for offering Jakarta as the site for the PC Secretariat. When Pepper Community countries wanted UNIDO to expand the scope of PC to cover both primary and secondary processing, UNIDO declined, and the proposal was not funded. Indonesia was then reluctant to get involved in PC.

The Asian Way principle of incrementalism prevailed when the Community reconvened in 1976, and member countries insisted on breathing life into the organization. India agreed to host the first session of the Community outside Bangkok in 1977, when a full-time Director was appointed, a budget drawn up, and Jakarta's offer to host the Secretariat was accepted. In 1980, PC was retitled the International Pepper Community to further welcome Brazil and Malagasy.

The Agreement Establishing the Pepper Community states its purpose as "to promote, coordinate and harmonize all activities relating to the pepper economy" (Article 3). It then goes on to specify detailed activities relating to production, processing, marketing, and research in the pepper industry.

The Session of the Community, the plenary organ, meets for about three days at least once each year (see Fig. 11.4). Each member designates a liaison officer and a research institution to facilitate contact with the Secretariat.

Before the 1977 Session, an expert group meeting of research liaison officers from member countries reviewed technical matters; this body became the Pepper Technical Panel (Peppertech) in 1978. Peppertech

Figure 11.4
Organization of the International Pepper Community

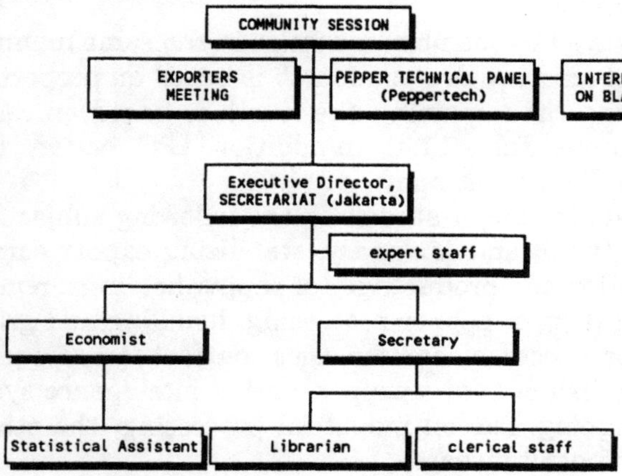

meets once each year. The Exporters Meeting is a group of private-sector representatives that discusses problems of marketing. Exporters Meetings began informally in 1980, two days before Peppertech; the body became a part of the organization in 1984, an Asian solution to an Asian problem of building a bridge between the private and public sectors. In 1985, IPC set up an International Council on Black Pepper Wilt, a disease affecting the pepper plant.

From 1972 to 1976, the Interim Secretariat and Interim Director were at ECAFE. After a full-time Director was appointed, the office moved to Jakarta in September 1976. In 1980, IPC's head was retitled as Executive Director. Various experts are seconded from time to time to the Secretariat from UN agencies to complete specific studies.

Three countries joined in 1972 (see Table 11.4). Singapore, Sri Lanka, and Thailand decided not to join after attending preliminary meetings. In 1979, Malagasy ratified, but it is not a member, since it has not

Table 11.4
International Pepper Community: Membership and Assessments

Year Joined	Member Countries	Assessment (1984)
1972	India	22.6%
	Indonesia	24.8
	Malaysia	24.8
1981	Brazil	27.8
Totals	4 Members	$129,140

deposited an instrument of accession with the United Nations in New York. Brazil joined in 1981. Malagasy, Sri Lanka, and Thailand are Observers at IPC Sessions.

The budget is defrayed by member countries in the same manner as APCC – one-half is shared equally, one-fourth is based on proportional shares of exports, and the remaining one-fourth is based on relative shares of production (see Table 11.4). In addition, IPC receives funds from UN agencies and West Germany.

IPC has completed nine major studies on the following subjects: the pepper economy in Brazil and Malagasy, stabilizing export earnings from pepper, production and productivity of pepper holdings, remunerative price levels for pepper, pepper processing, handling and grading of pepper, demand prospects, a common sales contract form for pepper export, and the establishment of a pepper market intelligence system. Two projects are ongoing, one on industrial processing, the other to assist in controlling footrot disease.

Due to black pepper wilt and other hazards, world pepper production of 160,000 tons per year lags behind demand. In 1988, the price of a pound of pepper averaged from $0.75 to $0.80, and prices may double in 1989, since IPC members have agreed to a minimum export price scheme. Consuming countries may thus consider a buffer stock arrangement along the lines of UNCTAD's Integrated Program of Commodities.

ASIAN RICE TRADE FUND (ARTF)[5]

More than 90 percent of all rice in the world is consumed in Asia. When rice shortages were anticipated in the late 1960s, ECAFE's Agriculture Division developed plans for a common fund so that rice could be purchased collectively in the region during periods of surplus, with a supply on hand in case of shortages. After meetings from 1969 to 1973, the Agriculture Division drafted the Agreement Establishing the Asian Rice Trade Fund, which was endorsed at the ECAFE session in April 1974, coming into force on December 1, 1974. Since no rice-exporting country has signed thus far, the Fund itself is not yet operational.

According to the founding agreement, ARTF's main objective is to "promote intraregional trade in rice among developing countries" (Article 2). Three functions are then set forth:

> (i) Undertake or arrange financing and refinancing facilities for rice sales transactions between the members involving deferred payments. . . . (ii) Perform such other activities as may be necessary for the furtherance of the activity

referred to in clause (i) above; and (iii) Initiate other schemes for cooperation in the field of intraregional trade in rice. (Article 2)

The Board of Directors is supposed to meet twice yearly to administer the Fund (see Fig. 11.5). A Director or Alternate Director from each member country is eligible to sit on the Board. The Chairman of the Board is the Chief Executive of ARTF. The Board may appoint a General Manager and staff to assist in carrying out ARTF operations, although no such persons have been appointed as yet.

Initially, ARTF was a project of the Agriculture Division of ESCAP, which served as the secretariat. Since no meetings of ARTF have been held since 1977, administrative responsibility for ARTF has shifted to the Economic Cooperation Among Developing Countries/Technical Cooperation Among Developing Countries (ECDC/TCDC) Unit at ESCAP.

Developing countries that are Members or Associate Members of ESCAP and either exporters or importers of rice were alone eligible for membership until 1978, when membership was made available to all ESCAP members. Five countries joined (see Table 11.5). Although the Khmer Republic, Laos, Singapore, and Thailand were at the 1973 preparatory meeting for ARTF, they did not join. Japan, also in attendance, is a developed country and thus was initially ineligible; it has financed some studies to assist ARTF in coming to fruition. Burma and Laos attended a session of the Board of Directors in 1977. Australia, Japan, Laos, and Pakistan were present at the Inter-Governmental Meeting on Regional Cooperation in Rice and on Operational Problems of the Asian Rice Trade Fund in 1977, convened by ESCAP. Thailand, where half of the agricultural population works in rice fields, in effect

Figure 11.5
Organization of the Asian Rice Trade Fund

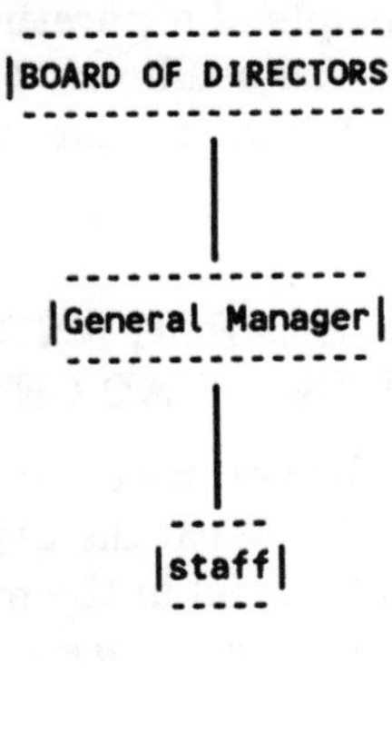

Table 11.5
Asian Rice Trade Fund: Membership

Year Joined	Member Countries
1974	Bangladesh India Sri Lanka
1975	Philippines Vietnam[a]
Totals	5 Members

[a]Joined as Republic of Vietnam; inactive since

vetoed ARTF by failing to join, since rice sales provide a significant portion of its foreign exchange.

The Fund becomes operational when it receives voluntary contributions from members or nonmember sources. Expenses for operating ARTF are eventually to be financed out of the income and receipts resulting from transactions. Meanwhile, ESCAP provides the interim secretariat to convene meetings and to administer studies related to ARTF.

ARTF will be able to negotiate contracts with rice-importing countries; payments then could be deferred for up to five years unless extended by the Board of Directors. Payment would come from the central bank of the importing country to ARTF, which would transfer the amount to the central bank of the exporting country.

The Association of South East Asian Nations (ASEAN) has a rice supply scheme of its own, involving nearly one million tons of rice, whereby countries with rice deficits are eligible to purchase rice from rice-surplus countries at preferential rates. Only the Philippines has had an interest in broadening the ASEAN rice scheme, as indicated by its membership in ARTF, although it is now self-sufficient in rice production. The Asian Way principle of separating politics from administration explains why ARTF was stillborn. The ASEAN rice scheme shows that pan-Southeast Asianism can take priority over pan-Asianism.

SOUTHEAST ASIA TIN RESEARCH AND DEVELOPMENT CENTRE (SEATRAD CENTRE)[6]

Most tin in Southeast Asia has been extracted from alluvial deposits close to the surface of the earth. With the discovery of large deposits deeper into the ground (as in Bolivia) in the mid-1960s, tin production in Southeast Asia appeared to enter a new era, requiring a new technology in Indonesia, Malaysia, and Thailand, countries responsible to date for about two-thirds of the world's tin. Technical assistance was required in order to locate new deposits.

The International Tin Council (ITC), concerned primarily with export prices for tin, convened a series of technical conferences on tin in the 1960s. At a 1969 conference, Professor K. F. G. Hosking, then Professor of Applied Geology at the University of Malaya, proposed the establishment of a regional center to develop tin production methods. After ECAFE accepted the idea in 1971, it commissioned Hosking to estimate the requirements for such an undertaking. In January 1972, ECAFE submitted Hosking's report to a meeting of Indonesian, Malaysian, and Thai representatives, who then agreed to apply to UNDP for funding for the proposed project. Although UNDP approved the project in 1974, the cash-flow crisis associated with increased oil prices meant that the amount of funding had to be renegotiated. The UNDP project then began in Ipoh, Malaysia, in February 1977, when a UNDP Project Manager arrived. Meanwhile, an Agreement Establishing the Southeast Asia Tin Research and Development Centre was signed at the ESCAP session on April 28, 1977, becoming effective in April 1978, whereupon the UNDP Project Manager became the Chief Technical Adviser of the new organization.

The founding agreement states that the principal aim of the center is "to promote, coordinate and harmonize all activities relating to the development of the tin industry in the member countries" (Article 2). The specific objectives are

> (a) to stimulate, conduct and coordinate research in the tin industry on technical and economic aspects of exploration, evaluation, development, and smelting; (b) to conduct studies on problems associated with the beneficiation of tin ores and complex ores containing significant percentages of fine-grained tin-bearing materials; (c) to collect, collate and publish statistics and data of importance for the continued prosperity of the tin industry; (d) to increase the technological knowledge within the industry by establishing training courses, promoting lectures, symposia on-the-job and other means of training and development for citizens of member countries; (e) to provide advisory services, and to carry out, commission, or promote the study of scientific, technological and economic aspects of development of the tin industry; (f) to provide a forum for the exchange of knowledge and discussion of problems relating to all aspects of the tin industry; (g) to engage in any undertaking, conduct any act, or do all such other things as may appear desirable, incidental or conducive to the attainment of the above objectives. (Article 2)

The plenary organ, the Board of Management, meets semiannually for about two days; each country supplies a plenipotentiary representative from the relevant government ministry, a national coordinator, and a representative of the tin industry to participate in meetings of the board (see Fig. 11.6). ESCAP and UNDP have ex officio seats on the board. In 1982, a Working Group meeting of national coordinators (representatives from government and industry in member countries), ESCAP personnel, and the professional staff of the center began to meet for three days before each meeting of the board to set priorities for proposals for adoption by the board; in 1986, the Technical Committee superseded the Working Group.

The head of SEATRAD Centre is a Director. Originally, each member country designated an Associate Expert, who was assigned to an Expert from outside the region to learn the skills required for the work of the center on an apprenticeship basis. This pairing of international and regional staff ceased in 1984, when the Asian Way principle of equality took over: regional experts now do all the work, also in teams of two professionals.

The headquarters facility is in Ipoh. The center carries out projects at various exploration and mining sites in close liaison with the member countries' national coordinators.

Three countries have joined (see Table 11.6). Although any tin-producing country may join, the distance between Ipoh and other tin-producing countries outside Southeast Asia precludes membership from Africa or Bolivia: much of the work involves collecting samples of minerals from areas of potential tin deposits and making site visits to existing tin mines.

Originally, UNDP provided equipment and supplies, as well as salaries for consultants, experts, and fellowships. Since 1984, members have shared administrative costs on the basis of the Asian Way principle of equality (see Table 11.6). UNDP provides project amounts, which

Figure 11.6
Organization of the Southeast Asia Tin Research and Development Centre

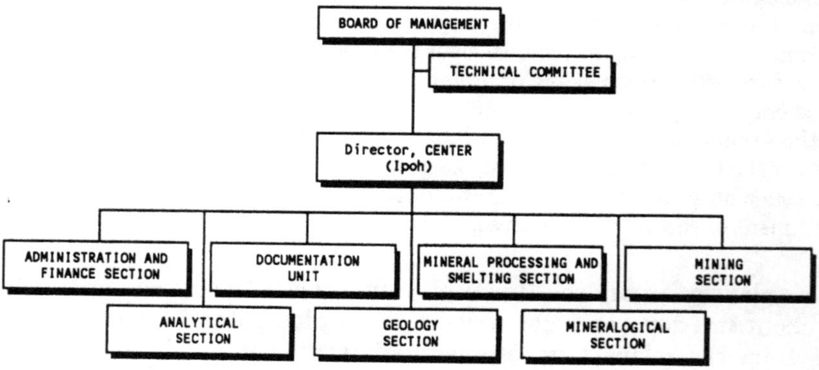

Table 11.6
Southeast Asia Tin Research and Development Centre: Membership and Assessments

Year Joined	Member Countries	Assessment (1984)
1978	Indonesia Malaysia Thailand	33.33% 33.33 33.33
Totals	3 Members	$643,725

are matched by member country contributions; France and Germany supply equipment and fellowships.

The Geology Section collects soil samples from potential exploration sites and seeks to perfect techniques of exploration and sampling in order to identify areas where tin might be present; channel sampling and geochemical analytical techniques have been studied as alternatives to traditional drilling and hand panning. The Mineral Processing and Smelting Section determines how to recover mineral byproducts from tin mining, such as niobium and tantalum; studies on the distribution, mode of occurrence, and amenability to separation of these minerals have been conducted from ore samples. The Mineralogy Section studies minerals in plant feed products and does liberation studies of different products obtained during metallurgical tests; a computerized ore mineral data base system identifies ore minerals in polished sections on the basis of microhardness, reflectivity, color, anisotropy, and internal reflections. A computerized particle-counting system has also been developed. Some 85,388 geochemical and chemical analyses were undertaken up to the end of 1983 by the Analytical Section; most of these were colorimetric determinations or atomic absorption spectrophotometric determinations, although some were classical assays. The Mining Section goes to mines in the region to observe operations; based on these visits, experiments have been carried out to lower production costs, and reports have been prepared with recommendations for more efficient methods.

In-service training is augmented by fellowships for training abroad. Workshops and group training courses, about one week in duration, have been held thrice yearly. Frequent seminars review research results.

The problems of tin go beyond technology. The development of a tin "OPEC," the organization described next in this chapter, emerged from the core countries involved in SEATRAD Centre.

ASSOCIATION OF TIN PRODUCING COUNTRIES (ATPC)[7]

When Indonesia and Malaya were still colonies, the international tin market was a small club of European-oriented tin-consuming countries and tin-producing colonies with many common interests. Regional cooperation in tin goes back to the Bandung Pool established in 1921 by the Federated Malay States and the Netherlands East Indies. When this effort to restrict exports did not work out, a Tin Producers' Association (TPA) was set up in 1929 in London, representing British interests in Burma, Malaya, and Nigeria. When TPA failed to stem the fall in prices resulting from the Great Depression, the first International Tin Agreement (ITA) of 1931–33 tried an International Tin Control Scheme from 1931–34 under the direction of the International Tin Committee (ITC) in London. Subsequent ITAs came in 1934–36, 1937–41, and 1942–46.

In 1932, meanwhile, the Tin Research Institute (TRI) was formed to encourage research on new methods of processing tin. TRI, which became the International Tin Research Institute (ITRI) in 1976, is located in Oxbridge, just outside London. In 1933, the International Tin Research and Development Council (ITRDC), later the International Tin Research Council (ITRC), was set up in London in 1933 to disseminate information on uses of tin and statistics of the tin industry.

During World War II, the United States developed a strategic stockpile of tin, and after the war Washington maintained its stockpile (still over 200,000 tons by 1981), thereby insulating the United States from upward fluctuations in price. In November 1945, the Combined Tin Committee (CTC) met in Washington to decide upon a method of allocating tin among consuming countries during the period of immediate postwar shortage. Composed of the main producing countries and some consuming countries, CTC existed until 1949, by which time it had allocated some 250,000 tons of tin among thirty-nine countries. The United States was allotted 127,000 tons; together with wartime allocations, this tin formed the basis of the postwar U.S. strategic stockpile. When ITC met in 1946 to consider an ITA, no action was taken and the organization became defunct, whereupon London paved the way for the International Tin Study Group (ITSG), which functioned from 1947 to 1956 as an informal body to study problems associated with the world tin market.

The UN Conference on Trade and Employment, held in Havana in 1947 and 1948, drew up guidelines for intergovernmental commodity agreements, and ITSG sought to draw up the framework for an ITA within the framework of the Havana Charter. ITSG prepared draft

ITAs; a UN negotiating conference met in Geneva in 1950, then resumed in 1953 when prospects were more auspicious. The first postwar ITA was negotiated in 1954, coming into effect in July 1956, with a new International Tin Council (ITC) at London in charge of the buffer stock. From 1956 to 1981, five ITAs were adopted, even though Washington had accumulated 350,000 tons of tin by 1955, an amount equal to two years of total world production and seven years of U.S. consumption. Tin, meanwhile, fell in price, as substitutions for tin were developed and the Western-dominated ITC insisted on an ITAs favorable to the interests of developed countries.

In 1970, Indonesia, Malaysia, and Thailand asked ECAFE to study the possibility of an organization of tin-producing countries. Since ITAs were reasonably successful after the ECAFE study was completed, there was little urgency for a producers' association; but in 1981, when the fifth ITA expired, the United States was still releasing tin from its stockpile, believing that the proposed sixth ITA put tin at an unrealistically high price.

Difficulties in negotiating the sixth ITA were the impetus for renewed interest in a tin-producer organization, and four ministerial meetings of tin-producing countries were held from 1980 to 1982. Meanwhile, continued U.S. stockpile releases had so depressed the price of tin that Malaysia secretly began to purchase tin on the London Metal Exchange in 1981; when this fact came out in February 1982, the price of tin fell from £9,000 per ton to about £7,000 per ton, the lowest price in 15 years. ITC, following its constitutional mandate, bought about 50,000 tons at the floor price, but there were so few buyers that the tin market shut down on October 24, 1985.

Meanwhile, in 1980, a liaison office in London exchanged ideas on the possibility of a tin-producers' organization. After a preliminary meeting in 1982, ministers of seven tin-producing countries adopted the text of the Agreement Establishing the Association of Tin Producing Countries on March 28–29, 1983.

The founding agreement specifies five objectives of ATPC:

> (a) to obtain remunerative and equitable returns to tin producers and adequate supplies to consumers at fair and stable prices based on the average cost of production and having regard to market forces; (b) to facilitate cooperation in the marketing of tin; (c) to maintain and extend the use and cost effectiveness of tin in modern technology through research and development; (d) to encourage processing activities and manufacture based on tin in Member countries with the view to promoting their industrialization and increasing their export earnings; (e) to promote the greater self-reliance and resilience of the Member countries in the tin industry. (Article 1)

ATPC sees itself as a mechanism to coordinate all tin organizations so that the tin industry can catch up with the role of aluminum and plastics in the world economy through increased product research and market development.

The plenary organ, the Conference of Ministers, meets at least once each year (see Fig. 11.7). The Executive Committee of subministerial officials meets quarterly for four-day sessions.

An Executive Secretary heads the Secretariat in Kuala Lumpur. In 1987, since a majority of ITRI countries belong to ATPC, ATPC in effect took over control of ITRI, although the latter is formally autonomous. ATPC countries are the only countries that give financial support to ITRI. ATPC also monitors producing countries' related organizations, including ITC, ITRI, and SEATRAD Centre. In 1986, ATPC asked UNCTAD to resuscitate the long-defunct ITSG to develop new options for the tin industry, including a new ITA.

The primary interest in establishing ATPC came from SEATRAD Centre countries, which account for about 70 percent of world tin production. Since an effective tin-producers' organization required more producer countries, negotiations brought four new members (see Table 11.7). The founding agreement also lists the following net exporters of tin as eligible for membership: Brazil, Burma, China, Niger, and Rwanda. None of these countries participated in the ITAs.

Although ATPC member countries have restricted production since 1983, two new tin producers—Brazil and China—have been able to expand production. In 1986, both countries attended the Conference of Ministers as Observers; they have promised to cooperate with the organization in the spirit of the Asian Way's principle of consensus building.

ATPC votes are based on a weighted formula. Out of a total of 1,000 votes, each member has twenty initial votes, while the rest is propor-

Figure 11.7
Organization of the Association of Tin Producing Countries

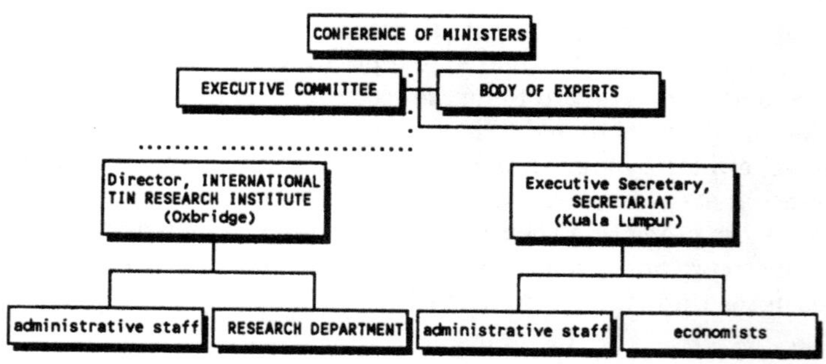

Table 11.7
Association of Tin Producing Countries: Membership and Assessments

Year Joined	Member Countries	Assessment (1985)
1983	Australia	8.5%
	Bolivia	15.8
	Indonesia	19.6
	Malaysia	32.0
	Nigeria	3.2
	Thailand	17.7
	Zaire	3.2
Totals	7 Members	c. $400,000

tionate to tin production. The same figures are used to calculate assessments of members to defray Secretariat costs (see Table 11.7).

As a coordinator of international efforts to encourage the use of tin, ATPC immediately sought to promote research and development on tin. The Secretariat collects basic data on the tin industry in order to pursue studies on joint approaches to the marketing of tin and on how to overcome financial, institutional, and other problems facing the tin industry.

The world glut of 75,000 tons of tin as of early 1987 meant that progress would take a while. ATPC first exerted pressure on the United States to sell off no more than 3,000 tons of tin per year, as it had agreed to do in an expired agreement of 1982. In 1987, the Kuala Lumpur Commodity Exchange offered long-term purchases of tin as a temporary stopgap outside the framework of ATPC. Then ATPC allocated an output quota of 96,000 tons for 1987 at amounts slightly below production figures for each country in 1986, with prices from $5,000 to $6,900 per ton. ATPC's supply-rationalization scheme was so effective, with cooperation from Brazil and China, that quotas increased to 101,900 tons for 1988, and prices recovered to $7,320 per ton by the end of 1988. Prices soared in early 1989 to about $9,000 per ton, so the quota system is expected to end, chalking up an important success for ATPC.

GOVERNMENT CONSULTATION AMONG JUTE PRODUCING COUNTRIES (GCJPC)[8]

Jute plant fibers, which are made into such products as rice bags and rope, provide some 70 percent of the foreign exchange of Bangladesh, one of the poorest countries in the world. Over the years, competition from synthetic sources has depressed the world jute market, and there is a worldwide glut in production at the level of four million metric tons per year.

In August 1971, UNDP's fact-finding mission on jute recommended the establishment of a Jute International, but the idea got nowhere. After adopting the IPC in 1975, UNCTAD convened several meetings from 1976 to 1980 to form a jute community. Meanwhile, ESCAP organized the first in a series of government consultative meetings of jute-producing countries with the aim of filling gaps in the eventual international agreement, and the countries drew up terms of reference on August 18–21, 1981, when they reconvened.

GCJPC countries agreed to the following goals:

> (a) to identify common problems and issues affecting the jute sector in the producing countries in its various aspects, including production, processing, trade, transport, training, and research and development; (b) to formulate proposals for specific regional cooperative activities, where necessary and feasible, to tackle the common problems and issues; (c) to formulate a common position on issues to be discussed at other international meetings on jute; and (d) to suggest an appropriate institutional arrangement for implementing the proposed cooperative activities at the regional level.

GCJPC countries then worked toward an agreement with jute-consuming countries, and an International Jute Organization (IJO) agreement was signed in 1983.

The Regional Consultative Meeting is the principal organ. Four-day sessions are held at least once each year. ESCAP's International Trade Division serves as the secretariat.

Six countries participate regularly as members (see Table 11.8). Brazil attends as an Observer from time to time.

The meetings set priorities for projects. The earliest, funded by the Netherlands and conducted by ESCAP, was an overview of the industry in Asia by ESCAP. A meeting on problems of standardizing grades of jute was held in 1982. The Netherlands supported the establishment of a computerized data system on production costs of jute and kenaf fibers in cooperation with the Food and Agriculture Organization of the UN (FAO); this project ran from 1985 to 1988, and included training workshops on data collection and computer processing. The Free University of Amsterdam has set up an econometric model on jute to develop production planning and marketing strategies and has provided technical assistance to enable the model to secure input from jute-producing countries. From 1984 to 1987, ESCAP set up national information services for jute products, combined with a study tour of European markets, to encourage jute-producing countries to meet the demand of consumers by diversifying jute products. Training courses on jute processing in India, retting and machinery-maintenance tech-

Table 11.8
Membership in Three Informal Commodity Communities: Government Consultation Among Jute Producing Countries; Intergovernmental Consultative Forum of Developing Tropical Timber Producing/Exporting Countries; and Regional Consultative Group on Silk

Year Joined	Jute Community	Tropical Timber Community	Silk Community
1979	Bangladesh India Nepal Thailand		
1980	Burma		
1982		Indonesia Malaysia Papua New Guinea Philippines Thailand	China India Malaysia South Korea Thailand
1983	China[a]		Philippines
Totals	6 Members	5 Members	6 Members

[a]Observer in 1982

niques in China, and factory management in Thailand have been opened to countries in the region. GCJPC currently awaits funds for quality-control projects.

INTERGOVERNMENTAL CONSULTATIVE FORUM OF DEVELOPING TROPICAL TIMBER PRODUCING/ EXPORTING COUNTRIES (ICFDTTP/EC)[9]

Hardwood from tropical rainforests in the Third World has almost vanished. Logging operations felled trees without restriction throughout the past century and with no provision to conserve or to replant. In two decades, the Philippine forest has declined from 16 million to 1 million hectares. Thailand, once an exporter, now imports tropical lumber. With the removal of the ecosystem connected with the forests, many farmers can no longer grow their crops, and many indigenous peoples have been forced to abandon ancestral homelands.

Foremost among the corporations engaged in this plunder after World War II were those from Japan, which consumes 20 percent and fells nearly half of all forest products sold on the world market. Japanese homebuyers want new, clean-looking houses, and Japanese restaurants buy nearly two billion disposable wooden chopsticks from Indonesia and the Philippines each year. In addition, Japan imposes a duty of 20 percent on imported plywood to protect its own domestic manufacturers, forcing suppliers in Southeast Asia to export unprocessed lumber or to cut the prices of their hardwood plywood. In the case of Sabah and Sarawak, price cuts of 30 percent were necessary in 1985, as Malaysia's largest foreign exchange source is the sale of tropical timber, both logs and sawn lumber.

UNCTAD originally identified tropical timber as an IPC commodity. In 1975, the nongovernmental South East Asian Lumber Producers' Association (SEALPA) was formed among Indonesia, Malaysia, Papua New Guinea, and the Philippines, but it was unable to forge a consensus. At about this time, ASEAN's Committee on Food, Agriculture and Forestry (COFAF) and FAO framed several tropical timber projects to bring technical personnel into the region. In 1978, ESCAP convened a meeting of country experts on tropical timber, where there was agreement on the need for an Asian and Pacific timber community. In July 1980, UNCTAD's preparatory meeting on tropical timber agreed on the components for a future organization, but Asian countries were eager to act before a transregional body could be formed. After an ESCAP meeting in 1981 and an ESCAP/SEALPA workshop in 1982, Malaysia hosted the first ICFDTTP/EC meeting in Kuala Lumpur later in 1982; three subsequent sessions have been held. The International Tropical Timber Organization (ITTO) was finally negotiated in 1983, and its Secretariat opened its doors in Yokohama in 1987.

ITCFDTTP/EC has no formal terms of reference. Instead, it meets at two- or three-year intervals to review technical assistance projects to the region. ESCAP's International Trade Division serves as the secretariat.

Five countries are members (see Table 11.8). Together they account for about 75 percent of the hardwood lumber in the world. Burma attended in 1982 as an Observer.

Country representatives and ESCAP, in collaboration with FAO, presented papers on problem areas to the 1982 meeting. The highest priority went to price stabilization through supply management and rationalization. Indonesia is now banning the export of plywood and rattan to ensure that some downstream processing will remain in the region, and it is prepared to buy Malaysia's sawn lumber as well, thereby encouraging other countries to follow suit. Laos and Thailand have stopped all logging as well. Other concerns are forest resource development, market information, processing capabilities, and standardization of logs, sawn lumber, and secondary wood products.

REGIONAL CONSULTATIVE GROUP ON SILK (RCGS)[10]

Silk, so prominent in trade between China and Europe nearly a thousand years ago that one of the trade routes was known as the silk route, is in short supply today. There is a need to modernize the industry.

The International Silk Association (ISA), formed in 1970, has tended to reflect the interests of consuming countries. ESCAP, accordingly, convened a meeting of silk-producing countries in Bangkok, where a Constitution of the Regional Consultative Group on Silk was adopted on December 15, 1982. The main objective, as set forth in the group's Constitution, is "to promote the production, processing and marketing of silk" (Article 4).

Sessions of RCGS, attended by trade ministers, meet every two to three years. The provisional agenda is drawn up by ESCAP's International Trade Division, which serves as the secretariat.

All silk producing countries of the ESCAP region that are Members or Associate Members of ESCAP are eligible to join. There are six members today (see Table 11.8). Indonesia and Iran attended the inaugural meeting but decided not to participate. Besides servicing member countries, RCGS technical assistance has also gone to Bangladesh and Nepal.

ESCAP provides administrative expenses. Project funds have been provided by ISA and the Netherlands.

RCGS coordinates technical assistance, which has consisted of the dissemination of information in regard to dyeing and finishing of raw silk, market promotion, pests and disease control, research, silkworm breeding, and the standardization and grading of raw silk. Although one difficulty appears to be silk processing, the only training arrangement was a two-month study tour of the industry in China in 1985. Two silk fairs have been organized to display silk products; the first, held in Hongkong in 1986, attracted orders of about $40 million.

SUMMARY AND CONCLUSIONS

Copra and crude coconut oil are today at their lowest levels of earnings since the 1930s, in part because of the use of synthetic substitutes. APCC has been a model for other commodity organizations in its use of the Asian Way principle of Asian solutions to Asian problems by focusing on the fourfold problems of research, production, processing, and marketing to advance the ailing coconut industry. APCC began by deciding that it would leave agricultural research to established centers in the Philippines and Sri Lanka, with the Secretariat responsible only for disseminating results. APCC then pursued economic studies. In regard to production, the Community found that coconut trees have a low return compared to alternative crops, so it encouraged coconut farmers to intercrop coconuts with other profitable crops, in that way increasing productivity rather than acreage. In relation to processing, productive methods were endorsed to extract oil from crushing, to market milk rather than raw coconuts, then using the coir for matting and the tree trunks for paper pulp. Marketing has been the stumbling block, due not only to high freight rates but also to inadequate advertising on uses of coconut products to manufacturers and consumers. APCC has had the effect of rationalizing the coconut industry. The days of the copra trade are virtually over; a more lean, vigorous coconut industry has arisen in its place.

The political significance of natural rubber goes beyond the economic realities, since most producers are smallholders; in Malaysia their economic security determines whether the governing coalition will survive politically. ANRPC's efforts have given the natural rubber industry a more competitive role in the world economy by rationalizing policies – first, by encouraging high-yielding rubber trees, then, by getting Japan to blend natural with synthetic rubber, and, in time, by drawing up a price stabilization agreement, attesting to the success of the Asian Way principle of incrementalism, as ANRPC emerged to revitalize the industry. ANRPC efforts paved the way for the establishment of the International Natural Rubber Organization (INRO), also in Kuala Lumpur, to supervise the INRA agreements of 1979 and 1986. INRO's buffer stock manager has now sold nearly all of the natural rubber accumulated in the early 1980s to halt the upward trend in prices.

AVRDC has extended the green revolution to vegetables. After collecting 25,000 germplasm varieties for six vegetables, only a few hybrids proved to be resistant to heat, insects, damp weather, and fungal as well as viral diseases while giving a high yield in a short growing season. AVRDC has distributed seed packets for retesting around the world. AVRDC's tropical tomatoes were an unusual success and are now exported to the First World. The ultimate success of AVRDC will come when vegetable farming, now intercropped between rice-growing seasons, is more profitable. Implementation remains a problem. The extension work required for farmers to experiment with new crops is a task beyond the scope of AVRDC but left to FFTC, as described in Chapter 5.

The pepper-seasoning industry has been pulling together over the years thanks to the efforts of IPC, but the struggle is uphill. Diseases, such as black wilt, threaten to reduce supply, and it has been reported that some Indonesian pepper is occasionally contaminated by agents that cause cancer, salmonella poisoning, tetanus, and typhoid. Pepper's problems, thus, are largely in production. Demand continues to outstrip supply, and consumers pay high prices around the world. Basic technical studies are ongoing, consistent with the Asian Way principle of incrementalism, but pepper is the only commodity besides natural rubber that is able to increase prices with impunity.

Thailand seeks to maximize income from rice; its participation in the ASEAN rice scheme is a major concession on its part, and it will go no farther in the interest of regional cooperation. Without Thailand, ARTF is doomed. Yet more countries have become self-sufficient in rice, thanks to IRRI's so-called miracle rice. Burma, meanwhile, is no longer a rice-exporting country, and India relies increasingly on wheat. One estimate of the cost of establishing a buffer stock of rice is $50 million, and bilateral two- or three-year arrangements have been suggested but never adopted. Even ESCAP has encouraged such Asian countries as Indonesia to develop "coarse grains" as inexpensive, nutritious alternatives to rice as a food staple. Nevertheless, as Thailand becomes more industrialized in the 1990s, it may find products with more lucrative export markets, and the role of rice may be reduced.

SEATRAD Centre did not find large new deposits of tin. The approach of having experts from outside the region train regional experts was successful but was phased out when tin prospecting seemed futile. SEATRAD Centre then attended to inefficiently operated mines, where owners were unaware of new labor-saving machinery. Making existing mining more efficient seemed the best way to proceed in a world market with a glut of tin. As in the Asian Way principle of separating goals from implementation strategies, it was easy to steer programs into more practical directions.

ATPC was long overdue. Before World War II, tin enjoyed a high level of prosperity, and the U.S. government bought large amounts of tin as a stockpile for use in wartime. After the war, the stockpile remained and industrial substitutes had been or were in the process of being developed. The aluminum and plastics industries, seeking a larger share of the world market, adopted aggressive and innovative sales campaigns, while the tin industry sat on its past laurels. In London, industrialists were more interested in cutting costs than in looking out for the welfare of tin-producing countries halfway around the world, and the tin industry hobbled along unconcerned about its future.

Countries in Southeast Asia, meanwhile, were pitted against producers in Africa, China, and South America in an effort to keep prices down. Since the tin industry lacked coherent leadership, merely reacting to developments in market forces beyond its control, the formation of ATPC represents an effort of Third-World countries to wrest control from London and to revitalize an industry all but abandoned by industrial powers. After the Asian Way principles of incrementalism and consensus building fashioned a reasonable program, Brazil and China cooperated with ATPC. In regard to modernizing the industry, new uses for tin are the province of ITRI, but breakthroughs have not emerged for decades. The decision to place ITRI under ATPC's wings may be a step in the direction of centralizing research, but only a step. An aggressive marketing effort is needed before the industry can truly compete with substitutes in the world market.

When IJO's Secretariat at Dhaka, Bangladesh, opened its doors in 1985, there were not enough ratifications for the organization to go into effect fully. Meanwhile, jute production is not going up, and prices remain unstable. GCJPC has pressured IJO to set up a price stabilization plan while seeking to make the jute industry more efficient, but to no avail.

With ASEAN, FAO, ITTO, SEALPA, UNCTAD, and UNIDO involved in studies on the tropical timber industry, ICFDTTP/EC has served thus far as a useful coordinating body for tropical timber in the region. The aim is to agree to common strategies for implementation so that the industry can maximize earnings while minimizing ecological difficulties and exploitation of the past. One country after another has ceased logging.

RCGS coordinates technical assistance for silk, a scarce commodity in the world market. The silk industry may experience a boom if it can modernize in the years ahead.

In July 1987, UNCTAD's Integrated Program of Commodities suddenly sprang to life. One of the latest developments in the new thinking of Mikhail Gorbachev's diplomacy is the decision to support the first window of the UNCTAD program, the Common Fund; contributions of the Soviet Union and its allies raised the monetary contributions from 59 percent to over the minimum 66.7 percent required to launch the fund. The Second World has come to the assistance of the Third World. This event comes so quickly that the full impact on Asian commodity communities has yet to be assessed, but it does bring good news indeed. The second window of the Integrated Program for Commodities, funds for research and development and marketing assistance, awaits implementation. Meanwhile, Asia has been "OPECized."

NOTES

1. For references to APCC documents, see Michael Haas, *Basic Documents of Asian Regional Organizations* (Dobbs Ferry, NY: Oceana Publications, 1979), vol. 7, pp. 290–93. For a bibliography of secondary sources for all the organizations described in this chapter, see pp. 285–89.

2. For references to ANRPC documents, see Michael Haas, *Basic Documents of Asian Regional Organizations* (Dobbs Ferry, NY: Oceana Publications, 1979), vol. 7, pp. 294–302.

3. For references to AVRDC documents, see Michael Haas, *Basic Documents of Asian Regional Organizations* (Dobbs Ferry, NY: Oceana Publications, 1979), vol. 7, pp. 303–6.

4. For references to IPC documents, see Michael Haas, *Basic Documents of Asian Regional Organizations* (Dobbs Ferry, NY: Oceana Publications, 1979), vol. 7, pp. 307–8.

5. For references to ARTF documents, see Michael Haas, *Basic Documents*

of Asian Regional Organizations (Dobbs Ferry, NY: Oceana Publications, 1979), vol. 7, pp. 309–12.

6. For references to SEATRAD Centre documents, see Michael Haas, *Basic Documents of Asian Regional Organizations* (Dobbs Ferry, NY: Oceana Publications, 1979), vol. 7. p. 313.

7. For references to ATPC documents, see Association of Tin Producing Countries, *A Milestone in Producer Collaboration in Tin* (Kuala Lumpur: ATPC, c. 1985) and later publications from this source.

8. For references to GCJPC documents, see UN Economic and Social Commission for Asia and the Pacific, *Report of the Government Consultation Among Jute Producing Countries* (Bangkok: ESCAP, 1979–).

9. For references to ICFDTTP/EC documents, see UN Economic and Social Commission for Asia and the Pacific, *Report of Intergovernmental Consultative Forum of Developing Tropical Timber Producing/Exporting Countries* (Bangkok: ESCAP, 1982–).

10. For references to RCGS documents, see UN Economic and Social Commission for Asia and the Pacific, *Report of the Regional Consultative Group on Silk* (Bangkok: ESCAP, 1982–).

12 CONFEROCRACIES

The Association of South East Asian Nations (ASEAN) and the Asian and Pacific Council (ASPAC) began as conferences among foreign ministers, with neither a formal agreement nor a secretariat. If we insist that an organization must have both components, then we could not talk about ASEAN until 1977, and ASPAC would be outside the scope of this volume. Rather than following such a procrustean definition, therefore, we must, to be consistent, include some lesser-known ministerial conferences: the Informal Meeting of Directors General of Civil Aviation, Asia and the Pacific (DGCA), the Asian Judicial Conference (AJC), the Conference of Asian and Pacific Labor Ministers (CAPLM), the Association for Science Cooperation in Asia (ASCA), and the Taxation and Customs Cooperation Conference (TCCC). In each case, power is vested in the conference itself, from which we derive the term *conferocracy*. All five organizations were proposed by the Philippines. Manila provided a secretariat in only one case, however.

INFORMAL MEETING OF DIRECTORS GENERAL OF CIVIL AVIATION, ASIA AND THE PACIFIC (DGCA)[1]

Matters of civil aviation are quite technical, involving air traffic, navigational equipment, and many other considerations. It is natural to expect that heads of civil aviation in Asian and Pacific countries would value opportunities for discussion of mutual problems and needs.

In 1961, Philippine Director General Vincente Rivera, Jr., convened an Informal Meeting of Directors General of Aviation in Asia and the

South Pacific at Manila to discuss civil aviation problems in the region and the role of the United Nations' International Civil Aviation Organization (ICAO) in meeting regional needs. Inasmuch as he wished to keep the sessions informal, a discussion ensued on a wide range of topics, without a fixed agenda or formal publication of proceedings. When the conference adjourned, participants agreed to a second meeting the following year, and the body has continued to the present, although somewhat more formally than originally envisaged.

Because the organization was to be informal, there is no official statement of objectives. According to Dennis H. Wilham, Deputy Representative for the ICAO Asia and Pacific Office at Bangkok in the mid-1980s, the apparent aim is as follows: "to provide a forum of an informal exchange of views, information and experience in coping with all aspects of . . . tasks and responsibilities in management, operation, regulation and control of civil aviation activities."[2]

Informal Meetings are held for a week about once each year. The host director general provided a secretariat for the first meeting. Later, DGCA asked ICAO's Asia and Pacific Office at Bangkok to serve as the Secretariat (see Fig. 12.1). Meetings have several Working Sessions to discuss specialized topics.

No records were kept initially, and there is no volume of proceedings of the second meeting, but by 1963, there were fifteen countries represented (see Table 12.1). Participation is tantamount to membership. The Republic of China (Taiwan) has not participated in DGCA since 1971, since its ICAO membership has terminated. Some countries have attended all the meetings, but others go from time to time. Vietnam, for example, resumed participation in 1984 after an absence of about 13 years, attesting to the pan-Asian spirit of the Asian Way.

Figure 12.1
Organization of the Informal Meeting of Directors General of Civil Aviation, Asia and the Pacific

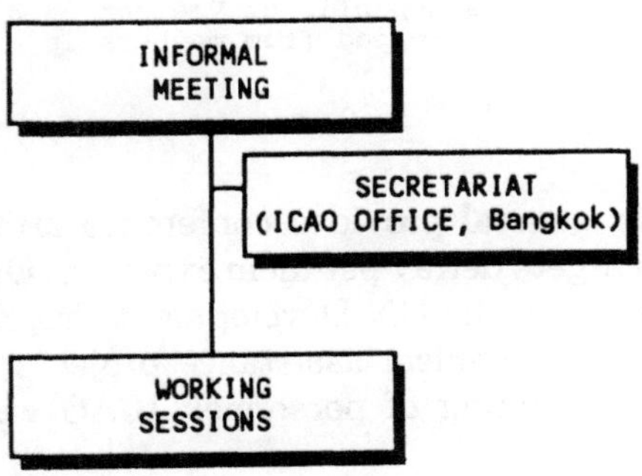

Table 12.1
Informal Meeting of Directors General of Civil Aviation, Asia and the Pacific: Membership

Year Joined[a]	Member Countries
1961	Australia
	Hongkong
	India
	Indonesia
	Laos
	Malaysia
	New Caledonia
	New Zealand
	Pakistan
	Philippines
	South Korea
	Taiwan (China) (d 1971)
	Thailand
	United Kingdom
	United States
1964	Japan
	Vietnam[b]
1967	Fiji
	Nepal
	Singapore
	Tahiti
1971	Brunei
1975	France
1976	Bangladesh
	Maldives
	Papua New Guinea
	Sri Lanka
1978	Afghanistan
	China
	French Polynesia
	North Korea
1981	Nauru
	Solomon Islands
	Tonga
1982	Canada
	Vanuatu
1984	Western Samoa
Totals	37-1=36 Members

[a]Dates for DGCA are uncertain: records begin in 1963 and are unavailable for 1973, 1974, and 1977
[b]Joined as Republic of Vietnam
Key: d = dropped from membership

The host director general provides conference arrangements. Civil aviation national budgets defray per-diem expenses. Outside the framework of the organization, the UN Development Program (UNDP) provided $20.6 million in technical assistance projects to the region in 1982–86, mostly for training of personnel; ICAO was the executing agent.

The main business of the Informal Meetings is the discussion of technical subjects relating to civil aviation. The principal topics are air navigation, including aerodromes and ground aids, aeronautical information services, air navigation, air traffic control, aircraft operations, meteorological services, and search and rescue services. Papers on other topics are also presented, including air transport, aviation security, and technical assistance. Comments on the papers generate discussion. ICAO often presents a paper on its international program of activities for the information of countries in attendance.

ASIAN JUDICIAL CONFERENCE (AJC)[3]

Newly independent Asian countries inherited systems of jurisprudence imposed by foreign powers on cultures that often operated by different principles. The development of modern legal systems in Asia has thus involved a blending of diverse influences. The Asian Judicial Conference (AJC) began in order to provide a forum for sharing these common experiences.

In 1963, Philippine Chief Justice Cesar Bengzon considered the idea of a joint forum among supreme court justices. He convened what he considered to be a preparatory meeting for this purpose at Baguio during May 1963. There was no formal agenda; instead, justices from eight countries had an informal discussion on jurisprudence. The justices, however, derived so much benefit from the meeting that they decided to call the meeting the First Asian Judicial Conference.

AJC began without a charter. In an address at the 1965 conference, Bengzon articulated his idea of the organization as "the betterment of the principles of justice in this part of the world." "Toward this goal," he continued, "the Conference seeks to establish a common ground for the interchange of information concerning the administration of justice in each of the participating countries." The functions, then, were "to learn from one another, and to develop a better, because more enlightened, jurisprudence for Asians out of the similarity of our common historical origins and traditions, even aspirations."

The Conference met about every other year for one week until its final meeting in 1973. The host chief justice provided the secretariat for the meeting and drew up an agenda based on correspondence with opposite numbers in other countries. The host chief justice selected a Secretary-General. A Pre-Conference Meeting handled problems of protocol, and participants read and discussed papers at Working Sessions (see Fig. 12.2).

Eight countries attended in 1963, and by 1973 eighteen countries were represented (see Table 12.2). The host chief justice issued invitations. The chief justice of Afghanistan agreed to attend in 1970, but at

Figure 12.2
Organization of the Asian Judicial Conference

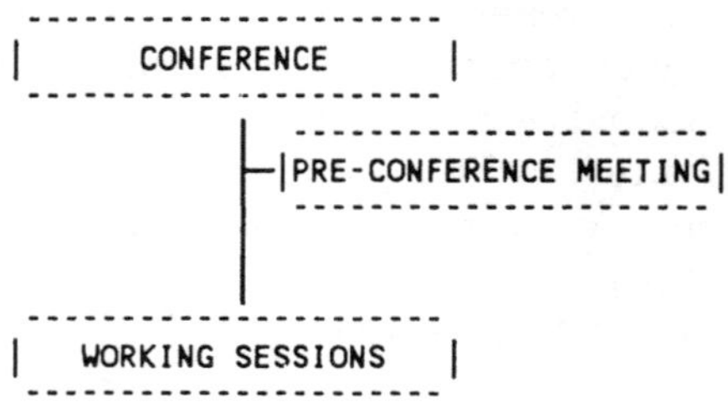

the last minute was unable to do so; his paper appeared anyway in the proceedings.

Host countries defrayed costs of holding the meetings, including publishing proceedings. Justices used their own national budgets to defray per diem expenses.

The chief justices presented a survey of the judicial system in their own countries, though not every year. Distinguished academic lawyers were also invited to present papers on assorted topics. There was al-

Table 12.2
Asian Judicial Conference: Membership

Year Joined	Member Countries
1963	India
	Japan
	Malaya
	Pakistan
	Philippines
	South Korea
	Taiwan (China)
	Thailand
1965	Australia
	Singapore
1969	Indonesia
	Laos
	New Zealand
	Sri Lanka
1970	Iran
	Nepal
	Western Samoa
1973	Fiji
Totals	defunct in 1973

ways at least one conference topic on which the justices wrote papers and compared experiences.

No conference was held after 1973 for reasons that are unclear. Asian justices met together in 1985 and 1987 at conferences organized by the Law Association for Asia and the Pacific (LAWASIA), which provided expenses for the meetings and did not consider their efforts to be a continuation of AJC.

CONFERENCE OF ASIAN AND PACIFIC LABOR MINISTERS (CAPLM)[4]

Established in Geneva under the terms of the Treaty of Versailles in 1919, the International Labor Organization (ILO) became a Specialized Agency of the United Nations at the end of World War II. Pursuing an idea proposed by the Indian ILO delegate in 1927, the first regional ILO conference was held in Santiago, Chile, in 1936. As the ILO, along with other UN agencies, began to decentralize operations by establishing regional offices throughout the world, the first Asian Regional Conference of ILO convened at New Delhi in 1947. The Regional Office for Asia, located at Bangkok, proceeded to convene regional ILO conferences at intervals of three to five years. Philippine Labor Secretary Emilio Espinosa convened the first Conference of Asian Ministers of Labor (CALM) in Quezon City, which met from December 12 to 16, 1966. Ministerial conferences have continued, and in 1976, CALM was renamed the Conference of Asian and Pacific Labor Ministers (CAPLM).

According to the Declaration issued at the first meeting, CAPLM exists "to provide a forum for free exchange of views and experiences" concerning

> 1. manpower policies, social security, labor administration and other related problems in the region, 2. formulation and implementation of regional projects and approved programs through international agencies involving Asian countries, 3. and the provision of such training and services as may be necessary for the proper development of labor administration in Asia and arrangements for utilizing such facilities existing in any country.

CAPLM, which has three-day sessions about every two years, consists of a plenary session and two Technical Panels (see Fig. 12.3). Originally, one of the Technical Panels, entitled "Regional Technical Cooperation," reviewed ILO activities in the region; the other Technical Panel discussed a special topic. In 1983, both panels reviewed ILO regional efforts and then went into a broad range of subjects. After the Technical Panels, the plenary session makes final decisions. Although Japan has offered a headquarters for the organization, and Pakistan

Figure 12.3
Organization of the Conference of Asian and Pacific Labor Ministers

supports the idea of a secretariat, there is no permanent office for CAPLM. The host country for the Conference provides secretariat services for the meeting.

Governments served by the ILO office in Bangkok are invited to attend. So far, forty-two countries have participated as members (see Table 12.3). Some of the countries that participated later are members of the region covered by the ILO Regional Office for the Middle East, which used to be in Beirut but now operates from Geneva. Taiwan (China) ceased participation after 1971, when it lost its seat in ILO. Hongkong has attended as an Observer. Host countries for CAPLM meetings absorb costs for conference arrangements. ILO already convenes regional ILO conferences, so it has understandably not volunteered to defray CAPLM costs.

Discussions are quite thorough and often lively. In recent years, the topics have included employment and human resources development, labor migration, labor productivity, training and mobility of labor, and working conditions and the environment.

ASSOCIATION FOR SCIENCE COOPERATION IN ASIA (ASCA)[5]

Scientists in government laboratories often work on similar problems throughout Asia, although with limited funds and in isolation from their opposite numbers in neighboring countries. The result is duplication of effort and sometimes of mistakes, without a more useful sharing of information and insights.

The Association for Science Cooperation in Asia (ASCA) grew out of an Asian Ministers of Science Conference held in Manila from November 16 to 20, 1970, convened at the suggestion of Dominador Reyes, Chief of the Office of International Relations at the Philippine National

Table 12.3
Conference of Asian and Pacific Labor Ministers: Membership

Year Joined	Member Countries
1966	Australia
	India
	Indonesia
	Iran
	Japan
	Laos (i 1975-)
	Malaysia
	Philippines
	Singapore
	South Korea
	Taiwan (China) (d 1971)
	Vietnam (i 1975-)[a]
1971	Afghanistan (i 1977-)
	Cambodia (i 1975-)[b]
	Pakistan
	Sri Lanka (o 1966)
1973	Bangladesh
	Fiji
	Nauru
	New Zealand (o 1971)
1975	Papua New Guinea
	Tonga (o 1973)
1976	Bhutan
	Mongolia
	Western Samoa
1978	Solomon Islands
	Tuvalu
1980	Cook Islands
	Kiribati
1983	Bahrain
	Iraq
	Jordan (o 1980)
	Kuwait
	Lebanon
	Nepal
	North Yemen
	Qatar (o 1980)
	Saudi Arabia
	South Yemen
	Syria
	United Arab Emirates
	Vanuatu
Totals	42-1=41 Members

[a]Joined as Republic of Vietnam
[b]Joined as the Khmer Republic
Key: d = dropped from membership
i = inactive
o = Observer

Science Development Board. Because science coordination is often handled below the ministerial level in Asian countries, a follow-up conference of senior officials met in Manila in March 1972, when ASCA was inaugurated.

The organization operates on an informal basis. During the first meeting in 1972, five Objectives and seven Policy Guidelines were adopted, which were modified by Working Guidelines, adopted in 1978. According to these documents, there are six aims:

> 1. exchange information in national scientific resources and research programs, 2. identify areas of common scientific or technological interest and assign priorities thereto, 3. examine means for providing solutions to priority problems . . . through the resources and facilities of existing agencies or by such other avenues as may be most appropriate and beneficial, 4. provide advisory services as requested in science and technology to the existing international and regional organizations, 5. review as necessary progress in the implementation of plans and programs for the advancement of science and technology in the . . . region, 6. consider other items which fall within the interests of the Association and may be mutually acceptable to members.

The Conference, the principal organ of ASCA, was held for three days annually up to 1976 (see Fig. 12.4). According to the Working Guidelines, Conferences are now held biennially. The host country for the forthcoming Conference furnishes a secretariat, a secretary general, and absorbs costs for running the secretariat until the succeeding host

Figure 12.4
Organization of the Association for Science Cooperation in Asia

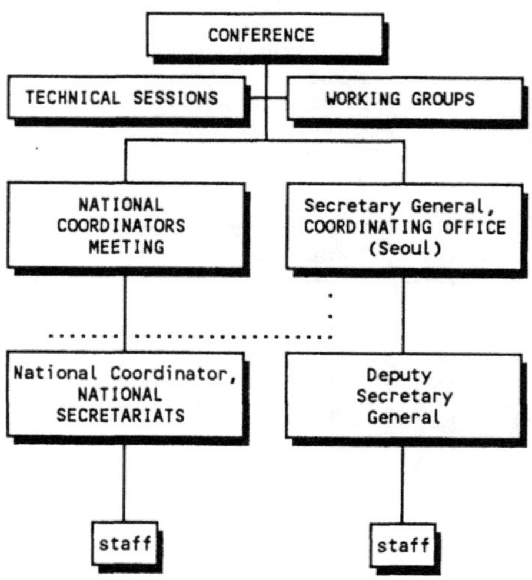

country takes over the responsibility. While this practice continues, in 1987 a permanent ASCA Coordinating Office was established in Seoul, financed by the Republic of Korea at about $357,000 per year. The Office has a Secretary-General, Deputy Secretary General, and a staff of six. Its tasks are to coordinate meetings, service projects, serve as an information clearinghouse for science and technology, and publish a newsletter.

Conferences consist of two parts: a plenary session, which begins with country reports, and a technical session, in which papers enable science coordinators and researchers to present and discuss research findings from project reports. Ad hoc Working Groups form to make recommendations to the plenary session. Ministers or their representatives make decisions at the final plenary session.

Between ASCA conferences there are special meetings on specific subjects. In 1988, South Korea held the first Asian Science and Technology Congress during the ASCA meeting. Seminars are organized by the various cooperative projects. Permanent ASCA centers in specialized fields are under study.

Each country has its own national ASCA secretariat. The procedure is for the country's science coordination board to name the ASCA Correspondent Institution, whose head or deputy is then the ASCA National Coordinator; since 1988, there has been a National Coordinators Meeting just before the Conference. Projects involving two or more countries designate a Lead Country or Countries to handle coordination.

Membership is open to all countries of Asia and the Pacific. Eighteen countries have participated so far (see Table 12.4), although there are several inactive members. The United States was an Observer in 1981. A Korean proposal to rename the organization the Association for Science Cooperation in Asia and the Pacific was rejected in 1988.

The host country defrays secretariat costs for each conference and seminar, although, on occasion, seminars have been sponsored by Australia and Japan on subjects for which other countries served as Lead Countries. Costs of being a Lead Country for a project are borne by the Lead Country or by an external aid donor, if any. Non-Lead Countries fund their own participation in particular projects or obtain external funding.

As of the 1988 Conference, countries were Lead Countries for new projects in the following fields: South Korea – meteorology and telecommunications; Malaysia – product testing, science and technology policy management training and technology transfer; Nepal – type culture collection; the Philippines – climatology; Japan – scientific and technical information.

Table 12.4
Association for Science Cooperation in Asia and Taxation and Customs Cooperation Conference: Membership

Year	ASCA	TCCC
1972	Australia	Philippines
	Indonesia	South Korea
	Japan	South Vietnam
	Philippines	Taiwan (China)
	South Korea	
	Thailand	
	Vietnam (i 1974-87)[a]	
1973	Bangladesh	
	Cambodia (o 1974, i 1975-)[b]	
	India	
	New Zealand (o 1972)	
	Pakistan	
	Singapore (o 1972)	
	Sri Lanka	
1974	Burma (i 1974-)	
	Nepal	
1976	Malaysia (o 1972-75)	
1979	Hongkong (i 1979-)	
1987	Brunei	
1988	Papua New Guinea	
Total	20 Members	defunct in 1975

[a]Joined as Republic of Vietnam
[b]Joined as Khmer Republic
Key: i = inactive
o = Observer

TAXATION AND CUSTOMS COOPERATION CONFERENCE (TCCC)[6]

Governments in developing countries need revenue, but elaborate methods for tax evasion, including smuggling, are widespread, and deny governments this revenue. TCCC was a forum to share experience and information on how to modernize tax and customs administration.

At a breakfast during the annual meeting of the International Monetary Fund (IMF) in 1972, the finance ministers of the Philippines, South Korea, Taiwan (China), and South Vietnam met informally. Cesar Virata, Philippine Finance Minister, noted that his country and the Republic of Vietnam were members of the Study Group on Asian Tax Administration and Research (SGATAR), a forum for discussing mutual problems in regard to tax policy (SGATAR is discussed in Chapter 6). Since the Republic of Korea and the Republic of China were not considered eligible for membership in SGATAR, composed as it was of Southeast Asian countries, a new organization was proposed.

Taiwan (China) invited the three other countries to the first Taxation and Customs Cooperation Conference (TCCC) in Taipei from May 30 to

June 2, 1972, when they agreed in principle to formalize the organization. TCCC, also known as the Four-Country Conference on Taxation and Customs Cooperation, met for the last time in 1975.

The Memorandum of Understanding that formalized TCCC was adopted on June 30, 1973. The aim was "to improve the tax and tariff systems and internal revenue and customs administration through effective research, planning and implementation," according to the preamble to the Memorandum of Understanding. The following functions are in the same document:

(a) serve as a clearinghouse for the exchange of information among the four member countries; (b) examine, conduct researches and studies on the tax and tariff systems and revenue and customs administration practices of the member countries; (c) gather, process, compile, and disseminate information; (d) issue publications; (e) coordinate requests for technical assistance, including the exchange of tax and customs officials, trainees and scholars among various countries; (f) perform such other related functions.

The Conference was the main body of the organization (see Fig. 12.5). The Conference had two main discussion groups – the Customs Group and the Internal Taxation Group – and lasted from three to seven days.

The headquarters, set up in 1973 in Manila, was called the Asian Secretariat for Taxation and Customs Cooperation. Although adminis-

Figure 12.5
Organization of the Taxation and Customs Cooperation Conference

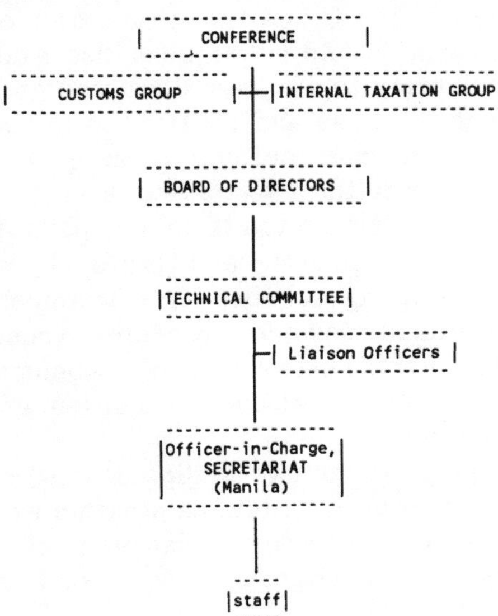

tratively in the Office of the Finance Secretary, in practice, it was headed by Dr. Angel Yoingco, Director of the National Tax Research Center. The Secretariat was supervised by a yearly two-day meeting of the Board of Directors, consisting of the heads or deputies of the Philippine Bureau of Customs, Bureau of Internal Revenue, and the National Tax Research Center. A Technical Committee—composed of a ranking official from the Philippine Department of Finance, the Bureau of Internal Revenue, the Bureau of Customs, and the National Tax Research Center—was also supposed to supervise the immediate work of the Secretariat; however, the latter body never met. For purposes of communication with member countries, liaison officers were designated outside the Philippines, to which the Secretariat in Manila addressed correspondence. Aside from the Officer-in-Charge, the Secretariat borrowed one professional and two general service staff on a part-time basis for TCCC duties.

From 1972 to 1975, there were four members (see Table 12.4). In 1975, the Republic of Vietnam ceased to exist. The Philippines established relations with the People's Republic of China in 1976, agreeing to have no further diplomatic relations with the Republic of China (Taiwan). As a result, TCCC could not continue.

The Philippine Department of Finance was responsible for financial support of personnel costs. Funds were part of the yearly budget of the National Tax Research Center, although the Bureau of Customs and Bureau of Internal Revenue were ready to share any additional costs that might have arisen.

The principal work of TCCC was the presentation of papers on customs and internal taxation and subsequent discussion at the annual conferences. The following topics were discussed on inland taxation: exemption of income from sea and air transport, taxation of foreign investments, taxing of tourism, automatic data processing, tax auditing, taxation in the agricultural sector, value-added versus turnover taxes, training of tax officials, and the establishment of a global income tax system. Discussion on customs and tariffs focused on the following: fraud due to smuggling, falsification of commercial documents, simplification of documentation and procedures in customs, removal of tax barriers to promote trade between member countries, promotion of tourism, tax incentives for export trade, valuation, and narcotics control.

Under an exchange program, two Philippine customs officials went to Taiwan for training. A more ambitious program was under preparation when TCCC collapsed. The Secretariat prepared a monthly newsletter and a report in 1974 on possible areas for treaty revisions on customs and taxation.

SUMMARY AND CONCLUSIONS

DGCA enables heads of agencies concerned with commercial aviation to keep abreast of changing developments in their fields, while informing ICAO of regional priorities. Although the discussions remain informal, proceedings are published, and attendance has increased over the years. Since ICAO provides technical assistance, there was no reason to set up DGCA as a more formal body, an Asian solution to the Asian problem of upgrading the quality of civil aviation.

It has now been more than a decade since AJC's last meeting, and memories of the reason for its expiration have faded. As long as the Law Association for Asia and the Pacific (LAWASIA) continues to finance ad hoc meetings of supreme court justices, AJC is unlikely to be reborn.

ILO's support of CAPLM is evident in three of its current programs. In 1971, under the Asian Regional Team for Employment Promotion (ARTEP), ILO began to provide regional training, seminars, and workshops as a part of the Asian Manpower Plan, the UNDP-funded Asian component of ILO's World Employment Program. The aim of these efforts was reducing unemployment, underemployment, and poverty by creating productive employment and improving the distribution of income. The Asian Regional Center for Strengthening Labor and Manpower Administration (ARPLA) is a second project in which ILO is the Executive Agency. Started in 1974, ARPLA seeks to improve the efficiency of national labor administration systems, including labor inspection and the extension of labor services to rural communities through advisory services, training, and fellowships for training, research, and regional seminars in the field of labor and manpower administration, with a focus on programs for integrated rural development. Although Asian countries urged ILO to establish an Asian manpower skill development institute, the response in 1978 was the Asian Regional Skill Development Program (ARSDEP), which serves as a clearinghouse for exchanging information and develops curriculum materials for vocational training. ARTEP and ARPLA originally operated out of facilities supplied by the Thai Ministry of Labor, while ARSDEP was at ILO's Bangkok office. ARTEP moved to New Delhi in 1986, and ARSDEP now is at Islamabad. Since Asian labor ministries are underfunded, the loose CAPLM was perhaps inevitable.

ASCA brings scientists together in a common forum to avoid the isolation of efforts and lack of cross-fertilization of ideas of scientists that frustrates science in Asia today. The need to pool research for external funding of similar projects in two or more countries has been well served by ASCA as a loose body that facilitates coordination.

TCCC existed because some countries could not attend SGATAR, since they were outside Southeast Asia. New developments in international politics in relation to both China and Vietnam caused the organization to collapse. SGATAR did not expand to include customs matters when TCCC folded, however.

Ministerial conferences well exemplify Asian solutions to Asian problems in providing regular activities without an ossified bureaucracy. These conferences have justified their existence.

NOTES

1. For references to DGCA documents, see *Proceedings of the Informal Meeting of Directors General of Civil Aviation, Asia and the Pacific*, published annually since 1965 by host civil aviation agencies.
2. Personal correspondence, June 12, 1986.
3. For references to AJC documents, see *Record of the First Asian Judicial Conference* (Baguio, May 1963) and later proceedings published by each subsequent host country.
4. For references to CAPLM documents, see Michael Haas, *Basic Documents of Asian Regional Organizations* (Dobbs Ferry, NY: Oceana Publications, 1979), vol. 7, pp. 469–71.
5. For references to ASCA documents, see Michael Haas, *Basic Documents of Asian Regional Organizations* (Dobbs Ferry, NY: Oceana Publications, 1979), vol. 7, pp. 472–76. See also Clarita R. Carlos, "An Analysis of Some Bases for Cooperation of Three Functional Organizations, Namely, Eastern Regional Organization for Public Administration, Asian Oceanic Postal Union and Association for Science Cooperation in Asia." Unpublished master's thesis, Department of Political Science, University of the Philippines, Quezon City, October 1976.
6. For references to TCCC documents, see Michael Haas, *Basic Documents of Asian Regional Organizations* (Dobbs Ferry, NY: Oceana Publications, 1979), vol. 7, pp. 476–78.

13 CONTINUING VITALITY IN ASIAN REGIONAL COOPERATION

The four most recent Asian regional organizations cannot be classified elsewhere but fill important gaps in cooperative efforts in the region: the First Agreement on Trade Negotiations Among Developing Member Countries of the Economic and Social Commission for Asia and the Pacific (known as the Bangkok Agreement); the Centre on Integrated Rural Development for Asia and the Pacific (CIRDAP); the Asian and Pacific Development Centre (APDC); and the South Asian Association for Regional Cooperation (SAARC). SAARC's potential is greater than almost all other regional organizations except ASEAN, as we point out below.

AGREEMENT ON TRADE NEGOTIATIONS AMONG DEVELOPING MEMBER COUNTRIES OF THE ECONOMIC AND SOCIAL COMMISSION FOR ASIA AND THE PACIFIC (THE BANGKOK AGREEMENT)[1]

Import substitution and export promotion are the two main development strategies followed by Third-World countries. Import substitution can be controlled through domestic politics, but export promotion requires superior products and marketing strategies to break down consumer preferences and tariff walls abroad. Most tariffs favor the import of raw materials and the export of manufactured goods, maintaining the international division of labor that locks Third-World countries into the role of primary producers. A reversal in trade patterns, where Third-World countries exchange goods with each other, requires a lowering of barriers to trade. It is the aim of the Bangkok Agreement to make Third-World trade possible, principally by negotiating mutual tariff reductions.

In 1963, the UN Economic Commission for Asia and the Far East (ECAFE, later ESCAP) organized the first meeting of the Council of Ministers on Asian Economic Cooperation to seek new approaches to development that would be more attuned to the needs of the region. In 1970, the Council adopted a resolution known as the Kabul Declaration, calling upon ECAFE to develop measures for intraregional trade expansion and other measures for economic cooperation. ECAFE's International Trade Division then set up an Intergovernmental Committee on Trade Expansion Program, which recommended the establishment of a Trade Negotiations Group (TNG).

In August 1973, some thirteen countries attended the third TNG session to consider requests for tariff reduction. After each country studied lists of requests from the other countries, three further TNG meetings were held in 1974, and by July 1975, seven countries agreed to a list of products for mutual tariff reduction. The result was a formal protocol entitled the First Agreement on Trade Negotiations Among Developing Member Countries of the Economic and Social Commission for Asia and the Pacific (ESCAP); it is known as the Bangkok Agreement because the founding meetings were at ESCAP headquarters in Bangkok. In 1985, ESCAP agreed to launch a second round of negotiations, known as the Seoul Round, with the aim of negotiating a new agreement to extend the first.

According to the Bangkok Agreement, its aim is

> to promote economic development through a continuous process of trade expansion among the developing member countries of ESCAP and to further international economic cooperation through the adoption of mutually beneficial trade liberalization measures consistent with their respective present and future development and trade needs, and taking into account the trading interests of third countries, particularly those of other developing countries. (Article 2)

The principal organ responsible for the Bangkok Agreement, the TNG, consists of representatives from countries participating in negotiations for regional trade liberalization (see Fig. 13.1). TNG met from 1972 to 1975, then again in 1979, and resumed work in 1985.

A Standing Committee of the Participating States was set up under the Bangkok Agreement. Composed of delegates from countries ratifying the agreement, it met for one-day sessions twice each year from 1975 to 1979 and once in 1982; the 1984 meeting decided to begin the second round, which got underway in 1986. The Standing Committee has the power to handle disputes between the members. Although the Agreement provides for an autonomous Director and Secretariat,

Figure 13.1
Organization of the Bangkok Agreement

ESCAP's International Trade Division has served as Secretariat for TNG and Interim Secretariat for the Bangkok Agreement since 1975.

Five countries ratified the Bangkok Agreement by 1976 (see Table 13.1). Laos restructured its economy after 1975 and has been inactive since. The Philippines and Thailand signed the Bangkok Agreement but did not ratify. Ten countries were in the TNG but neither signed nor ratified the Agreement: Afghanistan, Hongkong, Indonesia, Iran,

Table 13.1
First Agreement on Trade Negotiations Among Developing Member Countries of the Economic and Social Commission for Asia and the Pacific: Membership

Year Joined	Member Countries
1975	Bangladesh India Laos (i 1975-) South Korea Sri Lanka
Totals	5 Members

Key: i = inactive

Khmer Republic, Malaysia, Pakistan, Papua New Guinea, Singapore, and Vietnam. Most of these countries attended the TNG in 1985, but by 1988 only the People's Republic of China, Nepal, Pakistan, and Thailand were present, along with the four active members of the Bangkok Agreement.

Each country defrays its own costs for negotiations. ESCAP handles administrative expenses. The UN Conference on Trade and Development (UNCTAD) provides supporting information and staff for TNG, with funds from the UN Development Program (UNDP).

Negotiations for the Bangkok Agreement focused on items produced in surplus quantities by each country so that the impact of tariff reductions would be immediate. After each country identified products for possible bilateral tariff reductions, discussions expanded to a multilateral scope.

The Bangkok Agreement lists 146 products, with tariff reductions averaging 26 percent. Due to Laos' eventual nonparticipation (despite special concessions recognizing its landlocked status), 94 items were involved after 1975. There is an escape clause for emergency situations, such as immediate balance-of-payments difficulties and national defense.

During the initial ten-year period, ESCAP undertook special projects for the ratifying countries. One project was to standardize nomenclature so that the ninety-four items would be recognized as eligible for tariff reduction on entry into each country. Standardization of trade statistics was another project. ESCAP continued to identify items for intraregional trade within and outside the Bangkok Agreement countries. ESCAP is now working to encourage the development of long-term contracts between pairs of countries as an alternative to the hazards of securing foreign exchange by marketing products to developed countries in an era of increased First-World protectionism.

In 1986, a second round of negotiations began after a meeting in Seoul. Thus far, 364 items are on bilateral request lists, and offer lists are under preparation. ESCAP, meanwhile, is encouraging industrial joint ventures, industry clubs, regional chambers of commerce, and sectoral associations to keep pace with the progress of the Association of South East Asian Nations (ASEAN). ESCAP also proposed that countries consider foreign investment incentive schemes and is now setting up a regional investment information center.

Provisions of the Agreement also encourage the reduction or removal of nontariff trade barriers (NTBs), such as quotas and licensing restrictions. There has been no progress on this aspect of the Agreement.

Under the UN's General Agreement on Tariffs and Trade (GATT), trade concessions must follow the most-favored-nation principle, applying to all nations the most liberal concessions granted to any of a country's trade partners, unless they occur within an organizationally defined grouping of countries. In March 1978, the Bangkok Agreement countries were approved as establishing a valid grouping to qualify as an exception under GATT regulations.

Some of the countries that did not ratify the Bangkok Agreement were already involved in other trade groupings. Iran and Pakistan, for example, belonged to a trade liberalization scheme with Turkey through the now-defunct Regional Cooperation for Development (RCD) organization, headquartered in Tehran. Indonesia, Malaysia, the Philippines, Singapore, and Thailand adopted the Preferential Trading Arrangements (PTA) of ASEAN; Brunei joined later. Kampuchea, Laos, and Vietnam set up economic coordination commissions. Some thirteen countries participate in the South Pacific Regional Trade and Economic Cooperation Agreement (SPARTECA) under the South Pacific Forum (SPF), although SPARTECA primarily provides South Pacific island nations duty-free entry into Australia and New Zealand, which in turn have a free-trade agreement of their own called the Closer Economic Relations Trade Agreement (CERTA). Since three of the Bangkok Agreement countries belong to the Asian Clearing Union (ACU), there is a possibility that some of these organizations will merge in due course.

CENTRE ON INTEGRATED RURAL DEVELOPMENT FOR ASIA AND THE PACIFIC (CIRDAP)[2]

Rural development aid projects have tended to focus on only one element, such as community infrastructure, fertilizer inputs, irrigation, mechanization, and the like. Merger of these various elements into an overall package is what is known as integrated rural development (IRD), a concept stressed by the Food and Agriculture Organization of the United Nations (FAO) since the mid-1970s.

When FAO's Director-General came out in favor of regional IRD centers, the Asian Group of Permanent Representatives to FAO met in Rome in 1977. The delegates decided to plan the first of FAO's projected network of regional centers, and a Conference of Plenipotentiaries on the Establishment of a Centre on Integrated Rural Development for Asia and the Pacific convened on July 28, 1978, adopting the Agreement Establishing the Centre on Integrated Rural Development for Asia and the Pacific. The agreement went into effect one year later.

There are two objectives of CIRDAP:

(a) to assist national action and to promote regional cooperation relating to integrated rural development through a network of national institutions in Member States . . . with the aim, in particular, of improving the production, income and living conditions of small-scale farmers and other needy rural groups, and of encouraging their participation in social and economic life; and (b) to act as a servicing institution for its Member States with respect to integrated rural development, by providing them with technical support, by fostering the exchange of ideas and experience and by encouraging such joint or collaborative activities as may benefit those States individually or collectively. [Article I(2)]

CIRDAP's Governing Council has two-day sessions on a biennial basis (see Fig. 13.2). An Executive Committee, composed of five representatives from the Governing Council (including one from Bangladesh, the host country), meets at least once each year for two-day sessions to review CIRDAP's work; representatives of other member countries attend as Observers. A Technical Committee – composed of heads of national IRD centers, representatives of FAO and of the UN Regional Inter-Agency Committee on Rural Development for Asia and the Pacific, donor agencies and countries, and experts on rural development – meets with the Director once each year to provide advice on financial and technical aspects of CIRDAP programs.

Figure 13.2
Organization of the Centre on Integrated Rural Development for Asia and the Pacific

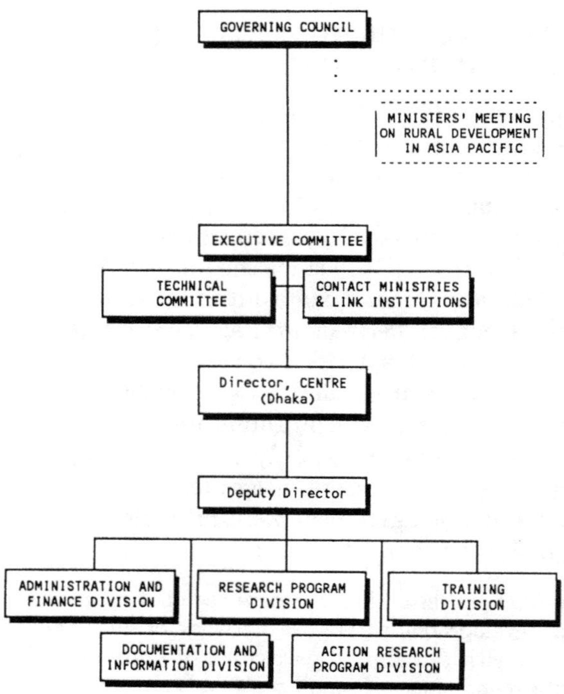

To facilitate liaison, CIRDAP's IRD network consists of the Contact Ministry and Link Institution in each country. The Contact Ministry is the government unit with IRD responsibility; the Link Institution is the academic locus of IRD research and training. (Four countries combined the two entities in one institution.) In 1987, a Ministers' Meeting on Rural Development in Asia Pacific convened; composed of CIRDAP members, participating nonmember countries, and donor countries and organizations, the body will have an advisory role in future years.

A Director manages CIRDAP, aided by a Deputy Director and a core professional and project staff. The Research Program Division identifies project needs for basic research, prepares project proposals, and evaluates results. The Action Research Program Division designs or helps governments to plan applied research, including programs for the rural poor, then evaluates projects. The Training Division provides ideas and support on training needs, prepares training materials, and trains the trainers of national IRD centers. The Documentation and Information Division publishes and disseminates materials on rural development, maintains a documentation archive, acts as an information clearinghouse, and aids national efforts to improve IRD information systems. The Administration and Finance Division handles accounting and housekeeping tasks, general administration, and supports the other divisions.

CIRDAP began operations in Comilla, adjacent to the Bangladesh Academy for Rural Development at Kotbari, the Link Institution for Bangladesh, with a small coordination office at Dhaka. In 1985, all CIRDAP offices moved to Dhaka.

Any member of FAO in the Asian and Pacific region is eligible for CIRDAP membership; eleven countries have joined (see Table 13.2). CIRDAP projects have attracted participation from several nonmembers: Bhutan, the People's Republic of China, Denmark, Fiji, Maldives, Papua New Guinea, North and South Korea, Tonga, and Western Samoa. Study tours have gone to Afghanistan, Botswana, Malawi, Nigeria, Tanzania, and Zambia. Canada, Japan, and Sweden, as donor countries, participate in the Technical Committee meetings.

CIRDAP's budget is in two parts. The General Fund is an administrative budget, mostly defrayed by member countries. Accounts of the Programme Budget are supported by a trust fund that places amounts from external sources for specific projects in time deposits until they are disbursed; the interest goes into a special reserve fund for other projects. For the 1986–87 biennium the amount in the trust fund was $913,740.

Although equal member contributions to the General Fund were anticipated, since 1984 all members have contributed an annual minimum – at present, $25,000. Bangladesh and India pay an enhanced rate

Table 13.2
Centre on Integrated Rural Development for Asia and the Pacific: Membership and Assessments

Year Joined	Member Countries	Assessment (1984)
1978	Bangladesh	$ 50,000 + $ 9,300
1979	India	50,000 + 100,000
	Indonesia	25,000 + 40,200
	Malaysia	25,000 + 27,900
	Nepal	25,000 + 3,100
	Pakistan	25,000 + 18,600
	Philippines	25,000 + 27,900
	Vietnam	25,000 + 6,200
1980	Laos	25,000 + 3,100
	Sri Lanka	25,000 + 3,100
1982	Thailand	25,000 + 24,800
Totals	11 Members	$325,000 + 264,200

of $50,000 each. The balance is based on UN budget assessments, with no country paying more than one-fourth of the total (see Table 13.2).

During each biennium, CIRDAP finances about six research studies that compare IRD experience in the region and six action research projects. Current priority areas are agrarian development, employment, institutional/infrastructural development, and resource development, including human resources.

There are about twelve training projects each year, mostly in member countries. Trainees include extension workers, organizers of the rural poor, ministry functionaries, supervisors and cadres of rural cooperatives, and field-level staff. Study tours facilitate exchanges of information and experiences, including expert advice. CIRDAP also prepares training manuals and other informational materials.

ASIAN AND PACIFIC DEVELOPMENT CENTRE (APDC)[3]

Newly independent Asian countries inherited colonial administrations that were designed to control indigenous peoples rather than to generate economic and social progress. In 1963, ECAFE set up the Asian Institute for Economic Development and Planning (AIEDP) in Bangkok, later called the Asian Development Institute (ADI). The Asian Statistical Institute (ASI) in Tokyo followed in 1970, and the Asian Centre for Development Administration (ACDA) began in 1971 in Kuala Lumpur. In 1977, ESCAP set up a Governing Council for these bodies, which were then renamed as follows: ADI became the Asian and Pacific Development Institute (APDI); ASI, the Statistical Institute for Asia and the Pacific (SIAP); and ACDA, the Asian and Pacific Development Administration Centre (APDAC). Then, in 1977,

ESCAP authorized the Asian and Pacific Center for Women and Development (APCWD) in Tehran and the Social Welfare and Development Center for Asia and the Pacific (SWDCAP) in Metro Manila.

By 1982, the five bodies were supposed to raise their own funds and thus would be able to leave the UN system. When new funding did not emerge by 1980, ESCAP integrated all but SIAP into a new Asian and Pacific Development Centre (APDC) in Kuala Lumpur on the assurance of UNDP support. ESCAP adopted a transitional Statute of the Asian and Pacific Development Centre in 1980, then drafted the Charter of the Asian and Pacific Development Centre, which went into effect on July 1, 1983.

APDC's aim, according to the Charter, is

> to assist Governments . . . and collaborate with governmental and nongovernmental research and training institutions and other institutions of public education in the Asian and Pacific region, in the study, formulation, implementation, management and evaluation of development strategies and policies. (Article II)

APDC's plenary organ is the General Council, which meets for about three days biennially, and selects the Director and the Management Board. The Management Board meets for a two-day session once each year (see Fig. 13.3). Membership on the Management Board consists of the Director, a representative of the host country (Malaysia), and up to seventeen persons from the region who serve in their personal capacity. UNDP, as a continuing contributor, has a seat on the General Council and Management Board; ESCAP sits on the latter body.

APDC staff are organized into long-term programs, headed by Coordinators. In 1984, APDC decided to establish liaison with national and regional institutions to form a network with its program and national focal points. So far, 190 institutions are part of this network.

Members of ESCAP are eligible to join; twenty countries have done so thus far (see Table 13.3). Although nonmembers, Afghanistan and Hongkong have contributed financially to APDC programs. APDC has established relations with national institutions in all member countries as well as in Fiji, Kiribati, Hongkong, Papua New Guinea, Singapore, the Solomon Islands, Tonga, and Vanuatu. Participants have also come from American Samoa, Micronesia, New Caledonia, Palau, Tuvalu, and Western Samoa.

APDC was launched on a commitment of $9.8 million from 1980 to 1985. UNDP offered $4.2 million, provided that the rest would come from member countries. No formula for member contributions has been drawn up. Instead, pledges were made during the 1982 and 1983 sessions of ESCAP, and additional pledges have been made at General Council meetings (see Table 13.3). Malaysia makes an additional grant

Figure 13.3
Organization of the Asian and Pacific Development Centre

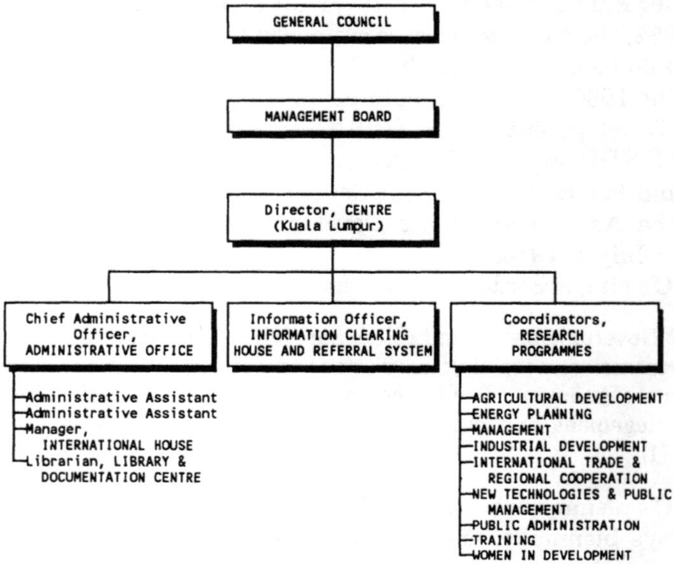

Table 13.3
Asian and Pacific Development Centre: Membership and Amounts Pledged

Year Joined	Member Countries	Amount Pledged (1985)
1983	Australia	$105,379
	Bangladesh	15,000
	Brunei	10,000
	China	50,000
	Cook Islands	
	India	55,000
	Indonesia	47,300
	Japan	350,000
	Laos	2,000[a]
	Malaysia	42,200
	Maldives	1,000[a]
	Nepal	1,500[a]
	New Zealand	10,765
	Pakistan	20,000[a]
	Philippines	40,205
	South Korea	35,000
	Sri Lanka	25,000[a]
	Thailand	40,000
	Vietnam	5,000[a]
1984	Brunei	
Totals	20 Members	$855,349

[a]Pledge pertains to 1984 or earlier

of about $165,000 each year and an in-kind contribution of the building for APDC. There is a reserve fund of $600,000 in case of future financial problems.

During 1986, the administrative budget of APDC was $497,000. The program budget is composed of contributions from various donor agencies plus rent charged by APDC's International House, and interest on bank deposits. In 1986, UNDP provided $1,879,000 to the program budget, and $120,856 came from other international sources.

Initially, research focused on planning and management, food security, human resources mobilization, and integration of women in development. In 1985, the focus shifted to agricultural development (including fisheries), industrial development (especially rural industrialization), international trade and regional cooperation, and new technologies and public management. In 1987–89, the themes were overcoming poverty, strengthening the capacity of development institutions to manage national development and change, increasing policy-making capabilities of governments, and adjusting to the changing world environment. Each research program consists of specific projects. Out of the forty-four projects in 1986, seventeen involved research, eleven involved training, and sixteen pertained to information exchange. In 1986, APDC was involved in over fifty meetings in conjunction with its programs; 857 participants were involved. In 1987, APDC began to offer a postdoctoral fellowship program.

In addition to these activities, APDC serves as the Secretariat for a nongovernmental regional organization, the Association of Development Research and Training Institutes of Asia and the Pacific (ADIPA). ADIPA, in turn, is the Secretariat for the Inter-Regional Coordinating Committee of Development Associations (ICCDA), an association of ADIPA counterparts in Africa, Europe, Latin America, and the Middle East.

SOUTH ASIAN ASSOCIATION FOR REGIONAL COOPERATION (SAARC)[4]

Since the partition of India, resulting in the formation of Pakistan, South Asia has been embroiled in conflict. India has felt threatened by the People's Republic of China and Pakistan. Bangladesh broke away from Pakistan in 1971. Insurgencies in the Maldives and Sri Lanka emerged in the 1980s. Bhutan and Nepal are landlocked and thus depend upon India for access to the sea. On the positive side, the Indus and Ganges rivers pass through several countries, all South Asians share a common cuisine, and the Indian rupee serves as a regional unit of exchange.

The idea of a South Asian community of states can be traced to April

1947, when the Indian Council of World Affairs convened the Inter-Asian Relations Conference in New Delhi. A Provisional General Council, including leaders or deputy leaders of delegations at the conference, was formed, with Indian Prime Minister Jawaharlal Nehru named President. A nongovernmental Asian Relations Organization office opened in New Delhi, and interested countries established affiliated national councils to coordinate efforts to build a pan-Asian organization. Out of the thirty-one countries attending the 1947 conference, only Burma, Ceylon, Malaya, and Pakistan followed through. The next meeting, scheduled for China in 1949, did not take place, and by 1957 the Asian Relations Organization was dissolved.

In 1949, Nehru convened an emergency conference of African and Asian countries to deal with the conflict between insurgent Indonesia and the Netherlands. Nehru reiterated his desire for a more permanent organization to respond quickly to situations of this sort, but again the time was not ripe.

In 1954, Prime Minister John Kotelawala of Ceylon invited government heads from the region to a conference in Kandy from April 28 to May 2 to exchange views and discuss problems of common interest. Known subsequently as the South Asian Prime Ministers' Conference, or the Colombo Powers Conference, the prime ministers of Burma, Ceylon, India, Indonesia, and Pakistan attended. Although they discussed events in Indochina at length, the prime ministers commented as well on atomic bomb tests, representation of China in the United Nations, problems of Tunisia and Morocco, and difficulties faced by Arab refugees in Palestine, and they considered proposals relating to economic cooperation and mutual aid. Since the conference set forth the idea of a meeting of African-Asian nations, the same five prime ministers met again in August and then in December in Bogor to finalize plans for the proposed Asian-African conference. The December meeting also approved the idea of a committee of experts among the Colombo Powers to consider economic questions of common interest. After the first Afro-Asian conference convened in Bandung in April 1955, the Colombo Powers never met again, believing perhaps that the task of building Third-World unity was on its way.

After 1955, the idea of a South Asian regional forum was discussed from time to time. The Bangladesh War of 1971 brought further urgency to the idea, but countries of the region proceeded as before. In December 1977, there was a passing reference to the idea of South Asian regional cooperation by King Birenda of Nepal in a welcoming speech to the Colombo Plan Consultative Committee, which met in Kathmandu. President Ziaur Rahman of Bangladesh, who was exploring similar ideas before the Colombo Plan meeting in 1977, was the first leader to take concrete steps; his vision was of a cooperative effort in cultural, economic, and technical fields that might ultimately build a framework for peace in the region. From 1977 to 1980, Rahman explained his idea during visits to India, Nepal, Pakistan, and Sri Lanka, and special envoys carried letters with further details to heads of governments in the region.

In 1977, research institutes in the region formed the Committee for Studies on Cooperation and Development in South Asia to develop ideas for specific projects. As results were encouraging, Bangladesh Foreign Minister Muhammad Shamsul Haq drafted a proposal in November 1980, including a projected summit meeting of South Asian government heads. Since there was consensus in the region that a summit should follow preliminary planning, seven foreign secretaries of the region convened at Colombo on April 21–23, 1981, when Study Groups were set up. The foreign secretaries then met again in 1982, to review reports from the technical groups, and in March and July 1983 they prepared for a meeting of foreign ministers.

In New Delhi on August 1–2, 1983, the foreign ministers adopted the Declaration on South Asian Regional Cooperation, formally beginning an organization known as the South Asian Regional Cooperation (SARC). The third Foreign Ministers Meeting on May 13–14, 1985, changed the name to the South Asian Association for Regional Cooperation (SAARC). Subsequently, the first Summit Conference of Heads of State or Government adopted the Charter of the organization on December 8, 1985.

The Charter of the South Asian Association for Regional Cooperation lists eight objectives:

> a) to promote the welfare of the peoples of South Asia and to improve their quality of life; b) to accelerate economic growth, social progress and cultural development in the region and to provide all individuals the opportunity to live in dignity and to realize their full potentials; c) to promote and strengthen collective self-reliance among the countries of South Asia; d) to contribute to mutual trust, understanding and appreciation of one another's problems; e) to promote active collaboration and mutual assistance in the economic, social, cultural, technical and scientific fields; f) to strengthen cooperation with other developing countries; g) to strengthen cooperation among themselves in international forums on matters of common interest; and h) to cooperate with international and regional organizations with similar aims and purposes. (Article 1)

The highest organ of SAARC, the Heads of State or Government Meeting (also known as the Summit Meeting), convenes for two days each year (see Fig. 13.4). Meetings of foreign ministers, called the Council of Ministers, are held for about two days twice each year to review SAARC's technical activities. India's fears that other states

Figure 13.4
Organization of the South Asian Association for Regional Cooperation

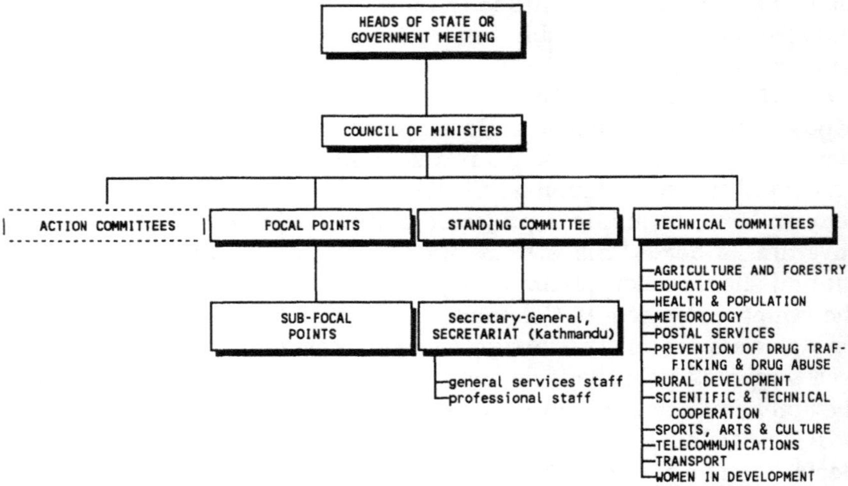

might gang up on it were relieved when SAARC agreed that all decisions require unanimity.

The Secretariat in Kathmandu opened in January 1987. The head, a Secretary-General, is assisted by one Director from each member country.

The Standing Committee, set up by the New Delhi Declaration in 1983, prepares for the Council of Ministers; composed of foreign secretaries, it meets at least once each year to identify new areas of cooperation, determine priorities, approve projects, mobilize resources for projects, and coordinate and monitor the work of SAARC.

The Study Groups, set up in 1981, became Working Groups late in 1981 and Technical Committees as of 1983. The first five Study Groups were in the fields of agriculture, rural development, telecommunications, meteorology, and health and population. Later, committees were set up in education; postal services; science and technology; transport; sports, arts, and culture; narcotics trafficking and drug abuse; and participation of women in development.

Each country's foreign ministry has a Focal Point to coordinate SAARC activities. Sub-Focal Points correspond to each Technical Committee and are usually in other ministries.

Seven countries make up SAARC (see Table 13.4). The smaller countries joined first, then India and Pakistan followed, so as not to be left out. A decision on India's sponsorship of membership for Afghanistan in 1987 was deferred in view of the ongoing internal struggle.

The least-developed countries (Bangladesh, Bhutan, Maldives, and Nepal) are given preferential status in regard to cost sharing; the more prosperous countries (India, Pakistan, and Sri Lanka) pay somewhat more of SAARC costs. In order to finance the Secretariat, there is a cost sharing arrangement in which each country pledges a certain portion of its foreign ministry budget to spend on SAARC projects. Each Technical Committee then requests funds from the Standing Committee (see Table 13.4).

Regional SAARC centers are being established at present in association with established national institutions. Under these arrangements, the host country will provide capital facilities and 40 percent of the operating expenses; the remaining 60 percent is shared on the same basis as the formula for the SAARC Secretariat. The Standing Committee is to raise external funds.

One of the ground rules of SAARC, as agreed at the initial meeting of foreign secretaries, is that no bilateral or political issue will be discussed at public sessions, although foreign ministers and government heads have issued statements calling for a nuclear test-ban treaty and about policies of various international organizations. Trade cooperation has also been ruled out because Pakistan insists that India first reduce import restrictions.

SAARC's earliest technical activities were seminars among experts in such areas as biomass, early warning systems for cyclones, environmental protection, handicrafts, poverty-focused rural development, and telecommunications needs. Short-term SAARC activities include training courses, conferences, and seminars, study tours, and expert exchanges. In 1988, there were 133 technical meetings.

For long-term cooperation, SAARC sets up regional bodies and links existing national institutions. In September 1984, the Technical Committee on Sports, Arts and Culture sponsored the first South Asian

Table 13.4
South Asian Association for Regional Cooperation: Membership and Assessments

Year Joined	Member Countries	Assessment (1987)
1983	Bangladesh	3% + 8.35%
	Bhutan	3 + 2.00
	India	3 + 29.10
	Maldives	3 + 2.00
	Nepal	3 + 8.35
	Pakistan	3 + 20.85
	Sri Lanka	3 + 8.35
Totals	7 Members	$400,000

Federation Games (SAFG). The SAARC Agricultural Information Centre has been established in Bangladesh, and the SAARC Meteorological Research Centre has been approved for India. Planning continues for the eventual establishment of SAARC facilities in the various areas covered by the Technical Committees. Other developments include a 50 percent reduction in intraregional airfare, direct dialing service via satellite, limited convertibility of national currencies for tourists from SAARC countries, and an agreement on the South Asian Food Security Reserve (SAFSR) of 200,000 tons of wheat and rice in national storehouses for emergencies. The 1986 summit recommended joint action to deal with hijacking, attacks on diplomatic personnel, and use of one country's territory to assist terrorism or civil strife in another SAARC country.

SUMMARY AND CONCLUSIONS

Trade among Bangkok Agreement countries increased 100 percent from 1975 to 1985, according to ESCAP calculations, which also estimate that the value of 1982 imports of Bangkok Agreement items totaled $52.5 million, accounting for about 8 percent of imports among the four countries. For this reason, the Seoul Round began in 1986. The need for more trade within the region with a minimum of bureaucratic negotiations followed the Asian Way principle of Asian solutions to Asian problems.

The need to develop agriculture in Asia, the most populous region of the world, is obvious. Fertile lands need trained farmers. CIRDAP's action research and training programs hold promise for success, but they must work through existing governmental structures in member countries. The network of Link Institutions aims for a long-term solution, consistent with the Asian Way principle of incrementalism. To the extent that bureaucratic impediments can be reduced and contact with individual farmers can be increased, CIRDAP will be able to point to important results in the years ahead.

APDC's precursors supplemented ESCAP by providing regular training in the field of development administration. Today, some observers believe that APDC may become an alternative or rival to ESCAP, as APDC has the potential for developing innovative programs. APDC has thus far steered away from ESCAP's institution-building mission, however, preferring to strengthen existing development administrators' knowledge and experience, thus pursuing Asian Way incrementalism.

The theory behind SAARC appears to have been that technical cooperation would spill over into friendly relations on politically sensitive matters. Some progress is occurring on technoeconomic issues, but efforts to establish a free-trade area are unlikely, since India could easily flood the region with its products, thereby frustrating plans for national development. Instead, SAARC has followed ASEAN in pursuing Asian Way consensus building and behind-the-scenes conflict resolution before moving into areas of more intense cooperation.

Ten days after the first summit, India and Pakistan agreed not to attack each other's nuclear facilities. In 1986, India quietly assured Bangladesh and Nepal that dissidents living in India would not be allowed to cross the border to disrupt elections. At the 1986 summit, India and Sri Lanka discussed problems relating to the Tamils in Sri Lanka, then Indian peacekeeping troops went to Sri Lanka, although India has yet to honor Colombo's 1989 request to arrange an orderly withdrawal. India and Pakistan discussed ways of decreasing military tensions, and the two assured each other that no attacks are planned despite massive U.S. aid to Pakistan in connection with problems in Afghanistan. Bangladesh, India, and Nepal are working out their differences in approach toward the development of the Ganges River basin. In 1988, India sent troops to suppress a revolt in the Maldives. Decisions on these matters were private and did not enter into the public record of SAARC, but they clearly result from the spirit of SAARC. The organization appears to have eased friction between regional rivals. Genuine progress in technoeconomic cooperation is now more likely than before, but more time is needed to put SAARC to the test.

NOTES

1. For references to Bangkok Agreement documents, see Michael Haas, *Basic Documents of Asian Regional Organizations* (Dobbs Ferry, NY: Oceana Publications, 1979), vol. 7, p. 560.

2. For references to CIRDAP documents, see Centre on Integrated Rural Development for Asia and the Pacific, *CIRDAP Report* (Dhaka: CIRDAP, 1980–). Published quarterly.

3. For references to APDC documents, see Asian and Pacific Development Centre, *Annual Report* (Kuala Lumpur: APDC, 1984–). Published annually.

4. For references to SAARC documents, see Secretariat, South Asian Association for Regional Cooperation, *SAARC Perspective* (Katmandu: SAARC, 1987–). Published irregularly.

14 THE "ASEANIZATION" OF ASIAN REGIONAL COOPERATION

THE RISE OF ASEAN

International relations in Asia today, to a large extent, consist of a set of mirrors reflecting the Association of South East Asian Nations (ASEAN). As more countries and organizations find that they must take ASEAN into account in their foreign policy planning, the result is the "ASEANization" of Asian regional cooperation.

What are so remarkable today are the dramatic shifts in foreign policy in so many parts of Asia regarding ASEAN. In 1971, for example, an employee of the UN Economic Commission for Asia and the Far East (ECAFE) unofficially referred to ASEAN as a "joke," because it pretended to be a strong regional organization but did not even have a secretariat or a set of operational programs with any degree of visibility. Yet that same organization, renamed the UN Economic and Social Commission for Asia and the Pacific (ESCAP) in 1974, was Executing Agency for a formal Dialogue between ASEAN and the UN system by 1978, and ESCAP's International Trade Division set up a special unit to help ASEAN with trade negotiations.

In the early 1970s, ASEAN was verbally attacked by the People's Republic of China, the Soviet Union, and Ho Chi Minh's Vietnam. By 1978, all three countries had begun to express admiration for ASEAN, the last even today, stating its readiness to join when the time is ripe. In contrast with the early lack of funds and concrete projects, ASEAN today has major financing from Australia, Canada, the European Community (EC), Japan, New Zealand, the UN system, and the United States, as well as from other sources.

THE ASEAN BREAKTHROUGH

The sharp contrast between early ASEAN and today's ASEAN is overshadowed by the impact that ASEAN has had on regional cooperation in Asia during the same period. ASEAN differed from most previous efforts at regional cooperation and established at least ten new trends that persist to the present.

Subregionalization. Perhaps ASEAN's most notable innovation was that it was subregional. The Association of Southeast Asia (ASA), its predecessor, consisted of three countries in Southeast Asia but had an important gap – Indonesia. The Central Banks of Southeast Asia, Australia and New Zealand (SEANZA) and the Anglo-Malayan (later Malaysian) Defence Agreement (AMDA) focused on Southeast Asian countries but their external members have been essential. Only ASEAN started with a core group of contiguous countries in a subregion. Since ASEAN began in 1967, some fourteen of the thirty-three newer Asian regional organizations have been subregional, including the Conference of Foreign Ministers of Kampuchea, Laos, and Vietnam and the South Asian Association for Regional Cooperation (SAARC).

Disrupted Transregionalism. Because of ASEAN's solidarity, international cooperation has become subregional outside Southeast Asia. For example, the decision of ASEAN to develop its own clearing arrangement meant that South Asian countries alone joined the Asian Clearing Union (ACU), and the Asian Reinsurance Corporation (Asian Re) nearly suffered the same fate when ASEAN decided to set up its own reinsurance pool. ASEAN withdrawal from organizations started by the Asian and Pacific Council (ASPAC) caused the latter to be centered largely in northeast Asia; these are the Cultural and Social Center for the Asian and Pacific Region (CULSOCEN) and the Food and Fertilizer Technology Center for the Asian and Pacific Region (FFTC). The same subregionalization by default almost befell the Asian Parliamentarians' Union (APU), but its Asian Development Center (ADC) began to do research for projects of the ASEAN-Japan Dialogue after 1977, and APU became APPU (Asian-Pacific Parliamentarians' Union) by adding another subregion of countries – those of the South Pacific – in 1980. Meanwhile, the Association for Science Cooperation in Asia (ASCA) has been unable to compete with ASEAN's better-financed Committee on Science and Technology (COST).

Sub-Subregionalization. Since Indochinese countries felt ASEAN hostility after 1975, several organizations originally consisting of all Southeast Asian countries now almost entirely are made up of ASEAN countries: the Southeast Asian Fisheries Development Center (SEAFDEC), Southeast Asian Agency for Regional Transport and Communications Development (SEATAC), Study Group on Asian Tax Administration and Research (SGATAR), Southeast Asian Ministers of Education Organization (SEAMEO), and the South-east Asian Central Banks Group (SEACEN). In some organizations, the Indochinese countries are still eligible to return; in other cases, Vietnam withdrew or was forced out. ASEAN, in short, served to subregionalize Southeast Asia.

Subregional Dynamism. An international organization in Asia will work if placed under the care of ASEAN countries. Two previously independent organizations that fell on hard times were revived as ASEAN projects: the Southeast Asian Promotion Centre for Trade, Investment and Tourism (SEAPCENTRE) and the Regional Organization for Inter-Governmental Cooperation and Coordination in Family and Population Planning in Southeast Asia (IGCC). The first folded in 1978, the second in 1982, only to become integrated later into ASEAN Dialogues as externally financed regional projects. Some regional organizations are executing agents for ASEAN projects, notably the Asia-Pacific Institute for Broadcasting Development (AIBD), SEACEN, SEAFDEC, SEATAC, and SEAMEO's Regional Language Centre (RELC) and its Regional Tropical Medicine and Public Health Project (TROPMED). In addition, ASEAN funds have laid submarine cables that comprise a part of the design of the Asia-Pacific Telecommunity (APT). Both the Southeast Asia Tin Research and Development Centre (SEATRAD Centre) and the Tripartite Council (TC) have three of the six ASEAN members. For these reasons, SAARC is trying to emulate ASEAN's dynamism in another subregion of Asia.

Magic of the ASEAN Name. Two organizations have ASEAN in their titles, although they are not affiliated with ASEAN itself: the ASEAN Inter-Parliamentary Organization (AIPO) and the Meeting of the Chiefs of National Police of the ASEAN Countries (ASEANAPOL). An ASEAN base for both newer and older organizations now has good prospects for success. Several nongovernmental organizations have been formed with ASEAN in their titles. There are thirty-one approved organizations linked to one of ASEAN's permanent committees. Starting in 1971, ASEAN foreign ministers encouraged the ASEAN Chamber of Commerce and Industry to form industry clubs in order to advance the ASEAN Industrial Complementation project; fifteen of these clubs now exist. In 1981, the ASEAN Association of Insurance Commissioners set up the ASEAN Reinsurance Pool (the ASEAN Reinsurance Corporation by 1988), and the ASEAN Committee on Finance and Banking (COFAB) took steps to launch the ASEAN Finance Corporation (AFC), both outside the formal structure of ASEAN. More unaffiliated, nongovernmental ASEAN-titled organizations exist in a variety of fields, even including an ASEAN Karate Federation. The ASEAN spirit has a magic that encourages successful organizations.

Subregional Solidarity. The cohesiveness of ASEAN countries provides strength to influence decisions at meetings of other international organizations. The ASEAN bloc openly caucuses together, then has the votes to prevail in such organizations as the Association of Natural Rubber Producing Countries (ANRPC) and the Association of Tin Producing Countries (ATPC). ASEAN countries lobby to have their diplomats selected as executive officers of UN and other international bodies. Thanks to ASEAN pressure, the International Civil Aviation Organization (ICAO) established a new air route in 1986 to ease congestion in the region. Most important of all, where there are differences between an ASEAN country and a non-ASEAN country, ASEAN countries rally together. The Cambodian seat at the United Nations, for example, was not occupied by a representative of the regime in Phnom Penh after 1978 but rather by a coalition of insurgent groups formed through ASEAN insistence. Australia's Qantas Airlines made concessions on overflights in Southeast Asia due to ASEAN pressure. Washington explains its policy toward Cambodia as support for ASEAN.

Subregionalization of Programming. ESCAP, which once resisted the idea, has established distinct programs for specific subregions in Asia. Asian Productivity Organization (APO) aid is now complementary to ASEAN's human resources development project. AIBD disburses funds for projects involving ASEAN countries. The International Labor Organization (ILO) supports the ASEAN Program on Industrial Relations and Labor Studies. About one-third of the Asian and Pacific Development Centre (APDC) projects are subregional, involving ASEAN, South Asia, and the South Pacific.

ASEAN Veto Power. Because of ASEAN, the following organizations collapsed: the Asian and Pacific Council (ASPAC) in 1972, the Asian Rice Trade Fund (ARTF) in 1974, the Ministerial Conference for the Economic Development of Southeast Asia (SEAMCED) in 1975, and the South-East Asia Treaty Organization (SEATO) by 1977. ASEAN's opposition to Japan's proposed Southeast Asian Medical and Health Organization (SEAMHO) meant that no such organization ever started. ASEAN resisted Japan's idea of a four-power Malacca Strait council; TC resulted instead. Due to ASEAN's pivotal role in Asia, in 1989 Australia proposed an Asia-Pacific cooperation council, but pointedly left development of the idea to ASEAN, if there was interest. Inasmuch as previous initiatives of this sort relegated ASEAN to a more passive role, they got nowhere. In July 1989, ASEAN decided to pursue the Australian proposal, and a report is expected in 1990.

Magnetism of ASEAN. Many countries seek to join ASEAN. Papua New Guinea, Sri Lanka, and Vietnam are ready to enter the organization. Only Papua New Guinea now attends meetings and has signed the ASEAN Treaty of Amity and Cooperation. The South Pacific Forum (SPF) is a Dialogue Partner; South Korea has sought the name status in vain. Burma has considered Observer status in ASEAN. Nepal, a member of SEACEN since 1967 and SEANZA since 1971, also joined IGCC in 1971, gravitating toward Southeast Asian organizations before the formation of SAARC.

Regional Development and Conflict Resolution. ASEAN is respected primarily because of its concrete accomplishments. In the economic and technical areas, it has forged ahead toward achieving elements of a new international economic order (NIEO) more fully than all other Asian organizations combined. In regard to conflict resolution, ASEAN has managed and resolved a large number of intra-ASEAN disputes.[1] SAARC is embarking along a similar path.

THE FUTURE OF THE ASIAN WAY

Academic observers have long debated whether integrative efforts among countries should begin with low-level (economic) or high-level (political) cooperation. In the history of Asian regional cooperation, First-World leadership of SEATO violated the Asian Way equality principle in the 1950s. India's political efforts during the same decade led to the nonaligned movement but not to a deepening of economic cooperation because these efforts went beyond pan-Asianism. APPU and ASPAC sought to push particular political policies in the 1960s, forsaking pan-Asianism.

ASEAN leaders first became acquainted on a personal basis, trying to achieve a cultural we-feeling before proceeding to tackle important economic or political problems. As soon as ASEAN foreign ministers developed mutual trust, they engaged in conflict resolution through consensus building, while finding Asian solutions to Asian problems in the form of modest functional cooperation on various technical matters that ranged from education to fisheries to labor productivity, initially within non-ASEAN organizations formed by ASEAN countries.

Asian cooperation in regard to banking, communications, and other technical areas went forward primarily because the core countries of ASEAN agreed on the value of new institutions in the 1970s. When ASEAN began to make bolder strides after 1976, a cooperative infrastructure grew through an incremental learning process, and greater elite expectations raised the level of commitment to regional cooperation. ASEAN then set forth important economic goals, deferring their implementation to a partnership between the private and public sectors as well as to joint projects with First-World or UN funding.

The mutual reinforcement among cultural affinity, elite political commitment, and technoeconomic institutions appears to explain why the

Asian Way has succeeded. In the 1980s, SAARC is now seeking to follow the ASEAN example, and Indochina is reaching out to ASEAN as well.

Asian regional cooperation has entered a new phase of activity. Having established the Asian Way as an operational code for proper diplomacy, Southeast Asian countries are now able to bring about peace and prosperity. Because intra-ASEAN conflicts are solved at a low-key level, and the six countries pledge not to compete with one another in cutthroat battles for markets, they enjoy exemplary progress. SAARC has a long way to go, but no farther than the ASEAN states when they began.

Staff members at Asian regional organizations have become the functional equivalents of Eurocrats in the offices of the European Community (EC). These Asiacrats carry the spirit of regional cooperation below the level of the ministers who make the key decisions. The press of Asia has also been a part of the story, dramatizing meetings so that the ordinary person today is keenly aware of regional aspirations, and thereby more reluctant to support conflict when the alternative is peace and increased mutual prosperity.

Today, Asian regional cooperation in some ways fulfills the goal of transnational integration more fully than does European regional cooperation, where economic motives have long taken precedence over community building.[2] The EC has revealed that its real aim is simply profits for certain economic sectors, so economic cooperation has not spilled over into increased political solidarity.[3] In Asia, the admiration for ASEAN is based on the development of a common we-feeling that led first to political then to economic cooperation, whereupon progress in development fed back to strengthen community bonds and thence strengthened regional political resolve.

Both ASEAN and SAARC have been active in conflict resolution. The People's Republic of China has been welcomed to many Asian regional organizations, while the EC has done little to bridge the gap between capitalist and socialist Europe. France decided to develop an independent nuclear deterrent force and asked the North Atlantic Treaty Organization (NATO) to move from Paris; in contrast, cooperation under the Five-Power Defence Arrangements (FPDA) is more intense now than ever. While negotiations for EC tariff reductions to Third-World countries have often given short shrift to the African-Caribbean-Pacific countries, ASEAN uses its Dialogues to exact more favorable trading arrangements with First-World countries. Meanwhile, the professional quality of the work at Asian technical organizations attracts funds from the First World and participants from outside Asia, further recognition of the success of Asian regional cooperation.

The Asian Way principles – Asian solutions to Asian problems, equality, consensus building, incrementalism, administration subordinated to politics, and Pan-Asianism – have proved to be realistic guides to regional progress. They comprise the wellspring for further regional efforts at a faster rate than perhaps any other grouping of countries in the world today. By focusing on the programmatic details of each organization in this volume, the benefits of regional cooperation at a technical level should now be clear. But there are gaps as well.

There is perhaps a long way to go before peace will come to every corner of Asia, but it has come to ASEAN countries – along with prosperity. Internal conflicts, even within ASEAN, remain. The Asian Way eschews interference in the internal affairs of other countries. Due to Asian solidarity, Indonesia and Malaysia have urged radical members of the world Islamic community to avoid meddling in the problems of Moslems in the southern Philippines, while India has come to the aid of the Maldives and Sri Lanka in cases of internal strife. At the same time, Asian solidarity did not resolve conflicts in Afghanistan and Cambodia in a peaceful manner. Both countries were isolated from Asian regional cooperation, so there is room for improvement in perfecting Pan-Asianism and other principles of the Asian Way. It is premature to predict whether ASEAN and its cousin SAARC will be building blocks for a new political order in Asia that will bring about a more lasting peace. But it is difficult to imagine any route to peace other than the continuing practice of the principles of the Asian Way.

NOTES

1. Estrella D. Solidum, *Towards a Southeast Asian Community* (Quezon City: University of the Philippines Press, 1974).
2. Johan Galtung, *The European Community* (London: Allen & Unwin, 1973); Leon N. Lindberg and Stuart A. Scheingold, *Europe's Would-Be Polity* (Englewood Cliffs, NJ: Prentice-Hall, 1970).
3. Ernst B. Haas, "Turbulent Fields and the Theory of Regional Integration," *International Organization* 30 (Spring 1976): 173–212.

BIBLIOGRAPHY

Anon. "The Geography of International Organization." *International Associations* 24 (1972): 175.

ASEAN Inter-Parliamentary Organization. *First General Assembly: Joint Communiqué* (Jakarta, January 8–11, 1975).

Asian Judicial Conference. *Record of the First Judicial Conference* (Baguio, May 1963).

Asian and Pacific Development Centre. *Annual Report*. Kuala Lumpur: APDC, 1984– (annually).

Association of Tin Producing Countries. *A Milestone in Producer Collaboration in Tin*. Kuala Lumpur: ATPC Secretariat, c. 1985.

Centre on Integrated Rural Development for Asia and the Pacific. *CIRDAP Report*. Dhaka: 1980– (quarterly).

Carlos, Clarita R. "An Analysis of Some Bases for Cooperation of Three Functional Organizations, Namely, Eastern Regional Organization for Public Administration, Asian Oceanic Postal Union and Association for Science Cooperation in Asia." Unpublished master's thesis, Department of Political Science, University of the Philippines, Quezon City, October 1976.

Galtung, Johan. *The European Community*. London: Allen & Unwin, 1973.

Gordon, Bernard K. *The Dimensions of Conflict in Southeast Asia*. Englewood Cliffs, NJ: Prentice-Hall, 1966.

Haas, Ernst B. "Turbulent Fields and the Theory of Regional Integration." *International Organization* 30 (1976): 173–212.

Haas, Michael. "The Aseanization of Asian International Relations." *Asia Pacific Community* 6 (1979): 72–86.

______. "The 'Asian Way' to Peace." *Pacific Community* (Tokyo) 4 (1974): 498–514.

______. *Basic Documents of Asian Regional Organizations*. Vols. 1-9. Dobbs Ferry, NY: Oceana Publications, 1974–80.

______. *The Pacific Way: Regional Cooperation in the South Pacific*. New York: Praeger, 1989.

Informal Meeting of the Directors General of Civil Aviation, Asia and the Pacific. *Proceedings, Directors General of Civil Aviation, Asia and the Pacific*, 1965- (annually).

Kende, Istvan. "Wars of Ten Years (1967–1976)." *Journal of Peace Research* 15(3) (1978): 227–42.

Lindberg, Leon N., and Scheingold, Stuart A. *Europe's Would-Be Polity*. Englewood Cliffs, NJ: Prentice-Hall, 1970.

Malaysia, Ministry of Foreign Affairs. "Straits of Malacca and Singapore – Joint Statement." *Foreign Affairs Malaysia* (November, 1971): 53–54.

Pentland, Charles. *International Theory and European Integration*. New York: Free Press, 1973.

Solidum, Estrella D. *Towards a Southeast Asian Community*. Quezon City: University of the Philippines Press, 1974.

South Asian Association for Regional Cooperation. *SAARC Perspective*. Kathmandu: SAARC Secretariat, 1987- (irregular).

UN Economic and Social Commission for Asia and the Pacific. *Report of the Government Consultation Among Jute Producing Countries*. Bangkok: ESCAP, 1979-.

______. *Report of Intergovernmental Consultative Forum of Developing Tropical Timber Producing/Exporting Countries*. Bangkok: ESCAP, 1982-.

______. *Report of the Regional Consultative Group on Silk*. Bangkok: ESCAP, 1982-.

Vietnam, Socialist Republic of. *Conferences of Foreign Ministers of Vietnam, Laos and Kampuchea*. Hanoi: Information and Press Department, Ministry of Foreign Affairs, 1981.

Wightman, David. *Toward Economic Cooperation in Asia*. New Haven, CT: Yale University Press, 1953.

Wright, Quincy. *A Study of War*. 2d ed. Chicago: University of Chicago Press, 1965.

INDEX

Acheson, Dean, 75
Administration, primacy of politics over, 9
Adviser on Intra-Regional Training, 27
African Development Bank (AfDB), 200
Afro-Arab Training Centre (AATC), 60
Afro-Asian Rural Reconstruction Conference, 59, 60
Afro-Asian Rural Reconstruction Organization (AARRO), 13, 52, 59–63; assessments in, 61, 62; functions of, 60; membership in, 60–61, 62; organization of, 60, 61; pilot projects in community development, 63; regional offices, 60; success of, 63–64; training centers, 60
Agreement Establishing the Asian Development Bank, 186
Agreement on Trade Negotiations Among Developing Member Countries of the Economic and Social Commission for Asia and the Pacific, 18, 265–69, 280; membership in, 267–68, 269; organization of, 266–67; programs of, 268–69
Agreement Relating to Malaysia, 40
Agreement Relating to the Separation of Singapore from Malaysia as an Independent and Sovereign State, 40
Agricultural Information Network for Southeast Asia (AgInfoNet-SEA), 163
Agricultural Special Fund (ASF), 190
Air Base Butterworth. *See* Butterworth Air Force Base
Air Defence Advisory Working Group, 43
Air Defence Council, 44–45
Anglo-Malayan Defence Agreement (AMDA), 12, 32, 37, 39–43, 50, 120, 183; membership in, 42
Arab Training Centre (ATC), 60
Arbitration, regional centers for, 57–59
Army Advisory Working Group, 43, 45
Asian-African Conference, 53
Asian African Legal Consultative Committee (AALCC), 13, 52, 53–59, 64; budget for, 56; and codification of international law, 56; and dispute resolution, 56–57; Disputes Settlement System, 56, 59; functions of, 53; growth of, 64; and Law of the Sea Treaty, 56; membership in, 54–56; organization of, 53–54; publications of, 57; regional centers for arbitration, 57–59; status of, under UN, 57; success of, 63; Trade Law Sub-Committee, 57
Asian and Pacific Center for Women and Development (APCWD), 273
Asian and Pacific Coconut Community (APCC), 17, 219, 220–23, 245–46; finances of, 221–22; functions of, 220; membership of, 221, 222; organization

Asian and Pacific Coconut Community (APCC) *(continued)* of, 220, 221; projects of, 222–23
Asian and Pacific Council (ASPAC), 14, 20, 65, 75–88, 90, 250, 283; aims of, 77; Asian and Pacific Maritime Cooperation Scheme (APMCS), 87–88; conferences, 79; Cultural and Social Center for the Asian and Pacific Region (CULSOCEN), 78–79; Economic Cooperation Center for the Asian and Pacific Region (ECOCEN), 83–84; exchange program of, 79; finances of, 77–78; Food and Fertilizer Technology Center for the Asian and Pacific Region (FFTC), 79–83; formation and termination of centers, 77; membership in, 77, 79; organization of, 76; origin of, 75–76; Registry of Scientific and Technical Services for the Asian and Pacific Region, 84–86; seminars of, 79
Asian and Pacific Development Administration Centre (APDAC), 272
Asian and Pacific Development Centre (APDC) (Kuala Lumpur), 18, 265, 272–75, 273, 285; aim of, 273; finances of, 273, 275; membership in, 274; organization of, 273, 274; programs of, 275
Asian and Pacific Development Institute (APDI), 272
Asian and Pacific Maritime Cooperation Scheme (APMCS), 14, 78, 87-88, 89–90
Asian and Pacific treaty organization (APATO), 75
Asian Broadcasting Union (ABU), 211
Asian Center for Tax Administration and Research (ACTAR), 110
Asian Centre for Development Administration (ACDA), 272
Asian Clearing Union (ACU), 16, 182, 196–99, 204, 269; membership of, 198; organization of, 197–98; origin of, 196; purpose of, 197; users of facilities, 198–99
Asian Coconut Community (ACC), 17, 219, 220
Asian College of Engineering, 93
Asian Culture Quarterly, 73
Asian Development Bank (ADB), 16, 103, 154, 182, 185–92, 205, 227; criticisms of, 202–4; finances of, 189, 190–91; membership of, 185, 188, 189; organization of, 187–89; origin of, 185–86; projects of, 192; purpose of, 186; subscriptions in, 189
Asian Development Equity Fund (ADEF), 192
Asian Development Fund (ADF), 190
Asian Development Institute (ADI), 272
Asian Finance and Investment Corporation (AFIC), 192
Asian Institute for Economic Development and Planning (AIEDP), 272
Asian Institute of Technology (AIT), 38, 93
Asian international history, 1–2
Asian Judicial Conference (AJC), 17, 253–55, 263; finances of, 254; membership in, 253–54; organization of, 253, 254
Asian Legal Conference at New Delhi, 53
Asian Legal Consultative Committee (ALCC), 13, 53
Asian-Oceanic Postal Training School (AOPTS), 16
Asian-Oceanic Postal Union (AOPU), 16, 206
Asian-Pacific Cultural Center (APCC), 71, 73–74
Asian-Pacific Development Center (APDC) (of APPU), 71, 74–75, 280
Asian-Pacific Parliamentarians' Union (APPU), 13, 69–71, 88–89, 148; aim of, 69–70; Asian-Pacific Cultural Center (APCC), 71, 73–74; Asian-Pacific Development Center (APDC), 74–75; assessments in, 73; central secretariat, 71; finances of, 71; membership in, 71, 72; organization of, 70–71
Asian-Pacific Postal Training Centre (APPTC), 209–210
Asian-Pacific Postal Union (APPU), 16, 69–75, 88, 206–9, 217; Asian-Pacific Postal Training Centre (APPTC), 209–10; finances of, 208; membership of, 207–8; organization of, 206–7; origin of, 206; programs of, 208–9
Asian-Pacific Tax and Investment Research Center (APTIRC), 112, 116
Asian Parliamentarians' Union (APU), 13, 65, 69, 88, 283
Asian Productivity Organization (APO), 13, 65, 66–69, 88, 90; assessments in,

67–68; budget for, 67–68; and improving productivity, 68–69; membership in, 67, 68; objective of, 66; organization of, 66–67
Asian Program of Educational Innovation for Development (APEID), 159
Asian Regional Center for Archaeology and Fine Arts (ARCAFA), 164
Asian Regional Center for Strengthening Labor and Manpower Administration (ARPLA), 263
Asian regional organizations, 10–12; banking organizations, 16; commodity communities, 17; communication organizations, 16–17; conferences without headquarters, 17–18; external initiatives, 12–13; Indian leadership, 13; later organizations, 18–19; Northeast Asian initiatives, 13–15; Southeast Asian leadership, 15–16. *See also specific organizations*
Asian Regional Skill Development Program (ARSDEP), 263
Asian Regional Team for Employment Promotion (ARTEP), 263
Asian Reinsurance Corporation (Asian Re), 16, 182, 199–202; activities of, 202; assets of, 202, 204–5; finances of, 200–1, 202; membership in, 200–1; organization of, 200, 201; purpose of, 199–200
Asian Relations Organization, 13
Asian Rice Trade Fund (ARTF), 17, 219, 232–34, 247, 285; finances of, 234; membership in, 233–34; objectives of, 232–33; organization of, 233; programs of, 234
Asian Round-Table Productivity Conferences, 66
Asian Secretariat for Taxation and Customs Cooperation, 261–62
Asian solutions to Asian problems, 5–6, 123, 245, 280, 288
Asian Statistical Institute (ASI), 272
Asian Vegetable Research and Development Center (AVRDC), 17, 219, 226–29, 246; finances of, 228; membership of, 227–28; objectives of, 226, 228; organization of, 226–27; programs of, 228–29
Asian Way, 2–3; administration subordinated to politics, 288; agreeing to long-term goals, 217; Asian solutions to Asian problems, 5–6, 123, 245, 280, 288; components of, 5; conflict resolution through, 19–20, 287; consensus decision making, 7–8, 247, 288; development of, 2–5; equality principle of, 6–7, 27, 37, 51, 183, 288; future of, 286–88; incrementalism, 8–9, 68, 121, 198, 230, 247, 280, 288; as new theory of international cooperation, 20–21; pan-Asianism, 9–10, 25, 77, 183–84, 200, 288; primacy of politics over administration, 9; of separating goals from bureaucracies, 171; of separating politics from administration, 66
Asia-Pacific Institute for Broadcasting Development (AIBD), 16, 206, 210–14, 218, 284; membership of, 212–13; objectives of, 211; organization of, 211–12; origin of, 210–11; training program of, 213–14
Asia-Pacific Telecommunity (APT), 17, 105, 214–17, 217, 284; activities of, 216–17; finances of, 216; membership of, 215–16; objectives of, 214; organization of, 215; origin of, 214; technical assistance from, 216–17
Association for Science Cooperation in Asia (ASCA), 17, 250, 263–64, 283; finances of, 259; membership in, 259–60; organization of, 258–59; origin of, 256–57
Association of Development Research and Training Institutes of Asia and the Pacific (ADIPA), 275
Association of Natural Rubber Producing Countries (ANRPC), 17, 219, 223–25, 246, 285; aims of, 223; membership of, 224; organization of, 223–25; programs of, 225; Technical Committee on South American Leaf Blight, 225
Association of Southeast Asia (ASA), 15, 119, 120–23; finances of, 123; membership in, 122; organization of, 121; projects of, 123; purpose of, 120–21
Association of Southeast Asian Institutions of Higher Learning (ASAIHL), 170
Association of South East Asian Nations (ASEAN), xvii, 4, 15, 17, 20, 39, 75, 119, 126–41, 145, 180, 234, 246, 250, 268, 282; accomplishments of, 146–48; Asso-

Association of South East Asian Nations (ASEAN) *(continued)*
ciation of Insurance Commissioners, 284; Bankers Acceptance (ABA) scheme, 135–36; Committee on Finance and Banking (COFAB), 284; Committee on Food, Agriculture and Forestry (COFAF), 244; Committee on Transportation and Communications (COTAC), 106; declaration of, 126; disrupted transregionalism, 283; Economic Ministers (AEM), 129; Finance Corporation (AFC), 284; funding for, 132–34; importance of outside forces to, 145–46; Industrial Complementation (AIC) projects, 137; Industrial Joint Ventures (AIJVs), 137; Industrial Projects (AIPs), 136; influence on other organizations, 140–41; Inter-Parliamentary Organization (AIPO), 15, 119, 141–43, 148; Japan Development Fund, 134; Karate Federation, 284; magic of the name, 284; magnetism of, 285–86; membership in, 131–32; and neutralization, 9; organization of, 127–31, 142–43; origin of, 126–27, 141–42; Pacific Cooperation in Human Resources Development (APC-HRD) Project, 133; Preferential Tariff Quota Scheme, 138; Program on Industrial Relations and Labor Studies, 285; projects of, 134–40; regional development and conflict resolution, 286; Reinsurance Corporation, 205; Reinsurance Pool, 136, 284; subregional dynamism, 284; subregionalization, 283–84, 285; subregional solidarity, 284–85; Swap Arrangement, 136; tasks of, 143; Tourism and Information Centre, 139; Trade, Investment and Tourism Promotion Centre, 115; Treaty of Amity and Cooperation, 286; veto power, 285; Zone of Peace, Freedom and Neutrality (ZOPFAN), 128, 134, 179, 180
Association of South-East Asian States (ASAS), 120
Association of Tin Producing Countries (ATPC), 17, 219, 238–41, 247, 285; membership of, 240, 241; objectives of, 239–40; organization of, 240; origin of, 238–39; programs of, 241
Australia and New Zealand Asian Command (ANZAC), 31–32
Australian, New Zealand, and Malayan Defence Committee (ANZAM Defence Committee), 12, 39
Australia-New Zealand-United Kingdom (ANZUK) force, 44

Baguio conferences, 32, 33, 34
Bahru, Johor, 45
Bandaranaike, Solomon, 186
Bandung Conference (1955), 75
Bangkok Agreement. *See* Agreement on Trade Negotiations Among Developing Member Countries of the Economic and Social Commission for Asia and the Pacific
Bangkok Declaration, 120–23
Bangladesh War (1971), 276
Banking organizations, 13, 16, 182; Asian Clearing Union (ACU), 16, 182, 196–99, 204, 269; Asian Development Bank (ADB), 16, 103, 154, 182, 185–92, 205, 227; Asian Reinsurance Corporation (Asian Re), 16, 182, 199–202; Central Banks of Southeast Asia, Australia, and New Zealand (SEANZA), 16, 182–85, 283; South-east Asian Central Banks Group (SEACEN), 16, 182, 193–96, 284
Bank for International Settlements (BIS), 136
Bayanihan, 9
Bengzon, Cesar, 253
Bidault, Georges, 33, 119
Birenda, 276
Black, Eugene, 102, 150, 186
Bureau for Technical Co-operation in South and South East Asia, 24–25
Business-suit diplomacy, 7
Butterworth Air Force Base, 41, 46, 47

Cable and Wireless Ltd., 216
Carnegie Endowment for International Peace, xvii
Central Banks of Southeast Asia, Australia and New Zealand (SEANZA), 16, 182–85, 283; finances of, 184; membership of, 183–84; organization of, 183, 184; programs of, 204; projects of, 185; purpose of, 183
Central Union of Agricultural Cooperatives and training, 61–63
Centre on Integrated Rural Development

for Asia and the Pacific (CIRDAP), 18, 265, 269–72; finances of, 271–72; membership in, 271, 272; objectives of, 269–70; organization of, 270–71; programs of, 272
Chandler, Robert, 17, 226, 228
Chiang Kai-Shek, 32
Chiba, Saburo, 69
Churchill, Winston, 31, 39, 118
Closer Economic Relations Trade Agreement (CERTA), 269
Cobbold, C. F., 183
Colloquium on Intra-Regional Technician Training (1969), 27–28
Colombo Plan Consultative Committee, 276
Colombo Plan for Co-operative Economic and Social Development in Asia and the Pacific (C-Plan), 12, 23–27, 29; Bureau for Technical Co-operation in South and South East Asia, 24–25; handling of aid requests, 24–25; organization of, 24; region, membership in, 25–27; technical assistance from, 27
Colombo Plan Staff College for Technician Education (CPSC), 27–29; activities of, 28–29; budget in, 28; location of, 28
Colombo Powers, 52; Conference, 13, 276
Combined Tin Committee (CTC), 238
Commission for Economic and Cultural Cooperation, 178
Committee for Studies on Cooperation and Development in South Asia, 277
Committee on Culture and Information (COCI), 133
Committee on Finance and Banking (COFAB), 135, 284
Committee on Food, Agriculture and Forestry (COFAF), 130, 136, 244
Committee on Industry, Minerals and Energy (COIME), 136
Committee on Science and Technology (COST), 130
Committee on Social Development (COSD), 130
Committee on Trade and Tourism (COTT), 135, 138
Committee on Transportation and Communications (COTAC), 106, 139–40
Commodity communities, 17, 219–20; Asian and Pacific Coconut Community (APCC), 17, 219, 220–23, 245–46; Asian Rice Trade Fund (ARTF), 17, 219, 232–34, 247, 285; Asian Vegetable Research and Development Center (AVRDC), 17, 219, 226–29, 246; Association of Natural Rubber Producing Countries (ANRPC), 17, 219, 223–25, 246, 285; Association of Tin Producing Countries (ATPC), 17, 219, 238–41, 247, 285; Government Consultation Among Jute Producing Countries (GCJPC), 17, 219, 241–43; Intergovernmental Consultative Forum of Developing Tropical Timber Producing/Exporting Countries (ICFDTTP/EC), 17, 219, 243–44, 248; International Pepper Community (IPC), 17, 219, 229–32, 246; International Rice Research Institute (IRRI), 17, 100, 226, 247; Regional Consultative Group on Silk (RCGS), 17, 219, 244–45; Southeast Asia Tin Research and Development Centre (SEATRAD Centre), 17, 219, 234–37, 284
Commonwealth Far East Strategic Reserve, 12, 39, 42–43
Communication organizations, 16–17, 206; Asian-Oceanic Postal Training School (AOPTS), 16; Asian-Oceanic Postal Union (AOPU), 16, 206; Asian-Pacific Postal Union (APPU) 16, 69–75, 206–9, 217; Asia-Pacific Institute for Broadcasting Development (AIBD), 16, 206, 210–14, 218, 284; Asia-Pacific Telecommunity (APT), 17, 105, 214–17, 284; International Telecommunication Union (ITU), 16–17; Universal Postal Union (UPU), 16
Communication theorists, 21
Communist International (Comintern), Baku (1920), 12
Confederation of Nations of Malay Origin, 124
Conference of Asian and Pacific Labor Ministers (CAPLM), 17, 250, 263; membership in, 256, 257; organization of, 255–56; origin of, 255; purpose of, 255
Conference of Asian Labor Ministers (CALM), 18, 255
Conference of Asian Ministers of Education and Ministers Responsible for Economic Planning, 150

Conference of Nonaligned Nations (1955), 52
Conference of the Foreign Ministers of Kampuchea, Laos, and Vietnam, 16, 149, 176–79; membership in, 178; organization of, 177–78
Conferences without headquarters, 17–18
Conferocracies, 250; Asian Judicial Conferences (AJC), 253–55; Association for Science Cooperation in Asia (ASCA), 256–60; Conference of Asian and Pacific Labor Ministers (CAPLM), 255–56; Informal Meeting of Directors General of Civil Aviation, Asia and the Pacific (DGCA), 250–53; Taxation and Customs Cooperation Conference (TCCC), 260–62
Conflict resolution, through Asian Way, 19–20, 287
Confucian doctrine, 6
Congress of the Nations of the Orient, 12
Consensus decision making, 7–8, 247, 288
Consultative Committee for Economic and Cultural Relations of Southeast Asian Nations, 119
Convention of the Asian Productivity Organization, 66
Convention on the Territorial Sea and Contiguous Zone (1958), 171–72
Coombs, H. C., 183
Coordinating Committee of Southeast Asian Senior Officials on Transport and Communications (COORDCOM), 14, 103
Copper Fabrication Project, 137
Co Thach, 177
Council of Agriculture, 61
Council of Technical Cooperation in South and Southeast Asia, constitution of, 23–24
Cultural and Social Center for the Asian and Pacific Region (CULSOCEN), 14, 78–79, 89, 283; conferences of, 79; exchange program of, 79; membership in, 79; organization of, 78–79; seminars of, 79

Data Communication Corporation of Korea, 216
Declaration on South Asian Regional Cooperation, 277
de Gaulle, Charles, 49
Deutsch, Karl, 21
Directors General of Civil Aviation, Asia and the Pacific (DGCA), Informal Meeting, 17, 250–53, 263; finances of, 252; membership in, 251, 252; organization of, 251; programs of, 253
Drug Advisory Program, 27
Dulles, John Foster, 33

East Asian Rural Reconstruction Conference, 59
Eastern Telecommunications Philippines, Inc., 216
Economic and Social Commission for Asia and the Pacific (ESCAP), 4–5, 16, 17, 18, 67, 185, 188, 214, 220, 221, 265, 282. *See also* ECAFE
Economic Commission for Asia and the Far East (ECAFE), 4, 5, 7, 8–9, 12, 16, 17, 124, 185, 196, 214, 220, 235, 239, 266, 282. *See also* ESCAP
Economic Commission for Europe (ECE), 12
Economic Cooperation Among Developing Countries/Technical Cooperation Among Developing Countries (ECDC/TCDC) Unit, of ESCAP, 233
Economic Cooperation Center for the Asian and Pacific Region (ECOCEN), 14, 83–84, 89; activities of, 83–84; organization of, 83, 84; purpose of, 83
Economics, primacy of, over politics, 19
Eden, Anthony, 33
Egyptian International Centre for Agriculture, 61
Egyptian Training Institute for Community Development, 60
Eisenhower, Dwight, 33
Emergency Petroleum Sharing Scheme, 137–38
Equality, Asian-Way principle of, 6–7, 27, 37, 51, 183, 288
Espinosa, Emilio, 255
European Economic Community (EEC), 20
European Productivity Agency (EPA), 66
Exclusive economic zone (EEZ), 56, 115
Expert Conferences for Economic Development in Asia and the Pacific, 75
External initiatives, 12–13; Anglo-Malayan Defence Agreement (AMDA), 12, 32, 37, 39–43, 50, 120, 183; Australian, New Zealand, and Malayan Defence Commit-

tee (ANZAM Defence Committee), 12, 39; Colombo Plan for Co-operative Economic and Social Development in Asia and the Pacific (C-Plan), 23–27, 29; Commonwealth Far East Strategic Reserve, 12, 39, 42–43; Economic and Social Commission for Asia and the Pacific (ESCAP), 4–5, 16, 17, 18, 67, 185, 188, 214, 220, 265; Economic Commission for Asia and the Far East (ECAFE), 5, 7, 8–9, 12, 16, 17, 185, 196, 235, 239; Five Power Defence Arrangements (FPDA), 12–13, 32, 43–49, 50, 51, 287; South-East Asia Treaty Organization (SEATO), 12, 32, 49–51, 75, 285

Far Eastern Commission, 12
Far Eastern Freight Conference (FEFC), 105
First Agreement on Trade Negotiations Among Developing Member Countries of the Economic and Social Commission for Asia and the Pacific, 18, 266
First Asian Judicial Conference, 253
Five Power Defence Arrangements (FPDA), 12–13, 32, 43–49, 50, 51, 287
Five Power Naval Advisory Working Group, 45
Five-Power Staff Agency, 33
Food and Agriculture Organization of the United Nations (FAO), 18, 59–60
Food and Fertilizer Technology Center for the Asian and Pacific Region (FFTC), 14, 79–83, 283; assessments in, 81; membership in, 80, 81; organizations of, 80–81; purpose of, 79–80, 82–83; training program of, 82–83
Four-Country Conference on Taxation and Customs Cooperation, 261
Franco-Siamese Conciliation Committee, 176
Fukuda, Takeo, 114, 132
Fukuda Fund, 132–33
Functionalist theories, 20

Garcia, Carlos, 120
General Agreement on Tariffs and Trade (GATT), 268–69
Geneva Conference (1962), 37, 77
Geneva peace treaty (1954), 33
Globe MacKay Cable and Radio Corp., 216
Gorbachev, Mikhail, 248
Gorton, John, 43
Goshi, Kohei, 66
Gotongroyoung, 9
Government Consultation Among Jute Producing Countries (GCJPC), 17, 219, 241–43; membership in, 242, 243; organization of, 242; projects of, 242–43
Greater East Asia Co-Prosperity Sphere, 12, 13, 31

Haas, Ernst, 20
Haq, Muhammad Shamsul, 277
Havana Charter, 238
Ho Chi Minh, 33, 119, 282
Holyoake, Keith, 43
Hongkong Telephone Co. Ltd., 216
Hosking, K. F. G., 235

Incrementalism, Asian Way principle of, 8–9, 68, 121, 198, 230, 247, 280, 288
Indian Agricultural Research Institute, 61
Indian leadership, 13, 52 ; Afro-Asian Rural Reconstruction Organization (AARRO), 13, 52, 59–63; Asian African Legal Consultative Committee (AALCC), 13, 52, 53–59, 64; Asian Legal Consultative Committee (ALCC), 13, 53; Asian Relations Organization, 13; Colombo Powers Conference, 13, 276
Indonesia-Malaysia-Singapore Traffic Separation Scheme Rules and Recommendations, 174
Institut Penyiaran Tun Abdul Razak (IPTAR), 211
Integrated Air Defence System (IADS), 48, 50
Integrated Program for Commodities, 219
Integrated rural development (IRD), 269
Inter-American Development Bank (IADB), 186
Intergovernmental Committee on Trade Expansion Program, 266
Inter-Governmental Consultations of Regional Cooperation in Pepper, 230
Intergovernmental Consultative Forum of Developing Tropical Timber Producing/Exporting Countries (ICFDTTP/EC), 17, 219, 243–44, 248; membership in, 244; organization of, 244; program of, 243–44

International Association of Chiefs of Police (IACP), 143
International Association of Universities (IAU), 168
International Bank for Reconstruction and Development (IBRD), 185
International Bureau of Fiscal Documentation (IBFD), 112
International Center for Settlement of Investment Disputes (ICSID), 58
International Civil Aviation Organization (ICAO), 17, 251, 263, 285
International Coordinating Committee, Southeast Asia Regional Cooperation in Family and Population Planning, 107
International Court of Justice (ICJ), 171
International Criminal Police Organization (INTERPOL), 143
International Development Association (IDA), 185
International Finance Corporation (IFC), 185
International Labor Organization (ILO), 17, 140, 255, 285
International Law Commission (ILC), 53
International Maritime Consultative Organization (IMCO), 174
International Maritime Organization (IMO), 174
International Monetary Fund (IMF), 260
International Natural Rubber Agreement (INRA), 223
International Natural Rubber Organization (INRO), 246
International Pepper Community (IPC), 17, 219, 229–32, 246; membership of, 231–32; organization of, 230–31; origin of, 229–30; projects of, 232
International Potato Center (Centro Internacional de Papas – CIP), 228
International Rice Research Institute (IRRI), 17, 100, 226, 247
International Rubber Research and Development Board (IRRDB), 225
International Rubber Study Group (IRSG), 223, 225
International Silk Association (ISA), 245
International Telecommunication Convention (1973), 214
International Telecommunication Union (ITU), 16–17
International Tin Agreement (ITA), 238, 239, 241
International Tin Committee (ITC), 238, 241
International Tin Control Scheme, 238, 241
International Tin Council (ITC), 235, 239
International Tin Research and Development Council (ITRDC), 238
International Tin Research Council (ITRC), 238
International Tin Research Institute (ITRI), 247
International Tin Study Group (ITSG), 238
International Tropical Timber Organization (ITTO), 244
Inter-Parliamentary Organization (AIPO) (of ASEAN), 15, 119, 141–43, 148, 284
Inter-Parliamentary Union (IPU), 69
Inter-Regional Coordinating Committee of Development Associations (ICCDA), 275

Japan-ASEAN Comprehensive Exchange Program, 134
Japan-ASEAN Cooperation Promotion Program (JACPP), 115; Fund, 133–34
Japan Association for Preventing Marine Accidents, 87, 172
Japanese National Group of Parliamentarians, 74
Japanese Shipowners' Association, 87, 172
Japan Productivity Center (JPC), 65, 66
Japan Scholarship Fund for ASEAN Youth, 133
Japan Special Fund (JSF), 190
Jayawardene, J. R., 23
Johari, Khir, 107
Johnson, Lyndon, 37, 102–3, 150, 186
Journal of Science and Mathematics Education in Southeast Asia, 161

Karnasut, Prida, 94
Keynes, John Maynard, 196
Khoman, Thanat, 4, 5, 6–7, 35, 120
Killearn, Lord, 118
Kishi, Nobusuke, 13, 69
Kokusai Denshin Denwa Co. Ltd., 216
Korean War, 32–33, 65, 75
Korea Telecommunication Authority, 216
Kotelawala, John, 276

Kuala Lumpur Commodity Exchange, 241

Lahore Convention, 5-6, 7
Laurel, J. B., Jr., 69
Law Association for Asia and the Pacific (LAWASIA), 255, 263
Law of the Sea Conference, 56
Law of the Sea Treaty (1982), 56, 115
Lee Tong Won, 75
Liberal Democratic Party (LDP) of Japan, 65
Link Institutions, 280
Longanthan, C., 186
Lon Nol, 37

Macapagal, Diosdado, 124
MacArthur, Douglas, 31, 32
McDonald, Malcom, 118
Magsaysay, Ramon, 34
Malacca Straits Council of Japan (MSC), 87, 172
Malaysian Fleet Operations Command, 48
Malik, Adam, 126
Manila Accord, 124-26
Manila Declaration, 124, 141-42
ManPac, 34
Mao Tse Tung, 3, 79
Maphilindo, 15, 119, 123-26, 145; membership in, 126; organization of, 125; origin of, 123-25
Marcos, Ferdinand, 38
Marine Fisheries Resource Development and Management Department, 98-100, 115
Mayaguez crew, 50
Meeting of the Chiefs of National Police of the ASEAN Countries (ASEANAPOL), 15, 119, 143-45, 148, 284; finances of, 144; functions of, 145; membership in, 144; organization of, 144
Miki, Takeo, 91
Military-oriented organizations in Asia, 12
Ministerial Conference for the Economic Development of Southeast Asia (SEAMCED), 14, 15, 91-93, 117, 285; membership in, 92; organizations of, 92-93; origin of, 91-92; purpose of, 92
Mitrany, David, 20
Mountbatten, Louis, 31, 118
Mufakat, 7
Multi-Purpose Special Fund (MPSF), 190
Mushawarah, 6
Mushawarah Maphilindo. *See* Maphilindo

Nairn, J. B., 183
National Broadcasting Centre of Malaysia, 211
National Groups of Parliamentarians, 71
National Institute of Small Industry Extension Training, 61
National Museum in Taipei, 73
National productivity organizations (NPOs), 66
Naval Advisory Working Group, 43
Nehru, Jawaharlal, 32, 52, 276
Neocolonialism, 32, 124
Neofunctionalist theorists, 20
New international economic order (NIEO), 29, 219
New Zealand Force Southeast Asia (NZForsea), 47
Nippon Telegraph and Telephone Public Corp., 216
Nixon Doctrine, 50, 172
Nonaligned movement, 52
North Atlantic Treaty Organization (NATO), 34, 287
Northeast Asian initiatives, 13-15, 65-66; Asian and Pacific Council (ASPAC), 14, 20, 65, 75-88, 90, 250, 283; Asian and Pacific Maritime Cooperation Scheme (APMCS), 14, 78, 89-90; Asian-Pacific Parliamentarians' Union (APPU), 13, 69-71, 88-89, 148; Asian Parliamentarians' Union (APU), 13, 65, 69, 88, 283; Asian Productivity Organization (APO), 13, 65, 66-69, 88, 90; Coordinating Committee of Southeast Asian Senior Officials on Transport and Communications (COORDCOM), 14, 103; Cultural and Social Center for the Asian and Pacific Region (CULSOCEN), 14, 78-79, 89, 283; Economic Cooperation Center for the Asian and Pacific Region (ECOCEN), 14, 83-89; Food and Fertilizer Technology Center for the Asian and Pacific Region (FFTC), 14, 79-83, 283; Ministerial Conference for the Economic Development of Southeast Asia (SEAMCED), 14, 15, 91-93, 117, 285; Regional Organization for Inter-Governmental Cooperation and Coordination in Family and Population

Northeast Asian initiatives *(continued)*
Planning in Southeast Asia (IGCC), 14, 15, 106–9, 284; Registry of Scientific and Technical Services for the Asian and Pacific Region, 14, 84–86; Southeast Asian Agency for Regional Transport and Communications Development (SEATAC), 14, 15, 102–6, 115–16, 283, 284; Southeast Asian Fisheries Development Center (SEAFDEC), 14, 15, 94–97, 115, 283, 284; Southeast Asian Promotion Centre for Trade, Investment and Tourism (SEAPCENTRE), 14, 15, 112–15, 116–17, 284; Study Group on Asian Tax Administration and Research (SGATAR), 14, 15, 110–12, 116, 260, 264, 283–84
North Korea, and border disputes, 20

Ohira, Masayoshi, 133
Organization of Petroleum Exporting Countries (OPEC), 219
Oshikawa, Ichiro, 66

Pacific Charter, 34
Pacific Islands Producers Association (PIPA), 221
Padu, Bersatu, 43
Pakikisama, 7
Pan-Asianism, Asian Way principle of, 9–10, 25, 77, 183–84, 200, 280, 288
Pan-Asiatic Conference (1926), 12
Park Chung Hee, 75
Payments union, 196
Pelaez, Emmanuel, 6, 124
Pepper Community (PC), 17, 219
Pepper Technical Panel (Peppertech), 230–31
Permanent Coconut Production and Productivity Panel (Cocopep), 220
Permanent Panels of Coconut Technology (Cocotech), 221
Philippine Global Communications Inc., 216
Philippine-Indonesian Coconut Commission (PICC), 220
Philippine Long Distance Telephone Co., 216
Philippine National Congress, 74
Philippine National Tax Research Center, 110–11
Philippines Communication Satellite Corp., 216
Pilot Project on Integrated Community-Based Human Resources Development, 155
Political organizations, 20; Asian and Pacific Council (ASPAC), 14, 20, 65, 75–88, 90, 250, 283; Association of South East Asian Nations (ASEAN), xvii, 4, 15, 17, 20, 39, 75, 119, 126–41, 145, 180, 234, 246, 250, 268, 282; South Asian Association for Regional Cooperation (SAARC), xvii, 18–19, 20, 265, 275–81; South-East Asia Treaty Organization (SEATO), 12, 32, 49–50, 50–51, 75, 285
Politics: primacy of, over administration, 9; primacy of economics over, 19
Pramoj, Kukrit, 38
Preferential Trading Arrangements (PTA), 138, 269
Preparatory Committee for the Establishment of an Asian Clearing Union, 196
Project Action, 158
Project CB-BLP (Community-Based Basic Learning Packages), 158–59
Project Clear, 158
Project Completion Assistance, 191
Project DELSILIFE (Development of a Learning System for the Improvement of Life), 159
Project IMPACT (Industrial Management by Parents, Community and Teachers), 158
Project NTR of T (Nontraditional Roles of Teachers), 159
Project Preparation Assistance, 191
Project Progress, 158
Project RIT (Reduced Instructional Time), 159
Protocol to the South-East Asia Collective Defense Treaty, organization of, 34–36
Punjab Agricultural University, 61

Quebec Conference of August 1943, 118
Quirino, Elpidio, 32

Rahman, Tunku Abdul, 43, 120
Rahman, Ziaur, 276–77
Ramos, Fidel, 143
Razak, Tun Abdul, 7, 103, 124
Razaleigh, 175

Recto, Claro, 5
Regional Consultative Group on Silk (RCGS), 17, 219, 244–45; finances of, 245; membership in, 245; organization of, 245; programs of, 245
Regional Cooperation for Development (RCD), 196, 269
Regional Language Centre (RELC), 161, 179, 284
Regional Institute of Higher Education and Development (RIHED), 149, 168–71, 179–80; assessments in, 170, 171; membership of, 170–71; organization of, 169–70; origin of, 168–69; projects of, 171
Regional Organization for Inter-Governmental Cooperation and Coordination in Family and Population Planning in Southeast Asia (IGCC), 14, 15, 106–9, 284; dissolution of, 107, 109; finances of, 109; membership in, 108; organization of, 107–8; seminars sponsored by, 109
Regional Project on Public Health and Pesticide Control, 93
Regional Tropical Medicine and Public Health Project (TROPMED), 153, 284
Registry of Scientific and Technical Services for the Asian and Pacific Region, 14, 84–86; membership of, 86; organization of, 85–86; projects of, 86
RELC Journal, 161
Research and Educational Center for Asia (RECA), 60
Reyes, Dominador, 256
Rhee, Syngman, 32
Rivera, Vincente, Jr., 250
Romualdez, Eduardo, 110
Roosevelt, Franklin, 31, 39, 118
Round-Table Meeting, 200
Rubber Research Institute of Malaysia (RRIM), 225
Rural reconstruction, 59
Rusk, Dean, 34
Rusk-Thanat communiqué, 35, 38

Saemul Undong Headquarters, 62
Sala Santitham, 17
Sarasin, Pote, 94
Sato, Eisaku, 91
Sattahip, 49, 50
Security Treaty Between Australia, New Zealand, and the United States (ANZUS), 32, 33, 37
Senanayake, D. S., 23
Sen, B. R., 60
Shang dynasty, 1
Shin Duck Lee, 206
Showa Maru oil spill, 175
Sihanouk, Norodom, 37, 176
Singaporean Headquarters Fleet Operations Command, 48
Singapore Reinsurance Corporation, 199
Sino-American Joint Commission on Rural Reconstruction (JCRR), 226
Sithi-Amnui, Paul, 186
Social Welfare and Development Center for Asia and the Pacific (SWDCAP), 273
South Asian Association for Regional Cooperation (SAARC), xvii, 18–19, 20, 265, 275–81; activities of, 279–80; Agricultural Information Centre, 280; finances of, 279; membership in, 278–79; Meteorological Research Centre, 280; objectives of, 277; organization of, 277–78; origin of, 275–77
South Asian Federation Games (SAFG), 280
South Asian Food Security Reserve (SAFSR), 280
South Asian Regional Cooperation (SARC), 277
South-East Asia Collective Defense Treaty, 34, 39; Conference, 33–34; purpose of, 34
Southeast Asia Community Organization (SEACOR), 120
Southeast Asia leadership, 15–16; Association of South East Asian Nations (ASEAN), xvii, 4, 15, 17, 20, 39, 75, 118–48, 180, 234, 246, 250, 268, 282; Conference of the Foreign Ministers of Kampuchea, Laos, and Vietnam, 16, 149, 176–79; Ministerial Conference for the Economic Development of Southeast Asia (SEAMCED), 14, 15, 91–93, 117, 285; Regional Center for Educational Innovation and Technology (INNOTECH), 156–59, 179; Regional Center for Tropical Biology (BIOTROP), 155–56, 179; Regional Centre for Archaeology and Fine Arts (SPAFA), 154; Regional Centre for Education in Science and Mathemat-

Southeast Asia leadership *(continued)* ics (RECSAM), 159-61, 179; Regional Institute of Higher Education and Development (RIHED), 149, 168-71, 179-80; Regional Language Center (RELC), 161, 179, 284; Regional Organization for Inter-Governmental Cooperation and Coordination in Family and Population Planning in Southeast Asia (IGCC), 14, 15, 106-9, 284; Regional Tropical Medicine and Public Health Project (TROPMED), 153, 284; Southeast Asian Agency for Regional Transport and Communications Development (SEATAC), 14, 15, 102-6, 115-16, 283, 284; Southeast Asian Fisheries Development Center (SEAFDEC), 14, 15, 94-97, 115, 283, 284; Southeast Asian Ministers of Education Organization (SEAMEO), 15-16, 19, 149-55, 179, 180, 284; Southeast Asian Promotion Centre for Trade, Investment and Tourism (SEAPCENTRE), 14, 15, 112-15, 116-17, 284; Southeast Asian Regional Center for Graduate Study and Research in Agriculture (SEARCA), 162, 179; Study Group on Asian Tax Administration and Research (SGATAR), 14, 15, 110-12, 116, 260, 264, 283-84; Tripartite Council (TC), 16, 149, 171-76, 180, 284

Southeast Asia Ministerial Conference on Family and Population Planning, 107

Southeast Asian Agency for Regional Transport and Communications Development (SEATAC), 14, 15, 102-6, 115-16, 283, 284; finances of, 105; functions of, 105-6; membership in, 105; organizations of, 104-5; origin of, 102-3; purpose of, 103-4

South-east Asian Central Banks Group (SEACEN), 16, 182, 193-96, 284

South-east Asian Central Banks Research and Training Centre (SEACEN Centre), 16

Southeast Asian Fisheries Development Center (SEAFDEC), 14, 15, 94-97, 115, 283, 284; Aquaculture Department (AQD), 100-2, 115; finances of, 96; function of, 96-97; Marine Fisheries Research Department (MFRD), 98-100; members of, 95-96; organization of, 94-95; purpose of, 94; Training Department (TD), 97-98

Southeast Asian Friendship and Economic Treaty (SEAFET), 120

Southeast Asian Journal of Tropical Medicine and Public Health, 168

South East Asian Lumber Producers' Association (SEALPA), 244

Southeast Asian Medical and Health Organization (SEAMHO), 92, 285

Southeast Asian Medical Information Center (SEAMIC), 93

Southeast Asian Ministers of Education Council (SEAMEC), 150, 151

Southeast Asian Ministers of Education Organization (SEAMEO), 15-16, 19, 149-55, 179, 180, 284; budget for, 154-55; Educational Development Fund (SEDF), 154; Endowment Fund, 154; membership in, 152-53; Nonformal Education Project (SNEP), 158; organization of, 151-52; origin of, 149-50; projects of, 153-55; purpose of, 150-51; Regional Center for Educational Innovation and Technology (INNOTECH), 156-59, 179; Regional Center for Tropical Biology (BIOTROP), 155-56, 179; Regional Centre for Archaeology and Fine Arts (SPAFA), 154, 164-66, 179; Regional Centre for Education in Science and Mathematics (RECSAM), 159-61, 179; Regional Language Center (RELC), 161-62, 179, 284; Regional Project in Archaeology and Fine Arts (SPAFA), 165; Regional Tropical Medicine and Public Health Project (TROPMED), 166-68, 179; Southeast Asian Regional Center for Graduate Study and Research in Agriculture (SEARCA), 162-64, 179

Southeast Asian Ministers of Education Secretariat (SEAMES), 105, 150

Southeast Asian Nuclear Weapon Free Zone (SEANWFZ), 134

Southeast Asian Promotion Centre for Trade, Investment and Tourism (SEAPCENTRE), 14, 15, 112-15, 116-17, 284; functions of, 114-15; membership of, 114; organization of, 113-14; origin of, 112-13; Tourism Division, 114; Trade and Investment Division, 114

Southeast Asian Science and Mathematics

Experiment (SEASAME), 160
Southeast Asia Tin Research and Development Centre (SEATRAD Centre), 17, 219, 234–37, 284; aim of, 235; Analytical Section, 237; finances of, 236–37; Geology Section, 237; in-service training, 237; membership in, 236–37; Mineralogy Section, 237; Mineral Processing and Smelting Section, 237; Mining Section, 237; organization of, 235–36; origin of, 234–35; programs of, 236–37
South-East Asia Treaty Organization (SEATO), 12, 32, 49–51, 75, 285; budget for, 37–38; end of, 38–39; military exercises, 38; origin of, 32–35; treaty area, 37
South Pacific Forum (SPF), 269
South Pacific Regional Trade and Economic Cooperation Agreement (SPARTECA), 269
South Pacific Resident Office, 188
Southwest Pacific Command, 31
Sports-shirt diplomacy, 7
Statistical Institute for Asia and the Pacific (SIAP), 272
Study Group on Asian Tax Administration and Research (SGATAR), 14, 15, 110–12, 116, 260, 264, 283–84; finances of, 112; membership of, 111–12; objectives of, 110; organization of, 110–11; research projects of, 112
Sukarno, 126
Summit Conference of Heads of State or Government, 277
Suzuki, Zenko, 133

Taipei, China, 188
Taiwan Sugar Corporation, 226
Tanco, Arturo, 100
Taxation and Customs Cooperation Conference (TCCC), 17, 250, 260–62, 264; membership in, 262; organization of, 261–62; origin of, 260–61; program of, 262
Technical Assistance Special Fund (TASF), 190
Technical cooperation among developing countries (TCDC), 29
Technical organizations, as arenas for conflict resolution, 19–20
Tengah Air Force Base, 41
Thailand Outreach Program (TOP), 227
Thanat (Thai Foreign Minister), 124, 126
Tin Producers' Association (TPA), 238
Tin Research Institute (TRI), 238
Tongyai, Chakratong, 94
Trade Negotiations Group (TNG), 266
Trade Preferences Negotiating Group (TPNG), 135
Traffic Separation Scheme (TSS), 173–74
Treaty of Amity and Cooperation, 130
Tripartite Agreement on the Safety of Navigation in the Straits of Malacca and Singapore, 174
Tripartite Council (TC), 16, 149, 171–76, 180, 284; finances of, 175; membership of, 175; organization of, 174; origin of, 173; projects of, 175–76; purpose of, 171–73
Tropical Agricultural Pest Biology Program, 156
Tropical Aquatic Biology Program, 156
Tropical vegetable information service (TVIS), 227

United Nations: Commission on International Trade Law (UNCITRAL), 56; Conference on Trade and Development (UNCTAD), 29, 199, 204, 219, 248, 268; Conference on Trade and Employment, 238; Convention on the Recognition and Enforcement of Arbitral Awards, 59; Development Program (UNDP) for ASEAN, 16, 17, 89, 252, 268; Economic and Social Commission for Asia and the Pacific (ESCAP) (*see* ESCAP); Economic Commission for Asia and the Far East (ECAFE) (*see* ECAFE); Educational, Scientific, and Cultural Organization (UNESCO), 16, 150, 211; Food and Agriculture Organization (FAO), 18, 59–60; Good Offices Mission (UNGOM), 2; India-Pakistan Observation Mission (UNIPOM), 2; Industrial Development Organization (UNIDO), 220–21; Institute for Training and Research (UNITAR), xvii; International Civil Aviation Organization (ICAO), 17, 251, 263, 285; Law of the Sea Conferences, 172; low profile of, in Asian conflict resolution, 2; Military Observer Group in India and Pakistan (UNMOGIP), 2

United States Agency for International Development (USAID), 105, 150, 154, 226
Universal Postal Union (UPU), 16
U Nyun, 4-5
Using Indigenous Learning Systems to Improve the Quality of Education in Deprived Communities project, 159

Vietnam Committee for Economic and Cultural Cooperation, 178
Vietnam War, 75
Villareal, Cornelo, 69
Virata, Cesar, 110

Waithayakon, Wan, 33
Whitlam, Gough, 86
Wilham, Dennis H., 251
Woodlands Naval Base, Singapore, 41, 43

Yew, Lee Kuan, 43
Yoingco, Angel, 110, 112, 262

Zone of Peace, Freedom and Neutrality (ZOPFAN), 128, 134, 179, 180

ABOUT THE AUTHOR

MICHAEL HAAS, a professor of Political Science at the University of Hawaii, has held visiting appointments throughout the world. The author or editor of twenty-three books and over one hundred articles, he is a major developer of the functionalist theory of international relations.

www.ingramcontent.com/pod-product-compliance
Lightning Source LLC
Chambersburg PA
CBHW071303180926
51613CB00001B/115
* 9 7 8 0 2 7 5 9 3 2 1 6 9 *